PEOPLE OF THE POTTERIES
a Dictionary of Local Biography
Volume 1

Edited by Denis Stuart

With an Appendix 'The Struggle for Federation'
by R. J. Edwards

Department of Adult Education, University of Keele, 1985

First published 1985
by the Department of Adult Education, University of Keele
ISBN 0 903160 23 4
Printed in Great Britain by
J. H. Brookes (Printers) Ltd.
141-149 Bryan Street, Hanley, Stoke on Trent

Cover design by Max Hammond

LIST OF CONTENTS

INTRODUCTION

This is a book for the people of the Potteries, about the people of the Potteries and by the people of the Potteries. It is intended as a contribution by the Department of Adult Education, University of Keele, to the celebrations of the 75th anniversary of the federation of the six towns in 1910. The book consists of about 600 brief biographies of local people of interest or importance who flourished before or in 1910. It is the first volume of what we hope will be a continuing series. It was written by the members of a number of classes organised by the Department of Adult Education from 1981 to 1984. One member of the group, Reg Edwards, has written an appendix on the struggle for federation in terms of the local personalities and issues involved.

Potters, inevitably and rightly, dominate our pages, but it was not our intention to write another book on ceramic history. We have made a selection of potters and have provided details of their domestic lives and personal interests. To these we have added examples of persons from a wide social spectrum and from the political right to the political left. Our approach has been based on the principle that local history concerns ordinary as well as newsworthy people. Thus we have included subjects who would not normally figure in a biographical dictionary—the butcher, the baker, the publican and the occasional sinner. To provide such a cross-section of society we have been forced to exclude many subjects whom others would have chosen. Any selection is likely to be an arbitrary one, and we invite readers to add to our store of biographies with articles which could be included in a later volume.

Our target readership has been those persons interested in the local history of the area. We hope, too, that the genealogical researcher will find the book useful. At the end of each article we have cited our sources and referred readers to longer works where these exist. It is not the function of a biographical dictionary to argue a thesis or make historical generalisations on the basis of our researches, although many ideas and themes suggest themselvs. We have not made any value judgments, but have let the facts speak for themselves; only occasionally have we offered a comment where this seemed desirable.

The educational objectives of the project were to provide an opportunity for persons to engage in local historical research, to practise the evaluation of historical material and to write the results of their researches in a compact form. My task as editor has been to ensure a uniformity of style and treatment.

The chief depository of the sources of information we have used has been the Horace Barks Library, City Library, Hanley, Stoke on Trent. We are indebted to the Staffordshire County Librarian, the Principal Area Librarian, Stoke on Trent, and to the members of the City Library staff, Derek Beard, Frank Edge, Mike Peterson and Kevin Reynolds; their knowledge and patience in servicing our class members over three winters were essential ingredients in the success of our project. We also thank the caretakers of the City Library for their willingness to work beyond their normal hours of duty.

Many persons, not members of our classes, have written, added to, or corrected our biographies. We thank Gaye Blake-Roberts, curator of the Wedgwood Museum, Frank Burchill and John Levitt of the Department of Adult Education, University of Keele, Rodney Hampson, Joan Jones, curator of the Minton archives, Royal Doulton, W. J. Chadwick of the Havergal Brian Society, Arnold Mountford, curator of the Stoke on Trent Museum and the members of his staff, and the librarians of the Royal College of Veterinary Surgeons Wellcome Library, the British Medical Association, the Royal College of Surgeons of England, the Pharmaceutical Society of Great Britain and the North Staffordshire Polytechnic. Numerous individuals who provided information are acknowledged in the relevant biography. We are grateful for publicity and for assistance with pictures to Bob Randall, editor of the *Evening Sentinel* and Barbara Mansfield, librarian.

The tutors involved in the first and second years of the project were Paul Anderton, Andrew Dobraczszyc and Robert Speake. Their contribution was decisive in getting the project under way. The names of the class members follow. To them belongs the major share of the credit. I trust they will forgive the cuts and alterations I have had to make in their carefully-compiled and vividly-written biographies in the interests of space and uniformity of style. An asterisk is placed after the names of those who attended all three years of the project and who were members of the final editorial group.

John Anderson*
Barbara Ardron
Joan Baker
Derek Benning
Margaret Boden
Ray Bourne
Elaine Bryan*
Frank Cooper*
F. S. Cooper
A. M. Crosbie
Nellie Davies
Vicky Degg*
Kay Derry
Florence Dodd*
Reg Edwards*
Miss L. A. Ellis
Mrs. E. Ellis
Lynne Franklyn
Carol Hanley
Miss C. A. Hassall
Elaine Holland*
William Holmes
Joan James
Les Jones
Rose Lovatt*
Joan MacPherson
Vilma Mainwaring*
Kathleen Manley*
Mary May*
Stuart Miles*
Sonia Mountford
L. G. O'Brien
Mary Phillips
Miss R. Shaw
R. C. Stones
Pamela Turner
Ernest Watkin
Mrs. H. W. Wood
Brian Woolley*

I am particularly indebted to Reg Edwards for extra help in the final stages of editing. Elaine Holland and Flo Dodd researched the pictures, and Barbara Stuart helped with typing, editing and proof reading.

DENIS STUART

Department of Adult Education
University of Keele
March 1985.

ACKNOWLEDGMENTS

We are grateful to the following for supplying photographs and/or permission to reproduce:

British Ceramic Society (Bernard Moore)
British Ceramic Research Association (J. W. Mellor)
Doris Robinson (Samuel Clowes)
Neale Harrison (Henry Pidduck)
Messrs. Twyfords Bathrooms (Thomas Twyford)
Tony Dyke (Oliver Dyke)
Minton Museum, Royal Doulton (U.K.) Ltd. (Herbert Minton)
North Staffs. Field Club (Charles Lynam)
I. Moxon, Messrs. Ellis Moxon and Co., and assistance of Bob Cooper, Messrs. Charles Butters and Co. (Walton Stanley)
Messrs. F. Geen and Co. (Frederick Geen)
W. J. Chadwick and the Havergal Brian Society (Havergal Brian)
The Evening Sentinel (Arnold Bennett, Josiah Clement Wedgwood, Sir Oliver Lodge, John Ridgway)
Newcastle Borough Library (Dinah Maria Mulock—Mrs. Craik—photograph by D. S. Dodd from A. L. Reade. *The Mellards and their Descendants)*
Stoke on Trent City Library (William Spanton, Lovelace Stamer, John Wilcox Edge, Thomas W. Harrison, Marie Reymond, A. R. Moody, Jesse Shirley)
Medical Institute, Hartshill and Dr E Isaacson (J. T. Arlidge)
Stoke City Museum Art Gallery (Enoch Wood)

ABBREVIATIONS

Some sources, frequently used, are cited in the references in the following abbreviated forms:

Adams	P. W. L. Adams, *History of the Adams Family of North Staffordshire* (1914).
Adams, *Notes*	P. W. L. Adams, *Notes on some North Staffordshire Families* (1910).
Anderton	P. Anderton, 'The Development of the Liberal Party of Stoke on Trent 1860-80' (Univ. of Keele M.A. thesis, 1974).
Briggs	J. H. Y. Briggs, *A History of Longton* (1982).
Census (+ year)	Population Census Enumerators' Schedules 1841 to 1881.
Dir. (+ year)	Directory e.g. White's *History Gazetteer and Directory of Staffordshire* 1851 (series in HRL).
DNB	*Dictionary of National Biography.*
Foster	J. Foster, *Alumni Oxonienses* (8 vols. 1887-92).
Huntbach	A. Huntbach, *Hanley, Stoke on Trent* (1910).
IGI Staffs.	*International Genealogical Index, Staffordshire.*
Jewitt	L. Jewitt, *Ceramic Art of Great Britain* (revised edition by G. Godden, 1972).
M & H	W. Mankowitz and R. Haggar, *The Concise Encyclopaedia of English Pottery and Porcelain* (1957).
Oldham	C. A. Oldham, 'Burslem: the development of statutory bodies and their interactions with local institutions 1850-1910', (Univ. of Keele M.A. thesis, 1977).
R and S	A. Rotherham and R. Steele, *A History of Printing in North Staffordshire* (1975).
S and L	M. Stenton and B. Lees, *Who's Who in British MPs 1832-85, 1886-1918,* (1976).
Shaw	C. Shaw, *When I was a Child* (1903).
Simms	R. Simms, *Bibliotheca Staffordiensis* (1894).
SHC (+ vol. no.)	Staffordshire Record Society (formerly William Salt Archaeological Society), *Collections for a History of Staffordshire.*
Townley	W. E. Townley, 'Urban Administration and Health: a case study of Hanley in the mid-19th century' (Univ. of Keele M.A. thesis 1969).
Turner	J. Turner, 'Stokeville Building Society', (Univ. of Keele B.A. dissertation 1974).
Venn	J. and J. A. Venn, *Alumni Cantabrigienses* (10 vols. 1922-54).
V and S	J. Vincent and M. Stenton, *McCalmont's Parliamentary Poll Book 1832-1918* (8th edition, 1971).
VCH (+ vol. no.)	*Victoria County History of Stafford.*
Ward	J. Ward, *History of the Borough of Stoke upon Trent* (1843).

Other abbreviations: c *circa* (about); *obit* obituary; HRL Hanley Reference Library (Horace Barks Reference Library, City Library, Hanley); PRO Public Record Office; q.v. *quem vide* (whom see, i.e. the subject of a biographical article in this volume); SRO Staffordshire Record Office; WSL William Salt Library.

ABINGTON, Revd. Leonard James (1785-1867), *pottery modeller,* Hanley.

LJA was born in London on 17 November 1785, the son of Leonard Joseph Abington. His paternal grandmother, a convert of George Whitfield, influenced him and he joined the Baptist church about 1800. He learned the trade of pottery modeller and Benjamin Wyatt, the architect, employed him in the decoration of Drury Lane theatre, London. He also executed much of the detail on Sir John Soane's Bank of England. Advised to leave London for health reasons LJA came to the Potteries in 1819 at the invitation of Jacob Phillips, a co-deacon with Abington at Little Wild Street Church, Bloomsbury, London. He worked at Phillips' pottery, Church Works, in Hanley and he also modelled for Joseph Mayer, Phillips' successor. From 1831 to 1838 LJA was in partnership with William Ridgway, acting as works chemist and improving the relief modelling on Ridgway jugs. He later entered into partnership with Edward John Ridgway (q.v.). Joseph Mayer left Abington £10,000 at his death and he retired from business. Church Works was demolished about 1948 and the site was later partly covered by the King George VI Club.

In 1820 LJA and Phillips reopened New Street (now Goodson Street) Baptist church, which had been closed for some years, and LJA and his father preached there for some years and at Burslem. A Baptist meeting house was registered in 1832 in the Ironmarket, Newcastle under Lyme, and LJA became its pastor. In an endeavour to heal a schism he also became pastor of Hanley Baptist church from about 1834.

LJA had a wide range of interests. With William Ridgway and Josiah Wedgwood II (q.v.) he helped to found the Hanley branch of the British and Foreign Bible Society and was a life governor of the National Society. In politics he had radical and Liberal opinions. He edited the *Pottery Mercury,* published by Thomas Allbut (q.v.), in 1824 and lectured to the Pottery Philosophical Society on topics in both the arts and sciences. In 1836 he helped to bring a lengthy strike in the pottery industry to an end.

LJA married (1) in 1807, Harriet Mundy (died 1808), and (2) in 1811 Sarah Sandys, daughter of a Baptist minister. He had six daughters and one son, also called Leonard James Abington, who operated the Victoria Sugar Refinery, London Road, Newcastle under Lyme. LJA died on 9 August 1867 at Northwood, Hanley.

Leonard James Abington, *Personal Recollections;* D. W. Adams, *The Victoria Sugar Refinery, Newcastle under Lyme;* G. Godden, *The Illustrated Guide to Ridgway Porcelain;* D. J. Lewis, *Baptists in Hanley;* A. Shelley 'The History of Ridgway' (Univ. of Keele Dept. of Adult Education local history certificate essay 1971): VCH viii.

ADAMS, Boyce (1833-97), *grocer,* Hanley.

BA was born in Uttoxeter in 1833, the son of Ralph Adams, maltster, of Carter Street, Uttoxeter and his wife Lydia. BA, in partnership with Joseph Lamb, acquired a grocery business at 1 Piccadilly, Hanley, in 1860. The shop had formerly been owned by John Buckley, grocer and miller (of Borough Mills, Marsh Street). BA and his partner expanded the business and eventually owned four shops, at Tontine Street and 32 Piccadilly, Hanley, at 59 High Street, Tunstall, and at 43 Market Place, Burslem. BA also acquired property in Snow Hill in 1872-5. The firm of Boyce Adams and Company continued until 1960 when it was acquired by Fine Fare. The original shop in Piccadilly was closed on 31 March 1973.

BA married twice. By his first wife, Jane née Buckley, daughter of John Buckley from whom he bought the shop, he had three children, all of whom died in infancy. Jane herself died in 1868, probably giving birth to her third child. In 1869 BA married Sarah, daughter of Robert Scrivener (q.v.). By her he had a number of children, two of whom married into the family of George Howson (q.v.), at Bethesda chapel. Robert, BA's son, was killed at Gallipoli in the first world war.

BA took no part in public affairs but served for 25 years as treasurer of Bethesda New Connexion chapel. By 1872 he was living at Crescent Villa, Cemetery Road, Shelton, where he died on 18 October 1897.

Census 1861, 1871, 1881; Dir. 1872; *Evening Sentinel* 31 March 1973.

ADAMS, Charles (1822-1912), *potter's miller,* Hanley.

CA was born in Keelings Lane, Northwood, Hanley, on 17 October 1822, the son of Thomas Adams. He was educated at Simeon Shaw's school and then at a school on Cannock Chase. He served an apprenticeship at the factory of Samuel Keeling, Market Place, Hanley, rising to become manager of this firm. Later he became a partner in his father's business, and then sole proprietor of Eastwood Mill Co.

CA was twice mayor of the social club called Ancient Corporation of Hanley. He was a director of Staffordshire Potteries Waterworks Company, and was created a freeman of the borough. In 1859 he joined the 1st Hanley company of volunteers and rose to become sergeant major of the battalion.

In 1850 he married Miss Forrester of Newcastle under Lyme, a daughter of the agent for Lord Granville's collieries, and by her had three daughters, one of whom married the Revd. W. S. Knowles, rector of Hanley and another Alfred Johnson, of Johnson Brothers, potters, of Hanley. CA's recollections of the history of Hanley were reported in the *Staffs. Sentinel* 9 March 1907. He died at his home in Charles Street, Hanley, on 21 July 1912. A stained glass window was erected to his memory in Hanley parish church.

Adams; *Staffordshire County Biographies; Staffs. Sentinel,* 22 July 1912 (obit.).

ADAMS, Jonathan Henry (1817-80), *chemist,* Stoke upon Trent.

JHA, the son of James Adams and Ann, née Taylor, was born in Hanley on 23 July 1817. His paternal grandfather, also Jonathan, was a timber merchant at Etruria Vale, whose business was impeded by the rail road built by John Rennie in 1805 from Hanley to the canal at Adams' wharf. Josiah Wedgwood II asked for compensation on his behalf. JHA was apprenticed to a chemist in Preston, Lancs., and with an inheritance from his grandfather in 1838, had opened a druggist's shop in High Street, Stoke upon Trent, by 1843. He was advertised as the agent for Schweppes' aerated waters in 1848. He qualified as a chemist in May 1853 and was registered with the Pharmaceutical Society until his death.

He was an original member of the Stokeville Building Society in 1850 and was living in a house at The Villas by 1861, having previously lived above the shop. In June 1853 he became an improvement commissioner for Stoke upon Trent and later supported the unsuccessful attempt of Oliver Lodge, senior to become Clerk. He asked, in May 1863, whether aid could be given to a public playground in London Road.

On 18 October 1842 at Preston, he married Elizabeth Chambers and the had five children. One son, Frank, qualified as a chemist in 1870 and continued the business. In 1907 the shop was on the corner of High Street and King (Consort) Street, the building which latterly housed Dale's Chemists, who some years ago exhibited some of Adams' prescription registers.

JHA died at The Villas on 13 April 1880.

Adams; Census 1861; Dir. 1907; *National Index to Wills and Administrations 1858-1931;* Stoke upon Trent Improvement Commissioners' Minute Book; Stoke upon Trent parish registers; Turner; letter from Josiah Wedgwood II to Trent and Mersey Canal Co., 1805, (HRL); information from Miss M. F. Mackenzie, Pharmaceutical Society of Great Britain.

ADAMS, Lewis (1805-50), *pottery manufacturer,* Stoke upon Trent.

LA was born at Bagnall on 11 July 1805, the 3rd son and 6th child of William Adams of Bagnall and Fenton Hall and Sarah née Heath his wife. He was educated at a school in Chapel Chorlton, Staffs. After his father's death in 1829 LA continued to live with his mother and unmarried sisters at Fenton Hall until 1835 when the family moved to the Mount, Stoke upon Trent, recently vacated by the Spode family. LA moved to The Watlands, Wolstanton, in 1842, where he lived for the rest of his life. He shared with his brothers in the family pottery business with factories in Stoke, Burslem and Tunstall.

LA was a churchwarden of Stoke upon Trent parish church in 1842 and master of the North Staffordshire Harriers from 1836 to 1842, when he sold his pack to William Davenport. The latter exchanged the pack for foxhounds and thus inaugurated the North Staffordshire Hunt. LA and his elder brother Edward subscribed to the building of Stoke town hall in 1834. In politics LA was a Whig. He supported his friend, John Lewis Ricardo, who was returned as Liberal member of Parliament for Stoke upon Trent in 1841. In 1839 LA became chief bailiff of Stoke upon Trent.

He died unmarried at The Watlands, on 24 September 1850. The Adams family crest was a boar's head, and this was adopted as the crest for the arms of the borough of Stoke upon Trent on its incorporation in 1874, and became part of the arms of Stoke on Trent after federation.

Adams; Adams, *Notes.*

ADAMS, Thomas (1807-83), *pottery manufacturer,* Stoke upon Trent.

TA was the fourth son of William Adams, master potter of Fenton Hall and Bagnall and Sarah née Heath. He was born in 1807, and educated, with his brothers, at a school in Chapel Chorlton run by Mr. Blount. Thomas and his brothers became partners in the pottery works started by their father, who rented three factories from Thomas Wolfe. TA visited Mexico on a number of occasions, building up a large trade there for printed wares, some pieces of which are today collectors' items. He later managed the Liverpool offices opened by his elder brother, William Adams (q.v.). Lewis Adams (q.v.) a third brother, died in 1850, William withdrew from the Stoke business in 1853 to run the Greenfield factory in Tunstall and Thomas and his elder brother, Edward, were left to manage the Stoke upon Trent factories. Thomas complained of the supervision of the firm by Edward's son, but his speculative ventures lost the firm much money. The business in Stoke upon Trent declined and was closed following Thomas's death in Liverpool on 12 March 1863. He was buried in Stoke upon Trent churchyard.

Adams; Adams, *Notes;* W. Turner, *William Adams, an old English Potter.*

ADAMS, William (1746-1805), *pottery manufacturer,* Tunstall.

WA was born in June 1746, in Burslem, the son of Edward and Martha Adams, of Bagnall and Burslem. He was born after the death of his father and his mother also died when he was young. WA was brought up by his uncle, Joseph Adams, who worked a pottery in St. John's Square, Burslem. WA served an apprenticeship in a pottery in Longport owned by a brother of James Brindley (q.v.) the engineer. He then went to work in the family pottery in Burslem. This pottery was sold to Anthony Keeling in 1778 and WA went into business on his own account, leasing a pottery in Tunstall which he rebuilt and renamed Greengates. He purchased the site between 1784 and 1794 and built Greengates Hall. WA's pottery became noted for jasper ware in various colours. His blue was more violet in tone than Wedgwood's and he preferred Roman to Greek models for figures. By the 1790s he was a severe competitor for Wedgwood, his prices often being 20% cheaper. One of WA's modellers was a Swiss, Joseph Mononget. WA also worked Newfield Pottery, Tunstall, in partnership with his brother-in-law, Caleb Cole. The manufacture of jasper ceased in 1805, after WA's death, and was resumed only on a limited scale in 1809. Benjamin, WA's younger son, sold the Greengates Works to Joseph Meir in 1822. It remained in the hands of the Meir family until 1896 when the Adams family bought it back.

WA married Mary Cole on 12 September 1771, and had numerous children. With his grandson William Adams (q.v.) he shares a commemorative clock tower in Tunstall Park.

Adams; D. Furniss, *William Adams, Potters, 1779-1979;* W. L. Little, *Staffordshire Blue;* W. Turner, *William Adams, an old English Potter.*

ADAMS, William (1748-1831), *pottery manufacturer,* Burslem.

WA was born in 1748, the son of John Adams (died 1757) and his wife Dorothy née Murhall. WA's mother was the daughter of William Murhall of Bagnall, who, according to tradition, captured and skinned alive a Scottish rebel during the Young Pretender's march through Staffordshire in 1745. WA was born in Brick House, Burslem, reputed to have been one of the first brick houses in Burslem and dating from before the middle of the 17th century. Brick House and works were let to Josiah Wedgwood from 1762 to 1770, during WA's minority. The property was eventually divided, part becoming the site of an Independent chapel in 1838 and another part passing to Burslem corporation about 1879 for an extension to the Wedgwood Memorial Institute.

WA married Mary Bourne, daughter of a Newcastle under Lyme shoe manufacturer, on 30 April 1769. They had five sons and eight daughters, none of the latter ever marrying. WA discouraged them from so doing by locking them in their rooms if ever he went from home. He is said to have lowered one of his daughters down a well to impede the access of suitors. His seventh daughter Mary, born in 1792, was engaged to Frederick Wright Tomlinson, son of John Tomlinson, of Cliffe Vale, for many years, but WA broke off the match abruptly for no apparent reason.

WA reclaimed Brick House works in 1770, potting there himself for some years. He had learned the skills of potting with his step-father, John Hales, at Cobridge. It was at the Cobridge works that WA successfully experimented with copperplate printing, a process which helped the area to gain its predominant position in the pottery industry. After his step-father's death WA obtained an interest in Cockshead colliery, Norton. He had previously encouraged a local engineer, Cope, to experiment with atmospheric engines, and eventually he bought two of James Watt's steam engines for use in the mine. He also had a watermill at Stanley, where much of his material was ground and in 1797 he built a papermill at Cheddleton to provide paper for transfer printing. About 1780 he built Cobridge Hall and came later to own most of the land in the Cobridge area. He owned five pottery factories but by 1820 had ceased potting in order to concentrate on coalmining, leasing numerous pits in Hanley, Sneyd and Cobridge.

When the parish of Burslem was created in 1807 WA bought the advowson, and later gave the land on which a rectory was built. He also donated the site for St. Paul's church, Dalehall. Always eccentric, towards the end of his life he became a religious fanatic. He died at Cobridge Hall on 16 February 1831, leaving among other things, 250 bottles of 30-year old port.

Adams; D. Furniss, *William Adams, Potters 1779-1979;* W. H. Little, *Staffordshire Blue;* W. Turner, *A Tour of the Low Countries and Germany;* VCH viii.

ADAMS, William (1772-1829), *pottery manufacturer,* Stoke upon Trent.

WA, son of Richard Adams and Elizabeth née Jackson, was born on 20 July 1772. He worked for and later became the partner of Lewis Heath, potter, of Burslem, whose daughter he married. The partnership ended when WA rented the Upper Cliff Bank Works, Stoke upon Trent, from John Davenport. On the death of Thomas Wolfe in 1818 WA leased the former's factories, Big Works and Bridge Bank Works, Stoke upon Trent. In one part of Bridge Bank Works WA produced painted and gilded ware designed by John Simpson, his chief artist. WA took his four surviving sons, William (q.v.), Edward, Lewis (q.v.) and Thomas (q.v.) into partnership in 1819. The firm was the largest in the Potteries, exporting much of its production to the United States and Central America.

WA was Tory in his political opinions, served as church warden in Bagnall and Stoke upon Trent, and made benefactions to several churches. He married Sarah, daughter of Lewis Heath, on 18 January 1793 and had eleven children. The family lived first in Bagnall then in Cliff Bank House, adjoining the pottery, and lastly in Fenton Hall. WA's hobbies were playing the violin, hunting and especially walking. His walk from Liverpool to Stoke is thought to have contributed to his death on 2 December 1829. His sons continued the business until 1853 when their partnership ended.

Adams; D. Furniss, *William Adams, Potters, 1779-1979;* W. L. Little, *Staffordshire Blue;* M and H; VCH viii.

ADAMS, William (1798-1865), *pottery manufacturer,* Tunstall.

WA was born at Bank House, Bagnall, on 9 November 1798, the eldest son of William and Sarah Adams née Heath of Bagnall and Fenton Hall. He was educated by the Revd. Edward Carless, curate of Wolstanton, and like his brothers, at Blount's school, Chapel Chorlton. After becoming his father's partner in 1819 he travelled extensively in the southern states of America between 1821 and 1823, and opened an office in New York. He returned to America on several occasions and on his last visit contracted an ague. Through his marriage to Jane Breeze on 9th May 1827 he came into part possession of Greenfield Hall, formerly Southfield, the home of Theophilus Smith (q.v.), and Greenfield Pottery, Tunstall. In 1832 WA opened a shipping agency in Liverpool, for the export of Adams' wares and also acting as shipping agent for other firms. The agency possessed its own fleet of barges for inland river and canal work. WA returned to Tunstall and assumed control of Greenfield Works. The factory produced printed ware, sponged ware for the eastern market, and sanitary ware. From 1842 ironstone ware was also made. On the dissolution of the partnership with his brothers in 1853, WA received Greenfield Works and the Hadderidge estate at Burslem, which had belonged to his maternal grandfather. His concern at his brother Thomas's reckless business dealings determined him to end the partnership. He closed the Liverpool agency in 1855 and concentrated on mining, working the Greenfield pits with his brother Edward. In 1858 he bought Newfield Hall, and leased Newfield Pottery from Smith Child (q.v.) from at least 1860, his son William finally buying the works in 1872.

WA was a Whig in politics and a strict churchman. By his wife he had two sons and five daughters. He died at Rhyl on 27 October 1865.

Adams; D. Furniss, *William Adams, Potters, 1779-1979;* VCH viii.

ADAMS, William (1833-1905), *pottery manufacturer,* Tunstall.

WA, son of William Adams (q.v.) and Jane née Breeze, was born in Everton, Lancs., on 13 June 1833. He was educated at the church school, Newchapel, Newcastle under Lyme grammar school and, from 1849-52, at Rugby school. With his brother Thomas he began refining paraffin from shale at Bradwell Wood, but the enterprise was ended by competition from petroleum imports from America. In 1865 on the death of his father WA took over the Greenfield Works and his brother Thomas the mines. In 1872 WA bought Newfield Pottery, which the family had rented from Smith Child from about 1860. The pottery was later leased to W. H. Grindley. Two of his sons later joined him in the family business, and when Greengates Pottery was taken over the Adams family once again began to produce jasper ware.

WA was chief bailiff of Tunstall in 1872, a county magistrate, one of the first members of Staffordshire county council and a member of the Wolstanton and Burslem Board of Guardians. In politics he was at first Liberal, but became a Liberal Unionist in 1886 and in 1888 was elected to the county council as a Conservative. He was a captain in the 1st Battalion Staffordshire Volunteers from its inception in 1859 and became lieutenant colonel in 1867. He was a churchwarden of Wolstanton parish church.

He married Laura Elizabeth Worthington, of Ball Haye Hall, Leek, on 26 May 1864, and had at least six children, two girls and four boys. The family lived first at Greenfield, Tunstall, then at Moreton House, Wolstanton, where WA died on 5 March 1905. He is commemorated by a mural tablet in Wolstanton church and by a clock tower in Tunstall Park, erected in 1907. He had given part of his Greenfield estate to form the park. There is an oil painting of WA in the uniform of a volunteer by John Nash-Peake, painted in 1863. WA's son, Percy W. L. Adams (died 1952), was the family biographer, a genealogist and a local historian.

Adams; C. Penn, *Staffordshire at the Opening of the 20th Century; Staffs. Sentinel* 5 March 1905 (obit.).

ADCOCK, George Frederick (1858/9-1924), *hatter and hosier,* Hanley.

GFA was born in Hanley on 30 April 1858, one of four children of George Adcock, a colliery clerk, and his wife Amelia. The family lived in Prospect Terrace, Northwood. GFA attended the Birch Terrace Academy and was then apprenticed to Johnson, drapers of High Street, a former employee of Michael Huntbach (q.v.). GFA's father started a hatter and hosier's business in Parliament Row and in 1879, on his father's death, GFA took over the business, having also worked at Huntbach's.

In 1897 he joined the Hanley School Board, remaining a member until 1902. He served as mayor of the county borough of Hanley from 1907 to 1910, and was the last mayor before federation, to which he was personally opposed. He nevertheless stood for election to the new county borough council and was elected. He resigned on 13 March 1914 having been made executor of a will the terms of which required him to buy shares and become managing director in a firm engaged in council contracts. For many years he was the chairman of the North Staffordshire Joint Schools Authority (Blind and Deaf), and from 1912-14 of the education committee. He attended Bethesda Chapel, Hanley.

He married Helen Foster in 1880. By his wife, who had also worked in Huntbach's shop, he had three children. She was later a member of the North Staffordshire Adult Deaf Society. The family lived in Trentham in 1912, at Sunnyside, Endon in 1916 and from 1921 at Westfield, Endon, where GFA died on 19 April 1924.

Census 1871; Huntbach; *Staffs. Sentinel* 11 November 1907.

ADDERLEY, Charles (1832-1902), *solicitor,* Longton.

CA, the son of Rupert Adderley and Sarah née Wood, was born in Commerce Street, Longton, being baptised on 16 December 1832. Rupert Adderley was a beerseller in 1834 and licensee of the Duke of York public house, Longton, in 1851. CA was articled to R. Heaton, of Burslem, and was admitted solicitor in 1856. He became a partner in the firm of Adderley and Marfleet, Market Street, Longton. He was appointed clerk to the Fenton commissioners in June 1863, in succession to Alfred Crewe, and ten years later became clerk to the Fenton Board of Health. In 1894 he was appointed clerk to the Fenton Urban District Council. He also served as clerk to the Longton School Board in succession to G. C. Kent. He retired in 1900.

CA married Annie Furber about 1860. She bore him three children while the family was living in Duke Street, Fenton, and a third daughter, Edith, born in Hilderstone Villa, Hilderstone, where they had moved by 1867. The family returned to Fenton by 1871, living at Heron Cottage, where another daughter, Constance, was born. Finally the Adderleys lived at Canterbury Villa, Lightwood, where CA died on 11 July 1902.

His son Rupert (q.v.) became clerk to the Fenton Urban District Council in succession to his father.

Adderley Family Tree, compiled by G. Cope-Cartlidge for the North Staffs. Branch of the Birmingham and Midland Society for Genealogy and Heraldry for an exhibition in the City Library, Hanley, June 1984; Census 1871; Dir. 1834-1904; Fenton Commissioners' Minutes; *Staffs. Sentinel* 28 February 1918.

ADDERLEY, Rupert (1864-1918), *clerk to council,* Fenton.

RA was born on 18 June 1864 at Heron Cottage, Heron Cross, the son of Charles Adderley (q.v.) and Annie née Furber. RA, who qualified as a solicitor in 1891, became his father's deputy, and succeeded him as Clerk.

He was an emphatic opponent of federation and though that no scheme would suit Fenton. In evidence to the House of Commons Committee on the Federation Bill in July 1908, he admitted that Fenton had no baths, markets or parks, but said that they were not necessary for Fenton. On federation, he insisted upon his full rights for loss of office and received £6,000 compensation.

RA married Mary Beech née Lewis, a cousin, on 24 January 1888 and there were three children of the marriage. The family lived at The Laurels, Cocknage Road, Dresden and RA had a practice in Normacot Road, Longton. He shot himself, at his office on 28 February 1918.

Staffs. Sentinel 28 February 1918 (obit.); Adderley Family Tree, one of exhibits mounted by North Staffs. Branch of Birmingham and Midland Society for Genealogy and Heraldry at City Central Library, Hanley, June 1984; Federation Newscuttings 1907-08 (HRL).

AIDNEY, Thomas (c. 1848-98), *colour manufacturer,* Stoke upon Trent.

TA, son of William Aidney and Elizabeth née Ryles, was born in Stoke upon Trent about 1851. His father was a colour, dye and paint manufacturer of Penkhull, and TA continued in this business. In 1880 he bought land from The Mount estate, Penkhull, for £217.18s.6d. on which he built Hartshill Hall, completed in 1881. In 1889 he bought an adjoining plot of land, with access from West Avenue, on which he built a colour works. This was the only industry allowed by Frederick Bishop who sold the Mount estate.

TA, who was married but for whom no children are listed in the censuses of 1871/81, died on 1 November 1898.

Census 1881; *Staffs. Sentinel* 2 November 1898; R. Talbot, *Penkhull Remembered.*

AITKEN Revd. Robert Ellis (1774-1849), *minister of religion (Church of England),* Hanley.

REA was born on 8 December 1774 in the parish of St. George's, Hanover Square, London. His father was Robert Aitken, a Scots army officer who was posted to India shortly after his son's birth and died soon after arrival. REA graduated from Trinity College, Oxford, in 1796 and was awarded an M.A. degree in 1800. Before coming to Hanley as successor to John Middleton in 1802, he served as a curate in Birmingham.

On his arrival he was faced with the need to improve the condition of the churchyard which was little better than a waste ground covered with broken pottery. He also bought additional land from Joseph Mayer.

Because of his identification with the establishment he became a target for the Chartist rioters. On 15 August 1842 a mob burnt down the Rectory three hours after REA had been persuaded to leave, having taken what valuables could be carried. The mob raided the cellar and then set fire to the house, destroying the library and several of the Hanley parish registers (some of which have no other record). REA received £2,000 compensation from the authorities. George Wilcox was transported for his part in the affair. He was unrepentant and said that his only regret was that he had not been able to find Parson Aitken to "frizzle" him in his bath chair.

REA retired from the curacy in 1848 and spent the last year of his life at his son's home in Stafford, where he also held the curacy of Castle Church. He died on 11 March 1849.

Burchill and Ross; Foster; Huntbach; memorial in Hanley parish church; *Staffs. Times* 18 March 1876, 20 May 1876; VCH viii.

ALCOCK, John (1809/10-86), *banker and pottery manufacturer,* Burslem.

JA, the second son of George and Sarah Alcock and the nephew of Samuel Alcock (q.v.) of Hill Top Pottery, was born about 1809 at Burslem. He and his brothers Joseph and George operated Alcock's Bank 1838-63 and, after George's death, to May 1865 when it was sold to the Manchester and Liverpool Bank. The firm acted as bankers to the Burslem and Tunstall Boards of Health, and was also a joint bank for the Staffordshire Potteries Waterworks Co. of which JA was a director. From 1832-8 JA, his brothers and his uncle were joint partners in Hill Top Pottery. With his brother George, JA took over the large pottery of Ralph Stevenson at Cobridge on Stevenson's bankruptcy in 1835. He extended the factory and the date 1848 and the initials 'J A' can still be seen on the entrance pillars. JA retired temporarily from business on the death of his brother George, but later joined his son in working Central Pottery, Burslem, (now Sadler's), and took over full control on his son's death in 1881.

JA qualified as an improvement commissioner in 1837 and later became a member of the Burslem Local Board of Health, representing Rushton Grange (Cobridge). He was involved in the building of Sneyd church, Nile Street, which he helped to furnish, and gave a house which he owned in Waterloo Road for use as a vicarage. In 1851 he lived at Elder House, formerly his uncle Samuel's home.

He and his wife Harriet had at least four children, Sarah, Harriet, Richard and John. He died at Bradwell Lodge, Porthill, on 23 June 1886.

M. Ashford, 'Hill Top, Burslem, and the Alcocks' (Univ. of Keele, Dept. of Adult Education, local history certificate essay 1971); Oldham; VCH viii.

ALCOCK, John (1833-98), *medical practitioner,* Burslem.

JA was the fifth son of Samuel Alcock (q.v.), of Hill Top Pottery, Burslem, He was born in Burslem but baptised at Kingsley, Staffs., on 8 December 1833. He graduated from King's College, London, and in 1857 was awarded the degrees of M.R.C.S. and L.S.A. After working as a house surgeon at the North Staffordshire Infirmary he opened a private practice at No. 1 Church (later William Clowes) Street, Burslem, having probably taken over the practice of Daniel Ball who retired in 1859. He retained his conection with the Infirmary, acting as honorary surgeon. He was also honorary surgeon to and governor of the Haywood Hospital. A District Nursing Association had been set up originally under the Haywood bequest but this was in abeyance from 1887 until 1892 when, thanks largely to Alcock's efforts, it was revived. A Nurses' Home, financed largely by the Victoria Jubilee Appeal, was opened in 1897.

JA married twice. His first wife, Emily, born in London c. 1830, bore him at least two children, Samuel King, born in 1862, and Reginald born in 1868. She died on 24 June 1876 and JA subsequently married again. By his second wife, Mary (died 11 August 1928), he had two sons, Frank, born in 1880, and Arnold, born in 1882. Arnold played rugby for England in 1906. Mary Alcock was the 'token' woman co-opted on to Burslem Education Committee in 1903.

JA lived first at 1 Church Street, then after his marriage at Sytch House, 33 Liverpool (later Westport) Road, and finally at Portland House, Newcastle Street, Burslem, the home of the Riley family in the early 19th century. He was a Conservative in politics and a member of St. Paul's church, Dalehall. He was appointed to the magistrates' bench in 1894. He died on 7 May 1898 and was buried in St. Paul's churchyard. His portrait, paid for by public subscription, was unveiled in the Wedgwood Institute in 1899. The Alcock Memorial Home in his memory provided a house at Ellastone, near Ashbourne, where young women and girls could recuperate after operations.

M. Ashford, 'Hill Top, Burslem and the Alcocks' (Univ. of Keele Dept. of Adult Education local history certificate essay, 1971); G. E. Lowndes, *Haywood Hospital 1880-1948;* Oldham; St. Paul's churchyard memorial inscription; *Staffs. Advertiser* 14 May 1898; VCH viii.

ALCOCK, Samuel (1799-1848), *pottery manufacturer and banker,* Burslem.

SA, the youngest of the nine children of Thomas Alcock, farmer, and his wife Katherine, was baptised at Kingsley, Staffs., on 21 July 1799. Much of Samuel's early life was spent with an uncle, who was a grocer and banker, of Market Square, Hanley. SA began in partnership with Ralph Stevenson of Cobridge, whose factory in the 1830s employed 600 persons. From about 1828 SA was operating Hill Top Pottery. With his nephew Joseph he bought the pottery from the Robinson family in 1832 and reorganised it as Hill Pottery, extending and rebuilding the premises, with a front range in classical style, completed about 1839. The building, in Westport (formerly Liverpool) Road, was admired by Arnold Bennett (q.v.), who called it Sytch Pottery in his novel *Clayhanger.* Samuel Alcock and Co. made porcelain and parian ware. Among his designers were Giovanni Meli (q.v.) and Hugues Protat. The firm's productions included jugs designed under the inspiration of the Gothic Revival. With his three nephews Joseph, George and John Alcock, SA operated the Burslem Commercial Bank until 1838, when their partnership ended.

On 20 June 1836 SA became one of Burslem's improvement commissioners. He was elected chief constable on 9 June 1842 and took a prominent part in quelling the Chartist riots of August of that year, for which the inhabitants of Burslem presented him with a silver salver.

Hill Pottery was mortgaged for £10,000 in 1848. The Alcock family connection with the pottery ended in 1851 and the company failed in 1859. The pottery was demolished about 1968 and the factory of A. G. Hackney and Co. was built on the site.

By the 1830s SA was living in Cobridge Cottage, in the area of the later Grange Street. Later he moved to Elder House, Rushton Grange, Cobridge. By his wife Elizabeth he had 11 children, several of whom were baptised at Kingsley, Staffs. SA died on 10 November 1848 and was buried at Kingsley.

M. Ashford, 'Hill Top, Burslem, and the Alcocks' (Univ. of Keele, Dept. of Adult Education local history certificate essay 1971); G. Godden, *British Pottery and Porcelain Marks;* Jewitt; M and H; VCH viii; memorial tablet in Hanley parish church.

ALEXANDER, Adolf (died 1933), *gentlemen's outfitter,* Hanley.

AA was the son of Jacob Alexander, who is described as the founder of the Jewish community in Stoke upon Trent in 1873. AA established Alexander's, a gentlemen's outfitters, in Hanley. Later he played a leading role in raising funds for the building of the synagogue in Birch Terrace, whose foundation stone he laid on 5 October 1922. He died early in February 1933.

I. Down, 'A History of Jewish Settlement in the Potteries', (Univ. of Keele B.A. dissertation 1984); *Staffs. Sentinel* 13 February 1933 (obit.).

ALFIERI, Charles (c. 1828-94), *schoolmaster,* Hanley.

CA was born in Soho, London, about 1828. He was the son of Antonio Bernardo Carlo Alfieri, a major in the Italian army, of Salerno, who later Anglicised his name and earned a living as a linguist. CA's mother was Sarah, born in Essex about 1796, and died 1871. CA founded a boarding school in Hanley about 1852, known as Northwood Academy. In 1871 the school was in Birch Street, Northwood, where CA lived with his wife Elizabeth Julia née Marriner, whom he married in 1855, seven children and five boarders, all of whom were born in or near the Potteries. The school continued for about 35 years until CA retired in 1894 to the south of England. Many prominent Potteries people attended Alfieri's academy.

CA was interested in the Potteries Mechanics' Institute and for many years was president of the North Staffordshire Photographic Society. He was a churchwarden of Northwood church. He died on 30 June 1894 at 5 Junction Road, Southsea, and was buried in Hanley cemetery.

Census 1871, 1881; Holy Trinity church, Northwood, marriage records; *National Index to Wills and Administrations 1858-1931; Staffordshire Advertiser* January 1846 advertisements; gravestone in Hanley cemetery.

ALLBUT, Thomas (1777-1857), *printer and publisher,* Hanley.

TA the son of John Allbut and his wife Mary was born at Ross on Wye, Herefordshire, on 31 March 1777. In 1796 John Allbut, his father, bought the printing business of John Mort of Hanley (founded in 1786 by John Strahan, first bookseller in the Potteries). Simms in his *Bibliotheca Staffordiensis* states that John Allbutt was the master of Bromsgrove School until 1806 though the history of that institution, *Bromsgrove School through Four Centuries,* does not confirm this. John Allbut became the proprietor of Meriden Academy, Warwickshire, about 1800, and his son, Thomas, took over his father's printing business. TA had several partners, George Gibbs between 1811 and 1813, his own son, Edwin, from 1832 to 1852 and Robert Hobson between 1848 and 1850. He published *A View of the Staffordshire Potteries* in 1800, Potteries directories in 1802 and 1822, and in 1824 he founded a newspaper, the *Pottery Mercury* with Leonard Abington (q.v.) as its first editor. A good deal of Allbut's printing was for local Methodist churches, especially the Bethesda Methodist New Connexion church for which he was a local preacher for 50 years. Apart from printing and bookselling TA sold a range of toiletries, dealt in tea and for a time, c. 1834, operated a post office. He succeeded his father as librarian and treasurer of the Pottery Subscription Library which in 1840 was housed in his shop in Market Square, Hanley. On TA's retirement the library was merged with that of the Mechanics' Institute. He retired from business on 31 December 1852 and was succeeded by his second son, Edwin.

TA married Sidney Ashford on 27 February 1798 at St. Martin's-in-the-Bull Ring, Birmingham, and had four sons and three daughters. He died on 29 December 1857 and was buried in Bethesda churchyard.

Allbut and Daniel, *Brochure*, 1897; Dir. 1834; R and S; Simms; *Staffs. Advertiser* 2 January 1858 and 5 January 1895.

ALLBUT, William (1809-79), *newspaper editor,* Hanley.

WA was born in Hanley about 1809, the son of Thomas Allbut (q.v.). By 1833 he was the proprietor of the *Staffordshire Mercury* (later styled the *North Staffordshire Mercury* and afterwards the *Potteries Mercury*), a moderately Liberal newspaper. He lived in Northwood, Hanley, moving to The Mount, Penkhull, in June 1844.

His first wife, Anne née Shirley, died in childbirth on 18 February 1833, aged 22. He married secondly Sophia Mort, who had opened a school for young ladies at Northwood in 1837. The school moved to The Mount and was open for the autumn term of 1844. In 1851 there were four teachers and 30 scholars between 9 and 17, of whom only two were local. The music teacher was Helen Mayer Ridgway.

About 1853 WA and his family left the Potteries for Cheshire. Later he retired to Middlesex, dying at Downhurst, Hendon, on 15 February 1879.

National Index to Wills and Administrations 1858-1931; Simms; R. Talbot, *Penkhull Remembered;* Staffs. County Council Study Book 9, *The Mount Estate, Penkhull.*

ANGUS, Robert Nicol (c. 1810-75), *railway engineer,* Stoke upon Trent.

RNA was born in Scotland about 1810. He was apprenticed to Bury, Curtis and Kennedy, engineers, of Liverpool, and about 1843 he may have been employed as engineer to the Preston and Wyre Dock Railway. He was appointed locomotive foreman to the North Staffordshire Railway in September 1847, responsible to the Engineer for the running and maintenance of the locomotive department. The company's first two engineers, S. P. Bidder (q.v.) and J. C. Forsyth (q.v.) made the decisions on which types of locomotive to buy. Thomas Dodds, the company's fourth engineer, appointed in 1870, was a devotee of the wedge motion of traction for locomotives, which his father had invented. Dodds bought several locomotives of this type and built others. They proved troublesome in practice and when Dodds left in 1874 and Angus was appointed to the newly-created post of locomotive superintendent, the latter's first task was to remove the wedge motion and replace it with the accepted link motion.

RNA married Margaret Ballantyne c. 1836, when he was working in Liverpool. A son, William, was born about 1843 and a daughter, Margaret, in 1848, by which time the family had come to Stoke. They lived first in Whieldon's Row and then at Whieldon's Hall, formerly the home of Thomas Whieldon the potter (q.v.). Part of Whieldon Hall formed the original station at Stoke, close to the locomotive works. Angus's brother-in-law, Alexander Ballantyne, was employed by the N.S.R. as a locomotive driver.

RNA did not long enjoy his new status as locomotive superintendent. He died, just a year after his appointment, on 10 July 1875.

Census 1861; R. Christiansen and R. W. Miller, *The North Staffordshire Railway.*

ANSON, General The Honourable George (1797-1857), *professional soldier and Member of Parliament,* Stoke upon Trent.

GA, younger son of Thomas I Viscount Anson, was born on 13 October 1797. He joined the army at an early age, serving in the 3rd Scots Fusiliers and was a major-general by 1851. He rose to be commander-in-chief in India by 1855. GA sat as Liberal Member of Parliament for Great Yarmouth from 1818 to 1835. He unsuccessfully contested South Staffordshire in May 1835, an election in which good electoral organisation by the Conservatives played a part. He was returned for Stoke upon Trent in 1836 and for South Staffordshire in 1837, holding the latter seat in the uncontested elections of 1841, 1846, 1847 and 1852. He accepted the Chiltern Hundreds in 1853, having been a member of the House of Commons for 34 years but having rarely spoken except to answer official questions.

In 1830 he married the Hon. Isabella Weld, daughter of 1 Lord Forester, and had two daughters. He died of cholera on 22 May 1857 at Karhal, during the Indian Mutiny.

F. W. S. Craig, *British Parliamentary Election Results 1832-85;* DNB; P. J. Doyle, 'The General Election of 1841: the representation of South Staffordshire', in *South Staffs. Archaeological and Historical Society Transactions, 1970-1, vol. xii.*

ARLIDGE, John Thomas (1822-99), *medical practitioner,* Newcastle under Lyme and Hanley.

JTA, son of John Arlidge, was born at Chatham on 17 July 1822. He was educated at Chatham and Rochester Classical and Mathematical School. He was apprenticed to a general practitioner in Rochester in 1838 and graduated M.B. and B.A. from King's College, London, in 1846. He was elected M.R.C.P. in 1847 and appointed resident medical officer at St. Luke's Hospital for Lunatics in the same year. In 1859 he published *The State of Lunacy and the Legal Provision for the Insane.* He was appointed consultant physician to the North Staffordshire Infirmary, then at Etruria, in 1862. He was awarded an M.D. (London) in 1867, and elected F.R.C.P. in 1869. He became an authority on occupational diseases, especially those connected with the pottery and mining industries. His chief work, *Hygiene Diseases and Mortality of Occupations* was published in 1892.

About 1859 JTA married Eliza Watts. He was appointed justice of the peace in 1873 and elected mayor of Newcastle under Lyme in 1878. he was a founder member of the North Staffordshire Field Club and was awarded the Garner medal in 1898. He lived at High Grove, Trent Vale, and practised in the Ironmarket, Newcastle. He died on 27 October 1899. He was no social reformer but it has been written of him that his greatest aim and his main ambition was the welfare of the working class.

British Medical Journal, 4 Nov. 1899, obituary; E. Isaacson, 'The Forgotten Physician, in *British Medical Association Annual Clinical Meeting,* Stoke on Trent, 1963 (with photograph on p.24).

ARMSTRONG, Revd. Dr. John Elchin (1806/7-72), *minister of religion (Church of England),* Burslem.

JEA was born in Dublin about 1806 and graduated from the University there in 1831. He was awarded further degrees, of M.A. (1841) LL.B. and LL.D. (1850) and D.D. (1853). A militant Protestant, he learned Gaelic to help him win converts among Catholics in Ireland. He continued similar work in England as honorary secretary of the Church Mission to Roman Catholics and visited the Potteries in that capacity. By 1855 he was vicar of Walsall and wrote a pamphlet accusing the Roman Catholic Church of kidnapping Henry Astropp, an English priest, who wished to renounce his vocation in order to marry.

In 1858 he became rector of St. John's, Burslem and was patron of the living. He was one of the founders of the Burslem Volunteer Rifle Corps and formed the Garibaldi Rifle Corps from amongst the boys of St. John's National School. This involvement was criticised by James Macintyre (q.v.) as "an unseemly perversion of a peaceful calling". He showed his peaceful side by organising entertainments to raise funds for the Wedgwood Institute by singing, playing the flute and conducting choirs which he had taught to sing by the Hullah method.

He caused controversy in 1863 by refusing to attend at the laying of the foundation stone of the Wedgwood Institute because he was expected to toast Roman Catholic clergy. At Christmas 1865 he offered a prize for an essay on an anti-papal theme. The winning entry was entitled "The World's Wail of Misery from Rome's Revolting Tyranny", by W. L. Evans (possibly William Evans editor of the *Potteries Examiner*). JEA published it as a pamphlet in 1866.

His wife, Julia, died in 1869 and he resigned as rector and left Burslem shortly afterwards. He was married a second time and died at Llanstadwell, Pembrokeshire on 10 September 1872.

M. W. Greenslade "Staffordshire—No popery 1850/1" in *Staffs. Catholic History* No. 21. 1982; *History of the Volunteer Force of Staffordshire 1859-1908;* Oldham; Census 1861; W. L. Evans, *The World's Wail of Misery from Rome's Revolting Tyranny,* (HRL Local Pamphlets No. 8); J. E. Armstrong, *The Astropp case* (HRL Local Pamphlets No. 34).

ARNOUX, Joseph Francois Leon (1816-1902), *pottery designer,* Stoke upon Trent.

JFLA was born in Toulouse in 1816, the son of Antoine Arnoux, porcelain and earthenware manufacturer and several times mayor of Toulouse. JFLA studied at the École Centrale des Arts et Manufactures in Paris. After qualifying as an engineer he worked with his father. He came to England in 1848 to study manufacturing techniques. While at Minton's he undertook research into encaustic tiles and impressed Herbert Minton who offered him the job of art director. Arnoux was responsible for Minton's display at the Great Exhibition of 1851 and his new majolica coloured glazes won a reputation both for Minton's and for Arnoux himself. He was later decorated with the Order of Franz Joseph and became a chevalier of the Legion of Honour. His reputation encouraged other French and continental artists to migrate to Minton's, including Solon (q.v.), Boullemier (q.v.) and Retchgitz. Arnoux encouraged local Potteries artists to familiarise themselves with continental styles and productions. His engineering background enabled him to effect several technical improvements in pottery making, including a down-draught oven. JFLA became a partner in Minton's on its incorporation as a limited company in 1885. He retired in 1892.

He married Suzanne Serac, born in St. Pierre in the West Indies, about 1840. They had two sons and two daughters, that last three of these children being born in Stoke upon Trent. They lived at 10 The Villas, Stoke upon Trent. JFLA continued in active association with Minton's after his retirement until his death on 25 August 1902. He was known popularly as 'The Man who made Minton's'.

P. Atterbury, *The Story of Minton;* Census 1871, 1881; Dir. 1875; G. Godden, 'Artists at Minton', in *Apollo,* 1962; *Staffs. Advertiser* 6 September 1902.

ASHWELL, John (born c. 1799), *colliery owner,* Longton.

JA was born in Coddington, Notts., about 1799. By 1834 he was living at Greendock, Longton. In 1845 he bought the Mossfield collieries for £20,000 and leased them to Messrs. Hawley, Bridgewood and Goodwin, who paid a minimum rental of £1,770 whether they worked the pits or not. Both Ashwell and the lessees were in dispute with the North Staffs. Railway Co. in August 1848 because of alleged damage to the property caused by land being taken for the Uttoxeter branch of the railway, which removed a wharf. JA claimed £4,220 and the Railway Co. offered £600. An arbitration awarded him £1,800.

He was the chief constable of Lane End (Longton) in 1837, when riots during the election lasted for a week and required the use of troops to quell them. In 1839 he was one of the original improvement commissioners for Longton and Lane End.

JA was living at Great Fenton in 1851 with his wife Mary and two children. He was farming 70 acres and worked a brick and tile yard in Anchor Road, Longton. Later he was working the Anchor Colliery. Another son was Michael Hoole Ashwell (q.v.) born at Coddington in 1825. He was Medical Officer of Health for the Borough of Stoke upon Trent from 1874 until his death in 1891 and the father of John Blow Ashwell (q.v.). The relationship between JA and MHA is not indicated in the obituary of MHA but is made clear by John Blow Ashwell in his acknowledgement that both sets of grandparents—Glovers and Ashwells—had connections with Longton.

Briggs; Census 1851; Dir. 1834, 1851; *Staffs. Advertiser* 12 August 1848; *Staffs. Sentinel* 17 March 1910.

ASHWELL, John Blow (1855-1910), *town clerk,* Stoke upon Trent.

JBA, the eldest son of Michael Hoole Ashwell (q.v.) and his wife Catherine Lydia née Glover, was born at Stoke upon Trent on 18 February 1855. He was educated in Malvern and at the Royal Medical College, Eton. After being articled to Keary and Marshall, solicitors, Stoke upon Trent, he was admitted a solicitor in 1878 and practised on his own account until 1887. On the death of William Keary (q.v.) JBA joined the practice of Keary and Marshall. He was elected a councillor for Stoke upon Trent south ward in 1884 but resigned in 1889 to become town clerk of Stoke upon Trent. He served in this office until federation in 1910, when he was elected a freeman of the borough of Stoke upon Trent. He presented Stoke upon Trent's case at the parliamentary committee hearings in 1908.

His political views were Conservative and he acted as agent for Conservative candidates at a number of parliamentary elections. He was secretary of the School of Art for 20 years. He married Mary Edith Bird.

JBA died at his home at The Quarry, Hartshill, on 19 October 1910. His previous ill-health was said to have been brought about by the stress incurred while preparing for federation. His family commemorated him by giving the clock in Penkhull church tower.

Federation Newscuttings (HRL); *Staffs. Advertiser* 22 October 1910 (obit.).

ASHWELL, Michael Hoole (1825-91), *medical officer of health,* Stoke upon Trent.

MHA, eldest son of John Ashwell (q.v.), farmer, of Great Fenton, was born at Coddington Manor, near Newark, on 24 November 1825. After graduating from University College Hospital, London, he was appointed house surgeon at Newark Infirmary. His degrees were MRCS(Eng) and LSA. He came to the Potteries in 1852 and entered into partnership with Dr. Robert Garner (q.v.) until 1879, and afterwards with Dr. Alexander McAldowie. On the incorporation of the borough of Stoke upon Trent in 1874 he was appointed medical officer of health. He was surgeon to the local militia and after this body was replaced by the volunteers in 1859 he served the latter until his death. He also acted as medical officer to the Stoke upon Trent Board of Guardians and was honorary physician to the North Staffordshire Infirmary.

Soon after his arrival in Stoke he married Catherine Lydia, daughter of John Glover (q.v.) of Longton, and had two sons, John Blow Ashwell (q.v.) and Albert Henry, later vicar of St. Mark's church, Jersey.

Up to 1874 MHA was a member of the board of improvement commissioners, and for some time was a member of the Stoke upon Trent school board. He died on 13 July 1891 at Stoke Lodge, Oakhill, and is buried in a family vault in Hartshill cemetery.

Staffs. Advertiser 18 July 1891; headstone in Hartshill cemetery.

AUDLEY, Robert (1860-1924), *licensed victualler,* Burslem.

RA was born on 8 June 1860 in Hanley, the son of James Audley, and educated at the Granville schools, Cobridge. He was first employed by the Shelton Coal and Iron Co., but later bought, among other public houses, the Granville Hotel (now Cobridge). In 1899 he became associated with Port Vale football club, who used the Granville as their headquarters. He was president of the North Staffordshire Licensed Victuallers Association, and helped to carry through to the House of Lords an action against a licensing assessment, which he won. In 1910 he founded New Hall Pottery Co., Hanley. He was a mason, and president of the Burslem Association for the Prosecution of Felons from 1913 to 1918.

He married Sarah Ann Cork on 9 October 1881, and remarried on his first wife's death. He had three children Robert James, and two daughters. He died, aged 64, on 9 December 1924 at Windycote, Longsdon, Staffs.

Pottery Gazette 1 January 1925; *Pottery and Glass,* December 1924.

AUSTIN, Jesse (1806-79), *pottery engraver,* Fenton.

JA the youngest of 12 children of William Austin, a tailor from Devonshire, was born in Longton on 23 March 1806. He was apprenticed to John Davenport of Longport. About 1840 he set up in business on his own, but because of the trade depression was unsuccessful and left the Potteries to work in Leicestershire. He returned in 1846 and joined F. and R. Pratt and Co. He collaborated with Felix Edward Pratt (q.v.) to produce and perfect multi-colour transfer printing on pottery. Davenports had made dinner services in 1836 which featured three-colour printing, said to have been invented by William Brooke, and it is possible that Austin may have learnt the technique and carried his knowledge to Pratt's. In 1859 a dispute with Thomas Pratt, the works manager, caused JA to leave and join T. C. Brown-Westhead, of Cauldon Potteries, Shelton, though he returned to Fenton in the following year.

He married Sarah Skinner on 22 March 1830 and his children included a son, Leonard. Leonard, who kept a private school for boys at 9 Gower Street, Longton, about 1867, later became school attendance officer for Longton school board. In 1841 JA and his family lived in Hope Street, Hanley, in 1851 in Heron Cross, in 1853 in Nelson Place, Hanley and in 1865 at 2 Spring Terrace. JA died on 30th March 1879.

Census 1841, 1851; Dir. 1865-6; Coysh and Honeywood, *Dictionary of Blue-Printed Pottery; Pottery Gazette* October 1955; C. William-Wood, *Staffordshire Pots and their Potters.*

AYNSLEY, Gerrard (1880-1959), *pottery manufacturer,* Longton.

GA, son of John Gerrard Aynsley and grandson of John Aynsley (q.v.), was born in 1880. He served an apprenticeship with the family firm of John Aynsley, Longton, china manufacturers, and eventually succeeded his father as managing director of Sampson Bridgwood. He saw active service in the South African War, 1899-1902, with the 22nd Company (Cheshire) Imperial Yeomanry and he also served in the First World

War. For some years he farmed in Australia. He returned to the Potteries, living at Spot Acre, near Stone, and travelled to work on horseback. He was a member of the North Staffordshire Hunt.

He died on 29 October 1959.

Evening Sentinel 30 October 1959.

AYNSLEY, John (1823-1907), *pottery manufacturer,* Longton.

JA was born in Union Street, Longton, in 1823, the son of James Aynsley and Charlotte née Anderson. His grandfather, also called John Aynsley, came to the Potteries from Northumberland, became chairman of the Fenton Park Colliery Co., and was afterwards in business as a maker of lustre ware, the first in Longton, in a factory on the site of Longton market. The family fell into reduced circumstances during JA's childhood, for reasons which are disputed. His mother went to work as a paintress and JA, after a short education in a dame school, began work at the age of nine, for twopence a day, at John Lockett's factory. Later he was employed in three different factories at the same time, working a 16-hour day. The trade depression of 1848 forced him to seek employment in Derby and the north of England. After some time he returned to the Potteries, acquired an interest in Cooper and Co., worked for Sampson Bridgwood and eventually became the latter's partner. In 1861 JA built the Portland works in Sutherland Road, Longton.

He was first elected to the Longton council in 1865. He served as mayor in four successive years from 1886, when he was instrumental in the creation of Longton Park, the first such park in the Potteries. The duke of Sutherland gave 45 acres of his estate in Dresden, JA donated £1,000 as well as trees and shrubs and raised funds to ensure that there was no charge on the rates during the development of the park, which was opened in 1888. JA also persuaded the duke of Sutherland to give land for the site of a new hospital. He used unorthodox methods of fund raising: he was offered a pig by the landlord of the Trentham Hotel on condition he drove it himself to Longton market; he completed the feat and raised a considerable sum of money in so doing. On another occasion he auctioned a donkey. The donkey died, JA calcined the bones and had a statue of a donkey made from the remains. The statue was used to collect funds for the cottage hospital for many years.

JA married Julia Gerrard at Bucknall on 27 March 1847. A son, John Gerrard Aynsley was born in 1855. JA died at Portland House, Blythe Bridge, on 7 February 1907.

Apollo, vol. 38 (1943); Briggs; *Staffs. Sentinel* 28 October 1899; VCH viii.

BADDELEY, George (1854-1934), *school teacher,* Burslem.

GB was born in Newcastle under Lyme on 23 June 1854 and educated at the British School there. He was a pupil teacher for five years then won a Queen's scholarship to study at the British and Foreign Bible Society's training college in London. He taught for some time in London before being appointed headmaster of Hill Top Boys' Board School, Burslem, in July 1877. He served as headmaster for 43 years, retiring in July 1920.

GB's reputation was such and his authority so accepted that on occasion the police sought his help in quelling disturbances in the town. His was the first school to provide midday meals for children during the pottery strike in the 1890s. Between 1900 and 1912 he was a member of the national executive of the National Union of Teachers.

GB served as a deacon in Burslem Congregational church for many years and held a number of other offices. He was a Rechabite, a member of the Tonic Sol-Fa Society and treasurer of Porthill Cricket Club.

He married Hannah Simpson on 26 December 1877 and there were eight children of the marriage. He died at his home Elim, Rushton Road, Cobridge, on 14 June 1934.

Evening Sentinel 14 June 1934; Oldham.

BAILEY, Revd. Granville Rowe (1843-1917), *minister of religion, (Church of England),* Tunstall.

GRB was born on 29 March 1843 at Shooter's Hill, Longton, the son of John Bailey and his wife Marianne née Rowe, colour manufacturer, and the grandson of William Bailey (q.v.), of Lightwood Lodge. He was educated at Hewitt's school, Tutbury, Staffs., and at Wharton's school, Appleby, Leics. He went to Trinity College, Cambridge, and graduated B.A. in 1866, M.A. 1891. Ordained deacon in 1867 and priest in 1868 he served as a curate in Sheffield before coming to Madeley, Staffs., as curate at Leycett church. A supporter of the High Church movement he introduced the use of the surplice by the choir. Towards the end of his curacy he astounded local opinion by inviting Blondin, the equilibrist, to a church garden party, but 13,000 people attended. A huge crowd of about 20,000 attended the garden party of 1888 when GRB had invited the band of the Royal Artillery. He made the same request for the services of the band in 1889, and when permission was refused questions were asked in the House of Commons and a petition was sent to the Duke of Cambridge, the commander-in-chief. The band was allowed to perform, and 26,000 people attended. Money from these ventures was used to pay for the services of a parish nurse for a number of years.

In 1890 GRB moved to Goldenhill, where he raised funds to enlarge the school, churchyard and to build a chancel. Fire destroyed the school in 1895 but GRB raised money for its rebuilding in the same year. He served as diocesan inspector of schools for the Archdeaconry of Stoke upon Trent 1884-7. He was vice-chairman of Tunstall Education Committee and a member of Stoke on Trent Education Committee from 1910. He favoured the annexation of Goldenhill parish to Tunstall in 1902, and was a prominent supporter of federation of the six towns. He acted as chairman of the Tunstall Federation Committee and gave evidence at the local government inquiry.

From 1896 he was a member of Wolstanton and Burslem Board of Guardians, resigning in June 1917. He served as chairman of Tunstall North Relief Committee.

In 1871 he married Henrietta Hewitt of Sheffield. They had two sons, Bernard who became a doctor and John who became a clergyman, and seven daughters. He died on 5 October 1917 at the Midhurst, Sussex, home of his son Bernard, and was buried at Goldenhill.

Federation Newscuttings 1907-8 (HRL); IGI, Staffs; *Staffs. Sentinel* 8 October 1917.

BAILEY, John Cuthbert (1856-1929), *pottery manufacturer,* Burslem.

JCB was born on 15 February 1856, the son of John Bailey, assistant agent to Rode Hall Estate in Cheshire, and was educated at Alsager Grammar School by Mr. Stonehewer. On leaving school at 14 he worked briefly for Henry Meir at Greengates Pottery, Tunstall and was then apprenticed for seven years to Bates, Elliot & Co., Dalehall Pottery. In 1878 at the age of 22 he became the London representative of the firm. While in London he attracted the attention of Henry Doulton. They had a common interest in music (JCB was a well known local singer) and Doulton appointed him manager of the Burslem works, to the astonishment of the Potteries people who confidently predicted disaster.

JCB took up his new position in June 1879 two years after Doulton had acquired the business from Pinder, Bourne & Co. With John Slater he transformed the existing premises. In 1884 a new wing was erected for the manufacture of china. Bailey travelled widely to represent the firm and was particularly successful in breaking into the American market. The factory, which employed 250 at the beginning of his career, employed 1500 at the close. In 1913 the King and Queen paid a visit to the factory, an event commemorated on film which still survives. JCB was chairman of the Staffs. Potteries Manufacturers Association and one of the founders of the British Pottery Manufacturers Association of which he was vice-president. He typified the evolution of pottery trades from the restricted craftmanship and conservative business methods of Victorian times to the adoption of scientific means of production and the highly developed business organisation of the 20th century.

He married Sydney Marie Alcock, a niece of Dr. John Alcock, in 1880, and by 1894 was living at Bradwell Lodge. There were five sons, Rev. Robert Cuthbert Steele Bailey, Cuthbert, Kenneth, John Hamilton, Dr. Bernard Cuthbert and three daughters. The last son became managing director in 1926 in succession to his father. He worked with Bernard Moore (q.v.) on experiments to perfect glazes such as 'sang de boeuf'.

JCB was Conservative in politics and in favour of tariff protection to keep out foreign ware. He died on 2 August 1929, having completed 50 years with Doulton & Co. at his home New Park, Trentham and was buried in Trentham Cemetery.

D. Eyles, *Royal Doulton 1815-1865; Evening Sentinel* 2 August 1929 (obit.); Newcastle High School Registers.

BAILEY, William (c. 1767-1855), *pottery manufacturer,* Longton.

WB was born in Staffordshire about 1767. He came to Lane End (Longton) as a journeyman tailor, and married a pottery paintress. By 1814 he had established a successful business in partnership with William Batkin, making *inter alia,* fine quality silver lustre ware and exporting lustre tea-sets to America. The partnership continued until about 1828. He had presumably retired by 1841 when he was described as of independent means.

When the Methodist New Connexion church was established in Longton in 1797 WB used his house in Stafford Street as a meeting place until a chapel could be built. A series of chapels was built culminating in Zion Methodist New Connexion church which was opened on 20 February 1842 in Commerce Street, and was registered by William Bailey of Lightwood, gentlemen, on 9 October 1843. WB subscribed £200 and his partner Batkin £100 towards the cost of this building. WB acted as a trustee for Zion church and also for Mount Tabor, Fenton. Zion chapel was amalgamated with Bourne chapel in 1938.

He married twice. His first wife, Anne, whom he married by 1801, died in 1836 aged 66; his second wife, Sophia, died in 1843 aged 70. In 1811 WB was living in Shooter's Hill, Longton. He died at Lightwood Lodge on 17 December, 1855, and was buried in Burslem churchyard. His two wives and a grandson, were buried in the same tomb. The Revd. Granville Rowe Bailey (q.v.), vicar of Goldenhill, was his grandson.

Bailey Family Memorial Cards (HRL); Jewitt; *Longton Sunday School Chronicle* 15 November 1892; M and H; Methodist Church membership lists, 1796-7, Swan Bank, Burslem; SHC, 4 ser. vol. iii; *Staffs. Advertiser* 22 December 1855; S. Shaw, *History of the Staffordshire Potteries;* VCH viii; Zion, Longton and Mount Tabor Methodist Church Trust Deeds.

BAKER, George (1796-1871), *wine and spirit merchant,* Burslem.

GB was born in Middlesex in 1796. He was established, with John Baker, as a wine and spirit merchant in the Market Place, Burslem, and in Hanley, before 1851. From 1853 he lived at Bradwell House, Wolstanton.

He had a range of personal business interests and engaged in a variety of public activities. He was a director of the Staffordshire Potteries Waterworks Co., and of the Burslem and District Gas Co.; he was a trustee of the Staffordshire Potteries Building Society and a local director of the Manchester and Liverpool District Bank. He was on the Burslem and Wolstanton Board of Guardians from its inception in 1838, and from 1848 to 1863 was chairman of this body. He was also a member of the Burslem Board of Health.

In politics GB was Conservative, and in religion an Anglican. He acted as secretary to the Burslem Auxiliary of the Bible Society, and was churchwarden at Burslem and Wolstanton churches. For some years he was on the committee of the North Staffordshire Branch of the Manchester School for Deaf and Dumb. He occupied a number of official positions within the Sutherland Freemason's Lodge and held other Masonic posts.

He died at Bradwell House in 1871, leaving £35,000, including land at Longport which gave him a rental of £681 7s. p.a.

Oldham; *Staffs. Advertiser* 2nd June 1860.

BAKER, John (born c. 1830), *wine and spirit merchant,* Hanley.

JB was baptised at Hanley on 30 September 1830, the son of John Baker (died 1864). The name Baker appears in a directory of 1802 as wine and spirit merchant, Old Hall Lane, Hanley. John Baker senior may have been the publican keeping the Grapes Inn, Market Place, Hanley, 1818, and a John Baker still kept the Grapes in High Street in 1872. JB and his brother George (q.v.) are listed in 1851 as wine and spirit merchants, Market Square, Hanley. Baker's wine vaults are listed in the 1881 directory but by 1884 JB had either retired or moved elsewhere or was dead.

JB was elected to Hanley borough council and in 1876 served as mayor. In 1861 he lived in Cemetery Road, Hanley, and by 1876 at Woodleigh House, Porthill. His wife, Betsy, was aged 46 in 1881, and had been born in Hanley.

It is suggested that Baker Street (later Lamb Street) was named after the family.

Census 1881; Dir. 1861, 1876; Huntbach.

BAKER, William (1800-65), *pottery manufacturer,* Fenton.

WB, the son of William Baker, was born in 1800. He succeeded to the family business founded by William Baker, architect of Audlem, Staffs., who had bought the estate and manor of Fenton Culvert, together with a pottery factory for his second son, William. This William married Sarah Bourne of the pottery family of that name and the two families were in partnership as pottery manufacturers until 1843. In that year the connection was severed and WB traded as William Baker & Company. The pottery later manufactured printed, sponged and pearl-white granite ware for export. There were two factories, situated on either side of City Road, Fenton, near the junction with Manor Road.

Following the establishment of the Fenton improvement commissioners in 1839, WB became the first chief bailiff of Fenton in 1840. He served as a commissioner until his death. The Baker family arms, which included a goat's head, formed part of Fenton's armorial bearings.

WB continued the family tradition of public benefaction. He financed the building of the Atheneum in 1853. The building comprised lecture and assembly rooms, library etc. and served subsequently as a school of art and then as a bank, being demolished in 1977. The building at the junction of Christchurch Street and City Road, is now a bank. He enlarged Christ Church, which had been founded by his uncle Ralph Bourne, (died 1835) who had left £3,500 to trustees for the erection of a new church. WB built the vicarage (now Glebedale House), and augmented the living. He became patron of the living in 1861. Among his other benefactions to the town were the infants' school (1839) and a drinking fountain.

In 1863 WB bought a large estate, Hasfield Court, in Gloucestershire. He died, unmarried, in August 1865, leaving his estates to his brother, the Revd. Ralph Bourne Baker, who erected a memorial tablet to him in the church. The tablet was transferred to the new church built on the site of the old one to the design of Charles Lynam (q.v.), in 1890.

Fenton Commissioners' Minutes (HRL); VCH viii.

BAKER, William Meath (1857-1935), *pottery manufacturer,* Fenton.

WMB was born at Hilderstone, Staffs., on 1 November 1857, the only son of the Revd. Ralph Bourne Baker. He was educated at Eton and Trinity College, Cambridge, and proceeded to his M.A. degree in 1886.

WMB's father inherited the estates of his unmarried brother, William Baker (q.v.), who died in 1865, and WMB took up the life of a country squire at Hasfield Court. He later became high sheriff of Gloucestershire. He maintained his connection with Fenton, however, to which he was a generous benefactor. He built Fenton town hall in 1888 at his own expense, leasing it to the Local Board of Health at a low rent. He inaugurated a building development in the area of the town hall and church, including shops and dwelling houses. Some of the terraced houses he built near the Baker factories, bear his monogram 'WMB' in the terracotta decoration above the first floors.

At his home in Gloucestershire WMB entertained the composer, Edward Elgar, and his wife. The fourth of Elgar's *Enigma Variations* is said to have been inspired by the memory of Baker striding out of the music room at Hasfield Court and inadvertently banging the door. Baker's brother-in-law, R. B. Townsend, is remembered in Variation III. The subject of Variation X, Dorabella, was the daughter of the Revd. A. Penny, vicar of Christ Church, Tunstall, who married William Meath Baker's sister.

WMB was a keen mountain climber and made several ascents in the Swiss Alps. He died on 15 January 1935 and was buried in Hasfield churchyard.

Burke, *Landed Gentry; Evening Sentinel* 4 June 1981; M. and H.; I. Parrot, *Elgar;* VCH viii; P. Young, *Elgar, O.M.*

BALL, Daniel (1800/1-95), *medical practitioner,* Burslem.

DB was born in Newcastle under Lyme about 1800. He worked first in the dispensary of the North Staffs. Infirmary, then studied at Barts Hospital, London, and qualified M.R.C.S. in 1824, and F.R.C.S. in 1844. He was in practice in Burslem from about 1825 to 1859, when he retired to Camp Hill, Whitmore. In 1823 he was a trustee of the Burslem Free School, honorary surgeon to the North Staffs. Infirmary 1835-59 and with Samuel Palmer Goddard medical officer of health to the Burslem and Wolstanton Poor Law Union. He chaired the committee drawn form the Burslem and Wolstanton guardians which replied to Edwin Chadwick's questionnaire and whose evidence was published in Chadwick's *Report on the Sanitary Condition of the Labouring Classes of Great Britain,* 1844. He was again involved in a public inquiry in 1849 on the issue as to whether Burslem should have a board of health. He argued that cholera, typhoid and typhus were not preventible by sanitary means alone but that their prevention needed also an improvement in people's habits and morals. He stated that he did however, expect great improvement in social and moral conditions from the provision of sanitary works, since these acted upon each other as both cause and effect.

In 1851 DB was living, unmarried, with his twin sister, Katherine, in Church Street, Burslem. Frederick Cooper was his assistant surgeon. He died at Cliff House on 17 March 1895.

Census 1851; Oldham; *Staffs. Advertiser* 23 March 1895 (obit.).

BARBER, George Herbert (1860-1946), *cinema owner,* Tunstall.

GHB, born in Tunstall in 1860, was left motherless in 1865. Two years later he and his younger brother were forced to enter Chell Workhouse when their father became too ill to work. The family moved to Milton in 1869. George worked on a farm at Brown Edge, then in coal mines first at Newchapel and in 1875 at Norton. He was a self-taught accordion player and to augment his income he played for dancing on four nights a week at public houses. He ws a teetotaller, however, all his life. He married in 1881. He left the mines during the strike of 1881 and worked for J. Hardman's chemical works in Milton. He worked his way up to become manager of the acid works and in 1886 moved to Talke Chemical Company as manager. Here he introduced many ideas which became standard practice in chemical and gas works in Britain and abroad, later patenting a hydraulic seal box widely used in both industries.

He taught himself reading, writing, arithmetic, shorthand and music. He was a member of the Wesleyan Methodist church, and served as a Sunday school teacher, superintendent and local preacher. He was largely responsible for the replacement of the 'tin pot' Wesleyan chapel at Talke by a brick structure. In 1900, after moving to Goldenhill, he began to give 'magic lantern' lectures on religious and temperance themes and became attracted by the possibilities of the moving pictures with which he replaced his slides. In 1909 he built Barber's Palace in Station Road, Tunstall's first cinema. within ten years he owned a chain of cinemas, two in Tunstall, one in each of Hanley, Fenton and Biddulph, and five in Buckinghamshire. He was enterprising in his advertisements, in 1922 taking regular air flights from Manchester, during which he threw cards out of the plane bearing the words "Barber's Message from the Sky. Prizes of £1 and 10s. notes will be given for one of these cards if presented to the manager of any of Barber's cinemas". He also learned, after the age of 60, to fly. He travelled to Palestine, all over Europe and to the Soviet Union.

He was elected a Labour member of Stoke upon Trent council, being particularly concerned with poverty and housing in the area. As chairman of the gas committee he was responsible for the installation of a benzole extraction plant at Etruria gas works which brought in an annual revenue of £12,000. In 1929-30 he served as lord mayor of the city of Stoke upon Trent. His public work was continued by his only son and by his two grandsons, one of whom, Leonard, also became lord mayor. GB died in 1946.

G. H. Barber *From Small Beginnings,* and *From Workhouse to Lord Mayor;* P. Gate 'The Cinema King' in *Staffs. Magazine* Oct. 1980; *The Sentinel Story 1873-1973* (picture).

BARKER, John (fl. 1750), *potter,* Longton.

JB, one of Thomas Whieldon's ovenmen in 1749, set up in business for himself about 1750 making salt-glazed stoneware at the Row Houses, near the Foley, Fenton. Later he made cream coloured earthenware, china glazed and blue wares at Lane End. He married Mary Plant on 21 May 1777 at Stoke church. Their eldest daughter married Josiah Spode. JB and his brothers William and Richard, are listed as potters in Lane End in 1781. In 1796 Richard alone of the brothers was still at Lane Delph. Barker Street, Longton, is probably named after the family. The company, Barker Brothers, built the present Meir Works in 1882.

M and H; VCH viii.

BARKER, Revd. Joseph (1806-75), *minister of religion (Methodist New Connexion and Christian Brethren),* Tunstall/Hanley.

JB was born in Bramley, Yorkshire, on 11 May 1806, and educated at James Sygstow School, Leeds. He worked in a woollen mill and taught himself Latin, Greek, Arithmetic and Grammar. William Ridgway (q.v.) heard him preach at a conference in Halifax and invited him to come to Hanley as minister at Mount Tabor Methodist New Connexion church, Tunstall. He served in this office from 1829 to 1841, when he was expelled from the Connexion for his Socinian views, taking a number of the Mount Tabor congregation with him. He preached in the meeting room of the Christian Brethren, who in the Potteries had associations with Unitarianism. He had moved back to Yorkshire by 1846 and worked as a printer from 1846-51 in Wortley. He spent the years 1851 to 1860 in America but returned to England in 1860. He joined the Primitive Methodists in Tunstall on his return, living from 1860-2 in Betley and from 1862-8 in Wolverhampton, Bilston and again in Tunstall. In 1868 he returned to America.

He was the secretary of a group calling themselves 'Independent Workmen', an organisation of non-trade unionists, in 1836 and held meetings in Betley and Hanley to try to bring the strike and lock-out of that year to an end. In Yorkshire he published the Barker Library of Cheap Books. He wrote the story of his own life *The History and Confessions of a Man*.

He died in Omaha, U.S.A., on 15 September 1875.

J. Barker, *Autobiography, The History and Confessions of a Man;* F. Burchill and R. Ross, *A History of the Potters' Union;* DNB; VCH viii; R. D. Woodall, *Midland Unitarianism and its Story.*

BARLOW, George (1845-1916), *accountant,* Hanley.

GB was born at Leek on 26 July 1845, the son of Benjamin Barlow. He was educated at Leek Grammar School, where his father was a master. Benjamin Barlow retired from teaching to devote himself to music, and was organist at Leek parish church. George, while still a boy, was his deputy. About 1860 he was apprenticed to his uncle, a stationer and newsagent in Bangor, North Wales. While there he was appointed organist at Menai Bridge and Llanfairfechan. He returned to the Potteries at the age of 21 and became cashier to Allbut and Daniel, the printers. In 1872 he applied for the position of borough accountant for Hanley. He was unmarried at the time and this was believed to be a barrier to his appointment, and he married Elizabeth Beaumont, headmistress of Hanley National Schools. GB served as borough accountant for 38 years. Shortly before his retirement, at federation, he was appointed borough treasurer.

For 30 years, until 1900, GB was organist at Hanley parish church, and was also organist to the Earl of Shrewsbury. He organised the Meakin concerts in the Victoria Hall, Hanley, from their inception in 1889. He was responsible for the Victoria Hall organ and severely rationed its use, a policy which annoyed some who wished to play it. He was treasurer of Hanley Park flower show and fete 1898, and acted as secretary of the 'Sentinel shilling fund' which raised £35,000 for the North Staffs. Royal Infirmary. He died at his home at 83 Park Road, Hanley, on 19th February 1916, leaving a widow and three surviving children. A daughter, Gertrude, who had died in 1914, had been one of the first women in the Potteries to graduate from university. She later taught at Hanley Secondary School.

Staffs. Sentinel 21 February 1916.

BARLOW, Thomas Waterhouse (1821-85), *pottery manufacturer,* Longton.

TWB was born in Longton and baptised on 7 October 1821 at the Methodist New Connexion chapel. He was the son of Thomas Barlow and Elizabeth née Poole. Thomas Barlow, one of the original Longton commissioners in 1839, was a manufacturer in Market Street, Longton, in premises once occupied by the Cyples family. TWB was apprenticed to Charles Harvey (q.v.) and by 1851 was in business on his own in Longton. In 1860 he occupied Coronation Works in Commerce Street. The firm was still working in Longton in 1940.

TWB became a member of Longton council on the incorporation of the town in 1865, and served as mayor of the borough 1871-3. He led the opposition to the Trent Purification Bill, saved the borough a large outlay and was presented with a gold watch and chain by his fellow councillors. He was chairman of Stoke upon Trent Liberal Association for some years before 1880.

He married twice. His first wife, Eliza, died in 1856 and by his second wife, Mary Hannah, he had seven children. The family lived, at various times, in Dresden, Hem Heath and Edensor Place. While in the Potteries TWB attended Methodist New Connexion churches, but after moving to the Mount, Stone, about 1872, he became a Congregationalist. He died on 2 July 1885 at The Cedars, Walton, Stone, and was buried in Christ Church, Stone.

Dir. 1851, 1860, 1867; IGI Staffs.; Jewitt; *Staffs. Advertiser* 4 July 1885; *Staffs. Sentinel* 3 July 1885.

BATE, Samuel (1817-91), *surveyor and land agent,* Stoke upon Trent.

SB, the son of Samuel and Martha Bate, of Styche Hall, near Market Drayton, Shropshire, was baptised on 1 June 1817. He became land agent to John Ayshfordwise of Clayton Hall, to Lord Camoys for the latter's property in Burslem and Biddulph and to Mrs Marsh Caldwell of Kidsgrove. He was surveyor of the Hanley and Shelton tithe map of 1850 and to the Newcastle to Blythe Marsh Turnpike Trust from c. 1870 to its disbandment in 1875. He also surveyed the agricultural lands of Stoke upon Trent in 1862. In 1851 he had an office in Commercial Street, Stoke upon Trent, and in 1884 an office in Brunswick Street, Newcastle under Lyme.

He served as an improvement commissioner for Stoke upon Trent in 1859, and acted as secretary of the North Staffordshire Agricultural Society founded 1846. SB wrote pamphlets on religious and agricultural topics some of which are preserved in HRL.

He was married between April and June 1844 at Shrewsbury, his wife Emma, born in Shropshire, bearing him seven children. The family lived at Camoys Lane, Knutton, in 1851 and in Springfields in 1861. SB eventually moved to The Firs, Aylestone, Leicester, because of his increasing commitments in that area. He died on 5 May 1891.

One of his sons, Samuel Stringer Bate, became an author. His works include a play about Cardinal Wolsey, which he dedicated to Queen Victoria. The dedication was unauthorised and had to be withdrawn. Another son, Alfred, became a mining engineer.

Census 1851, 1861, 1871, 1881; Dir. 1851; Simms; *National Index to Wills and Administrations 1858-1931; Staffs. Sentinel* 8 May 1891 (obit.); Stoke upon Trent Improvement Commissioners' Minutes.

BEARD, William (1869-1950), *pottery engraver,* Stoke upon Trent.

WB, son of a nightwatchman at Minton's was born on 27 June 1869 and educated at Boothen Church of England School. He left school in 1882 and was employed at Minton's as an errand boy and feldspar washer. In 1884 he was apprenticed as an engraver, his indentures being signed by Thomas Minton, Herbert Minton and Samuel Simpson.

One of WB's main leisure interests was swimming, and for some years he acted as trainer to Stoke Swimming Club team.

He died at James Street, Stoke upon Trent, before 6 May 1950.

The Beard family was one of those who served Minton's for long periods of time. His mother had worked as a paintress at the factory for 70 years.

J. Steel 'William Beard (Engraver)' (Minton Archive 616).

BEBBINGTON, James (1831-93), *bookseller and printer,* Hanley.

JB was baptised at Hanley on 26 October 1831, the son of Charles Bebbington and his wife Anne, née Jones. He was in business as printer, bookseller and newsagent prior to 1860. He acted as secretary to Samuel Pope, who stood as Liberal candidate on a temperance 'platform' for Stoke upon Trent in 1859. Later Bebbington transferred his support to George Melly, the successful Liberal candidate of 1862. JB published poll books for both elections, possibly to allow temperance supporters to know which tradespeople had been politically opposed to them. He was Liberal registration agent and secretary of the Liberal Council, which dissolved in acrimony in 1869.

JB was elected to Hanley borough council in 1871, and served on the school board in 1873. He championed the working class cause in the council chamber and in the local press, and had a sharp eye for financial irregularities. Thanks to his efforts Hanley was granted the right to hold a separate quarter sessions. He spoke against the idea of a Potteries county which was mooted when the County Councils Act came into force in 1888, supporting the idea of county borough status for Hanley.

JB's passion for politics and public work was at the sacrifice of his personal prosperity, and led to his bankruptcy, followed by his resignation from the council on 23 September 1883. He returned to the council in November 1887 but was forced by ill-health to retire in 1890. He successively lost his sight and his hearing, but learned to communicate by using wooden letters which he carried in a small portmanteau, and he taught himself to read in this fashion with accuracy and rapidity.

His business premises were in Broad Street, then in Tontine Square, where he lived in 1871, and finally in Market Place, Hanley. In 1881 he was living at 6 Church Street with his wife Susannah and a nine year old daughter, Ada. Among the books he printed was H. C. Wedgwood, *Up and Down the County.*

He died at his home in Sun Street, Shelton, on 27 June 1893 and was buried in Hanley cemetery.

Anderton; Census 1871, 1881; Dir. 1867, 1880, 1884; Hanley Council Minutes; *Staffs. Sentinel* 1 July 1893 (obit.)

BENNETT, Sarah (fl. 1893-1908), *trade unionist and suffragette,* Burslem.

SB was educated at Queen's College, London. In 1884 she started a co-operative society in the New Forest. She came to the Potteries about 1893, possibly as a result of a campaign by the Women's Trade Union League led by Gladys Tuckwell and was active in unionising women in the pottery industry.

With the support of the Potters' Union she was elected to the Burslem School Board in 1898 and 1901 and to the Burslem and Wolstanton Board of Guardians. A pamphlet attacking certain teachers was thought to have cost her the seat of the "token" woman when Burslem Education Committee was formed in 1903. The seat went to Mrs. Mary Alcock, widow of Dr. John Alcock.

SB was an active suffragette and campaigned with Christabel Pankhurst against the Liberal candidate in the North-West Staffs. by-election in July 1907. On 3 January 1908 she was arrested during a suffragette demonstration in London and sentenced to three weeks' imprisonment. She took advantage of The Qualification of Women (County and Borough Councils) Act 1907 to stand at the Burslem council elections in November 1907, again with union support, although there was some criticism of this because she had campaigned against the Liberals in the by-election. She called for the municipalisation of abattoirs and for the council to supply milk. She favoured federation. In May 1908 a distraint was levied upon her goods because of her refusal to pay rates on the grounds that women did not have the vote.

Burslem School Board minutes (HRL); Oldham; *Staffs. Sentinel* July 1907, November 1907, 30 January 1908, 19 February 1908, 26 February 1908.

BENNETT, Enoch Arnold (1867-1931), *writer/journalist,* Hanley/Burslem.

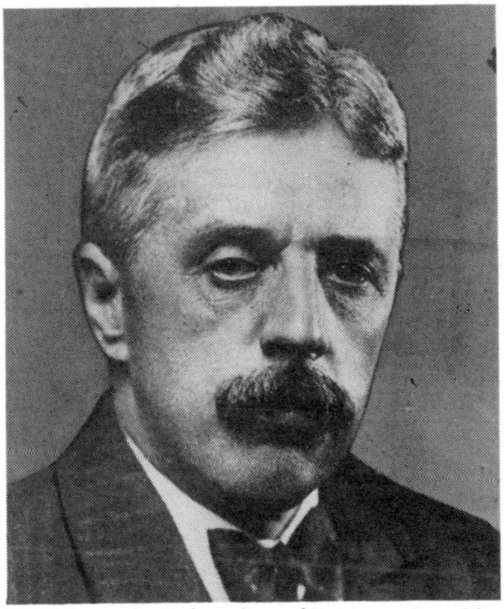

AB was born 27 May, 1867 at 90 Hope Street, Hanley, a pawnshop, eldest child of Enoch and Sarah Bennett. His early childhood was spent in various homes of increasing poverty while his father studied to be a solicitor. He spent much time in the draper's shop of his maternal grandparents in St. John's Square, Burslem, later recreated as the Baines shop in *The Old Wives Tale.* The family moved to 198 Waterloo Road, Burslem, in 1879 after his father's success as a solicitor. They moved again in 1881 to a new house, 205 Waterloo Road.

AB was educated at Wesleyan Infants School, Burslem Endowed School in the Wedgwood Institute, then Orme School, Newcastle under Lyme. In 1882 he passed Cambridge Junior Local Examination which qualified him to transfer to Newcastle under Lyme High School and university. He left school, however, in 1883 and entered his father's office. He began to write short articles for the *Staffordshire Knot* (a newspaper venture of which his father was a shareholder). After failing, to the disappointment of his father, to pass his law examinations, AB moved in 1889 to London where he was employed as a shorthand clerk.

In 1890 he met Frederic Marriott, an art teacher, and became the Marriotts' lodger, with access to musical evenings, art and theatricals. In 1891 he won 20 guineas for an article in a *Tit-Bits* competition. He began to write freelance, though many of his articles were rejected. In 1893 he became assistant editor to a weekly magazine, and editor in 1896, and began to achieve a reputation for his book reviews. In 1898 he moved to a house of his own with his sister Tertia as housekeeper. His first published novel was *A Man from the North* (1898). In the same year he began to write a daily journal which he continued with only a few breaks, until near his death.

He resigned his post in 1900 to devote himself to writing. He produced short stories for the press but found serial writing more profitable. *The Grand Babylon Hotel* (1900) made his name as a novelist.

From 1903 to 1911 he lived mostly in Paris, producing many novels and plays. He continued his work as a freelance journalist. In 1907 he married Marguerite Soulie from whom he separated in 1921. He became increasingly prosperous and this was reflected in his life-style which included a large house and a yacht. From 1923 he had a permanent relationship with Dorothy Cheston, later Dorothy Cheston Bennett. They had one daughter, Virginia, born on 13 April 1926. He died of typhoid fever in London on 27 March 1931. His ashes lie in his mother's grave in Burslem cemetery. Memorial plaques are in Burslem town centre and on his birthplace in Hope Street.

Throughout his life he was plagued by a stutter. He appeared to be a hypochondriac and an insomniac. He had a strong determination to succeed, with reputation and finance vying for importance. He was obsessed with the number of words he could turn out in a year. He influenced many other writers, acknowledged or not. Many of his characters, events and places actually existed or happened in and around Burslem in the 19th century. His most popular and well-known works include: *Anna of the Five Towns* (1902), *The Old Wives Tale* (1908), *The Card* (1909), *Clayhanger* (1910), *Riceyman Steps* (1923).

Dudley Barker *Writer by Trade* (1966); Margaret Drabble *Arnold Bennett* (1974); E. J. D. Warrillow, *Arnold Bennett and Stoke upon Trent.*

BENNETT, John (born c. 1826), *workhouse governor,* Tunstall.

JB was born in Stockport, Cheshire, in 1826. He was a trustee of St. Margaret's Lodge of the Potteries and District Independent Order of Oddfellows, and was the Chell workhouse governor in 1862, his wife, Nancy being matron. They held these posts until at least 1871 and probably until 1876.

Census 1871; Dir. 1862; *Independent Order of Oddfellows Rules of St. Margaret's Lodge* (HRL); Stoke on Trent Historic Buildings Survey, *Workhouses in the Potteries;* VCH viii.

BENTLEY, William (1777-1833), *engraver,* Hanley.

WB was born in 1777. By c. 1818 he had set up an engraving workshop, with William Wear and Samuel Bourne, in Vine Street, Shelton. He opened the first art gallery in the Potteries at his workshops in October 1825.

He died in May 1833.

M. and H.; *Pottery Mercury* 12 October 1825; *Staffs. Advertiser* 1 June 1833 (obit.).

BERESFORD-HOPE, Alexander James (1820-87), *Member of Parliament,* Stoke upon Trent.

AJB-H was born in London in 1820, the youngest son of Thomas Hope, Esquire, of Deepdene, Surrey and the Honourable Louisa, youngest daughter of the 1st Baron Decies, Archbishop of Tuam. He was educated at Harrow and Trinity College, Cambridge, and received the degrees of LL.D. (Cambridge), Hon. D.C.L. (Oxford) and Hon. LL.D. (Dublin). In 1842 he married Lady Mildred Cecil, eldest daughter of the 8th marquis of Salisbury. He was a president of the Institute of British Architects and a trustee of the British Museum. In politics he was Conservative. He sat in Parliament for Maidstone from 1841-52 and from 1857-9. He unsuccessfully contested Stoke upon Trent in 1862, but was elected in 1865, and sat for the borough until 1868, when he was elected for Cambridge University. He spoke in favour of the established church 'both as a divine institution and as an estate of the realm'. He died on 20 October 1887.

Stenton; V and S.

BERRINGTON, Robert (1825-84), *grocer,* Burslem.

RB was born at Ripley, Derbyshire, in 1825. By 1841 he was apprenticed to William Eley, of Market Place, Burslem, and by 1851 he was in business on his own account as a grocer and provision dealer. He was elected to the Burslem Board of Health in 1855. By his wife, Rebecca, aged 30 in 1861 and born in Uttoxeter, he had three children.

RB died on 16 May 1884.

Census 1841, 1861; Oldham; memorial inscription in Burslem cemetery.

BESWICK, James Wright (1845-1920), *pottery manufacturer,* Longton.

JWB was born in Tunstall in 1845, the son of Robert Beswick (q.v.). He began potting in Albion Street, Longton, about 1890 then moved to the Britannia Works, High Street and afterwards to Gold Street works, which he was working by at least 1899. The firm of J. W. Beswick Ltd. was still there in 1984.

JWB was elected to Longton borough council and served as vice-chairman of the School Board. He later became a member of Stoke upon Trent borough council. For 15 years he represented Kidsgrove on Staffordshire county council. He played a leading part in the building of the Stone Road Primitive Methodist church. He was a member of Florence Bowling Club.

By his wife Esther Annie he had four sons and four daughters. He was living in Belgrave House, Dresden from 1900, and died there aged 75 on 5 May 1920, just after attending a meeting at Chesterton where he had been chosen as a delegate to the national synod at Hull.

Census 1851, 1861; Dir. 1890; Jewitt; *Staffs. Sentinel* 6 May 1920.

BESWICK, Robert (born c. 1804), *earthenware manufacturer and coalmaster,* Tunstall.

RB was born in Halliwell, near Bolton, Lancs. By 1841 he was living in Watergate Street, Tunstall, with the trade of joiner and builder. By 1851 he was working a coal and ironstone mine at Great Chell, trading as the Chell Coal and Iron Co. He also manufactured earthenware and bricks and tiles, as well as continuing with his work as a builder. His brick and tile manufactory was at Dale Hall and his pottery was Church Bank Works, Tunstall which he built in 1842 and continued until 1860.

He was a member of the Tunstall Local Board of Health from 1855 to 1860, again in 1863, and was chief bailiff in 1864. By his wife Rachel he had at least five children, including James Wright Beswick (q.v.).

Census 1841, 1851; Dir. 1851; Jewitt; *Tunstall Local Board of Health Annual Reports;* VCH viii.

BETTANY, Frederick (1860/1-1924), *fire brigade officer,* Burslem.

FB was born in Burslem about 1860. After leaving school he entered the offices of A. R. Wood, architects and surveyors. From about 1900 he was engineer and surveyor to Burslem town council and held this position until federation in 1910. Under his supervision a number of large public buildings were erected, including St. John's Market Hall, Moorland Road Baths and Burslem sewage works. On federation he was appointed captain of the new county borough fire brigade, having served as fire officer for Burslem since 1895. A disastrous fire at Grimwade's Pottery prompted a motion in the council for a reduction in his salary, but this was lost. As a result of the fire the first motor fire engines were brought to the Potteries. The Burslem appliance appears in a film shot in Burslem about 1918 (shown in the North Staffs. Polytechnic Film Centre in the 1980s).

For more than 30 years FB was involved in the volunteer movement, becoming a sergeant in the cyclist section. He was a provincial grand master of the freemasons and a member of the Independent Order of Foresters. He captained Stoke Football club in the 1880s and later played for Port Vale.

He married and had two daughters. The younger, Ethel, served as a V.A.D. in the first world war in Salonika. FB died at Hamil House, Burslem, on 9 June 1924.

J. Allcock, *Notes on Burslem Fire Brigade 1895-1900; Staffs. Sentinel* 11 June 1924.

BEVINGTON, Samuel (before 1808-1863), *pottery manufacturer,* Hanley.

SB, son of Richard and Hannah Bevington, was baptised at Shelton on 8 May 1808. He established the Swan Works, Elm Street, Hanley, about 1835. In 1851 he was described as a china painter and gilder, of Brunswick Street. He exhibited porcelain tea services at the 1862 Exhibition. The firm, which had traded as S. Bevington and Son, passed after SB's death to his son, John, and in 1866 to W. L. Evans and Co. From them it passed in 1871 to Neale Harrison and Co., and after them to T. A. Simpson, of Burslem and Stoke upon Trent.

SB was a Chartist, and helped Thomas Cooper, the Chartist leader, to escape through the cordon of police, soldiers and special constables set up after the riots of 15-16 August 1842. Cooper was later arrested in Leicester. SB made two unsuccessful attempts to secure election to Hanley council, in August and October 1857. He was opposed to the introduction of the Public Health Act in Hanley.

By his wife Eliza he had nine children. He died on 8 November 1863 and was buried in Hanley cemetery.

F. Burchill and R. Ross, *A History of the Potters' Union;* IGI Staffs.; Jewitt; *Staffs. Advertiser* 24 June 1854.

BIDDER, George Parker (born 1806), *railway engineer,* Stoke upon Trent.

GPB, the son of a stonemason, was born at Moretonhampstead, Devon, in 1806. His abilities at mental calculation attracted the attention of Sir John Herschel and Sir Henry Jardine, and through them he obtained an education at Camberwell and at Edinburgh University. He worked first for the Ordnance Survey, then, about 1837, with Robert Stephenson on the London and Birmingham Railway. He was appointed consulting engineer to the North Staffordshire Railway in 1845, and in that year, with Stephenson, surveyed the proposed extension of the N.S.R. to Liverpool, a project which was abandoned. Among his other works GPB designed and erected the first swing bridge, at Reedham, on the Norfolk and Lowestoft Railway, of which company he was chairman about 1858. He also worked on the construction of the Victoria Docks. With J. L. Ricardo (q.v.) he founded the Electric Telegraph Company. GPB, Samuel Parker Bidder, his younger brother, and Sir George Elliot worked the Newcastle and Lawton collieries.

He had two children, George Parker Bidder and H. J. Bidder. His brother, Samuel Parker Bidder, resident engineer for the N.S.R. was living in Stone in 1851.

G. P. Bidder *'Harecastle and Lawton Collieries'* (HRL); Bidder Papers, Science Museum Library, London; R. Christiansen and R. W. Miller, *The North Staffordshire Railway;* R. D. Woodall, 'Peeps into the Past, in *Stoke City Times* 26 April 1961.

BILL, John (c.1789-1878), *farmer,* Stoke upon Trent.

JB was born in Trent Vale about 1789. He may have been the son of Richard Bill of Black Lion Farm, Hanford, living in 1800. On 9 October 1822 he married Mary Robinson and was living at Black Lion Farm at the time of his marriage. There were at least seven children of the marriage. In 1834 JB was listed in a directory as a seedsman and lime burner. He became a Stoke improvement commissioner in 1839, and an arbiter in a compensation case between Mossfield Colliery and the North Staffordshire Railway in 1848. He is described as a farmer in 1851. In 1861 he farmed 250 acres, of which he owned about 120 acres and rented the remainder from the Duke of Sutherland and John Ayshford Wise in Clayton, employing 11 men. In 1867 he was appointed to the Stoke Board of Guardians.

He died at Trent Vale Farm on 18 May 1878.

S..Bate, *A Survey of Agricultural Lands in the Parish of Stoke upon Trent;* Census 1851, 1861; *Stoke Improvement Commissioners Minutes.*

BILLINGTON, Charles (c. 1836-1902), *brass founder,* Burslem.

CB was born in Lancashire about 1836. He travelled widely before settling in the Potteries. In 1871 he took over the Vulcan Foundry at Longport, and was in partnership with Newton some time before 1875. By 1881 the foundry employed 55 men.

By his wife, Martha Margaret, who he married by 1860, he had a son, Charles, born in Birmingham about 1860, a second son Gideon Morley born in Brazil about 1865, a daughter Martha born in Leeds about 1867, another daughter, Sylvia, born in Newcastle under Lyme about 1869 and a third daughter, Lydia, born in Shelton about 1871. He was an active supporter of the temperance movement. He died at his home in Woodlands Parade, Wolstanton, on 3 January 1902, and was buried in Wolstanton churchyard.

Census 1881; Oldham; *Staffs. Sentinel* 11 January 1902 (obit.); Wolstanton churchyard memorial inscription.

BIRBECK, William (born about 1799), *ceramic artist,* Stoke upon Trent.

WB was born in Worcester about 1799, and served an apprenticeship there with Chamberlain's (later Royal Worcester Works). He began working for Minton's about 1841, specialising in heraldic devices, crests and monograms on dinner ware. By his wife Anne, born in Staffordshire, he had a least two children, William, born in Coalport about 1824, and Mary born in Staffordshire in 1846. William Birbeck junior also became a potter's artist, specialising in flowers and butterflies, and lodging at 134/5 Old Market Square, Stoke upon Trent, in 1861. William Birbeck junior may also have been the artist of that name working at Coalport about 1875.

Census 1861; G. Godden, *British Pottery and Porcelain;* Jewitt; W. Scarratt, *Old Times in the Potteries.*

BIRCHALL, John (born c. 1808), *police officer,* Stoke upon Trent/Burslem.

JB was born in Bellymore, Co. Cork, Ireland, about 1808. He served in the London police force and in the police force set up for Stoke district by the Act of 1839. He was injured during the riots in Longton that occurred not long after the force was established. He was appointed to Staffordshire county police in 1843 as a sub-inspector 2nd class, reduced to 3rd class in 1844 and promoted again to 2nd class in 1847.

His children's birthplaces provide clues to his movements: one was born in Stoke in 1840, others in Wolstanton 1844-6, Betley 1847 and in Burslem 1851-1860. In 1861 he and his family were living in Ellgreave Street, Dalehall.

He was pensioned off on 15 April 1872.

Briggs; Census 1861; Staffs. Constabulary Force Book, CRO, Stafford; VCH viii.

BISHOP, Frederick (c. 1815-91), *solicitor,* Stoke upon Trent.

FB was born on 15 December 1815 at Shelton, the son of William Bishop, an attorney, of Shelton Hall and Mary Ann née Chatterley. FB was articled to his father, and in 1841 was appointed clerk to Shelton Gas Co. Ltd. By 1851 he was in practice as a solicitor and partner in the firm of Bishop and Blakistone. He acted as solicitor for the Staffordshire Potteries Building Society in 1854 and was a director of the Potteries Street railway in 1862 and also of the Chatterley Iron Company. His father retired from practice about 1866.

FB served as chief bailiff of Hanley in 1847. He bought the Mount estate, Penkhull, from the Spode family in 1856, and laid out Prince's Road with good-class terraced housing. He sold land to Hanley council for use as a cemetery about 1860, and also sold ten acres of the Mount estate as a site for the new North Staffordshire Infirmary, to which he gave £1,000. He was patron of the church of St. Thomas the Apostle, Penkhull, about 1883.

In August 1842 he married Eliza Agnes Watson at St. Pancras church, London, the ceremony being conducted by his brother, the Revd. William Chatterley Bishop, of Northampton. There were at least eight children by the marriage. From about 1855 to 1875 the family lived at the Mount, Penkhull. Two of FB's children who died in infancy were buried in Penkhull churchyard.

FB died at Portman Square, London, on 25 August 1891.

Census 1861; Dir. 1851; A. Dob, *The Mount Estate;* R. Talbot, *Penkhull Remembered Again;* VCH viii.

BLACKHURST, Richard (1810/11-77), *pottery manufacturer,* Tunstall.

RB was born at High Carr about 1810. He was in business as an earthenware manufacturer at Tunstall (or Church) Works in 1857, with a partner, Dunning, exporting to the home and South American markets. After Dunning's death in 1867 RB carried on the business by himself. He may have been the partner of Heath in the firm of Heath and Blackhurst who acquired the Hadderidge Pottery in 1859.

In 1841 he was living in Paradise Street, Tunstall, and was described as potter. In 1851, still in the same house, he was described as potter's printer, widower, living with his unmarried sister-in-law, Ellen Povey. By 1860 he was living in Wesley Place.

In 1862 he served as chief bailiff of Tunstall. From 1867 to 1872 he was treasurer of Wesley Place Methodist Sunday School. He died on 5 September 1877 and was buried in Tunstall cemetery. He had married again and his widow was still living in 28 Wesley Place, in 1881.

Census, 1841, 1851, 1881; *Tunstall Board of Health Annual Reports; Wesley Place Centenary Souvenir* 1799-1899.

BLACKWELL, Revd. John (died 1863), *minister of religion, Wesleyan Methodist church, Burslem*

Little is known about John Blackwell. He was a missionary in the West Indies and before 1862 was appointed superintendent of Burslem and Hanley Wesleyan Methodist circuit. He died suddenly, in Burslem, in 1863, the Revd. F. W. MacDonald preaching at his funeral.

MacDonald, F. W., *Reminiscences of my early ministry.*

BLACKWELL, Joseph Andrew (1798-1881), *diplomat,* Burslem.

JAB was born in 1798 in Cobridge. He represented the British government in Hungary before and during the Hungarian revolution of 1848. He was unable to establish a consulate in Budapest and returned to England. He became vice-consul at Lubeck in 1854. He married Agnes Warmuth, an Austrian.

He was a boyhood friend of Francis Emery of Cobridge, with whom he continued to correspond.

He died in Lubeck in 1881.

Evening Sentinel 14 September 1982; *The Guardian* 17 September 1982.

BLOOR, Charles (born c. 1840), *hollow-ware presser and trade unionist,* Burslem.

CB was born about 1840 in Burslem and worked as a hollow-ware presser. By 1873 he was secretary of the Hollow-ware Pressers' Society. He also became secretary of the Federation of Operative Potters and was one of the leaders of the strike in 1881 against a reduction in wages of one penny in the shilling. He wrote a letter to the *Sentinel* saying "an employer has no moral right to sell his goods at a price at which he cannot meet the just demands contracted in the working of the business". Later he bemoaned the lack of union membership which caused the strike to collapse after six weeks.

He was elected to Burslem School Board in July 1875 and served until 1883. In 1884 he was elected to Burslem council and continued to serve until 1897. By 1891 he had given up his union activities and gone into business in Waterloo Road as a colour manufacturer and flint grinder.

In 1881 he was living in Bridge Street, Burslem with his wife Hannah and four children.

F. Burchill and R. Ross, *History of the Potters' Union;* Census 1881; Dir. 1896; Oldham; *Potteries Examiner* 13 September 1873; *Staffs. Sentinel* 28 November 1881.

BODEN, James (c. 1756-1841), *minister of religion (Congregationalist),* Hanley.

JB, born about 1756, was the first minister of Tabernacle Congregational chapel, High Street, Hanley, from 1785-96. He helped to found Stafford Congregational chapel and the London Missionary Society. He left the Potteries to serve in Sheffield in November 1796, but returned to Hanley in September 1835 to attend the jubilee celebrations of the Sunday School which he had helped to found, and which was the first Sunday School opened in Staffordshire (September 1785).

He died at Sheffield, aged 84, on 4 June 1841.

A. G. Matthews, *Congregational Churches of Staffordshire; Staffs. Advertiser* 8 June 1841; VCH viii.

BODLEY, Edward Fisher (1815-81), *pottery manufacturer,* Burslem.

EFB was born in Lapford, Devonshire, in 1815. By the age of 24 he was living in Steeple Bumpstead, Essex, where he was an Independent minister of religion given to revivalist sermons. He moved to Rochford, Essex, where he married and had three children. After the death of his wife he came to Shelton and is listed as an accountant and as a commercial traveller in directories from 1864 to 1876. He also engaged in pottery manufacture, opening the Scotia Pottery in 1862. The building had originally been the Burslem workhouse and been converted by James Vernon into a pottery. The firm traded as Bodley and Harrold, changed to Edward F. Bodley and Co., and in 1880 to Edward F. Bodley and Sons. In 1881 the business moved to New Bridge Pottery, Longport. It ceased in 1898. Bodley had supplied pottery to the Confederate navy in the American Civil War. He was in partnership with Diggory in the manufacture of china 1870-4, using the china department of Samual Alcock's Hill Top Pottery. He was still using this pottery in 1881, when his two factories employed between them 350 people.

EFB had married again, in 1852, Mary Ridgway, by whom he had eight children. He was Liberal in politics, and served as mayor of Hanley 1872-3. On his retirement he removed to Dane Bank House, Congleton, where he died, on 17 April, 1881. He was buried in Christ Church, Eaton, near Congleton. His son Edwin James Drew Bodley carried on the business until 1892 when he was declared bankrupt.

Census 1871, 1881; Dir. 1864, 1867, 1875/6; Jewitt; VCH viii.

BOON, Edwin (1806-82), *builder and grocer,* Burslem.

EB, possibly the son of John and Ann Boon, was baptised on 29 June 1806. Nothing is known of his early career but in 1851 he was a builder and also secretary of a provident society. In 1860 he was living at 110 Liverpool Road and was described as shopkeeper; in 1867 he was a grocer and builder; and in 1870 a grocer and joiner.

He served on the Burslem Local Board of Health from 1853 to 1868 and was chairman 1866-7. Liberal in politics, he was one of the nominees of Samuel Pope, the temperance candidate, in the parliamentary election for Stoke upon Trent in 1857. He attended the local Congregational church.

By his wife Diana he had a daughter, Mary, born about 1837. He died at Melbourne Street on 24 August 1882.

Anderton; Oldham; *Staffs. Sentinel* 24 August 1882.

BOOTE, Richard (1823/4-93), *earthenware and tile manufacturer,* Burslem.

RB was born in Cheshire about 1823. With Thomas Latham Boote he founded the firm of T. and R. Boote in 1842, and manufactured parian statuary and vases at the Central Pottery, Burslem. Later he moved to Kilncroft Works and then to Waterloo Pottery. After 1865 the manufacture of all decorative wares was discontinued and the firm confined itself to ordinary granite ware for the American market. From about 1850 RB was making tiles and the Blackwall Tunnel, under the River Thames, at London, was lined throughout with Boote tiles. In 1894, after RB's death, the firm became a limited liability company, continuing into the 20th century with the manufacture of tiles.

RB lived at Bleak Hill, Cobridge, where he died on 13 September 1893.

Census 1851; Jewitt; M and H.

BOOTH, Thomas Gimbert (1850-1907), *earthenware manufacturer,* Tunstall.

TGB, born about 1850, was the son of Thomas Booth, pottery manufacturer, of Knowles Works, Burslem in 1864 and of Church Bank Works about 1870. TGB succeeded his father about 1876, for a short time in partnership with his brother Fred. The business was registered as a limited company about 1898, and TGB acted as managing director until 1904 then as chairman. The firm was noted for its Royal Semi Porcelain, Silicon China and in the 20th century for its reproduction, in opaque earthenware, of 18th century Worcester porcelain. The factory employed 95 men in 1881. The firm continued until the 1940s.

TGB was elected to the Tunstall Local Board of Health in 1882 and served a chief bailiff from 1886-90. He supported the idea of a separate Potteries county and was one of Tunstall's first representatives on Staffordshire county council in 1889. His portrait, by John Nash Peake, hung in the council chamber. He was a churchman, a Conservative and bred racehorses.

He lived in Wolstanton, then at Bradwell Lodge, Porthill, at May Bank Cottage in 1881, for some time after 1904 in Wellington, Shropshire and for the last six months of his life at Grace Dieu, 17 Knowsley Road, Southport, where he died on 7 September 1907 leaving a widow, Eliza.

Census 1881; Dir. 1907; *Staffs. Sentinel* 17 October 1907 (obit.).

BOOTHROYD, Benjamin (1808-86), *medical practitioner,* Hanley.

BB was born in Spalding, Lincolnshire, in 1808. He was apprenticed to a local doctor, continued his studies at Guy's Hospital, London, and became a member of the Royal College of Surgeons. He came to the Potteries in 1832, at a time when there was a cholera epidemic in the area, a fact which helped to focus his interest on matters of public health. He practised at 26 Market Place, Hanley.

Throughout his adult life he was active in local government and in local community projects generally. He served as an improvement commissioner, a turnpike trustee and a member of the highway board. In 1857, on the incorporation of Hanley as a borough, he was elected to the council, and immediately appointed alderman, a position which he occupied until his death. In 1861 he was appointed mayor and was also placed on the borough's commisssion of the peace. As chairman of the sanitary committee he was one of the first to stress the need for smoke abatement. He played an important role in the abolition of the 22 tollgates in the borough in the period 1871-81. BB promoted a land allotment scheme at Northwood. He was interested in art education and at his death left £5,500 worth of stock to pay off any debt incurred by Hanley School of Art and for prizes and scholarships. He served as chairman of the Committee of the Joint Hospital Board for Infectious Diseases for Hanley, Stoke and Fenton, set up in 1880.

For his time he had a progressive view about child labour. In giving evidence to the Children's Employment Commission in May 1862, he stated that no child under ten years of age should be employed in a pottery, nor if under 14 be employed more than ten hours a day including one and a half hours for meals. He also urged that children under 15 who were unable to read well or write legibly should attend school for three hours a day, such attendance to be subtracted from the hours of work. He also criticised working conditions in some factories, complaining of faulty construction, imperfect ventilation and overcrowding.

In politics Boothroyd was a Liberal, and he was a member of Hanley Tabernacle church (Congregationalist).

He died at the end of September 1886.

Census 1851; *Report of Child Employment Commission, Parliamentary Papers, 1863; Staffs. Advertiser* 2 October 1886; E. J. D. Warrilow, *History of Etruria*.

BOSTOCK, Lewis (1776/7-1842), *iron founder,* Stoke upon Trent.

LB, the son of David and Mary Bostock, was born about 1776, at the time when his father began iron founding in Cross (Epworth) Street, Stoke upon Trent. The foundry first provided castings for the Grand Trunk (Trent and Mersey) Canal then being built, and occupied the south-west side of Epworth Street, between Church Street and Hill Street.

His parents were probably original members of a Wesleyan Society in the town and he was one of the trustees who bought land from Thomas Wolfe to build Cross Street chapel in 1799. He registered the chapel for worship in 1801. LB bought more land from Wolfe in 1805 on which he built the Sunday School and two houses. Two years later he built a house for himself in Market (Hide) Street, which later became the minister's house and ultimately the chapel caretaker's. Both chapel and house were demolished in September 1983.

In 1839 LB was one of the Stoke upon Trent improvement commissioners. On 25 January 1828 he married Dorothy Key of Uttoxeter. He died in 1842.

Cox's Pottery Annual 1926; E. Beech and A. Curtis: *A History of Wesley Chapel, Stoke upon Trent;* Uttoxeter Parish Registers (SRO); SHC 4 ser., iii; Stoke upon Trent Improvement Commissioners Minute.

BOUGHTON, Richard (born 1803/4), *draper,* Burslem.

RB, the son of John and Mary Boughton, was born in Newton Longville, Buckinghamshire, about 1803. He had moved to the Potteries by 1836 and was in business as a linen and woollen draper, Market Place, Burslem, in 1841. He was living in Hill Street in 1861 and at Bleak Hill in 1862.

RB served on the Burslem Local Board of Health from 1863 to 1865, and was a trustee of Burslem Free School in 1859. In politics he was a Liberal/Independent and in religion an Anglican.

He married Ann Hammond in London on 10 August 1835 and there were three children of the marriage. At the time of his marriage his business was a partnership, Cox and Boughton, of Hanley. RB sent his daughters to the Misses Cotton (Boarding) School, Bleak Hill. His son Richard was an articled potter in 1861.

Census 1841, 1851, 1861; Dir. 1851, 1860; Oldham.

BOULLEMIER, Antonin Hilaire (1838-1900), *ceramic artist,* Stoke upon Trent.

AHB was born in Metz, France, in 1838. He studied in Paris then worked for various decorating establishments and at the Sèvres factory. He came to England in 1872 to work for Minton. After a dispute with Colin Minton Campbell (q.v.) AHB set up his own business in Penkhull New Road. He continued to accept commissions from Minton's, however. He also painted and some of his canvases were exhibited at the Royal Academy.

AHB was an accomplished singer and had been offered the position of principal bass at the Opera Comique, Paris. In the Potteries he conducted amateur operatic performances and organised 'Penny Popular Concerts' at Stoke town hall.

He married before 1877 and had two children, Henri and Lucien (q.v.) both of whom painted for Minton in a style similar to their father's. AHB died on 26 April 1900 at 64 Penkhull New Road.

G. Godden, *Victorian Porcelain;* Minton Mss; *Pottery Gazette* 1 May 1900 (obit.); *Staffs. Sentinel* 26 April 1900 (obit.).

BOULLEMIER, Lucien Émile (1877-1949), pottery artist, Stoke upon Trent

LEB was born in Penkhull New Road, Stoke upon Trent, in 1877, the son of Antonin Boullemier (q.v.). Like his father LEB worked as a pottery artist for Minton's and later became art director of Malings Pottery, Newcastle upon Tyne. He spent some time in the United States of America, where he worked for Lennox Pottery, in Philadelphia.

He was a talented portrait painter and two of his portraits of Queen Victoria were bought by the royal family. He also painted the Duke of Windsor, as Prince of Wales, in 1932.

In his youth LEB played football for Chesterton, Newcastle under Lyme, for Stoke, then in the first division, and for Port Vale. He was a member of Port Vale's team when they defeated Sheffield United, then leaders of Division 1, in the F.A. cup competition of 1897-8. While in America LEB played for Philadelphia Hibernians. He was chairman of Stoke Swimming Club and a water polo referee.

Later in life LEB developed his musical interests. He was a member of several amateur operatic societies. During the Second World War, as Labour and Welfare Officer at Radway Green Royal Ordnance Factory, he was a member of the Radway Jollees group.

He was married in 1896 at St. Peter's Roman Catholic church, Stoke upon Trent, and had one son. He lived at 20 Eleanor Crescent, Westlands, Newcastle under Lyme, where he died on 15 January 1949.

Evening Sentinel 15 January 1949; M and H; Minton Mss; *Staffs. Sentinel* 2 February 1898.

BOULTON, William (1825-1900), *engineer,* Burslem.

WB was born at Seabridge, Clayton, Newcastle under Lyme, on 21 February 1825. In 1852 in partnership with Benjamin Brough he set up as ironfounder in Moorland Road, Burslem. The firm moved in 1856 to the site of its present premises in Navigation Road, Burslem. For 40 years WB employed his inventive talents in devising machines to improve the processes of pottery manufacture. Between 1860 and 1897 he took out 23 patents including a rope-drive jigger (1868), a blunger (1874), lathes, thrower's wheels, an encaustic tile apparatus, a dish-washing machine and a machine for making electric insulators under presssure. Arnold Bennett (q.v.), with whom the Boulton family had close associations, called him 'a lone and wonderful genius'.

In politics WB was a Liberal. He served on the local board of health 1872-8 and was mayor of Burslem in 1881 and again in 1892. He was a lifelong member of the Wesleyan Methodist church, a Staffordshire county magistrate and a governor of Haywood Hospital.

By his two wives WB had 13 children. In 1876 he lived at Grange Cottage, Waterloo Road, Burslem, two doors away from the Bennett family's house at 198 Waterloo Road. WB's eldest son William Henry became engaged to Tertia Bennett, Arnold Bennett's sister, but was drowned at Barmouth while on holiday with his fiancée and her two brothers, Frank and Septimus.

WB died on 29 October 1900 and was succeeded by his son Frank Dunning Boulton as head of the firm. He was the last of the Boulton sons and when he died in 1945 the direct family interest in the firm ceased. The firm continued in the Boulton tradition and in 1952 produced a filter for the coal industry which made it possible for pure water to be returned to the washing plant. Today the company controls a number of subsidiary firms.

Oldham; *Potteries Gazette* 1 October 1896; *Staffs. Sentinel* 13 September 1897; VCH ii; headstone in Burslem cemetery.

BOULTON, William (baptised 1832), *pawnbroker and clothier,* Stoke upon Trent.

WB was baptised at Trentham 18 March 1832, where William Boulton and Hannah Naylor, probably his parents, were married in 1831. He served an apprenticeship with Carryers Brothers, pawnbrokers, of Newcastle under Lyme, and set up on his account in business about 1860 in Stoke upon Trent. He was still in business as pawnbroker and clothier, at 45, 47 and 49 Liverpool Road and 5 London Road, in 1900. He served as president of the North Staffordshire Pawnbrokers' Association. He was elected to Stoke upon Trent borough council in 1874, served continuously until 1901, being appointed mayor twice, in 1888-9 and 1889-90, and was a chairman of the finance committee. He was attached to London Road Baptist chapel, for which he acted as treasurer for over 40 years.

In 1880 he was living, with his wife, Elizabeth, at Park Cottage, Bath Street, Stoke upon Trent, at Field House, Boothen, in 1900, and at The Villas, Stoke upon Trent, at the time of his death, on 15 November 1901. He acted as returning officer for the borough elections only a fortnight before he died. He was buried at Hartshill.

Dir. 1872-1900; Fenn's *Stoke Borough Almanac; Staffs. Sentinel* 16 November 1901 (obit.).

BOULTON, William (fl. 1900), *tile manufacturer,* Tunstall.

WB owned Midlands and Port Vale Tileries c. 1867, trading as Boulton and Co. The firm made pressed paving tiles, garden edging, ridge and roofing tiles, sanitary tubes and other items. From 1872 the firm was styled Brownhills Tileries but in 1892 the premises were at Summer Bank, Tunstall. WB also owned Hawthorne Tileries, Trent Vale, by 1884. He became a member of the Tunstall Local Board of Health in 1892, became chief bailiff and also chairman of the urban district council 1896-1900. He served as county councillor for the southern division of Tunstall in 1907. In that year he was living at Dimsdale House, Alexander Parade. He may have been the William Boulton living in Watlands Avenue, Porthill in 1912.

Dir. 1872-1912; *Men of the Period* (c. 1897).

BOURNE, Charles (1775/6-1836), *pottery manufacturer,* Fenton.

CB was baptised on 21 November 1776, the son of James Bourne. He was in business at the Foley c. 1805, manufacturing high quality porcelain. He retired in 1830, his factory being bought by Elkin, Knight and Elkin.

He married Mary Edwardes, of Lane Delph, in 1798 and by her had at least two children. He died at Stafford, aged 60, on 18 October 1836. His tomb in Stoke churchyard survives today.

G. Godden, *Antique Dealer and Collectors' Guide,* May 1967; Jewitt; M and H; *Potteries Mercury* 1 November 1828; *Staffs. Advertiser* 13 November 1830; VCH viii.

BOURNE, Hugh (1772-1852), *carpenter and founder of Primitive Methodism,* Burslem.

HB was born at Ford Hays Farm, Stoke upon Trent, on 3 April 1772, the son of Joseph and Ellen Bourne. In 1788 the family moved to Bemersley, Norton-le-Moors, where Bourne worked as a carpenter. By his own efforts he acquired an extensive education, including a knowledge of Greek, Hebrew, Latin and French. He joined the Methodist Society at Ridgway, near Bemersley, in 1799, and soon began, with Daniel Shubotham and Matthias Bayley, to evangelise among the colliers in the Harriseahead area. A chapel was built, largely at Bourne's expense, in Daniel Shubotham's garden, and early in 1802, the chapel and its three classes were united to the Burslem Methodist circuit. Amongst the converts of 1805 was William Clowes (q.v.).

In 1807 Bourne heard an American travelling preacher, Lorenzo Dow, speaking about camp or open-air meetings in America. Bourne and his colleagues decided to hold a similar meeting on Mow Cop to provide a counter attraction to disreputable activities during Wakes week, the annual Potteries holiday. The meeting was held on 31 May 1807, and attracted a large crowd. Its success prompted the organisers to hold three more meetings in that year, but by this time the local Methodist circuit authorities and the Methodist annual conference had become alarmed at the emotional character of the gatherings and by their possible political implications during the Napoleonic war, then in progress. They forbade the holding of such meetings, and when Bourne defied the ban he was expelled from the Burslem society on 27 June 1808, together with his brother James. They continued to evangelise, independently, and in 1809 employed James Crawfoot, of Delemare, Cheshire, as a full-time missioner. Bourne and his followers established their first separate society in 1810 at Standley, a village near Bemersley. William Clowes was excluded from Tunstall Methodist society in that year and he and his followers amalgamated with Bourne. They adopted the name Primitive Methodist in 1812, by which time the movement had 34 preaching places and 23 preachers. The new denomination owed much to Hugh Bourne's talents and energy, and the close identification of Primitive Methodism with the working class established by Bourne in the early years remained a dominant characteristic of the movement. From 1818-42 Bourne edited and published a quarterly magazine. He visited missions in the United States of America from 1844 to 1846. He died unmarried, on 11 October, 1852, in which year the Primitive Methodists numbered 110,000 and had 560 travelling preachers.

VCH iii and viii; J. T. Wilkinson, *Hugh Bourne, 1772-1852.*

BOURNE, Ralph (1772/3-1835), *pottery manufacturer,* Fenton.

RB was born about 1772. He became principal partner in the firm of Bourne, Baker and Bourne of Fenton. He carried on the business alone after 1833, following the death of William Baker (q.v.), and John Bourne.

During the pottery workers' strike of 1834 RB reported to the government and to the local Staffordshire authorities on the state of affairs in the Potteries.

He left £3,500 for the erection of Christ Church, Fenton, and contributed to the building of Hilderstone church. He lived at Hilderstone Hall. He died in November 1835.

M and H; *Staffs. Advertiser* 5 December 1835; J. Thomas, *The Rise of the Staffordshire Potteries.*

BOURNE, Samuel (1788/9-1864), *pottery designer,* Fenton.

SB was born in Norton-in-the-Moors about 1788. He was apprenticed to Wood and Caldwell of Burslem and about 1810 worked at Mason's pottery. Three of the vases which he painted for Mason were sold at Sotheby's on 4 February 1975. He became chief designer at Minton's from 1828, holding this post until his retirement in 1863.

He married Elizabeth (probably née Taylor) on 13 December 1813 at Fulford, and had at least five children. He was a Fenton improvement commissioner. By 1841 he was living in Duke Street and by 1861 in Queen Street, Fenton, where he died on 26 November 1864.

Census, 1841, 1851, 1861: R. Haggar and E. Adams, *Mason Porcelain and Ironstone;* IGI Staffs.; *National Index to Wills and Administrations 1858-1931.*

BOWERS, George Frederick (1808/9-1867), *pottery manufacturer and coalmaster,* Burslem.

GFB was born at Audley, Staffs., about 1808. He is first documented in 1834 when he was the landlord of the Blue Bell Inn, Nile Street, Burslem. In 1841 he was potting at Brownhills Pottery formerly Marsh and Haywood, in partnership with Edward Challinor, having leased the works from Samuel Marsh. The firm made porcelain tea wares with painted decoration and was awarded a gold medal at the 1851 Great Exhibition. By 1861 he was employing 97 men, 19 boys and 12 girls. He built a flint-grinding mill in Chester Street, Brownhills, in or shortly before 1853.

On 11 August 1839 GFB married Mary Buxton, widow of a glass and china merchant of Boston, Lincs. He was living in Brownhills Cottage at the time of his marriage, from which there were at least three children. He served on the Burslem Local Board of Health from 1857 to 1863 and was a trustee of Burslem Free School in 1859. He was Conservative in his political opinions and a member of the Church of England. He died at Brownhills Cottage on 1 January 1867 and was buried in St. Paul's churchyard, Dalehall.

His son Frederick F. Bowers took over the running of the pottery in the early 1860s but the business failed in 1871, was bought by James Eardley and continued as The Brownhills Pottery Co. until 1896. GFB's grandson, C. H. Bowers (died 1934) became managing director of Booths Ltd. in 1904 (now part of Staffordshire Potteries).

Census 1861; Jewitt; M and H; *National Index to Wills and Administrations; Oldham; VCH viii.*

BRADFORD, George Percival (1820-93), *draper,* Hanley.

GPB was born in Alderley, Cheshire, on 27 September 1820, according to the 1871 census (although his gravestone in Hartshill cemetery states he was born in Knutsford). He was in business as a draper in Macclesfield, Cheshire, where he promoted penny readings and other recreative pursuits before coming to Hanley in 1855. In his shop in Market Square, Hanley, which he maintained until he retired in 1890, he employed nine men and 15 women.

He leased the Potteries Street Railway from its builder, George Train, in 1864, and continued as a director of the North Staffs. Tramway Co., when it bought the P.S.R. in 1879. He claimed he was one of the most experienced tramway managers in the country.

He served as a councillor from 1862 to 1864, then in 1870 became a member of the inaugural Hanley School Board, serving on this body, with a break from 1882 to 1885, until his death, and becoming chairman in 1890. In 1891 T. W. Harrison replaced him in this office, with the support of the majority of the members who were opposed to Bradford's policy on the Higher Grade School (later Hanley High School).

He returned to Hanley council in 1878 where he was often in the centre of controversy. One local Hanley historian has characterised him as 'better known for his opposition than for any constructive qualities'.

On retiring from business GPB farmed Birches Head Farm, where he had lived since 1875. In 1889 was elected to represent Bucknall on Staffordshire county council.

He married Mary Kay, of Liverpool, and by her had two sons and four daughters. One son, Peter, became a doctor in Southport. GPB died on 30 January 1893 at his brother's home in Manchester. He was buried in Hartshill cemetery.

Census 1871; J. Wentworth Day, *Wheels of Service: the story of PMT; Staffs. Sentinel* 30 January 1893; *Staffs. Advertiser* 4 February 1893.

BRAIN, Elijah (1845-1910), *pottery manufacturer,* Fenton.

EB was born in Fenton on 24 November 1842. He was educated at Fenton and Stoke National Schools and later attended the Fenton and Stoke Athenaeums to improve his education. He began work as a jigger and mould runner for Baker and Co., Fenton, and worked his way up to cashier for the firm. He left in 1855 and became a partner in Robinson and Son, The Foley (King Street). From 1885 he was in partnership with A. B. Jones and W. Hawker. He served as president of the English China Manufacturers Association.

He was elected to the Fenton Local Board of Health in 1855 and was first chairman of the Fenton Urban District Council in 1894 and again in 1897. He was instrumental in securing the erection of a bridge at Fenton railway station in place of the level crossing, and was one of the founders of the Fenton Nursing Institution. He was a strong Liberal and an advocate of tariff reform. A member of the Fenton Education Committee from its inception and of the committee which helped to establish the Hanchurch Holiday Home pioneered by Millicent Duchess of Sutherland (q.v.).

From 1875 EB was a conductor of the Mount Tabor chapel choir and was also one of the founders of the Stoke Philharmonic Society. In 1878 he inaugurated the Fenton Children's Religious Services, with an annual festival at Fenton town hall. He served on the Stoke upon Trent school board. In 1910 he failed to gain election to the federated council of Stoke on Trent, trailing Phillip Elliot and John Shaw Goddard (q.v.).

By his wife Mary Julia he had two daughters and a son. He died on 23 October 1910 and was buried at Fenton cemetery.

Staffs. Sentinel 24 October 1910 (obit.).

BREGAZZI, Charles (born 1796/7), *carver and gilder,* Hanley.

CB was born about 1796 near Lake Como, Italy. He is first documented in the Potteries in 1834, with Sebastian Bregazzi, as carver, gilder, looking-glass and barometer manufacturers, etc. in High Street, Hanley. In 1860 he was in Tontine Square, Hanley, and in 1862 at 36 Tontine Street, after which date there is no further record of him in the area.

In 1841 he was living in Parliament Row, Hanley, with his wife, Marianne, born in London, and a child, Dominic aged ten. This suggests that he had emigrated to England before 1831.

Census 1841, 1861; Dir. 1834, 1862; Hanley Rate Book 1862.

BRIAN, (William) Havergal (1876-1972), *composer,* Longton.

WB was born at 35 Ricardo Street, Dresden, in 1876, the third child of Benjamin Brian, a potter's turner. He was baptised William but later changed his name to Havergal, a name possibly derived from a family of Worcestershire hymn-writers. HB's musical talents were displayed at an early age. He became a choirboy at the local church of St. James the Less, Longton, and also joined other choirs and orchestras, including that of George Hawley, son of George Hulme Hawley (q.v.). He learned to play the violin, cello and piano, using the small salary he earned as an organist at St. James's church, then at Holy Trinity church, Meir, and also at Odd Rode church, Cheshire, to pay for his music lessons. He was apprenticed to a joiner but abandoned this and earned a precarious living as a clerk, then as a traveller for a timber merchant. He had some lessons in harmony from Theophilus Hemmings (q.v.), but as a composer Havergal Brian was largely self-taught. He began composing at the age of 12. Later he sent one of his compositions, an anthem, to Edward Elgar. Elgar remarked that the work was original, if involved, and urged him to continue composing.

In 1899 HB married Isobel Alice Priestley at St. Peter's church, Stoke upon Trent. By her he had five children, one of whom died in infancy. The family lived at 11 Gordon Street (now Dominie Street), Hartshill, and it was in this house that he wrote his setting of Shakespeare's sonnet 'Shall I compare thee to a summer's day', his first musical success outside the Potteries. The family moved later to 9 Lefield Road, Trentham and then to 50 James Street, Stoke upon Trent.

He found a patron in Herbert Minton Robinson (q.v.) who helped him and his family financially for 14 years. He was also befriended by Sir Granville Bantock, professor of music at Birmingham University. He made his London debut, with Sir Henry Wood, at a promenade concert in 1907. Success now began to change him. He took to drink, became estranged from his wife and in 1913 the marriage finally broke up. Robinson withdrew his patronage and Brian moved to London where he lived with Hilda Mary Hayward, marrying her in 1933 after the death of his first wife. He had five children by this second marriage.

For some years HB fell into obscurity, though he continued to compose. Little more was heard of him until 1954, when Robert Simpson, a BBC music producer, helped to get Brian's 8th Symphony performed. His musical comeback was climaxed in 1966 when his Gothic Symphony was performed at the Albert Hall under the conductorship of Sir Adrian Boult.

HB moved to Shoreham on Sea in 1958, and it was here that he died on 28 November 1972. His musical output had been prodigious. He wrote 32 symphonies, five operas, five suites, two violin concertos, a cello concerto, more than a hundred songs and various other works. Brian is the most important composer hitherto produced by the Potteries. His works have been frequently broadcast by the BBC, he has been the subject of a play, *Awkward Cuss,* produced in the Victoria Theatre, and a number of books have been written about him. The Havergal Brian Society exists to promote his music and to perpetuate his name.

R. Nettel, *Havergal Brian, the man and his music;* K. Easthaugh, *Havergal Brian, the making of a composer;* R. L. E. Foreman, *Havergal Brian and the performance of his orchestral music;* M. MacDonald, *The Symphonies of Havergal Brian* (3 vols.); H. Brian, *The Faraway Years.*

BRIDGWOOD, Sampson (c. 1798-1876), *pottery manufacturer,* Longton.

SB may have been the individual baptised at Stoke upon Trent parish church on 25 December 1801, the son of Nathaniel and Elizabeth Bridgwood, although the 1871 census suggests that he was born in 1793. The family had established a business in Market Street, Longton, at the beginning of the 19th century. By 1838 SB was occupying a pottery works in Stafford Street, Longton, formerly in the occupation of George Forrester. This factory was demolished to make way for the new market in 1863. SB opened another factory in Bridgwood (formerly Wharf) Street about 1853, where he manufactured bone china. He was also working Gom's flint mills in 1851 and opened the Anchor Mills, adjoining the Anchor Pottery, in 1867. These mills had ceased operation by the mid-1950s. SB was a partner of Hawley and Goodwin in Mossfield Colliery in 1845.

He married by about 1820 and had a son Samuel, born about that year. In 1871 SB, a widower, was living in Lightwood Road, and was described as a china manufacturer and colliery owner. He was appointed to the Longton borough commission of peace. He died at Lightwood on 2 June 1876.

Census 1871; Dir. 1872; Jewitt; VCH viii.

BRIGGS, Michael (c. 1799-1862), *draper,* Stoke upon Trent.

MB was born in Atherstone, Warwicks., about 1799. In 1837 he started a drapery business in High Street, Stoke upon Trent. He may have been the partner of Samuel Keys in a pottery factory in Copeland Street, Stoke upon Trent, in 1862, which exhibited in London in that year. In 1860 he indicated his intention to build a new inn in the town, on the corner of Liverpool Road and High Street.

He qualified as an improvement commissioner in 1841 and was an original member of the Stokeville Building Society in 1850 and served on the committee. On 1 February 1837 he married Elizabeth Ottey at Rugeley, Staffs., and they had at least seven children. One son, William Ottey Briggs was mayor of Newcastle under Lyme in 1875 and 1891. The family were living in Hill Street, Stoke upon Trent by 1849 and at The Villas by 1861, by which year MB was a widower.

He died on 1 October 1862.

Census 1861; Jewitt; *Staffs. Advertiser* 16 June 1900 (obit. of W. O. Briggs); Stoke upon Trent Improvement Commissioners' Minutes; Stoke upon Trent parish registers; Turner.

BRIGHT, William Leatham (1851-1910), *Member of Parliament,* Stoke upon Trent.

WLB was born in Rochdale, Lancs. on 12 August 1851, the son of John Bright, the anti-corn law leader and Margaret Elizabeth Leatham. He became a colliery agent and shipbroker. A Liberal like his father he successfully contested Stoke upon Trent in the parliamentary election of November 1885 and won the seat again, as a Gladstonian Liberal in favour of Home Rule for Ireland, in 1886, though with a reduced majority. He withdrew from the seat in 1890, but came back into politics to contest Rochdale in 1895.

He married, on 28 March 1883, Isabella McIvor, daughter of Alfred Taylor, of Carshalton, Surrey. He died on 23 September 1910.

S and L; V and S.

BRINDLEY, James (1716-72), *canal engineer,* Tunstall.

JB was born at Tunstead, in the parish of Wormhill, Derbyshire, in 1716, the son of James and Susannah Brindley. He set up in business as a millwright in Leek, Staffs., in 1742. In addition to constructing mills and steam engines he became famous for his work as a canal engineer. He was involved in the surveying and construction of the Bridgewater Canal, the Trent and Mersey Canal, the Staffordshire and Worcester Canal, and numerous others. He had a share in Golden Hill colliery and was a partner of his brother John in the Longport Pottery.

He married Anne Henshall on 8 December 1765 at Wolstanton church, and had two daughters, Susannah and Anne. He also had a natural son, John Bennett (1760-99), from whom Arnold Bennett the novelist descended. He died at Turnhurst on 27 September 1772 and was buried in the churchyard at Newchapel.

C. T. G. Boucher, *James Brindley, Engineer, 1716-72.*

BRINDLEY, Thomas (born c. 1814), *coal and iron master,* Burslem.

TB, son of Thomas and Ann Brindley, was baptised in Burslem on 28 December 1814. His father was a farmer, living at Sneyd Green in 1851. TB was listed as a coal and iron master of Cobridge Colliery, employing 40 men and boys and living at Cobridge Cottage, Elder Road, Burslem. He was then a widower, his wife, Emily, having died after 1851/2 when his youngest child, Frank, was born.

TB served on the Burslem Local Board of Health from 1852 to 1864.

Census 1851, 1861; IGI Staffs.; Oldham.

BROADE, Philip Barnes (died 1852), *landowner,* Fenton.

PBB, son of Thomas Broade and Sarah née Cartledge, owned the manorial rights of Fenton Vivian. He had inherited four fifths of the manor from his father who died in the early 1840s, and had purchased the remaining fifth, which comprised lands in Botteslow, from William Kelsall Tait. He married Charity, daughter of William Baker of Fenton Culvert, and was living at Fenton Manor House in 1851. The house, which had a stone pedimented doorway, was built about 1800 and had been much improved by the early 1840s. It was demolished in the 1960s. PBB is documented as in favour of granting a licence to a theatre in Hanley, to which T. B. Rose the stipendiary magistrate (q.v.) was opposed. He died on 12 August 1852.

Staffs. Advertiser 14 Feb. 1852; R. Talbot, *History of Fenton;* VCH viii.

BROADHURST, Henry (1840-1911), *Member of Parliament,* Stoke upon Trent.

HB was born at Littlemore, near Oxford, on 13 April 1840, the youngest of the 12 children of Thomas and Sarah Broadhurst. His father was a stonemason and keen Methodist, and HB served his apprenticeship as a stone mason under his father. He worked in Norwich and London and in 1872 gave up his trade to become a full time official in the Stonemason's Union. In 1873 he became secretary of the Labour Representation League. In the following year he stood for election for the borough of Chipping Wycombe but was defeated. In 1875 he was appointed secretary to the parliamentary committee of the Trades Union Congress. He was adopted as Liberal candidate for Stoke upon Trent in 1880 and became the first working class candidate to be elected in the Potteries. When the Stoke constituency was divided in 1885 HB was doubtful of the wisdom of fighting a Potteries seat single-handed and moved to the Bordesley seat in Birmingham. He served as under-secretary for the Home Department for a short period. Later he sat for a Nottingham seat and as a 'Lib-Lab' for Leicester, retiring from public life in 1906. He visited the Potteries in November 1907 and spoke in favour of federation.

In 1860 he married Eliza Olley, of Norwich, and as there were no children of this marriage he adopted his wife's niece. In collaboration with Sir Robert Reid (later Lord Loreburn) he wrote a book on household enfranchisement in 1885.

He died in October 1911.

J. M. Bellamy and J. Saville, *Dictionary of Labour Biography,* vol. 2; *Staffs. Sentinel* 11 October 1911; V and S.

BROADY, John (1833/4-1900), *brewer's agent,* Stoke upon Trent

JB, son of Charles and Mary Broady, was born in Stoke upon Trent about 1833. His father was agent for Allsop's Brewery and for Soresby and Co., wharfingers and canal carriers. JB after first working as a railway clerk, became the local Allsop's agent. He lived in Glebe Street in 1851.

He was elected auditor for the borough of Stoke upon Trent, with G. H. Stringer, in 1874 and served in this office until 1889. He was on the Stoke School Board from 1892. He acted as secretary for the Stoke upon Trent Conservative Club, was a superintendent of the parish church Sunday School for 30 years, hon. librarian of the Stoke Athenaeum and associated with the North Staffordshire Philharmonic Society. He died at Glebe Street on 6 May 1900 and was buried in Stoke churchyard. There is a memorial to him in Stoke parish church.

Census 1851; *Fenn's Stoke Borough Almanac; Staffs. Sentinel* 7 May 1900.

BROMLEY, John (c. 1830-1915), *pottery manufacturer,* Hanley.

JB was born about 1830. By 1873 he was in business at the Victoria Works, St. James Street, Hanley, trading as Adams and Bromley. The factory produced jasper, in quality and character a good imitation of Wedgwood, and above average majolica. Green-glazed dessert ware was also produced in quantity. The firm continued until 1894.

JB was elected to Hanley borough council in 1873 and served as mayor from 1879 to 1881. He was elected an alderman in 1887 and created a freeman of the borough in 1895. A freemason he served as master of Menturia Lodge in 1894, founded Gordon Lodge and was its first grandmaster in 1886 and became senior grand warden of the province of Staffordshire. He was one of the first persons to be enrolled in the volunteer Shropshire and Staffordshire Artillery. He was elected president of the North Staffordshire Provident Society.

He lived at The Mount, Penkhull, and apparently served on both Stoke upon Trent and Hanley councils at the same time. He died at Shelton on 22 July 1915.

Dir. 1904; Huntbach; Jewitt; *Potteries Year Book* 1902; *Staffs. Sentinel* 22 July 1915.

BROOKE, Ernest (1861-1908), *engraver,* Stoke upon Trent.

EB was born at Park House, Stoke upon Trent, on 18 July 1861, the son of William Brooke, an engraver, and a grandson of William Brooke who worked for Davenports at Longport and is said to have invented three-coloured printing on pottery, engraved plates for Simeon Shaw's *History of the Staffordshire Potteries* and helped to found the Potteries Mechanics' Institute.

EB was educated at the Middle School, Newcastle under Lyme, and the Wedgwood Memorial Institute, Burslem. He eventually continued in the family business of engraving, working from an office in Sutherland Chambers, Stoke upon Trent. He owned a large art collection and lent paintings, engravings and pottery to the museum at Stoke.

His political career began in 1900 when he was elected to a casual vacancy on Stoke upon Trent council. He became a keen supporter of federation. He challenged the majority of Stoke councillors to poll the ratepayers for their opinions on the council's action in rejecting the Draft Provisional Order in February 1908; he fell into dispute with friend and angling companion Rupert Adderley, clerk to Fenton Urban District Council (q.v.) over the question as to whether Fenton's opposition to federation might be overcome by the offer of special terms to Hanley.

EB was a humorous and witty speaker, sang comic songs at concerts and worked for charities. In 1908 he organised a benefit concert at the Stoke Hippodrome in aid of the mayor of Wigan's Colliery Disaster Fund.

In 1894 he married a daughter of Robert Bates of Newcastle. The family lived at Harding House, Penkville Street, Stoke upon Trent, where EB died on 16 November 1908. He was buried in Hartshill cemetery.

Staffs. Sentinel 16 November 1908.

BROUGHAM, Mary (born 1794), *printer,* Burslem.

Mary Brougham, the wife of Stephen Brougham, whom she married on 26 September 1816 at Burslem was daughter of William and Mary Lea. She was baptised at Burslem on 26 October 1794. She was in business with her husband as a printer in the Market Place, Burslem before 1828, but subsequent directories mention only her name. In 1834 she was bookseller, binder, printer, operated a circulating library and acted as sub-distributor of stamps. By 1841 she was selling sheet music and by 1851 was manufacturing "elegant parian brooches and bracelets which have most deservedly received patrongage of Her Majesty, Duchess of Sutherland and Jenny Lind, etc." In 1851 she lived at the premises in Market Place with her sons William Henry and Joseph and daughter Mary Jane. There were at least two other children—John Fownley and Hannah. By that year MB had also added a Bible depot to the list of her business interests.

By about 1861 the business was in the hands of Richard Timmis (q.v.). The old post office was later taken over by Warwick Savage.

Census 1851; Dir. 1834, 1841, 1851; IGI Staffs; R and S.

BROWN, William (1825-1900), *miner,* Hanley.

WB was born in Rothwell, Yorkshire on 6 March 1825, the son of a farm labourer. His early life and career were passed in the Yorkshire coalmining area, where he worked underground for 25 years. He was involved in a strike in 1844 that lasted for 17 weeks. He was dismissed from his job because of his trade union activities and began a greengrocery business with money he had earned singing at concerts and at services for the local Methodist New Connexion chapel. In 1866 he became a full-time agent of the local miners' association.

He moved to the Potteries in 1870 to become the agent for the newly-formed North Staffordshire Miners' Federation, at a salary of £2 10s. a week. He opened his union meetings with prayers and singing and advised against strike action during times of high unemployment and depression. When, in 1876, the mine owners announced a 10% reduction in pay, WB, at a mass meeting in the Circus, Hanley, recommended arbitration. The union split over the issue, Brown leading the southern area of the Association. He ceased his union activites in the late 1880s.

WB was a Methodist all his life and a Liberal. At times he displayed a condescending attitude to his union members but miners in the district owed much to his abilities.

He married twice, in 1845 and 1851. In 1893 he was appointed to the local bench of justices of the peace. He died at St. John Street, Hanley, on 21 September 1900.

Census 1881; *Staffs. Sentinel* 22 September 1900.

BROWNFIELD, Douglas Harold (1856-1917), *potters' miller,* Hanley.

DHB, son of William Brownfield, pottery manufacturer (q.v.), was born in Hanley on 30 March 1856. He was educated at Rugby School, where he excelled at sport. He worked in his father's firm, of which he became a partner in 1879, taking over the milling part of the business, at New Hall Mills, in 1886. He was the greatest all round sportsman in the Potteries in the later Victorian period: he played cricket for Stoke upon Trent 1873, Hanley 1875, Trentham Park 1876, Staffordshire 1885-98 and England 1888, including a match against the Australians in 1890. He played football for local teams and for Staffordshire 1879-80. He acted as first reserve for the England rugby team, and he competed at the Stoke Victoria Athletic Club sports 1878-82.

He married in August 1883 and had two children. He died at Llandudno on 5 August 1917.

Northern Ceramic Society Journal, vol. 4; *Staffs. Sentinel* various issues 1872-1900; information from Rodney Hampson and John Edmunds.

BROWNFIELD, Edward Arthur (1853-1939), *pottery manufacturer,* Hanley.

EAB was born at Chatterley House, Old Hall Street, Hanley, in 1853. He was the fourth child of Wiliam Brownfield (q.v.), master potter, of Cobridge. He was educated at Rugby School, and hoped to enter the ministry, but came to work in the family business after the death of his father in 1873, becoming a partner in the firm with his two brothers. He was interested in the chemistry of potting and invented an adventurine glaze in 1881. He and Ludwig Jahn created the largest single piece of china ever made, overcoming great technical difficulties to make an 11 foot high vase. It was exhibited at the Crystal Palace in 1884 and in Paris in 1889, but was destroyed by a fire at the works in 1894. By 1886 EAB was in sole control of the pottery, his brother Douglas (q.v.) running the flint mills. The eldest brother, William Etches Brownfield, left the firm and went to Australia, where he died unmarried in 1903. In 1892 EAB turned his works into a co-operative concern, the workers holding shares in Brownfields Pottery Society Ltd. The enterprise had only luke-warm support from the co-operative movement and the business was wound up in 1898. EAB became a pottery agent in London until 1904, when he went to Australia and opened a pottery in Lithgow, New South Wales. He married there in 1905 and had one son, Harold. He died in Australia in 1939.

R. and E. Hampson 'Brownfields, Victorian Potters' in *Northern Ceramic Society Journal,* 4, (1980-1).

BROWNFIELD, William (1812-73), *pottery manufacturer,* Hanley.

WB was born in Hanley on 13 February 1812, the son of Ralph Brownfield, earthenware manufacturer and Sarah née Meigh. After working as a commerical traveller for his father's firm WB joined Robinson and Wood, using a works in Douglas Street and Arthur Street (in 1981 the Alexandra Pottery). The firm, employing 500 people, made earthenware, blue-printed and iron-stone ware and hand-painted wares. WB exhibited at the major international exhibitions from 1862. In 1871 a new china works was built in Crane Street and a former Minton artist Ludwig (Louis) Jahn (q.v.) was engaged as art director. From 1846 WB also operated New Hall Mills in Brook (now Century) Street, Hanley.

WB was a Liberal and supported J. C. Ricardo's candidacy in the parliamentary election for Stoke upon Trent in 1841. He was also a member of Bethesda Methodist New Connexion church. He served as a market trustee and commissioner for Hanley and was chief bailiff in 1844. He favoured Hanley's incorporation as a borough and in 1858 became Hanley's mayor in succession to John Ridgway. He was a borough and county magistrate and later a deputy lieutenant. He was a director of the Staffordshire Potteries Waterworks Company and of the North Staffordshire Railway. He gave £500 towards the building of a working men's reading room in the Mechanics' Institute in 1859 and in the same year presented the drinking fountain in Fountain Square to the town.

WB lived in Market (now Huntbach) Street, Hanley, until his marriage to Ellen Etches, daughter of a Derby cheese factor, on 14 January 1847. The family lived subsequently at Chatterley House, Old Hall Street, Hanley, where their seven children were born. They moved to Barlaston Hall, Barlaston, about 1869. WB died there on 12 July 1873. A red marble obelisk in Hanley cemetery commemorates him.

Daily Sentinel 17 July 1873; R. and E. Hampson, 'Brownfield, Victorian Potters', in *Northern Ceramic Society Journal,* 4, (1980-1); Jewitt.

BRYAN, John (1816-82), *builder and contractor,* Stoke upon Trent.

JB, son of John Bryan and Sarah (possibly née Burton) was born at Alton, Staffs., in 1816. He was established in business as a builder in the Potteries by 1842, when he was responsible for the alterations to the Stoke police station lock-up. In 1850 he obtained the contract to build the first 16 houses for Stokeville Building Society (The Villas). His other works included the Church of our Lady of the Angels and St. Peter in Chains, Cliff Bank, Stoke upon Trent, opened in 1857, the Granville Schools at Cobridge and a number of sewers including those in Penkhull, North Street and Flash Lane.

He married about 1848 and had four children. The family lived at Bryanstone Place, Stoneyard, Liverpool Road, Stoke upon Trent, in 1848, and later in Copeland Street. JB died on 25 March 1882 at Registry Street, Stoke upon Trent and was buried in Stoke churchyard. His tomb was surviving in 1984.

Census 1841, 1851, 1861; N. Malkin, *A Grand Tour; Stoke upon Trent Improvement Commissioners' Minutes;* VCH viii.

BULLER, Ernest (c. 1841-97), *industrial porcelain manufacturer,* Hanley.

EB was the son of James Wentworth Buller, M.P., and brother of (Sir) Redvers Buller, later commander-in-chief in Natal in the South African war, 1899-1902. EB, a civil engineer by profession, met with an accident while in the employ of the Indian government and returned to England. He set up in practice in Hanley as a consulting engineer and surveyor. His cousin had acquired the Bovey Tracey Pottery (Devon), where with other articles he manufactured stilts and spurs. Finding the cost of carriage to the Potteries, his main market, too heavy, he moved to Hanley by about 1860. EB joined his cousin and in 1866-7 they began to manufacture telegraph insulators. EB became sole owner in 1869. He acquired the telegraph engineering business of Jobson Bros., of Dudley, in 1885, and the firm became Buller, Jobson and Co. They produced insulators for the first London underground railways and in the early decades of the 20th century were supplying insulators to concerns all over the world. The original factory was in Joiner's Square, Hanley, but in 1920 a new factory was built at Milton.

From about 1880 to about 1895 EB lived at 2 Spur Street, Hanley. He retired in 1896 and died in London on 4 June 1897.

Huntbach; Jewitt; J. C. Wedgwood, *Staffordshire Pottery and its History;* VCH ii.

BURNDRED, William George (1878-1939), *veterinary surgeon,* Hanley.

WGB was born in Hanley on 9 June 1878. He was educated at the Wesleyan Higher Grade School, Hanley, and graduated at the New Veterinary College, Edinburgh on 21 May, 1900, being First Fitzwygram Prizeman. He set up in practice in Hanley, and acted as honorary surgeon to a number of local organizations, including the Potteries and District Collie Club and the North Staffordshire Terrier Club. At the outbreak of the First World War he was veterinary officer in charge of remounts. He joined the Royal Army Veterinary Corps, and served in India, commanding a veterinary hospital. After the war he acted as veterinary officer with the artillery and eventually retired with the rank of major.

His published works include an essay *Antiseptics and Wound Treatment,* for which he was awarded a silver medal. He was a member of Menturia Masonic Lodge.

He married and had two sons, Captain W. H. Burndred, who served with the British Army in India, and G. F. Burndred, a solicitor with the firm of P. J. McKnight and Sons, Hanley. He lived in Hope Street, Hanley. He died on 24 March 1939.

Evening Sentinel 27 March 1939; *The Veterinary Record* (8 April 1939), No. 14, vol. 51; C. Penn, *Staffordshire at the Opening of the 20th Century.*

BURTON, William (1863-1941), *ceramic chemist,* Hanley.

WB was born on 19 March 1863, the son of David Burton, a grocer of Droylesden Road, Newton Heath, Manchester. He was educated at a Methodist day school, became a pupil teacher and later an assistant science master at a central higher grade school. In 1885 he won a scholarship to the Royal College of Science, London. There he met H. G. Wells, the novelist, also on a similar scholarship.

WB left London without graduating, and began work at Wedgwood's, Etruria, as a works chemist. He taught technical pottery part-time at Burslem and Hanley. About 1914 he worked as manager and later as managing director for Pilkington's pottery and tile works. He led the discussions on behalf of the manufacturers on the adoption of lead regulations. Whilst at Pilkington's he recruited Gordon Forsyth (q.v.) and other artists, and produced fine lustre and glaze effects. He retired in 1915 and devoted his time to writing on ceramics.

He married Eliza Nicholls and from 1887 to about 1892 they lived at 18 Victoria Street, Basford. The house bears a plaque recording a visit made by H. G. Wells in 1888, a visit which provided Wells with the background for his short story *The Cone,* inspired by Shelton steelworks, and for other stories. WB left one daughter, Mary, who married Professor F. C. Ormerod.

For his writings on ceramics WB was awarded the honorary degree of M.A. from Manchester University in 1908. His major works include: *A History and Description of English Porcelain* (1902); *A History and Description of English Earthenware and Stoneware* (1904); *Porcelain, a sketch of its Nature, Art and Manufacture* (1906); *A General History of Porcelain* (1921); *Josiah Wedgwood and his Pottery* (1922).

R. S. Hampson 'H. G. Wells and the Staffordshire Potteries' in *The Wellsian* (Journal of the H. G. Wells Society), New Series, No. 3, (1980).

BUTTERS, Charles (1832-91), *auctioneer and valuer,* Hanley.

CB was born in Hanley in 1832. He served an apprenticeship to a pawnbroker in Hanley and started his own business as a pawnbroker before setting up in 1856 as an auctioneer and valuer. It has been stated that most of the property in Hanley passed through his fingers at some time or another.

He married and had three children. He was a member of the local Wesleyan Methodist church and a freemason. He lived at Bellfield, May Bank, Newcastle under Lyme.

He died on 16 February 1891.

Huntbach; *Staffs. Sentinel* 21 February 1891.

CADDIE, Alfred J. (born 1843), *librarian,* Stoke upon Trent.

AC was born in London about 1843. He gained a 2nd class teacher's certificate and was appointed assistant master at St. Thomas's School, Penkhull, on 5 May 1871. He took charge as headmaster on 1 February 1872 and held this post until his retirement on 6 September 1878, when he took up the appointment of borough librarian at the new Stoke upon Trent library and museum. This had been built in 1877/8 on land given by Colin Minton Campbell (q.v.). The nucleus of the library's books was the stock of the Athenaeum, hitherto housed in the south wing of Stoke upon Trent town hall. Caddie held the post of librarian until his resignation on 17 May 1888 when he was succeeded by his son A. J. P. Caddie (q.v.).

AC married his wife Louisa in Islington, London in June 1868. In 1870 they were living in Norbury, near Rocester, Staffs., and in 1871 at 5 Bath Terrace, Stoke upon Trent. There were four children, Alfred, Ernest, Albert and Minnie.

Census 1871; 1881; St. Thomas's National School, Penkhull, log book 1862-90; *Woolley's Almanack* 1888; VCH viii.

CADDIE, Alfred J. P. (1870-1953), *librarian and museum curator,* Stoke upon Trent.

AJPC was born on 22 April 1870 in Norbury, near Ashbourne, the son of Alfred Caddie (q.v.). He was appointed Stoke borough librarian in succession to his father on 21 June 1888. The borough librarian also doubled as museum curator, and Caddie began what was to become a unique collection of local and foreign pottery. He was the first curator to obtain a grant from the Board of Education for London-approved articles. As a member of the Council of Museums Association he read a paper which urged co-operation between the Victoria and Albert Museum and the provinces. He believed that museums should specialise, and that great industrial areas should first of all confine themselves to collecting materials illustrative of local industries. He lectured on pottery both locally and nationally. On Federation Caddie became chief curator of the Potteries' Museums. At a special librarians' conference held in Stoke upon Trent he proposed that small town libraries should co-operate in the establishment of reference libraries.

He married Catherine Elizabeth Toft, youngest daughter of W. H. Toft, on 30 July 1891 at Stoke parish church, and there was one son, Colin Roy, who died at the age of nine. AJPC lived first at 5 Bath Terrace, then at 32 Sheppard Street and afterwards at 126 Oakhill. In 1891 he was elected honorary secretary and treasurer of the Staffordshire Photographic Survey Society.

He died in Stoke upon Trent on 1 March 1953.

Census 1881; Dir. 1882-1892; *Staffs. Sentinel* 14 June 1911.

CAMPBELL, Colin Minton (1827-85), *pottery manufacturer, and Member of Parliament,* Stoke upon Trent.

CMC the son of John and Mary Campbell, was born in Liverpool on 27 August 1827. He came to the Potteries in 1842 to work for his uncle, Herbert Minton (q.v.), who took him into his partnership with M. D. Hollins in 1849. When Herbert Minton died in 1858 CMC took over direction of the firm. The partnership with Hollins was dissolved in 1863, CMC taking the china works and Hollins the tile works. Herbert Minton had employed Leon Arnoux (q.v.) as art director and CMC continued the policy of employing continental artists. Minton majolica was decorated by Emile Lessore, Edouard Rischgitz, Louis Jahn (q.v.) and Antonin Boullemier (q.v.). Among the technical improvements which CMC introduced was the acid gold process which made possible the use of gold decoration in bas relief. Louis Marc Solon (q.v.) who came to Minton's in 1870, introduced the technique of pâte-sur-pâte decoration, one of Minton's major contributions to 19th century ceramics. The firm won medals at the Great Exhibition in 1851, again in 1862, in Paris in 1853, Vienna in 1867 and elsewhere. CMC also founded the Campbell Brick and Tile Co. in 1875.

CMC married Louisa Wilmot Cave-Brown-Cave, whose mother was a daughter of Thomas Minton (q.v.). They had eleven children of whom a son and three daughters survived to adult life. CMC's business interests other than pottery included the North Staffordshire Railway, of which he was chairman 1873-83, and the Staffordshire Potteries Waterworks Co., of which he was a director.

CMC served as mayor of Stoke upon Trent 1880-3. He contributed to the building of the public baths, a new sewage system and other public works, and gave the land for a new public library. He presented a fountain to the town in 1859. He unsuccessfully contested the election for Stoke upon Trent in 1868 in the Conservative interest but was returned for North Staffordshire in the uncontested election of 1874. He was a captain in the Newcastle and Potteries Troop of Yeomanry, a captain in the Stoke Rifle Volunteers and a major in the 1st Staffordshire Battalion Rifle Volunteers. He attended the Church of England and contributed to the cost of the rebuilding of Holy Trinity church, Hartshill, in the 1860s and 1870s, and to the restoration of St. Michael's parish church, Rocester. He was appointed a deputy lieutenant of Staffordshire in 1868 and high sheriff in 1869.

He died at Woodseat, near Uttoxeter, on 8 February 1885. A statue to his memory by Thomas Brock was unveiled in 1887 in Campbell Place, but it was moved in 1954 to a site near the modern factory in London Road, Stoke upon Trent. In 1968 Minton's became a member of the Royal Doulton Tableware Group.

P. Atterbury, *The Story of Minton;* J. Barnard, *Victorian Ceramic Tiles;* M and H; *Pottery and Glass* February-March 1951; *Staffs. Sentinel* 9 February 1885; VCH ii and viii.

CAMPBELL, William (born 1860), *architect,* Hanley.

WC was born on 2 June 1860 and educated at a private school run by William Shawcross in Hanley and later at Wellington School. He was articled to Ambrose Wood of Hanley. Later he established his own business, working principally on business, hotel and residential buildings. He drew the maps for the *Potteries and Newcastle Directories* of 1907 and 1912, and offered to supply a map of the district to the government inquiry on federation, of which he was a supporter.

He was a member of the Society of Architects, a freemason and a Conservative in politics.

Staffs. County Biographies.

CAPPER, Joseph (1788-1860), *blacksmith,* Tunstall.

JC was born near Nantwich, Cheshire, about 1788. His family moved to Tunstall where he learned the trade of a blacksmith. He is stated to have been converted to Primitive Methodism at a camp meeting on Mow Cop in 1807. He became a local preacher for this denomination. He sometimes preached out of doors, his sermons including exhortations to his listeners, to use his own words, 'to be virtuous, to leave off drunkenness, to cease swearing and not to commit adultery'. He was a member of the first building society to be established in Tunstall, and later lived in one of the houses built by the society, 29 Piccadilly, Tunstall. By his wife Sarah he had three children, John, Henry and Joseph, the last born on 29 June 1817.

He early developed radical political views and was a popular and humorous speaker at reform meetings. In the parliamentary election for Stoke upon Trent in 1832 he supported George Miles Mason, the (unsuccessful) radical candidate. After the Chartist riots in the Potteries in August 1842 Capper was arrested and charged at the special Stafford assizes with incitement. Although the speeches he had made were delivered weeks before the riots he was found guilty and sentenced to two years' imprisonment. In 1843, while still serving this sentence, he was again brought to trial on a charge of sedition. He was found guilty but there was a recommendation to mercy and no additional sentence was imposed. Prison broke his health and destroyed his political commitment to Chartism; though on his release and return to the Potteries he was welcomed by a large crowd he took little or no further part in the reform movement.

He died on 10 January 1860 and was buried in Tunstall churchyard.

F. Burchill and R. Ross, *History of the Potters' Union;* J. Epstein and D. Thompson (edit.) *The Chartist Experience;* H. A. Wedgwood, *People of the Potteries.*

CAREY, John (c. 1803-43), *pottery manufacturer,* Fenton and Longton.

JC was born about 1803, and was probably the son of John and Sarah Carey. With Thomas Carey he operated three factories in Lane End, the Anchor Works in Market Street, Longton, and a pottery in King Street, Fenton. The partnership ended in January 1842.

He married Harriet Cartwright, at Trentham, on 26 June 1823, and there was at least one child, John, of the marriage. JC was the patron of St. James's church, Longton, for which he built a rectory house in 1840. This house was attacked during the Chartist riots of 1842. He served as chief bailiff of Longton 1840-1.

He died at Parkfield, Barlaston, on 12 November 1843.

Dir. 1818, 1834; Jewitt; *Staffs. Advertiser* 18 November 1843; VCH viii; memorial tablet in St. James's church, Longton.

CARTER, Roger (1867-1936), *chief constable,* Hanley.

RC was born in 1867 in Kendal, Westmorland, where his father was a builder and timber merchant. He was educated at Kendal Grammar School. He joined his father's business, but the death of both his parents in a short space of time led him to join the local police force at the age of twenty. He moved to Rochdale and quickly won promotions. In 1898 when a detective-inspector, he was appointed chief constable of Windsor. Twice in the next three years his abilities were tested, when during the celebration of Queen Victoria's eightieth birthday and the occasion of her funeral he was responsible for controlling large crowds.

He was appointed chief constable of Hanley in September 1901, in succession to Herbert Windle (q.v.) and made improvements in the force's working conditions, increasing leave and meal breaks on night duty. He believed that tact was better than force in controlling crowds, and his experience in Windsor enabled him to improve the control of Saturday night crowds in Hanley.

On federation, RC was appointed chief constable of the Stoke on Trent County Borough and organised the integration of the Hanley force and those of the county force in the other towns to create a force of 250. Amongst his innovations were road safety lessons for children. He was made a member of the Royal Victorian Order in 1913 for his previous services to Queen Victoria and later received the King's Police Medal.

He was married twice, with five sons. He was a freemason, a skilled horseman and a member of Newcastle Golf Club. At the time of his death he was still chief constable having been a policeman for almost fifty years.

He died on 13 April 1936 at "Helme", The Avenue, Basford, Newcastle under Lyme.

Evening Sentinel 13 April 1936.

CARTLIDGE, George (born 1868), *art teacher,* Hanley.

GC was born in 1868. He studied at the Hanley School of Art in 1878, and began teaching art in 1897. He had a reputation as a portrait modeller and pottery painter, and his portrait of Thomas Hardy was used as the frontispiece of Macmillan's Standard edition of Hardy's works. He also painted the barbotine portraits over the entrance to the eastern extension of Hanley Art School, in Pall Mall. Later he became a partner in the pottery firm of Sherwin and Cotton, of Hanley.

R. Haggar, *A Century of Art Education in the Potteries;* M and H; VCH viii.

CARTLIDGE, Samuel J. (born c. 1857), *art teacher,* Hanley.

SJC, born about 1857, became a pupil at the Wedgwood Institute, Burslem, about 1871. At the age of 17 he obtained a certificate qualifying him to take charge of a school of art. He was appointed headmaster of Hanley School of Art in 1882, holding this post until 1900. He also taught at the Victoria Institute, Tunstall. Later he became a chief inspector to the Board of Education.

R. Haggar, *A Century of Art Eduaction in the Potteries.*

CHADWICK, Thomas (c. 1775-1841), *surgeon,* Longton.

TC qualified as a surgeon about 1800 and was in practice in Longton from at least 1809, when he was living in High Street. He was one of the original improvement commissioners in 1839. He died on 13 November 1841 and is commemorated by a memorial in St. James's church, Longton and by the name of Chadwick Street, where he lived in a cottage beside the present Gladstone Pottery Museum, now occupied by Staffordshire Crystal.

Briggs; Dir. (Holden) 1808-10, 1834, 1841; Gladstone Museum exhibit.

CHALLINOR, Arthur (died 1914), *town clerk,* Hanley.

AC was the son of Edward Challinor, the first town clerk of Hanley. He qualified as a solicitor in 1875 and in the same year became town clerk of Hanley on the death of his elder brother Charles. He was appointed the first Clerk of the Peace in 1880. He was made a freeman of Hanley in December 1900 and retired as town clerk in 1910 upon federation.

AC married his cousin Miss Notley on 16 January 1878. There were no children of the marriage.

He died in Cornwall in March 1914.

Staffs. Sentinel 24 March 1914.

CHALLINOR, Charles (1829-93), *colliery owner,* Fenton.

CC was born in Leek on 19 July 1829, the son of William Challinor and Mary née Shelmerdine. His numerous business interests included the managing directorship of John Challinor and Co. Ltd., Glebe Colliery, and interests in E. and C. Challinor and Co., Fenton Pottery, Baker and Co., earthenware manufacturers, Gimson and Co., Fenton, Stilt and Spur Works, Wallace and Co., Railway Stilt Works, Charles Challinor, Pinnox Works, Tunstall (employing 3,000 people), Charles Challinor, Fenton Tileries and E. and C. Challinor, Stoke upon Trent, flint and stone mills.

He was a churchman and a Conservative, served as an improvement commissioner and on the Fenton Board of Health. He was a vice-president of the North Staffs. Infirmary.

On 19 April 1855 he married Lettice Adams, daughter of William Adams of Greenfield, and had four sons and six daughters. He lived at the Lodge, Oakhill, in 1861, and later at Basford Hall.

He died on 13 February 1893 at Fenton, following an accident involving a steam engine at Glebe colliery.

Adams; Adams, *Notes; Staffs. Advertiser* 18 February 1893.

CHALLINOR, Edward (1792-1879), *pottery manufacturer,* Tunstall.

EC was born on 18 July 1792, the son of William Challinor, attorney of Pickwood, Leek, and Mary née Bagnall. He was apprenticed to J. and R. Riley, of Burslem, whose factory occupied the site of what later became Hill Top Pottery. EC began in business on his own account at Overhouse Pottery, Burslem, which he bought in 1819. From about 1828 he leased the works to a succession of potters. He joined in partnership with John Wood, making pottery at Brownhills then at Woodlands, Tunstall. In 1869 he rebuilt Overhouse, installing the latest machinery.

He died, unmarried on 16 April 1879.

Staffs. Advertiser 19 April 1879; Adams, *Notes;* Jewitt; VCH viii.

CHALLINOR, Edward (1817-69), *solicitor,* Hanley.

EC was the son of William Challinor of Derby and Elizabeth née Glass, daughter of J. Glass, earthenware manufacturer of Hanley. He was articled to a Manchester solicitor and in 1839 set up his own practice at 30-2 Cheapside, Hanley. On the incorporation of the borough of Hanley he was appointed town clerk and held that office until his death.

EC had Liberal political opinions and acted as parliamentary election agent for the Liberal party in Hanley in the 1860s. With Edmund Oswald, Samuel Taylor and John Keates (q.v.) he helped to found the *Staffordshire Weekly Sentinel* in 1854.

His two sons, Charles Edward and Arthur, also served as town clerks of Hanley.

Anderton; *The Sentinel Story 1873-1973.*

CHARLESWORTH, James (died 1900), *medical practitioner,* Hanley.

JC came from a family which had lived in Longnor, Staffs., since at least 1676. He practised medicine in Hanley, succeeding Boothroyd as a fashionable ladies' doctor. He was appointed a justice of the peace in 1880, elected to the Hanley council in 1882 and served as mayor 1884-5. He was elected alderman in 1890.

He died in 1900.

Huntbach.

CHATTERLEY, Ephraim (1744-1811), *pottery manufacturer,* Hanley.

EC was baptised on 20 February 1744, the son of John and Joyce Chatterley. He was in business with his brother Charles until 1793 when they gave up in favour of their nephews, James and Charles Whitehead. The brothers manufactured earthenware, and through their agent Elijah Mayer built up an extensive foreign trade.

The brothers built Shelton Hall (also known as Chatterley Hall) in 1782. Ephraim was living there c. 1790 and after his death in 1811 his widow Mary lived there until her death in 1832. The house, a square three-storied building with a lower wing to the north, stood between Cemetery Road and Caledonian Road. It was demolished in 1959. By a deed of 1803 EC left a rent-charge of £8 8s for bread for the poor of Hanley and Shelton to be distributed on Christmas Day and Good Friday. Later it was paid to the North Staffs. Deaf and Dumb Society.

EC died in 1811. His heiress was Mary Ann Chatterley, mother of Frederick Bishop (q.v.). There is a memorial tablet to EC in St. John's church, Hanley.

M and H; VCH viii.

CHILD, Smith (1730-1813), *naval officer,* Tunstall.

SC was born in 1730, the son of Smith Child of Miles Green, Audley. He entered the navy in 1747 and first went to sea in the *Chester* commanded by Richard Spry. he also served on the *Devonshire* under Captain Matthew Buckle. He was appointed junior lieutenant on the *Princess Royal* commanded by Sir Charles Saunders. He served at the siege of Pondicherry in 1761 and at Louisbourg. He commanded the *Europe* in 1781 in actions off the Chesapeake capes in the American War of Independence. He attained flag officer rank on 14 February 1799. He acted as regulating officer for the impress service at Liverpool, where he was granted the freedom of the borough.

In 1764 he married Margaret Roylance, and established his home in Newcastle under Lyme. In 1770 he inherited Newfield Hall, Tunstall, from his uncle, Thomas Baddeley. He rebuilt the hall and prior to 1800 added a pottery works to it. The hall was demolished about 1948. In 1958 its site was occupied by Beresford Transport Ltd.

SC died at Newfield on 21 January 1813. He left his estate to his grandson, (Sir) Smith Child, then a minor. He was buried in St. Margaret's churchyard, Wolstanton.

P. Adams, *Wolstanton;* J. Haydn, *Book of Dignities;* VCH viii; Ward.

CHILD, Sir Smith (1808-96), *Member of Parliament,* Tunstall.

SC was born on 5 March 1808 at Newfield Hall, Tunstall, the son of John George Child and Elizabeth née Parsons. He was the grandson of Admiral Smith Child (q.v.). SC's father died in 1811 and he became heir to the Newfield and other estates which had originally belonged to the Baddeley family of Tunstall. In 1851 he was returned unopposed to Parliament as Conservative member for North Staffordshire. He won the election for West Staffordshire in 1868, retiring from politics in 1874. He served as high sheriff of Staffordshire in 1865 and was a deputy lieutenant and county magistrate. He was created a baronet in 1868.

Smith Child was a major philanthropist in the Potteries area and made contributions to many charitable institutions. He contributed annually to the North

Staffordshire Infirmary, served as president and vice-president of its general management committee and was elected a patron in 1895. In 1877 he built and endowed the Smith Child ward, originally intended for incurable patients but eventually opened as a children's hospital. Two years earlier he had founded the North Staffordshire Incurables Fund, for sending patients on holiday. He also supported, in Tunstall, the local Nursing Society and the Samaritan Society, and at Longton the Cottage Hospital.

His benefactions extended to other fields. He supported the Tunstall Choral Society; the Victoria Institute, Tunstall, was built largely as a result of his efforts and support and accommodated, at various times, a museum, an art school, a technical school, a high school for girls, a library and a reading room. Nor were his benefactions confined to Tunstall. He supported the establishment of the Wedgwood Institute, Burslem, gave £200 to the North Staffordshire Chamber of Commerce to encourage the teaching of Spanish and Portugese, the languages of the expanding pottery markets in South America, and £1,000 towards the establishment of a girls' industrial school at Lichfield.

He was ready to help with immediate relief as well as with longer term constructive projects. He subscribed to the fund for the victims of the Talke colliery disaster in 1868, helped to start the North Staffordshire Miners Permanent Relief fund in 1870 and gave to the Leycett colliery disaster fund in 1880.

He married Sarah Hill at Fulford church on 28 January 1835, and had three children, the eldest of whom, Smith Hill Child, who died aged 30, gave his name to the ward in the North Staffordshire Infirmary. In 1841 the family moved from Newfield Hall to Rownall Hall, Wetley, and in 1853, on the death of his father-in-law, Richard Clarke Hill, SC came into possession of Stallington Hall. Smith Child died in Stallington Hall on 27 March 1896.

Tunstall clock tower was erected in 1893 in his honour, the money being raised by public subscription. A tablet on the tower has an inscription memorialising his philanthropy. A stained glass window was erected to his memory in Goldenhill church, of which he had been a founder member in 1913.

P. W. L. Adams, *John Henry Clive;* P. W. L. Adams, *Wolstanton; In Memoriam Sir Smith Child* (Local Pamphlets vol. 43 HRL); *Staffs. Sentinel* 6 February 1912.

CLARKE, Revd, Adam (1832-86), *minister of religion (Church of England),* Longton.

AC was the son of the Revd. Joseph Butterworth Bulmer Clarke, rector of West Bagborough, Somerset. He graduated B.A. from Exeter College, Oxford, and was appointed curate of St. Neots, Cambridgeshire, 1856-8, curate of Long Preston, Yorks., 1858-63 and on the death of Benjamin Vale (q.v.) was presented to the living of St. James the Less, Longton, by his mother, who was the patron. He removed the side galleries and old screen of the church and abolished pew rents. He organised the erection of new church schools. In 1864, with George Farmer, he instituted a dispensary system for medical care. With William Webberley he founded the Longton Cottage hospital, opened in 1868, for the benefit of the manufacturing, labouring and other classes of the borough of Longton and neighbourhood. The hospital was located in Mount Pleasant (now Lawley Street). In 1879 it was moved to the other side of the street and in 1889-90 was replaced by the present cottage hospital in Upper Belgrave Road on land given by the Duke of Sutherland.

AC was a member of the School Board and of the Stoke upon Trent Board of Guardians. He married Beatrice Margaret Edwards, daughter of J. J. Edwards of Trentham and had four children of whom three survived. He died on 16 January 1886 at 20 Carlton Hill, London.

Briggs; Foster; *National Index to Wills and Administrations 1858-1931; Staffs. Sentinel* 18 January 1886.

CLEMENTSON, Joseph (1794-1871), *pottery manufacturer,* Hanley.

JC was born on 15 July 1794 at Carrigill, Cumberland. He came to the Potteries in 1811 and worked first as a collier. In 1820 he apprenticed himself to J. and W. Ridgway, and by 1832 was able to set up his own business at the Phoenix Works, Shelton, in partnership with Jonah Reed. The partnership ended in 1839. JC continued on his own, enlarging the works in 1845 and also buying the Bell Works in 1856. Early on in his partnership with Reed JC had travelled to Canada, and this laid the foundation for a successful commercial career. He retired from business in 1867 in favour of his four sons and his son-in-law, Edward Baxter, minister at Bethesda chapel, Hanley, who had married his youngest daughter Lucy.

JC served as chief bailiff of Hanley 1849-51, being unsuccessful in his promotion of the adoption by Hanley of the Public Health act. He was an early advocate of amalgamation of the Potteries towns.

He married Martha Phillips in 1816 and had eight children. He was a member of Bethesda New Connexion church.

He died at Prospect House, Shelton, in 1871. His name is continued in Clementson's Mill car park, off Clough Street, Hanley. Francis Clementson, in 1834 a contractor of Joiners' Square, Hanley, and an elder brother of JC, is buried in Bethesda churchyard.

IGI Staffs ; Jewitt; *Staffs. Advertiser* 26 August 1871; Townley.

CLIFF, Clarice (1899-1972), *pottery designer,* Tunstall.

CC was born in Meir Street, Tunstall, on 20 January 1899, the middle child of seven brothers and sisters, the children of Harry Thomas Cliff and Ann née Machine. She attended the High Street Elementary and Summerbank schools in Tunstall and was apprenticed as an enameller at Lingard Webster's factory, at a wage of one shilling a week. After three years she moved to work as a lithographer at Hollinshead and Kirkham. She attended evening classes in Tunstall, and at the age of 17 went to work for A. J. Wilkinson, where her decorating manager, Jack Walker, noticed her artistic flair. he called Colley Shorter's attention to her and she was allowed to experiment with designs. Her first productions were brightly coloured and made up of diamonds, oblongs and squares. She had the idea of painting imperfect ware with these designs, and the designs and crude colours began to sell. The early designs were called Bizarre. Cliff pottery was shown at many exhibitions and her design, Tibetan, won the diploma of honour at Ghent in 1913.

In the 1920s and 1930s Clarice with her cloche hat, cigarettes and ruby-coloured Austin Seven, seemed to be typical of the times. Towards the end of her life she became a celebrity among Art Deco collectors.

She married Colley Shorter who had first provided the opportunity for her to express her talents.

She died in 1972. In that year Brighton Museum staged a Clarice Cliff exhibition.

P. Wentworth-Shields and K. Johnson, *Clarice Cliff; Evening Sentinel* 24 May 1976.

CLIVE, John Henry (1781-1853), *pottery manufacturer,* Tunstall.

JHC was born in Bath on 20 March 1781, the son of Richard Clive, younger brother of Robert Clive of India, and Sarah. The Clive family shunned Sarah who took her son to live with the Heathcotes at Longton Hall. Richard, her first husband, died in a debtor's prison, and Sarah married Charles Simpson, of the firm of Turner, Clover and Simpson, in 1793. Her son John was apprenticed to Turner. The family moved to Newfield Hall where John joined Admiral Smith Child in running Newfield Pottery, Tunstall, trading from 1811 to about 1828 as Child and Clive. The Newfield factory was taken over by Joseph Heath & Co. about 1828. In 1825 he went into business on his own. He was successful, particularly in his mines at Clanway, which had an ingenious method of drainage into the Trent and Mersey Canal. JHC was a pioneer in the introduction of ornamental engraving on blue printed wares. Later he acquired a tile works near Tunstall.

He had a wide range of interests. He evolved a system of shorthand, part of which was adopted by Pitman; he designed and built a large-scale model of a suspension bridge which was accepted for the Great Exhibition of 1851; with another he patented, in 1825, a double sextant for observing lunar distances to obtain longitudinal readings for ships; in 1835 he published *A Glossary or Short View of the Dialect of North Staffordshire;* in 1836 he founded, with others, the Potteries Theatre Royal.

He also played a part in public affairs. He was appointed Tunstall's first chief constable in 1816 and was largely responsible for the plan to erect a town hall and the laying out of the market place.

JHC married Lydia Cash on 30 September 1805, and there were five children by this marriage. His first wife died by 1824 when he married again, his second wife being the widow of Henry Roylance and a member of the Child family. JHC lived in Chell House (now the Victory Club) and for part of the year in London. He moved from Chell House to Clanway Hall, rented from Thomas Wedgwood and from 1827 to 1846 he owned the Bridestones estate at Biddulph. He also bought the Brownhills estate (now Tunstall cemetery), and owned land, houses and shops in Tunstall, as well as property in London.

He died in Hastings on 24 October 1853, and was buried in Bath. He left £5 to the poor of Tunstall.

P. W. L. Adams, *John Henry Clive 1781-1853;* VCH viii.

CLIVE, Robert Henry (1846-1930), *colliery owner,* Tunstall.

RHC was born on 18 January 1846 the son of Henry and Ann Clive. After attending Congleton Grammar School he entered the office of Robert Heath, coalmaster, at Biddulph. On his father's death in 1865 he became manager of Clanway Colliery. He was also the head of Clive Brothers, Newfield Brick and Marl Works, and later the director of J. Gimson and Co., and chairman of Furlong Mills Co., Burslem.

In 1871 he was elected to the Tunstall Board of Health and became chief bailiff in 1873. He continued to serve on the board until 1902. He was a member of the Wolstanton and Burslem Board of Guardians and chairman in 1877. Later he became a county councillor and a trustee of Coton Hall Asylum. He joined No. 13 Kidsgrove Company of Volunteers in 1867 and eventually rose to command the 5th North Staffs. Battalion. He served on the local bench of magistrates. He was one of the pioneer supporters of the North Staffs. Cripples' Aid Society founded by Millicent Duchess of Sutherland (q.v.) and in 1917-18 was president of the North Staffs. Royal Infirmary. He inaugurated the Woore District Nursing Association, becoming its president.

He married Mary Dale Peake on 13 July 1876 and had at least four children by the marriage. The family was living at Mere Cottage, Lawton, in 1873, and in 1899 at Gravenhunger, Woore. RHC was a church warden of Tunstall, Lawton, Hartshill and Woore churches over the course of time, made a special study of church music and was a musician of some ability.

He died on 14 April 1930 following a road accident and was buried in Hartshill cemetery. There is a stained glass window to his memory in Hartshill church.

P. W. L. Adams, *John Henry Clive;* Dir. 1882, 1892; *Evening Sentinel* 15 April 1930.

CLOWES, Samuel (1864-1928), *trade unionist and Member of Parliament,* Hanley.

SC was born at Milton on 17 September 1864, the son of James Clowes, a miner and innkeeper. The family moved to Hanley when SC was 12 and he worked, first as a mould runner, secondly as a hollow ware presser at Cauldon Pottery and at Dunn Bennett and Co., and eventually in the sanitary ware works of George Howson and Sons.

From his apprenticeship he was an active trade unionist and worked his way up from membership of his local lodge committee to become general secretary of the National Society of Pottery Workers. He helped to achieve final amalgamation of all the unions associated with pottery manufacture. He built up the membership, negotiated wage increases, helped to secure the abolition of the 'good from oven' system in 1919, and was active in the promotion of safeguards for pottery workers' health. During the First World War he was a member of the Trade Advisory Committee which was responsible for advice on manpower and raw materials. He served as president and later treasurer of the North Staffordshire Trades and Labour Council.

He was prominent in local affairs. He was appointed a justice of the peace in 1910, elected to the Stoke on Trent council in 1911 and was made a city alderman in 1927. Associated with the North Staffordshire Royal Infirmary from about 1914 he became its president from 1924 to 1927, during the period of large extensions, and organised the collection of the large sums of money required. He inaugurated the Hanley Blind Welfare Committee and served as its vice-president. He was elected Labour member of Parliament for Hanley in 1924, and was the first operative potter to sit in Parliament.

SC married Jane Muckley and had nine children, two of whom died in infancy. One son, Harold, served on the city council and aldermanic bench, was awarded the O.B.E. in 1955, was elected lord mayor in 1959, and received a knighthood in 1960 for services to the local community. One daughter, Doris, later Mrs. Robinson, also had a distinguished record of local service, became lord mayor and was awarded the C.B.E.

SC, 'Honest Sam' as he was known locally, died at his home in Hill Street, Hanley on 25 March 1928.

F. Burchill and R. Ross, *History of the Potters' Union; Pottery Gazette* 1 May 1928 (obit.); *Staffs. Sentinel* 27 March 1928.

CLOWES, William (1780-1851), *minister of religion (Primitive Methodist),* Burslem.

WC, son of Samuel Clowes and Ann née Wedgwood, a distant relation of Josiah Wedgwood I (q.v.), was born at Ball Bank on 12 March 1780. At the age of ten he was apprenticed to a potter. He moved to Hull about 1800 where, according to his own account, he lived a dissolute life. Returning to the Potteries he attended a Wesleyan Methodist service in Burslem and was converted. He joined the Tunstall Methodist society, came to know Hugh Bourne, and attended the first camp meeting on Mow Cop on 31 May 1807. He wrote an account of the meeting, describing how 'it continued full of glory and converting power . . . and at the close which took place about half-past eight o'clock in the evening, several souls were set at liberty'. Clowes came to the second camp meeting on Mow Cop, held on 19 July 1807, but was then temporarily discouraged by the Methodist official attitude of disapprobation towards such large open-air meetings. He continued his own evangelistic work, however, and on 3 June 1810 attended a camp meeting held at Ramsor. His name was omitted from the preachers' plan of the Burslem circuit and in September 1810 he was excluded from the connexion. Towards the end of 1810 the work of the 'Bourneites' and the 'Clowesites' began to merge and in May 1811 the two groups united and issued a uniform ticket of membership. Later that year the Burslem society invited the camp-meeting Methodists to return but the invitation was rejected. On 13 February 1812 they adopted the name Primitive Methodist. The name was suggested by James Crawfoot, a farm labourer who recalled the term being used by John Wesley many years before.

William Clowes a gifted preacher, played a major role in the subsequent spread of the Primitive Methodist movement, in Hull from 1819 and especially in London and Cornwall.

WC married Hannah Rodgers on 28 July 1800.

He died in Hull on 2 March 1851.

G. M. Morris 'The Origin of Primitive Methodism in North Staffordshire 1800-1812' in *North Staffs. Journal of Field Studies,* vol. 9—1969; Staffs. C.C. Education Dept. Local History Source Book G.26 *Some Staffordshire Characters;* VCH iii and viii; J. T. Wilkinson, *William Clowes.*

COATES, Herbert (born 1849), *grocer and baker,* Hanley.

HC was born in Hanley on 20 July 1849, the son of George Coates. He was educated at the British School, Etruria. He set up in business in John Street, Hanley as a grocer and baker by 1884 and was still there in 1912.

HC, a Liberal in politics, was elected to the council in 1886 and served as mayor of the county borough in 1901. He attended the coronation of King Edward VII and Queen Alexandra in 1902, and presented to the town the mayoral robes and hat worn at this ceremony, for use by his successors.

He was a member of the Methodist New Connexion church and served as a local preacher in the Hanley district for over 30 years. He was a supporter of the local temperance movement. He married Elizabeth Cliffe, of Talke-o'-the Hill, in August 1873. He lived at Fashoda House, Trentham Road, Longton, in 1913.

F. A. Barnes, *Mayors of England and Wales 1902;* Dir. 1884; VCH viii; E. Warrilow, *A Sociological History of the City of Stoke on Trent.*

COGHILL, Douglas Harry (1885-1928), *Member of Parliament,* Stoke upon Trent.

DHC, son of Harry Coghill and Mary Jane née Fuller, was born in 1885. He was educated at Cheltenham College and Corpus Christi College, Oxford, and was called to the bar at the Inner Temple in 1879, joining the Oxford circuit. He was elected for Newcastle under Lyme in 1886, standing as a Liberal Unionist, but was defeated in the election for that constituency in 1892. He stood for Stoke upon Trent as a Liberal Unionist is 1895 and was successful. He stood again, in 1900, this time as a Conservative, and was again returned. He was defeated, however, in the election of 1906.

He argued the manufacturers' case over the question of government regulation of the use of lead in the manufacture of pottery glazes.

Anderton; V and S.

COLE, Samuel (born c. 1818), *police officer,* Hanley.

SC was born in Ipswich about 1818. He joined the Staffordshire police in 1843 and by 1847 had risen to the rank of inspector. In that year the Hanley commissioners refused to give him and Superintendent Betts a testimonial until certain improvements they had required in the service were forthcoming. He was appointed superintendent in 1854, and also acted as sanitary inspector (including common lodging houses), inspector of nuisances and superintendent of the fire brigade for an extra salary totalling £52 a year. In 1856 he was dismissed from the police force at the instigation of two magistrates, Loxdale and Twemlow. The Hanley commissioners appealed to the Home Office, there was an inquiry and Cole was reinstated. The county police committee and chief constable resigned in protest at this decision.

SC lived in 1861 at the Town Hall, Market Square, Hanley, with his wife Anne, (born in Ipswich) and his children (born in Hanley). He retired on a pension in 1865 and died on 14 November 1885.

Census 1861; Hanley Commissioners' Minutes; Staffs. Police Force Book (SRO); Townley.

COLE, Samuel (c. 1826-1906), *glass manufacturer,* Hanley.

SC was born either in Worcestershire or in Audley, Staffs. about 1826, and was established in business as a glass agent, in Marsh Street, Hanley,.by 1851. In 1862 he traded as Samuel Cole and Co., Falcon Glassworks, Cauldon Place, and had a house and shop in Broad Street, now the R.A.C. centre. He was in partnership with Horton Yates from 1864 to c. 1874 and had a house on Snow Hill from c. 1870 to c. 1880. Cole was the largest manufacturer of glass in the Potteries. By 1900, if not earlier, the factory had been closed because of a prolonged strike.

SC served as a councillor for Hanley borough from 1857 to 1871. He was a justice of the peace, Conservative in politics, and married with at least one child, Sarah. He gave up his shop about 1896, and died on 28 October 1906.

Census 1851, 1881; Huntbach; *National Index to Wills and Administrations 1858-1931; Staffs. Sentinel* 28 October 1906.

COLSELL, Henry (1819/20-after 1881), *canal carrier,* Stoke upon Trent.

HC, born in Aldgate, London, about 1819, lived a peripatetic life and had a variety of occupations. He was still living in London, at Shoreditch, in 1841, married to Louisa Ann, who had been born about 1799, and who bore him a son, Frank, in 1841. By 1844 he was living in Chester and by 1851 he was in business as a beerhouse keeper, grocer and provision dealer in Liverpool Road, Stoke upon Trent. His wife Louisa died in 1853 and he married again, by his two wives having at least eight children. He prospered sufficiently to be appointed an improvement commissioner for Stoke upon Trent by 1869. In 1861 he is listed as a canal carrier, of Glebe Street, in 1871 he operated as Colsell, Whalley and Co., and in 1873-4 as Mellor, Colsell and Co. In 1881 he was living in Clyde Street, Stoke upon Trent, his occupation given as railway clerk.

Census 1851; Stoke upon Trent Improvement Commissioners' Minutes.

COOKE, John Roddy (1839-1900), *clothier,* Hanley.

JRC was born on 14 September 1839 in Taunton, Somerset. His father came to Hanley as a Baptist scripture reader and JRC was apprenticed as a clothier to T. and R. Gilman. He was a partner in two businesses, Hill and Cooke, pawnbrokers and jewellers of Hanley, and Gilman and Cooke, clothiers and outfitters, of 19 Market Square, Hanley. After his death it was reported that a petition of bankruptcy had been filed against his estate.

He was elected to the Board of Guardians in 1870 and served until 1900, acting as chairman 1891-7 though he did not attend regularly. He was made a freeman of the borough in 1867 and elected mayor in 1876 and alderman in 1885. He married Edna née Booth and was living at Steward's Lodge, Sandon in 1884 and at Orsett House, Barlaston, from 1892. He died on 7 September 1900 at Stoke Road, Shelton, and was buried in Hanley cemetery.

Dir. 1867-1900; Huntbach; *National Index to Wills and Administrations 1858-1931; Staffs. Sentinel* 8 September 1900.

COOKE, William (1806-84), *minister of religion (Methodist New Connexion),* Burslem.

WC was born on 2 July 1806 at the New Inn, Burslem. The family moved to Cobridge and he attended the Wesleyan Sunday School at Burslem, then a day school kept by Steven Brougham at Tunstall (later at Zoar chapel, Burslem). When WC was 13 the family moved again, to Shelton, and he went to Bethesda Sunday School. He became in time a Sunday School teacher, prayer leader, tract distributor and class leader. He opened a free night school for adults in reading and understanding the scriptures. At the age of 18 he was on the plan as a local preacher and at 20 he was a candidate for the ministry. He qualified, and was sent to Newcastle on Tyne, where he began writing one of his major theological works, *Christian Theology,* an answer to ideas promulgated in the Barkerite controversy of the time. In 1836 he was superintendent of the Irish Mission and in 1843 he was elected president of the Methodist New Connexion conference. For 22 years he was editor of the Connexional magazine. He was elected president of the conference twice more, in 1859 and 1869.

WC was in Hanley, for a year, in 1848, where he worked as editor and secretary of missions. The Cooke Memorial School was built at Bethel chapel, Burslem in 1877.

WC died on 25 December 1884.

O. A. Beckerlegge, *United Methodist Ministers and their Circuits;* H. Smith, *Sketches of Eminent New Connexion Ministers;* J. Young, *After 100 Years.*

COPE, John (1879-1962), *musician,* Hanley

JC, the son of James Cope a coalminer, was born at Cinder Hill, Milton on 31 May 1879. While still a schoolboy his musical talents attracted the attention of Madam Marie Reymond, (q.v.), a music teacher, living in Burslem. She assisted him to study the organ under Rheinberger, in Munich, and he eventually also became a conductor Back in the Potteries he conducted the Burslem Orchestral Union which Madam Reymond had established at her own expense. The orchestra later became the North Staffordshire Orchestra. JC conducted for the Carl Rosa Opera Company in Sheffield and other cities, and he joined this company in 1919. In 1924 JC returned to the Potteries and resumed his conductorship of the North Staffordshire Orchestra. He was also organist at the Congregational church, Newcastle under Lyme, at St. Paul's church, Burslem and at Leek parish church. He was later appointed city organist to the Stoke on Trent corporation and was visiting music master at Newcastle High School and the Orme Boys' School, Newcastle. He also acted as mucical director and conductor of the Stoke on Trent Amateur Dramatic Society, and for some years was musical director of Sheffield Grand Opera.

He married, had a daughter, Moyna, and died in April 1962 at his home in Charles Street, Hanley. He was buried in the same grave as Marie Reymond in Hanley cemetery.

Census 1881; R. Nettel, *Music in the Five Towns 1840-1914; Evening Sentinel* 2 June 1959 and 6 April 1962.

COPELAND, Richard Pirie (1841-1915), *pottery manufacturer,* Stoke upon Trent.

RPC was the son of William Taylor Copeland (q.v.) and Sarah Yates. He was educated at Harrow and Trinity College, Cambridge. With his brothers he was taken into partnership by his father in 1867, the firm trading as W. T. Copeland and Sons.

He played an active role in local Potteries and in Staffordshire affairs. He was councillor and alderman of Stoke upon Trent corporation, and represented the town on the county council. He was a justice of the peace for the locality from 1876, and for the county from 1904, a deputy lieutenant and in 1902 high sheriff of the county. In politics he was a Conservative and he was a supporter of the Church of England. The Copeland arms, on a field or two bars gules, bearing three trefoils vert, overall a bend charged with three boars' heads, became part of the seal of Stoke corporation.

He married Emily Henrietta Wedgwood in 1868, and had three children. He lived at Kibblestone Hall, Oulton, where he died in 1915.

Rickwood and Gaskell, *Staffordshire Leaders; Cox's Potteries Annual and Yearbook, 1925; Stoke upon Trent Parish Magazine Souvenir Supplement,* May, 1930.

COPELAND, William Taylor (1797-1868),
pottery manufacturer and Member of Parliament, Stoke upon Trent.

WTC was born in 1797, the only son of William Copeland, (d.1826) who was a partner in the Spode firm c. 1800. In 1833 WTC acquired the Spode factory from the executors of Josiah Spode III. He took Thomas Garratt into partnership and the firm, Copeland and Garratt continued until the partnership was dissolved in 1847, and the firm was renamed W. T. Copeland, late Spode. In 1867 WTC took his four sons into partnership with him, trading under the name of W. T. Copeland and Sons. Apart from such prestigious products as the Prince of Wales' Service made in 1866, the firm's 'ivory body' ware was one of the greatest improvements made in earthenware. Among Copeland's achievements in colour was a new turquoise—Cerulean blue. The firm produced painted and enamelled tiles, and about 1842 introduced Parian ware. The firm's artists included Hurten, Abraham and Brayford.

WTC was involved in the London interests of the Spode business taken over by Copeland. He was sheriff of London 1828-9 and served as lord mayor 1835-6. He contested the Coleraine constituency in 1831 and 1832 and succeeded on petition in both years. He was again elected for Coleraine in 1835. At the general election of 1837 he stood, successfully with J. Davenport, for Stoke upon Trent, in the Conservative interest. He was elected again in 1841 and 1847, was defeated in 1852 but won the seat back from the Liberals in 1857 and retained it in the election of 1859.

WTC had a large interest in the Fenton Park Colliery and played an important role in the establishment of the North Staffordshire Railway Company in 1846, and his other interests included a racing stable. His collection of sporting paintings of J. F. Heming led to his commissioning Heming for other paintings, some of which were reproduced in full colour on Spode table services.

WTC married Sarah Yates in 1826. He had four sons, to two of whom, Richard Pirie and A. G. Copeland, he left the business when he died at Russell Farm, Watford, on 12 April 1868. There is a memorial tablet to him in Stoke parish church.

DNB; G. Godden, *Victorian Porcelain;* G. Bernard Hughes, *The Story of Spode;* Jewitt; M and H; S and L; VCH viii; J. C. Wedgwood, *Staffordshire Pottery and its History.*

CORDON, Richard Ash (1797-1878), *surgeon,* Fenton.

RAC was baptised on 27 August 1797 at Tutbury, Staffs., the son of James Cordon and Mary née Ash. In 1841 he was in business as druggist, insurance agent and surgeon in Market Street, Longton. He also acted as registrar of births, marriages and deaths. In the 1851 census he was described as surgeon, and had presumably qualified by reason of being a surgeon before 1815.

By his wife, Margaret, he had at least four children. He died in April 1878 and was buried in Fenton churchyard.

Census 1841, 1851; Fenton parish registers.

CORK, Benjamin (1797/8-1875), *earthenware manufacturer,* Burslem.

BC was born about 1797 in Burslem. From 1846-60 he was in partnership with Joseph Edge in Queen Street Newport Pottery, making earthenware. From 1860-70 the firm was styled Cork, Edge and Malkin, and as Edge, Malkin and Co., from 1870 to 1902. The earthenware, though aimed at the cheapest market, was in good taste, with differently coloured inlaying patterns in the ground body. Cork and Edge exhibited at the Great Exhibition in 1851.

BC served on the Burslem Local Board of Health from 1855 to 1860. In 1851 he and his family were living in Newport Lane. By his wife Mary he had three daughters, one of whom, Mary, married Frederick William Macdonald (q.v.).

Jewitt; Oldham; *National Index to Wills and Administrations 1858-1931;* VCH viii.

CORK, William (1804-56), *innkeeper,* Burslem.

WC appears in 1851 as innkeeper of the Queen's Head, Queen Street, Burslem. A Liberal in his political opinions he served on the Burslem Board of Health from 1850 to 1856. By his wife, Margaret, he had a son, William. He died on 23 September 1856.

Dir. 1851; Oldham.

CORN, Alfred Henry (1866-1916), *tile manufacturer,* Tunstall.

AHC was born in Burslem on 25 July 1866, the son of Edward Corn and grandson of Edward Corn (q.v.). He and his brother Edmund Richard were educated at Newcastle Grammar School. They succeeded to their father's business at Top Bridge Works, Longport, where they experimented in the production of glazed tiles. In 1900 they acquired the sanitary ware business of Edward Johns and Co. (founded at Armitage, Staffs., in 1817), and Edmund took over this business while Alfred remained at Longport. In 1902 the business was moved to Pinnox Works, Tunstall and concentrated on tile manufacture. The company produced many Art Nouveau designs which were registered to prevent pirating. In 1911 a new factory adjoining the Pinnox Works was built for the production of floor tiles, and the company acquired Burslem Mills Co., where their raw materials were prepared. The business was now known as the Henry Richards Tile Co. Ltd., reduced in 1931 to Richard's Tiles.

AHC was a Burslem councillor for six years, travelled widely and was keen on outdoor sports. On 22 October 1902 he married Floris L'Anson, of Saltburn-by-the-Sea, Yorkshire, and the family lived at Selwyn, Trentham. AHC died in 1916, and his brother Edmund took control in Tunstall, helped by his newphew Geoffrey Corn. Edmund died in 1945.

Richards Tiles (1837-1953); *To Commemorate the Centenary of Richards Tiles;* J. B. Austwick, *The Decorated Tile;* C. Penn, *Staffordshire at the Opening of the Twentieth Century.*

CORN, Edward (1804-69), *earthenware manufacturer,* Tunstall.

EC was born in 1804 in Tunstall. He served an apprenticeship to Hancock and Lithcoe's earthenware factory, Burslem, and in 1837 bought the factory. His business flourished and he transferred to a larger factory in Navigation Road, Burslem. He left two sons, William and Edward, who carried on the business as W. & E. Corn. The works was noted for its white granite ware and Queens ware, made mostly for export to the United States of America. William died about 1885 and Edward in 1891, the latter leaving the business to his two sons, Alfred Henry and Edmund Richard. In 1890 the factory was moved to Top Bridge Works, Longport.

Jewitt; *Richards Tiles 1837-1953; To Commemorate the Centenary of Richards Tiles;* inf. from D. Malkin, H. and R. Johnson Ltd., Highgate Tile Works, Tunstall.

CORNES, James (c. 1863-1935), *housing engineer and planner,* Hanley.

JC was born in Hanley about 1863, the son of Cornelious Cornes, a builder of Lichfield Street. He worked for his father until 1888 and with the experience gained began to study domestic engineering. The death of his sister through the explosion of a domestic boiler led him to design a safer system of heating.

He founded the firm of Cornes and Heighton, London and became associated with the garden village movement. His expertise contributed to the design of Letchworth Garden Suburb, Port Sunlight and Bournville. In 1905 he wrote *Modern Housing in Town and Country.* He was a founder member of the Housing and Town Planning Council. His friendship with W. R. Sutton resulted in the Sutton Trust building some 800 houses in North Staffs.

For many years he lived at Leek and there built 300 model homes which were rented at 5/6d. per week to prove that decent accommodation could be built and let for that price. He latterly lived at Cheadle and sat as a representative on the county council.

He died on 1 June 1935.

Evening Sentinel 2 June 1935.

CORNWELL, Thomas Chinsura (1857-c. 1939), *chemist,* Hanley.

TCC was born on board the SS Chinsura off the coast of Madagascar on 2 October 1857, the son of Thomas Cornwell, the ship's captain and his wife Louisa. Thomas spent several years at sea after leaving school, twice sailed round the world and once suffered shipwreck. He left the sea eventually to study and qualify as a pharmaceutical chemist. He bought the business of Arthur Baines, of Piccadilly, Hanley, in 1884. He was honorary secretary of the local branch of the Pharmaceutical Society for many years, and president of the North Staffordshire Chemists' Association in 1913 and 1914. A founder of the North Staffordshire Traders' Association, he became the president of this organization in 1913. He sold his business to his partner, H. G. Shaw, in 1921, and retired to live in Penzance, Cornwall, where he died on 20 November 1940.

His local sporting interests included water polo, and he kept goal for Hanley, and also played bowls for Hanley and Basford.

Staffs. Sentinel 22 September 1922; PRO, Births at Sea, BT 158 piece 1; info. from Mrs. Walsh, T. C. Cornwell Ltd.

COTTON, Arthur (1856-1937), *estate agent,* Tunstall.

AC was born in Goldenhill in 1856. He was established as an estate agent at 27 Market Square, Tunstall, by 1900, but had been in business from about 1886. He was elected to Tunstall council in the 1890s, was chief bailiff of Tunstall 1905-6-7 and a Staffordshire county councillor 1902-10. He had supported the idea of federation for about 20 years but from 1908 was publicly opposed to the move, on the grounds that it would be forced upon unwilling participants. He argued that Tunstall's share in government would be lessened by the proposed reduction from 27 to 12 members and that councillors would have less power in the federation and officials more. For this inconsistency he was much criticised by federationists like Leonard Grimwade (q.v.).

AC was a member of Wolstanton and Burslem Board of Guardians and became an advocate of reform of the poor law. He argued for the use of cottage homes to separate children from the aged, infirm and mentally handicapped in workhouses, and spoke at the annual poor law conference in London c. 1900 on the subject. He was president of the Burslem and Tunstall Liberals and a member of Wesley Place Chapel.

In 1935 he offered six acres of land at Sandyford to the city for the construction of a park, but the city council refused the offer on the grounds that the cost of levelling the site would be excessive.

Shortly after 1910 he moved to Alsager but returned to Tunstall in 1932. By his wife Gavina Martha he had four sons and two daughters. One son, Arthur, became borough surveyor of Newcastle under Lyme.

AC was elected recorder of the Old Tunstall Council, an unofficial body similar to the Ancient Corporation of Hanley. He had an extensive knowledge of the town's history. He died at York Villas, Stanley Street, Tunstall, on 23 December 1937, and was buried in Tunstall cemetery.

Dir. 1900-1936; *Evening Sentinel* 24 December 1937 (obit.); Federation Newscuttings (HRL); *National Index to Wills and Administrations 1858 to date.*

COTTON, Margaret (1800/1-74), *schoolmistress,* Burslem.

MC, born in Hanley about 1800, was the daughter of Charles Cotton, who kept the Legs of Man Inn, Burslem. She conducted a boarding school, helped by her two sisters, Ann and Esther, at Bleak Hill House, Cobridge, from before 1850 to her death. In 1851 two of her boarding pupils were Sarah and Elizabeth Boughton, daughters of Richard Boughton (q.v.), who was then living above his shop in Market Place, Burslem.

MC died at Bleak Hill House in 1874.

Census 1851; Dir. 1851.

CRANMER, Horatio (1812/13-95), *registrar and rate collector,* Stoke upon Trent.

HC, son of William Cranmer, a farmer, was born about 1812, probably in Penkridge, Staffs Prior to 1843 he was a collector of the poor rate in Fenton. He appears in the Stoke Improvement Commissioners' Minutes on 1 February 1843, when there is recorded a complaint to the Board of Guardians that he had persuaded people not to pay their police and lighting rates. In 1847 he was assistant overseer to the guardians, living at Upper Cliff Bank, Stoke upon Trent. He was still living there, as collector of the poor rate, in 1851. In 1859 he was living at West Bank.

He married Emma Heath on 7 September 1847, and had three children, William, Thomas and Frances. The last named may have been the Frances Cranmer who married Thomas Aidney, colour manufacturer of Hartshill.

HC died at 32 Hill Street, Stoke upon Trent, on 23 October 1895.

Dir. 1851; *National Index to Wills and Administrations 1858-1931;* parliamentary election poll book, Stoke upon Trent, 1859; Stoke upon Trent Improvement Commissioners Minutes; Stoke upon Trent parish registers.

CRAPPER, John Sugden (baptised 1825-91), *dental surgeon,* Hanley.

JSC was baptised on 3 March 1825 in Halifax, Yorkshire, the son of Hanson Crapper and Mary née Gaukroger. Hanson Crapper was a boot and shoe maker of Bridge Street, Halifax. JSC became L.D.S. of the Royal College of Surgeons of Ireland and in 1882 received a doctorate in dental surgery from Pennsylvania College, U.S.A. With a partner, Brierley, he established a porcelain tooth manufactory in Broad Street, Hanley, and remained as managing director when the business was bought by the Dental Manufacturing Company in 1873. He is stated to have been one of the old school of dentists to whom cocaine and after care were unknown.

He was elected to Hanley council in 1858 for a three year term but failed to gain re-election. A member of Stoke upon Trent Board of Guardians he initiated the practice of taking workhouse boys to Hanley Baths. Afterwards he would entertain them in his own home. He was a Conservative in politics and a freemason. He became a member of the Ancient Corporation of Hanley and was the author of its history, published in 1876.

He married Harriet Ann, possibly née Brierley, and they lived at the White House, Broad Street, Hanley, on the site of which the Mitchell Memorial Theatre now stands, and which he had bought from the executors of Richard Hicks. He died at his home on 20 February 1891.

Baines Dir. (for Halifax) 1823; Census 1871; J. S. Crapper, *The Ancient Corporation of Hanley* (1876); Hanley Borough Council minute book; *National Index to Wills and Administrations 1858-1931; Staffs. Advertiser* 21 February 1891; VCH viii.

CREWE, SAMUEL (born 1815/16), *licensed victualler,* Stoke upon Trent.

SC, the son of William and Elizabeth Crewe, was born in Nantwich, Cheshire, about 1815. William Crewe was the licensee of the Talbot Hotel, Stoke upon Trent, and also a farmer, of Hanford. SC was employed as a counting house clerk in 1843, living in Liverpool Road, and by 1846 was the licensee of the Wheatsheaf Hotel, Stoke upon Trent. From 1860 to 1867 he was the licensee of the Castle Hotel, Newcastle under Lyme.

In 1850 SC called a meeting at the Wheatsheaf which resulted eventually in the setting up of Stokeville Building Society. He was one of the original committee members. In this year he was also farming in Penkhull. SC was a Stoke Improvement Commissioner by 1859.

He married, on 13 June 1839, Sarah Outrim, by whom he had at least eight children, William, Elizabeth, Isabella, Sarah, Rosa-Emily, Constance, Mary Outrim and Alice Maud. His son, William Outrim Crewe, was a solicitor in Newcastle in 1867.

Census 1841, 1851; Stoke upon Trent parish registers; Turner.

CROSBIE-DAWSON, George James (1841-1914), *railway engineer,* Stoke upon Trent.

GJC-D was born at Abercrombie Square, Liverpool, on 30 April 1841, the son of Richard Crosbie-Dawson. He was educated in Solihull, Warwickshire, and then articled to Robinson-Wright, of Duke Street, Westminster. He joined the staff of Euston station, London, in January 1862 and served with the London and North Western Railway Company for 21 years, eventually becoming resident engineer. In 1886 he was appointed chief engineer to the North Staffordshire Railway Company, a post which he retained until his death. Under his direction nearly all the company's lines were relaid, the Manifold Valley line between Leek and Waterhouses constructed (opened 1904) and the Trentham to Trentham Park extension built. He was also involved in the repairs to Harecastle Tunnel.

He was a Fellow of the Geological Society and a member of the Institution of Civil Engineers, the Royal Statistical Society and the Numismatic Society. He married Catherine Webber on 7 August 1872 and had a son and a daughter. He died at May Place, The Brampton, Newcastle under Lyme on 14 June 1914.

R. Christiansen and R. W. Miller, *The North Staffordshire Railway;* G. J. Crosbie-Dawson, *A Brief Sketch of the Introduction of Railways into this Country and the wonderful results thereof* (Local Pamphlets, vol. 37, HRL); R. Keys and L. Porter, *The Manifold Valley and its Light Railway; Nuneaton Chronicle* 17 February 1872; *Staffs. Sentinel* 18 June 1914.

CUMBERLIDGE, George (1825-1904), *grocer,* Tunstall.

GC, born in Burslem in 1825, was apprenticed to the pottery trade in Tunstall but in 1847 began trading as a general grocer and tea dealer in Burslem. In 1857 he returned to Tunstall to open a large tea, grocery and provision business. He retired in 1887 and his business was taken over by his sons, Walter and E. G. Cumberlidge. The shop stood on the corner of Peel Street and Windmill Street.

GC was active in local government. He was a member of the Tunstall Local Board of Health from 1872 to 1889; in 1882 he was elected chief bailiff, and laid the foundation stone of the new town hall during his period of office. In 1892 he was elected a county councillor and in 1894 placed on the commission of the peace for the county. He served on the Wolstanton School Board for 18 years and was chairman for three of these years.

A Liberal in politics, he was vice-president of the local Liberal Club. He was a deacon of the Baptist chapel, Burslem, for some years.

By his wife, Sarah (died 1928 aged 92), he had three sons. He lived at Providence Cottage, Tunstall, and died there on 28 December 1904. He was buried in Burslem cemetery. His children contributed to the erection of a fountain in Tunstall Park to his memory.

Census 1881; Dir. 1882; *Evening Sentinel* 1 December 1938; *Men of the Period; Tunstall Local Board of Health Annual Reports.*

CURRIE, John (1883-1914), *artist,* Hanley.

JC was born in Newcastle under Lyme on 14 May 1883, the son of Michael Currie and Barbara née Sherlock. He was educated at the Roman Catholic elementary school in Newcastle and from 1897 to 1903 he attended Newcastle Art School. He worked as a decorator at Minton's in 1903, attended Hanley Art School 1904-5 and from there won a British Institution scholarship to study engraving at the Royal College of Art. In 1907 he was appointed master of life drawing at Bristol School of Art. He had a studio in Wicklow Street, Dublin, where he was an inspector of art. In 1910 he was employed by London County Council to teach art, but in the summer term of that year he enrolled at the Slade School of Fine Art. Here he made the acquaintance of Augustus John, Jacob Epstein and other artists. Currie found patrons in Edward Marsh and Sir Michael Sadler and with their help exhibited in London at the Friday Club and the New English Club. He staged his own one-man show at the Chenil Gallery in July 1913. On visits to Ireland, where he was drawn by his ancestral roots, he made several drawings of Irish peasants. A picture of Penkhull, Stoke upon Trent, done in post-impressionist style, was presented to Hanley Museum by Arnold Bennett. A small mural, painted in 1908, hangs in the refectory of the Cistercian College, Roscrea, County Tipperary.

JC married Jessie Brandon, of Wolstanton, a fellow student at Newcastle Art School, in July 1907. A son, Mark, was born in Wolstanton on 11 September 1908. In 1911, however, Currie separated from his wife, lived with Dolly Henry in St. George's Square, and later in 3 Heath Passage, Hampstead, London. He and Dolly had violent quarrels and for a time he returned to Staffordshire. He came back to London and on 8 October 1914 at 50 Paulton Square, shot Dolly Henry dead then turned the gun on himself. He lived for a few hours but died on 9 October in Chelsea Infirmary.

Hanley Museum Exhibition Catalogue, November 1980.

CUTTS, John (1772-1851), *pottery artist,* Hanley.

JC, born in 1772, was a ceramic painter of 'free' Derby type landscapes at Pinxton, Derbyshire and elsewhere. He became a partner in the business until 1813 when the factory closed and he moved to Staffordshire. He established a business in Lane End (Longton) and decorated some of Josiah Wedgwood II's teawares. By 1834 his firm was trading as Cutts and Sons, enamellers and gilders, of New Street, Hanley. By 1842 the firm described as manufacturers of pottery figures, was employing 50 workpeople.

JC married a sister of Edward Rowland, the Derby painter. She died aged 66 in 1837 and JC's sons pre-deceased him. He died in 1851. Cutts Street, Snow Hill, Shelton, is probably named after his son James Cutts.

Jewitt; M and H.

CYPLES, Lydia (1775-1845), *pottery manufacturer,* Longton.

Lydia Steel, born in 1775, married Jesse Cyples at Norton in the Moors on 8 December 1793. The Cyples family potted in Market Street, Lane End, and ran one of the oldest established factories in that area. Joseph Cyples is recorded as manufacturing general earthenware and Egyptian black ware in 1787. Jesse Cyples was listed as a maker of Egyptian black in 1805. He died in 1810 and his widow, Lydia, continued the business, her sons assisting her, until her death in 1845. The business was listed as R. and W. Cyples, Barlow and Cyples, and finally, in 1849, Thomas Barlow.

Jewitt; M and H.

DANE, Ralph (1830-1915), *architect,* Burslem.

RD was born at Lilleshall, Shropshire, on 22 July 1830. By 1860 he had established an architect's practice at 70 Liverpool Road, Burslem, and had an office in Shakespeare Buildings, Piccadilly, Hanley, by 1872. He was professionally associated with the erection of a number of large buildings in the country generally, including the gaols at Leeds and Manchester and the Free Trade Hall, Manchester. His commissions in Staffordshire included the county asylum, Stafford, Hanley public baths and buildings on the Sneyd estate at Keele. One of his last commissions was the entrance gates for Sneyd church.

RD was a trustee of Sneyd National school, subscribed to the North Staffordshire Infirmary, and held high office in St. Martin's Lodge, one of the oldest freemason's lodges in the county. He was also Provincial Grand Junior Warden. A member of Burslem Conservative Club, he was appointed to the commission of the peace in Burslem in 1900.

Married with two sons and two daughters he died at his home in Liverpool Road, Burslem, in July 1915.

Staffs. Sentinel 12 July 1915 (obit.).

DANIEL, Charles (1833-1915), *clerk to Board of Guardians,* Stoke upon Trent.

CD was born on 30 May 1833 at Newcastle on Tyne. His father, a traveller for Minton's, brought his family to Hanley when CD was aged three, and CD was educated at Dr. Haslem's School, Eastwood House, Hanley. He was apprenticed to Charles Jones, a chemist of Lamb Street, Hanley, in 1848. He worked for some time in Worcester, then returned to Hanley and joined his elder brother, Henry Porter Daniel, in the printing firm of Allbut and Daniel. On 16 October 1867 he was appointed from 24 applicants as clerk to the Stoke upon Trent Board of Guardians, and held this post until he retired in 1910, gaining a reputation as an authority on Poor Law matters. He also acted as clerk to the Stoke upon Trent Rural District Council, Superintendent Registrar, and clerk to the Assessment committee. He was a member of the 'Ancient Corporation of Hanley', a social club holding an annual dinner, and was 'mayor' of this body in 1890.

He was living, unmarried, in Caledonia House, Cemetery Road, in 1881. Subsequently he married a Miss Yates, niece of the Revd. E. Duncan Boothman, rector of Shelton, but had no children.

He died at Shelton Old Hall on 25 September 1915.

Huntbach; *Staffs. Sentinel* 20 September 1915 (obit.).

DANIEL, Henry (1765-1841), *pottery manufacturer,* Stoke upon Trent.

HD, the eldest son of Thomas Daniel and his wife Fanny née Moore, was born in 1765. Thomas Daniel was an enameller and colour maker who had been apprenticed to Warner Edwards of Bell Bank Works, Shelton, and Henry followed his father's trade, working for John Mayer from 1789. He established himself in his own business, with a partner, about 1796, trading as Daniel and Brown, enamellers and potters, Market Place, Hanley. They supplied Worcester with cream-coloured earthenware. By 1805 HD was renting an enamelling workshop in the Spode factory. He designed and built his own enamelling kilns, purchased undecorated ware from Spode, decorated it, and sold it back. His employees included John Hancock of Derby, whom he hired as a layer of grounds. The partnership with Brown was dissolved in 1806. By the time HD ended his association with Spode, in 1822, he was employing 200 people, one third of the work-force on the site. In 1823 he opened his own porcelain factory in London Road, Stoke upon Trent, in 1826-7 producing a number of services for the earl of Shrewsbury. He owned two other factories, in Bedford Row, Shelton, producing stone china. He took his son Richard (q.v.) into partnership in 1841.

HD married Elizabeth possibly née Dyer and had three sons and one daughter. He rented his house from Spode but owned six houses and land in Shelton.

M. Berthond, *H. and R. Daniel 1822-1846;* Jewitt; M and H; *Staffs. Advertiser* 17 April 1841 (obit.).

DANIEL, Richard (1799-1884), *pottery manufacturer,* Stoke upon Trent.

RD, the son of Henry Daniel (q.v.) and his wife Elizabeth, worked potteries in Waterloo Road, Burslem and at Hanley, before joining his father in business in 1840. RD gave up his own potteries on succeeding to his father's business in 1841, and worked the Daniel factory in Elton Place, Stoke upon Trent, until 1846. By this year he was at the peak of his career and also a member of several railway management committees. He transferred the factory to Boothen Road in 1846 and in the following year opened another factory in Fenton. He had over-reached himself financially, however, and was imprisoned for debt for nine months until December 1847. On his release he returned to the Boothen Road factory, which he worked until 1854. There was a further business reverse and RD had to find employment as manager at Hill Pottery, Burslem. He became bankrupt again in 1866 and moved to London where he became a commission agent.

He died in London in 1884.

M. Berthond, *H. and R. Daniel.*

DAVENPORT, Charles Thomas (1818-64), *medical practitioner,* Tunstall.

CTD was born in Astbury, Cheshire, in 1818, the son of Charles Davenport, a surgeon, by his wife Ellen. In 1841 he was living with his father and mother in Well Street, and was himself listed as a surgeon. In 1861 he was living in Paradise Street and in 1864 in High Street.

He was a member of the Tunstall Board of Health in 1858 and in 1861 was appointed medical officer of health, succeeding James Troutbeck in this post.

By his wife Mary Jane he had a son and daughter. He died on 16 December 1864.

Census 1871; IGI Staffs.; *Tunstall Board of Health Annual Reports.*

DAVENPORT, John (1765-1848), *pottery manufacturer and Member of Parliament,* Stoke upon Trent.

JD was born in Derby Street, Leek, Staffs., on 29 September 1765, the son of Jonathan and Ellin Davenport. His father died when he was six years old, and he was sent to work soon after. Later he moved to Newcastle under Lyme where he was employed at Kinnersley's bank until 1785. He then joined Thomas Wolfe in Stoke upon Trent, and became Wolfe's partner at a china works in Liverpool. In 1794 he bought his own business, Brindley's Longport Pottery, and the partnership with Wolfe ended. By the 1840s his four works in Longport employed over 1,500 people. He produced earthenware, porcelain and flint glass and in 1806 patented a method of ornamenting glass in imitation of engraving or etching. He bought Cliff Bank Pottery from John Harrison in 1804, and also acquired a large earthenware factory in Newport, Shropshire.

JD's sons joined him in the business in the 1820s and he became increasingly absorbed in political affairs. He stood as a Conservative candidate in the parliamentary election for Stoke upon Trent in 1832 and was returned, together with Josiah Wedgwood II (q.v.). He was returned again in 1835 at the uncontested election of that year.

In 1813 JD bought Westwood Hall, Leek. He retired from public life in 1838, having served as a magistrate and deputy lieutenant for Staffordshire. He married Diana Ward in 1795 and by her had two daughters and three sons. John Davenport junior became a lawyer, Henry died in 1835 and William (q.v.) took over effective control of the business. The family interest was maintained until about 1887 when the last of the Davenport factories was sold to Thomas Hughes. Most of the surviving factory buildings were demolished in 1961.

JD has been described as a 'hard, gritty capitalist'. He participated in the victory parade of 1815 from Longport to Burslem, heading the procession with his works manager James Mawdesley, both wearing glass hats and carrying glass walking sticks specially made for the occasion.

JD died at Westwood, Leek, on 12 December 1848 and was buried in Leek parish church graveyard.

Anderton; T. A. Lockett, *Davenport's Pottery and Porcelain 1794-1887;* V and S; VCH ii and viii.

DAVENPORT, William (1805-69), *pottery manufacturer,* Burslem.

WD was born in 1805, the second son of John Davenport (q.v.) and Diana née Ward. With his brother Henry he was taken into partnership by his father. He became sole owner in 1848 although he had been in effective control for more than ten years previously. He did not handle his affairs well, and when he died he left severe financial problems for his son Henry.

In 1832 WD married Marianne Wood, by whom he had nine children. The family lived first at Longport Hall but later moved to Maer Hall which they bought from the Wedgwoods. WD enjoyed the life of a country gentleman. He was master of the hounds at Baddeley Edge and in the 1840s was responsible for the revival of the North Staffordshire Hunt, of which he was master for 27 seasons. He was high sheriff of Staffordshire in 1859 and also served as deputy lieutenant and magistrate. He helped to promote the Staffordshire Potteries Waterworks Company, becoming first chairman of the board. One of the pumping engines was named Davenport after him.

In C. Shaw's autobiography *When I Was A Child* WD is portrayed unsympathetically as the person who had forced him into the workhouse by sacking his father.

He died at Maer Hall on 6 June 1869. The Upper and Lower Bridge Works at Longport were sold between 1876 and 1881 to meet heavy mortgage payments.

T. A. Lockett, *Davenport Pottery and Porcelain 1794-1887;* Oldham; *Staffs. Sentinel* 12 June 1869 (obit.).

DAWES, William (1830-1902), *medical practitioner,* Longton.

WD was born in Longton on 27 September 1830, the son of Dr. William Dawes, who had an extensive practice in the neighbourhood. WD junior began his medical career at the North Staffordshire Infirmary and was elected M.R.C.S. in 1854. He was one of the promoters of the original Longton Cottage Hospital in Mount Pleasant (Lawley Street), and became honorary physician there and at the new hospital in Normacot opened in 1890. In 1879 he was sued by a patient, Hughes, for alleged negligence, but he won the case and the people of Longton gave him a public dinner and presented him with a silver casket containing £120 as an expression of their confidence in him. He was appointed Medical Officer of Health for Longton in 1880, in succession to Dr. James Weaver, and continued in this post until his death. He had previously been both an improvement commissioner and a councillor. In his annual reports he often condemned the council for 'playing at sanitation' and demanded the abolition of earth privies.

WD was Conservative in politics and Catholic in religion. He played a foremost part in the erection of St. Gregory's church, Heathcote Road, in 1869. His hobby was photography and he served as president of Longton Photographic Society.

He died while on one of his periodic recuperations at the Imperial Hydro, North Shire, Blackpool, on 19 September 1902, leaving a widow Frances, and two sons, Joseph, his deputy as M.O.H., and Stephen, chaplain to the Connaught Rangers in the South African War.

Staffs. Sentinel 19 September 1902 (obit.).

DAWSON, Joseph (1843-1910), *printer,* Burslem.

JD was born in Preston in 1843, the son of William and Elizabeth Dawson. His father was minister at Hill Top Wesleyan Methodist Church, Burslem. JD was apprenticed to Bowering, printer, of the Old Post Office, in Burslem. He set up his own business using various premises in the town until he built the Caxton Printing Works in Newcastle Street. He was connected with William Owen (q.v) and Enoch Bennett, father of Arnold, in the production of a newspaper *The Staffordshire Knot,* which failed in 1892.

JD provided Arnold Bennett (q.v) with information on the history of Burslem, and Bennett may have used Dawson's printing works as the model for those of Darius Clayhanger in his novel *Clayhanger.* Dawson printed three Christmas gift books for Bennett between 1906 and 1908, and Bennett dedicated his novel *The Grim Smile of the Five Towns* to Dawson.

JD was opposed to federation believing it would result in increased power of officials, but particularly because Burslem might become merely a suburb of Hanley. It is possible to see Dawson's fears reflected in those of Constance Baines about federation in Bennett's *The Old Wives' Tale.* He printed a manifesto *Fifteen reasons why Burslem ratepayers should oppose and vote against Federation,* in the summer of 1907, and gave evidence to the House of Lords select committee in 1908.

In 1894 JD wrote and published *The Wedgwood Memorial Institute.* He was a member of Burslem School Board, a justice of the peace and a local preacher and Sunday school teacher at Hill Top Methodist Church. He was a Liberal in politics, and Arnold Bennett in his *Journal* writes of talking politics with Dawson and Edmund Leigh (q.v).

JD married but had no children. He died on 5 July 1910 and was buried in Burslem cemetery.

A. Bennett, *The Old Wives' Tale;* N. Flower (edit.) *The Journals of Arnold Bennett;* J. Hepburn, *The Letters of Arnold Bennett;* letters to *Staffs. Sentinel* 13 May 1907 and 28 August 1907; *Staffs. Sentinel* 6 July 1910 (obit.); J. Dawson, *Wedgwood Memorial Institute* (Burslem Public Library).

DE RENZIE, Revd. Geoge Castriot (1851-1928), *minister of religion (Church of England),* Tunstall.

GCDR was born in Leeds on 22 May 1851, the eldest son of the Revd. George Birks De Renzie, chaplain of Pentonville and Wandsworth prisons. The family was descended from George Castriot Skanderbeg, prince of Epirus, an Albanian hero of the 15th century. GCDR was educated at the City of London School, where Herbert Asquith, prime minister 1908-16, was his contemporary. He graduated from Trinity College, Cambridge, and was ordained in 1874. He served first among the chain makers of Cradley, in the Black Country, then in 1898 accepted the living of St. Mary's Tunstall.

He raised £1,200 for the restoration of the church at its jubilee in 1909, and helped to save the Church schools in Lascelles Street, Tunstall, when the Board of Education required £5,000 to be spent on new building, by pledging his insurance policies as security. The sum took ten years to raise and the effort contributed to the failure of his health. He resigned in 1920, was appointed to Blurton, but retired in 1924.

The family lived at Kenwood, Keele Road, Newcastle under Lyme, and later GCDR and his wife lived with a married daughter at Huntley Lodge, Bothwell, near Glasgow. He died on 2 August 1928 and was buried in Tunstall cemetery.

Staffs. Sentinel 2 August 1928.

DEAN, James (born 1826), *printer,* Burslem.

JD was baptised at Burslem on 10 December 1826, the son of John Dean (q.v) and Sarah possibly née Handley. He was established in business at 33 Market Place, Burslem as bookseller, printer, and stationer in 1851, and in 1860 he was listed as printer, bookseller, stationer, bookbinder, newsagent, artist's colourman, chemist, druggist and stamp office, to which, in 1861, was added account book manufacturer.

He served on the Burslem Board of Health 1867-70. By his wife Maria, born about 1823, he had at least seven children. He lived at Hamill Cottage from before 1861 to at least 1881. In 1861 he was employing three men and five boys.

Census 1861, 1881; Dir. 1851, 1861, 1874; Oldham.

DEAN, John (born c. 1799), *brick and tile manufacturer,* Burslem.

JD was born in Wolstanton about 1799. In 1851 he was a brick and tile manufacturer of Church Street and Hamill. In 1861 his occupation was shown as brick manufacturer and mine agent, employing 10 men, five boys and one girl. He may have married twice. His first wife, Sarah, possibly née Handley, whom he married in 1823, bore him a number of children including James Dean (q.v). In 1864 he was living in Ellgreave Street. He served on the Burslem Board of Health 1850-3.

Census 1861; Dir. 1851, 1864; Oldham.

DEAN, William (1812-75), *printer,* Stoke upon Trent.

WD was baptised at Audley on 13 December 1812, the son of John Dean, farmer, of Butters Green, Bignall End, and Elizabeth his wife. In 1837 he was in business as a printer in partnership with Richard Cyples Tompkinson, then became sole owner on the latter's retirement. His firm printed the map which was issued with Ward's *History of the Borough of Stoke upon Trent* and from 1852-5 the *Staffordshire Potteries Telegraph,* a Liberal newspaper. About 1867 WD moved to Longton where his business was in Trentham Road (now Stafford Street). He also published a set of engravings of local buildings.

He qualified as a local improvement commissioner in 1840 and served for a number of years on various committees. He was the first secretary of the Stoke Athenaeum in 1846 and served as a trustee of Wesley chapel, Stoke upon Trent;

He married Martha Greatbach on 10 January 1839 and by her had three daughters and a son. He died at 5 Trentham Road, Dresden, on 8 February 1875.

Audley parish registers; A. Curtis and E. Beech, *History of Wesley Chapel;* Dir. 1871; IGI Staffs.; *National Index to Wills and Administrations;* Oldham; R and S; Stoke upon Trent Improvement Commissioners' Minutes; Stoke upon Trent parish registers.

DICKENSON, Christopher (died 1904), *cornmiller,* Stoke upon Trent.

CD was born in Coalbrookdale, Shropshire, the son of Barnard Dickinson. From about 1851 to 1880 he owned a cornmill in Eldon Place (later Campbell Place), by the side of the canal. He claimed in answer to a complaint in 1853 that his boiler was so constructed as to consume nearly all its smoke.

CD's brother-in-law was Joseph Sturge, the Birmingham Chartist. CD was chairman of the local Liberal council in 1868, was elected to Stoke upon Trent council after the incorporation of the town and served as mayor 1874-5. He was a nominee for Samuel Pope, the Liberal temperance candidate in the parliamentary election of 1859.

By his wife Sophia, whom he married in Luton in 1844, CD had at least four children. In 1851 he lived at High Grove, Trent Valley (now St. Joseph's), in 1861 at Fenton Manor House, in 1871 at The Grove, Penkhull, in 1881 at 52 King Street, Newcastle under Lyme, and about 1900 at 25 Hartshill.

He died at Hartshill on 2 July 1904.

Anderton; Census, 1851, 1861, 1871, 1881; Stoke upon Trent Improvement Commissioners' Minutes.

DIGGORY, Thomas (1811/12-78), *potter's agent,* Burslem.

TD was born in Hanley about 1811. In 1851 he was a pottery foreman, living in the Grange, Cobridge, and married to Elizabeth, with one son, Thomas, born about 1842 in Burslem. In 1874 TD was listed as a commercial agent, of Clifton Terrace. He died in 1878.

Census 1851; Dir. 1874; Oldham.

DIMMOCK, John (c. 1819-66), *pottery manufacturer,* Hanley.

JD was born at Shelton under Harley near Swynnerton, Staffs about 1819 and was baptised at Marsh Chapel, Newcastle under Lyme, on 26 December 1819, the son of John Baddeley Dimmock and his wife Margaret Mary née Spearman.

He was connected with the firm which became John Dimmock and Sons from about 1836 and may have been related to Thomas Dimmock, living in Albion Street in 1842, who escaped the depredations of the Chartist mob because he was known to be a friend of the working class. JD rebuilt the Albion Works which stood on the site of the later Palais de Danse and Essoldo Cinema (now C and A Department Store and Coral Social Club) in 1862. He changed his ideas so much during the rebuilding, that the extra improvements he called for cost more than the original estimate.

He was chief bailiff of Hanley 1853-4 and mayor in 1860. He rose to the rank of captain in the 1st Company of Hanley Volunteers.

In 1851 he was living in Broom Street and in 1861 in Lichfield Street. By his wife Catherine he had at least six children. He died at Seabridge on 8 October 1866, and was buried at Swynnerton.

Census 1851, 1861; Huntbach; IGI Staffs.; *Staffs. Advertiser* 13 October 1866; *Staffs. Mercury* 20 August 1842.

DIMMOCK, Josiah (1820/1-92), *timber merchant,* Stoke upon Trent.

JD was baptised in Hanley on 10 November 1820, the son of Josiah Dimmock and his wife Margaret née Smith (married in 1818). In partnership with his younger brother, Timothy, he traded as a timber merchant at Shelton wharf on the Trent and Mersey Canal. The business had formerly been that of William Kenwright (q.v.).

He was a member of Stoke upon Trent Board of Guardians from 1856 until 1891 and chairman from 1863 to 1866 and from 1869 to 1891. One of the managers of the Staffordshire Industrial School for Boys at Werrington, he initially opposed its enlargement, preferring that a new school be built in the south of the county.

JD qualified as an improvement commissioner for Stoke upon Trent in June 1860 and was immediately elected chief bailiff. He declined to take any part in the affairs of the borough on its incorporation in 1874. He stood as a county councillor for Stoke upon Trent in 1889 and although defeated was elected an alderman. He was treasurer of the Stoke upon Trent Athenaeum on its foundation in 1846 and secretary of the Minton Memorial Buildings in London Road at their inception in 1858. He replaced Jonathan Henry Adams as a member of the committee of the Stokeville Building Society in 1853.

He was married, by 1851, to Ellen Mackenzie and was living at Upper Cliff Bank, Stoke upon Trent. There was one daughter of the marriage. He married a second time and the family lived at Fradswell Hall, Stone for many years. JD died at Fradswell on 23 September 1892.

Census 1851; Dir. 1851; IGI Staffs.; *Staffs. Advertiser* 1 October 1892; Stoke upon Trent Improvement Commissioners' minute book.

DIX, Harry Stuart (1861-1918), *brewer,* Hanley.

HSD was born at Grove House, Shelton, in 1861, the youngest of four sons of Alexander Mills Dix and Anna Marie Josephine. The Dix family, after an association with Southwark Brewery, bought Shelton Brewery, Sun Street, in 1851 from Samuel Loney. HSD was educated at Hemming's School, Stoke upon Trent, and at Leamington College. On his father's death he and two of his brothers took over the family business and developed it into one of the the most up-to-date and largest breweries in North Staffordshire.

He rented a tennis court in Cemetery Road, and as a young man gained a reputation for his mountaineering in Switzerland. He was an active member of the old Stoke Philharmonic Society, whose conductor was Dr. Swinnerton Heap (q.v.). HSD was a freemason and a member of the Church of England. He was elected to Hanley council in 1857 and served, with a break of only one year, until 1870. He was chairman of the general committee of Hanley Red Cross. He married Mildred Burghope of Malvern. Their son was one of the first officers of the 1/5 Bn. North Staffs. Regiment to be killed in the First World War.

He died at Trent Vale House on 21 February 1918, and was buried in Hanley cemetery.

Staffs. Sentinel 22 February 1918 (obit.); Hanley Rate Books.

DIXON, James (born c. 1817), *dentist,* Hanley.

JD was born in Antigua about 1817. He obtained a medical degree in New York and was in practice in Liverpool Road, Stoke upon Trent, in 1864.

In 1855 he was elected chairman of the Shelton Highways Board but the election was disputed. He led the opposition to the creation of a Hanley Board of Health. At a public meeting in June 1854 he described the Public Health Act as arbitrary, despotic and centralising. He argued that it would give unlimited power to a few persons and deny any voice in local government to the masses. He also opposed the incorporation of Hanley in 1867.

In June 1854 he was sued by the Apothecaries Company for practising as an apothecary without the requisite certificates of qualification, and was ordered to pay £20.

In 1861 he was living in High Street, Hanley, with his wife Sarah and a daughter, Rachel, aged 13.

Census 1851, 1861; Dir. 1864; *Staffs. Advertiser* 6 April and 26 May 1855; *Staffs. Sentinel* 25 June 1854 and 2 June 1855; Townley.

DOBELL, George Thomas (born c. 1854), *publican,* Hanley.

GTD was born in Witton, Cheshire, about 1854. The 1879 directory shows him as a beer seller, Hampton Street, but later he kept a beerhouse in West Terrace and by 1886/7 the George public house in West Terrace. The census of 1881 lists him as a cabinet maker, of West Terrace.

He was probably the most successful athlete in the Potteries in his time. He played football for Stoke, and won races at Stoke Victoria Athletic Club sports in 1878, earning £100 in prizes in 1879. He convened a meeting to found the Hanley Hare and Hounds (forerunner of the North Staffordshire Harriers) at the George and Dragon public house, Joiners Square, Hanley, in October 1878.

By his wife, Mary, GTD had two sons, William and George.

Census 1881; Dir. 1879, 1886; H. P. Mawdesley 'The Development of Athletics in the Potteries 1850-1900' (University of Manchester dissertation 1977).

DOBSON, Sir William Warrington (1861-1941), *brewer,* Burslem.

WWD was born at Cheetham Hill, Manchester, in 1861, the son of Matthew Dobson, hop merchant, and Louisa née Warrington. He was educated at Old Trafford School, learnt the technical side of brewing at Senior's, Barnsley, and the office routine in Manchester. In 1880 Matthew Dobson became the partner of Henry Parker, of Burslem Brewery, WWD represented his father's interest in the brewery in Burslem and assumed direction on Parker's death in 1884. He became managing director when the firm was incorporated in 1889.

In 1881 he joined the North Staffs. volunteers and began a part-time military career which culminated in his appointment as colonel of the 1st Battalion from 1900 to 1908, and honorary colonel of the 5th Battalion in 1909. During the first world war he helped in recruiting. He was awarded the Territorial Decoration in 1921.

From 1889 he represented Burslem on Staffordshire county council. He also served on Burslem council until federation, being mayor in 1897-8 and 1889-90. He was elected an alderman on Stoke on Trent council in 1910. He had at first been opposed to federation and had served on Burslem anti-federation committee in 1907, but subsequently changed his opinions.

He married Alice, daughter of William Meakin of Westwood Manor, Wetley Rocks, Staffs., in 1887. He lived first at Tittensor then at Seighford Hall, becoming chairman of Seighford parish council from 1906 to about 1931. He was chairman of the Stafford Division of the Conservative Association, and high sheriff of Staffordshire in 1915. He acted as Master of the Foxhounds of the North Staffordshire Hunt in 1903 and 1907.

He was knighted for political and public services in 1933.

Oldham; *Staffs. Sentinel* 15 May 1913, file in *Evening Sentinel* cuttings library.

DODD, John (died 1910), *superintendent of police,* Tunstall.

JD joined the Staffordshire police on 6 January 1868. He was stationed at Stoke, Longton, Kingsley and Uttoxeter before returning to Stoke as sergeant in 1874. He transferred to Burslem and then to Silverdale in 1878. He moved to Rugeley on his appointment as inspector in 1883. In the following year he was transferred to Tamworth where he served until 1898 when he was appointed superintendent at Tunstall. He retired on 31 March 1910 and died on 21 April 1910 at his home in Victoria Park Road.

Staffs. Sentinel 22 April 1910.

DODD, William (born 1795/6), *proprietor of houses,* Hanley.

WD was born in Cheshire about 1796. He had moved to the Potteries by at least 1820, when his eldest child was baptised in Hanley. In 1851 WD was described as a proprietor of houses. He bought the windmill, built about 1795 and still in use as a mill about 1837, sited on high ground at the east end of the present Windmill Street. By 12 August 1848 he had converted it into an observatory, equipped with a telescope and a camera obscura affording visitors a wide prospect of the surrounding countryside, and he served refreshments in the grounds. Unfortunately the telescope was stolen only a few days after Prospect Tower, as it was called, had been opened. William Dodd had relinquished the property by 1854 but the location was described as pleasure grounds and museum of art in 1866. In 1865-6 Dodd still owned a beerhouse and four other houses in the present Windmill Street.

By his wife Anne he had at least four children of whom John was listed in 1851 as a colour manufacturer, of Northwood.

Census 1851, 1861; Dir. 1851, 1854, 1860; IGI Staffs.; Map of Hanley 1866 (HRL): *Staffs. Advertiser* 12 and 16 August 1848; VCH viii.

DUDSON, James (1812-82), *pottery manufacturer,* Hanley.

JD was born in Shelton on 12 March 1812, the son of Thomas Dudson, potter, and Elizabeth née Penny. James's grandfather, Richard Dudson (1768-1833) had begun the family pottery business with a factory in Broad Street in 1800. A second works, in Hope Street, was opened in 1809 with Thomas Dudson in charge. Thomas (1786-1845) ran the factory until his death in 1845, when James took it over. The pottery produced jasperware and stoneware in various colours. In a letter to the *Potteries Examiner* in 1846 James was falsely accused of installing a 'whispering pipe' in his workshop, by means of which he could hear what his workpeople were saying. He offered £1,000 for the name of the anonymous writer of the letter. What he had done was to instal a speaking tube from his office down to the workshop for ease of communication. The speaking tube was invented in 1796 and adapted in the middle of the 19th century for use in houses to allow the owner to speak to the servants' quarters.

JD exhibited at the Great Exhibition in London in 1851 and again in 1862. The works employed 33 persons in 1851. He was an improvement commissioner for Hanley, but failed to secure election to the council in 1857.

He married Jane née Spilsbury in March 1838. By 1841 the family was living in Clarence Street, Hanley. They moved to Alsager in 1862 and JD died there on 6 June 1882. His son James Thomas Dudson married Elizabeth Ann, daughter of Robert Scrivener (q.v.), the ceremony being performed at Bethesda Methodist New Connexion church in September 1864. James Thomas took over the family business on his father's death. The firm contines today, in the control of the eighth generation of the Dudson family, and specialises in the production of wares for the hotel and restaurant market.

F. Burchill and R. Ross, *History of the Potters' Union; Census 1841, 1851; information provided by Miss Audrey Dudson; Evening Sentinel* 2 September 1975; Jewitt; M and H.

DYKE, Oliver (1860-1924), *draper,* Hanley.

OD was the eldest of ten children of Ralph Dyke, a Cheshire farmer, and was born on 4 September 1860. He was apprenticed in the drapery trade and gained experience in several provincial towns and in the large establishment of James Schoolbred and Co., Tottenham Court Road, London. He came to the Potteries in 1890 and in partnership with Henry Bratt bought Dudley's mantle business, in Stafford Street, Hanley. They traded as Bratt and Dyke in a wide range of goods. In 1896 they acquired the Roebuck public house on the corner of Stafford Street and Trinity Street, together with several old cottages, and there erected a three-storey block. Some of the shop assistants lived on the premises, and were subject to strict regulation. They were expected to take a weekly bath, attend a place of worship and no courting or familiarity was allowed in business hours. Bratt and Dyke were good employers, ahead of many of their competitors in their attitudes to their workpeople; they adopted the proposal to close the shop at 8 o'clock each week night and at 10 o'clock on Saturdays whether other firms in the town did so or not.

OD was president of the local traders' association, a vice-president of the National Chamber of Trade and a county representative on the Drapers' Chamber of Trade. He attended the Bethesda United Methodist church, of which he was a trustee and circuit auditor, and was treasurer of the Bucknall Road Mission. He was appointed a justice of the peace in 1914 and in 1922 was elected to Stone Urban District Council.

He married Caroline Mably, born in Cornwall, and later the family moved to Stone. OD died at 'The Woodlands', Stone, on 22 September 1924, and was buried in Stone cemetery.

Staffs. Sentinel 20 September 1901, 22 September 1924 and 30 September 1975.

EDGE, John Wilcox (1844-1923), *tile manufacturer,* Burslem.

JWE was born about 13 February 1844 in Queen Street, Burslem, the sixth child of Joseph Edge (q.v.) and Eliza née Davis. He attended the Wesleyan Day Infants' School begun by his mother, then the school at Shelton Hall run by Charles Osmond. At the age of 16 he entered his father's tile manufacturing business. Visiting Italy for health reasons he met Albert Wenger (q.v.), a meeting which may have encouraged Wenger to settle in the Potteries later. On his return JWE became a partner in Edge, Malkin and Co., and also acquired an interest in Sneyd Colliery.

He was elected to Burslem town council in 1880 and served as mayor in 1889-90 and 1890-1. During his mayoralty he supported Burslem's annexation of Wolstanton. He was an original member of Staffs. County

Council and was elected an alderman in 1889. Although he had hoped that a Potteries county council might be formed he became a supporter of federation, though he argued for non-county borough status for the federation, so that it might be subject to county council control. At the time of the federation inquiry he was chairman of the county council boundaries committee, but resigned in July 1908 because the county council was opposed to federation. He gave evidence to the Local Government Board, the House of Commons and the House of Lords during the inquiry. His views were given prominence by the promoters of federation because he came from Burslem whose council had an anti-federation majority.

In 1877 he married Anne Edge, daughter of his cousin Stephen Edge (q.v.) and the honeymoon was spent travelling in the Eastern Mediterranean region. He was involved in the running of the Wedgwood Memorial Institute, and his initials are included in the tiled design of 1902 in the entrance hall. His political opinions were Liberal and he was thought of as a possible parliamentary candidate for North Western Staffs. in 1907. He attended the local Wesleyan Methodist church and was a supporter of the temperance movement. He lectured on the history of Burslem, his recollections being published in the *Staffordshire Knot* in 1888 and the *Staffs. Sentinel* on 13 February 1923. To commemorate his 79th birthday he was awarded the freedom of the borough. Before his death he was living in Woburn Sands, Bedfordshire. He died at Hastings on 6 May 1923.

Federation News Cuttings (HRL); *Staffs. Sentinel* 13 February and 7 May 1923.

EDGE, Joseph (1805-93), *earthenware and tile manufacturer,* Burslem.

JE was born in Burslem on 14 July 1805, the son of William Edge and Anne née Willcocks. He began his working life as a confectioner but by 1846 was in partnership with Benjamin Cork (q.v.), manufacturing earthenware at Newport Pottery, Queen Street, Burslem. In 1860 the name of the firm changed to Cork, Edge and Malkin and an additional factory was opened at New Wharf. In 1870 the firm was trading as Edge, Malkin and Company and continued in this style until 1903. They exhibited teapots and other articles at the Great Exhibition in 1851. By 1875 they were producing encaustic tiles by a new patented process and obtained large contracts for buildings including Southport public baths. The factory was bought by Newport Pottery in 1920.

JE's other business interests included the Burslem Gas Works, the Staffordshire Potteries Waterworks Board and the North Staffordshire Tramway Company. JE was Conservative in politics. As a superintendent of Wesleyan Methodist schools in Burslem he was host to Matthew Arnold, the poet, when the latter came to North Staffordshire as a government inspector of schools. JE served as an improvement commissioner and on the local Board of Guardians. From 1875 he was a justice of the peace and in 1887 he sat on the committee of the Wedgwood Memorial Institute.

By his wife Eliza née Davis he had eight children including John Wilcox Edge (q.v.). He died at Wolstanton on 21 May 1893.

Joseph Edge, Chief Bailiff of Burslem (HRL); M and H; *Staffs. Advertiser* 27 May 1893; VCH viii.

EDGE, Stephen (c. 1817-86), *corn merchant,* Burslem.

SE was born in Burslem about 1817. He lived in Rathbone Street, Tunstall, in 1851, when his occupation was stated to be cheese factor. From 1860 he traded as a provision merchant, at the Market Place, Burslem.

SE served on the Burslem Board of Health from 1863-9. By his wife Elizabeth, born in Tunstall about 1822 he had two daughters and one son. He died in 1886.

Census 1851; Oldham.

EDWARDS, Aaron (1832-1908), *pottery manufacturer,* Longton.

AE was born in Longton on 1 August 1832. He was co-founder in 1858 of the firm of Cartwright and Edwards, Warren Street, Longton. In 1868-9 they built the Borough Pottery in Trentham Road, Longton, making use of machinery for nearly all processes. In the 19th century the firm produced most classes of earthenware and extended their range to bone china in the 20th century. Cartwright and Edwards also held the Victoria Pottery by 1912. The firm became a subsidiary of Alfred Clough Ltd. in 1955 and both the Victoria Pottery and the Borough Pottery were sold to the Manor Engineering Company. The Victoria Pottery was demolished and the Victoria Foundry built on the site. In 1960 Cartwright and Edwards Ltd. occupied the newly-built Newborough and Sutherland Potteries, not far from the former Borough Pottery.

AE served on the Longton Board of Guardians and was mayor of Longton in 1874, 1896-9, and 1907-8. He was created alderman in 1875. He represented Longton on Staffordshire county council. He was a member of the Methodist New Connexion, and was associated with Zion chapel, Longton. He served on the board of several local building societies. In politics he was a Liberal, supporting sanitary reform and borough extension. He played a leading role in securing the Sutherland Institute as the Central School for Science and Technology and School of Art.

He died on 8 July 1908.

Briggs; Jewitt; VCH viii.

EDWARDS, Enoch (1852-1912), *miner, trade union official, Member of Parliament,* Burslem.

EE was born in Talke-o'-the-Hill in 1852, the son of James Edwards, a miner. His parents were members of the Primitive Methodist church and EE went to the local P.M. school until the age of nine, when he began work at nearby Hollingwood Colliery for sixpence a day. At the age of 18 he became treasurer of the local lodge of the North Staffordshire Miners' Association. He suffered an accident at work in 1873. He rose rapidly within the ranks of the trade union movement, becoming treasurer of the N.S. Miners' Association in 1875 and general secretary in 1878. He was elected president of the Midland Miners' Federation in 1886, in 1890 he became treasurer of the Miners' Federation of Great Britain and from 1904 until his death president of the Miners' Federation. During the coal strike of 1883 he favoured conciliation and arbitration.

His local activities were many. He was district secretary of the Ancient Order of Shepherds, 1892, and a member of the Ancient Order of Foresters; he served nine years on the Burslem School Board, was elected to Burslem council then created an alderman. He served as mayor of Burslem 1899-1900, and was appointed a justice of the peace for Burslem and then for Staffordshire. Later he was elected to Staffordshire county council. He unsuccessfully contested the Hanley constituency as a Liberal candidate in the parliamentary election of 1900, but standing as a 'Lib-Lab' won the seat in 1906. In the two elections of 1910 he was again elected as a Labour candidate with Liberal support.

In 1875 he married Elizabeth Alice Rathbone and had three sons. He moved to Burslem in 1883 and lived at 38 Price Street. He was a member of Clowes Memorial Chapel.

He died at Southport on 28 June 1912 and was buried in Burslem.

Dictionary of Labour Biography; Oldham.

EDWARDS, John (1816-93), *pottery manufacturer,* Fenton.

JE was born in Blurton in 1816, probably the son of James and Mary Edwards. By 1850 he was established in the King Street works as a china manufacturer. He took out a patent for the improvement of methods of stacking wares for firing in 1859. The factory produced semi-porcelain and white granite ware for the American market by the early 1880s. The firm of John Edwards was still occupying the premises in 1900. By 1960 the building was in use as a tea warehouse.

From 1856 to 1873 JE served as an improvement commissioner for Fenton, giving land in Park Lane and Market Street for road improvements. He was chief bailiff 1872-3. In 1863 he had supported the idea of a Potteries Junction railway to free the district from the North Staffordshire Railway monopoly. He was Conservative in politics.

By his wife Cicely he had five sons and one daughter. He died at The Woodlands, Hartwell, on 5 December 1893.

British Ceramics Review, Spring 1975; *Staffs. Sentinel* 6 December 1893; VCH viii.

EDWARDS, Joshua Price (1835/6-91), *surgeon,* Tunstall.

JPE was born in Wales about 1835. He graduated L.F.P.S. at Glasgow and in 1864 was appointed Medical Officer of Health to the Tunstall Local Board of Health on the death of Charles Davenport. He also served as Medical Officer of Health to the Urban Sanitary Authority until his death in 1891.

In 1871 he was living in High Street, Tunstall. By his wife Diana Margaret he had three children. He died at Greengates House, Tunstall, on 2 December 1891.

Census 1871; Dir. 1879; *Tunstall Board of Health Annual Reports.*

EDWARDS, Thomas (1838-1910), *trade union official,* Burslem

TE was born at Hot Lane, Burslem, the son of Edward and Susannah Edwards, and was baptised at St. John's church, Burslem, on 30 September 1838. He began work at Davenport's factory at the age of eight, earning sixpence a week. Later he was apprenticed as a placer. When he was sixteen he was orphaned and was left responsible for six younger brothers and sisters. He joined the Ovenmen's Society at the age of 19, was a member for over 50 years and agent for 20. He worked as a fireman for Twyford's in Bath Street, Hanley, and a glost fireman for Dudson's. He was involved in the strike of which helped to bring about the end of annual hiring in 1865. He helped to achieve increases in wages in 1900 and 1908. In the latter year the Home Secretary appointed him a member of the Departmental Committee on Lead Poisoning.

TE was elected to Burslem council in 1892, became an alderman in 1903 and served as mayor 1908-10. He was a member of the School Board between 1899 and 1903 and of the Education Committee from 1903 to 1906. He was opposed to federation, believing that Burslem had made all the improvements it required. He also opposed expenditure on new buildings, including a new town hall for Burslem. After the new county borough of Stoke on Trent was created TE argued for a distribution of the offices throughout the six towns, with a medical officer of health in Burslem.

He married Elizabeth Cooper, who as a child had been taken to America by the Potters' Emigration Society. There were eight children of the marriage. TE was a member of Bethel Methodist church, Burslem. He lived at Cemetery Lodge, Holden Bridge, Burslem and later at 351 Sneyd Street, where he died on 24 December 1910.

Dir. 1907; Oldham; *Staffs. Advertiser* 31 December 1910; *Staffs. Sentinel* 13 November 1907 and 26 December 1910 (obit.).

EGERTON, Albert Edward (1897-1966), *miner,* Longton.

AEE was born in Longton on 10 November 1897, the son of Thomas Henry Egerton. He was educated at Cooke Street School in Longton and Blurton Church of England School. He worked as a haulage hand at Florence Colliery before volunteering, at the age of seventeen, to join the 3rd Battalion North Staffs. Regiment. Later he transferrd to the 1st Battalion in France and then to the 16th Battalion Sherwood Foresters (Notts., Lincs. and Derby), with whom he fought on the Somme in 1916. During the third battle of Ypres, on 20 September 1917, he gained the Victoria Cross for his reckless bravery when, under heavy fire, he launched a solo attack on a heavily defended enemy dug-out. He killed three Germans and, with support, captured twenty-nine more. His action was said to be in revenge for the death in action of his brother William in August, the news of which had reached him only that morning.

He was invested with his medal by King George V on 5 December 1917 and came to Longton three days later to an ovation and a civic reception, where he was presented with a testimonial and a purse of money. The celebrations were partly overshadowed by the news of the death of the other Potteries V.C., John Harold Rhodes (q.v.) a week before. AEE was later promoted to the rank of sergeant, suffered severe gassing and spent a year in hospital recovering.

On his return to the Potteries he became a salesman for work produced by ex-servicemen. Later he worked for the Potteries Motor Traction Company as a conductor and then as an inspector. During the Second World War he was security officer at the aircraft works at Meir and later worked for the Staffordshire Potteries Ltd.

By his wife Elsie he had three daughters. He died at his home in Uttoxeter Road, Blythe Bridge, on 14 February 1966 and was buried at Forsbrook.

Evening Sentinel 14 February 1966, 26 November 1984; *Staffs. Sentinel* 5 December and 8 December 1917.

ELEY, William (c. 1810-86), *grocer and tea dealer,* Burslem.

WE was born in Burslem about 1810. By 1851 he was in business in Swan Square, Burslem, as grocer and provision dealer. He lived with his wife, Anise, and four children, at 1 Queen Street.

WE served on the Burslem Board of Health from 1853 to 1855. He died on 15 December 1886. Robert Eley, solicitor, of 11 Queen Street, may have been his son.

Census 1851; Oldham.

ELLIOT, Liddle (1807-69), *civil engineer,* Burslem.

LE was baptised at Trentham on 1 November 1807, the son of Thomas and Jane Elliot. In 1827 he was appointed surveyor to the trustees of the Talke-Darlaston turnpike road. In 1846 was appointed engineer to the Staffordshire Potteries Water Board, a post which he held until his death. He acted as adviser and consultant to Tunstall Board of Health on the disposal of sewage. He put forward a plan, in 1866, for sewering all the Potteries, but nothing came of this.

LE was involved in pottery manufacture with Mayer Brothers, making earthenware. In 1860 he traded as Liddle Elliot and Son and in 1867 as Bates, Elliot and Company, Stubbs Street, Dalehall. He married Mary Ann Cork on 22 April 1834 and by her had at least two sons, John, who died aged three and another son who succeeded him as engineer.

LE died at his home in The Beeches, Liverpool Road, Newcastle under Lyme, on 1 March 1869.

Dir. 1860, 1867; J. W. Edge, *Memoirs;* IGI Staffs.; Jewitt; *Pure and Wholesome Water* (HRL); *National Index of Wills and Administrations; Tunstall Board of Health Annual Reports.*

ELLIOT, Phillip (1860-1929), *draper,* Fenton.

PE was born on 31 August 1860 in Newcastle under Lyme, the son of Walter Elliot, draper, of High Street, Newcastle. He was educated at the Middle School and apprenticed to James Myatt, a draper of the Ironmarket, Newcastle. By 1884 he was in business in High Street East, Fenton, and later opened a branch in Victoria Road.

He was elected to Fenton council in 1898 and to Stoke upon Trent school board in 1895. As chairman of the education committee in 1904 he called a conference to attempt to obtain agreement on a unified scale of salaries for Potteries teachers. He was strongly opposed to federation on the grounds that it would entail large contributions from Fenton in paying other people's debts, and that Fenton's low rates encouraged industry. During the parliamentary proceedings which led to the federation bill, counsel for the federationists asked Elliot why, if he was able to represent Fenton as an earthly paradise, he chose to live in Longton.

PE served as mayor of Stoke on Trent 1913-14 and 1914-15 and was chairman of the education committee from 1910 to 1926. By his wife Sarah Sophia, he had two sons and four daughters. He was Liberal in politics and a Congregationalist in his religious opinions. He died at Hartshill Close (now Close School), Princes Road, on 23 July 1929. The house was sold to Stoke on Trent education committee in 1932.

Federation newscuttings 1907-8; *Staffs. Sentinel* 23 July 1929 (obit.).

ELLIS, Arthur (1849-1941), *solicitor and town clerk,* Burslem.

AE was born in 1849 at Longport, Burslem, the son of the Revd. Phillip Brabazon Ellis (q.v.), Vicar of St. Paul's, Dalehall and his wife Mary née Nimmo. The family trace their descent from Robert Alis who came from Normandy in 1066. AE was educated at King William College, Isle of Man and at Liverpool College. He began working in an office in Liverpool but returned to Burslem as an articled clerk in his brother Brabazon Wood Ellis's practice at Overhouse (formerly that of W. E. Twigg). He qualified in 1875 and on the death of his brother in the same year, took over the practice.

In 1891 he became town clerk of Burslem in succession to J. W. Powell (q.v.) and served until 1910. He prepared the case for Burslem's opposition and the indications are that he was personally opposed to federation. One councillor accused him of being prejudiced and implied that he had influenced the decision by counsel for Burslem to withdraw from the Inquiry in January 1908. He dismissed similar criticism by declaring that he was used to being slandered by councillors.

He was clerk to the Burslem and Tunstall justices from 1901 to 1923 when he retired from that post and from his practice. In 1924 he went to live in Weston super Mare. He married Eleanor Victoria Tennant, daughter of Frederick Tennant (q.v.) on 21 July 1880 and in 1881 the couple were living at Vale View, Porthill. Later they lived at Wolstanton and from 1908 at Alsager. There were six children of the marriage and the couple had been married for almost sixty years when Mrs. Ellis died in June 1940. AE died on 31 March 1941 at Weston.

Adams; *Evening Sentinel* 2 April 1941; Federation newscuttings; information from Mr. H. B. Ellis (grandson), of Ellis, Moxon and Co., Burslem.

ELLIS, George (1841-1912), *builder,* Hanley.

GE was born in 1841 and educated at St. John's National School, Hanley. He served an apprenticeship with Benjamin Buxton of New Street, Hanley, and set up as a builder on his own account in 1862 in premises at 52 High Street, Hanley. His buildings included the Birmingham and District Bank, Hanley, Lloyds Bank, Newcastle under Lyme (now Williams and Glynns), Twyford's Manufactory, Cliff Vale, Albert and Daniels Printing Works, Hanley (now Webberleys) and Huntbach's, Hanley. He was also involved in the restoration of St. John's church, Hanley and the erection of four Hanley board schools. He served as secretary of the Newcastle and Potteries Branch of the Master Builders' Association.

GE was a member of the Church of England, a Conservative and a freemason. He served as secretary of the Hanley Society for the Prosecution of Felons. He was elected for the east ward to Hanley council in 1890 and served as mayor from 1898 to 1901. He was made an honorary freeman in 1907. He died at his home in Highfield House, High Street, Hanley, on 9 January 1912.

Huntbach; *Staffs. Sentinel* 19 November 1898 and 9 January 1912.

ELLIS, William (born 1810/11), *potter,* Burslem.

Little is known about William Ellis's early life. He is first documented as a member of the board of management of the Potters' Union in 1836, newspaper reports showing him as a follower of the principles of Robert Owen. In 1841 he was living with his wife and two children (there were two more children later) in Upper Pitt Street, Burslem. In the following year he took a prominent part in the local Chartist movement; he addressed a meeting in Hanley Market Place on 13 June which pledged itself to support local strikes, and in July led a party of Chartists to Stafford where they interrupted a meeting of the aristocracy and gentry in the Shire Hall. On Monday 15 August a meeting, led by local Chartist Leaders, including John Richards and George Hemmings, and stimulated by the presence of the national Chartist leader, William Cooper, called for a general strike until the People's Charter should become law. Riots involving the looting and destruction of a number of buildings, broke out on the night of the 15-16 August. Soldiers were called in, the Riot Act was read, and many people were arrested. William Ellis fled to Glasgow, where he was apprehended, and brought back to Stafford. The Home Secretary, Sir James Graham, at first hoped to bring a charge of high treason against him, but the charge was changed to one of conspiracy. Ellis was accused of participating in the burning of Hanley parsonage. Despite the fact that he established an alibi, he was found guilty and sentenced to be transported for 21 years. On his arrival in Australia he was not set to work with other convicts but given a teaching job. Within six months of his arrival he was virtually set at liberty within the district, and in a few years was completely free. Unlike some other Chartists, however, he did not receive a pardon and never returned to England. He engaged in business, prospered and eventually became a magistrate and a member of the legislative assembly. What happened to his wife Emma and his children is not known, nor the date of his death in Australia.

R. Fyson, 'The Crisis of 1842: Chartism, the Colliers' Strike and the Outbreak in the Potteries' in J. Epstein and D. Thompson, *The Chartist Experience.*

ELPHINSTONE, Charles George Walker (1851-1931), *theatre proprietor,* Hanley.

CGWE was born in London in 1851, the son of James Elphinstone (q.v.). On his father's death in 1892, he became proprietor of the Theatre Royal in Hanley and in 1894 employed Frank Matcham to design substantial alterations, which included the installation of private boxes and increased seating. Matcham had been joint architect with C. F. Phipps of the re-building in 1887, by which the building was enlarged so that the stage of the new theatre covered the whole area of the old theatre. He also designed the Empire Theatre in Commerce Street, Longton in 1896.

CGWE also took over the circus in Tontine Street (on the site of the present Post Office) and when Hanley council ordered the wooden building to be demolished because of its unsafe condition, he again turned to Frank Matcham to design a theatre and circus combined.This was the Grand Theatre in Trinity Street, although it appears never to have been used as a circus, an adaptation which could be performed in twenty four hours. CGWE's connection with both theatres lasted until 1920. Both buildings were later destroyed by fire, the Grand in 1932, after becoming a cinema, and the Theatre Royal in 1949. The Grand was re-built as the Odeon cinema (now in Piccadilly—the former Gaumont and original Regent). The Theatre Royal was re-built in 1951 and was recently re-opened as a theatre after many years as a bingo club.

CGWE expanded his theatrical empire in Hanley with the purchase of the King's Palace Theatre (the former Alexander Music Hall) in New Street (now Goodson Street) in 1901 and later opened the Empire Picture Palace (now Piccadilly Arcade). He owned theatres in Keighley, Yorks. and Douglas, Isle of Man.

He was elected to Hanley council and by 1904 was living at High Grove, Trent Vale. He died there on 12 February 1931 and in the following year the house became St. Joseph's College.

Evening Sentinel 14 February 1931; *Staffs. Advertiser* 6 August 1887; *Staffs. Sentinel* 10 August 1898; VCH viii; B. Walker (edit.) *Frank Matcham : Theatre Architect (1980).*

ELPHINSTONE, James Henry Walker (1826/7-92), *theatre proprietor,* Hanley.

JHWE was born in London about 1826. He became the lessee of the Pavilion Theatre there but its destruction by fire forced him to return to his first occupation of acting. He appeared at the Royal Pottery Theatre, Hanley, in 1860, and was billed as the 'celebrated London actor'. He prospered, acquired the Liverpool Coliseum, and in 1873 became the proprietor of the Theatre Royal, Hanley (the former Royal Pottery Theatre) in succession to James Rodgers (q.v.). He rebuilt the theatre in 1887. The building was destroyed by fire in 1949.

In 1877 JHWE took Thomas Rogers, proprietor of the People's Music Hall, to court. JHWE complained that Rogers had put on a pantomime without a stage play licence. Rogers, a Hanley councillor who later ran the Alexandra Music Hall in New Street (Goodson Street) Hanley, was fined £90.

By his wife, who had died when the family lived in London, JHWE had at least two sons, Charles (q.v.) and James, both of whom became theatre proprietors. Charles bought the Theatre Royal after his father's death and James leased the Queen's Theatre, Longton, in 1888, after the death of Matthew Wardhaugh (q.v.). James (junior) was adjudged bankrupt in 1890 and blamed the high rent of the Longton theatre for his failure. He later ran the Lyceum Theatre, Stafford, but with little more success.

JHWE was living at Far Green Cottage, Providence Square, Hanley, by 1879, and at 161 Bucknall New Road, Hanley, by 1884. Subsequently he moved to the Isle of Man, where the family also had a theatre, and died at Douglas on 12 September 1892. He was buried in Bow churchyard, London.

P. Butters, *Stafford, the story of a thousand years;* Census 1881; Dir. 1879, 1884; *Staffs. Advertiser* 3 March 1877, 15 September 1892; *Staffs. Sentinel* 13 September 1892 (obit.) and Summer Number June 1906; *Theatre Royal Souvenir Programme, Re-Opening* 14 August 1951; VCH vi and viii.

EMBERTON, Hamlett (died 1890), *street musician,* Hanley.

HE was a native of Smallthorne, born about 1818. Details of his early life are lacking but in the 1880s he was a local 'busker' playing a variety of instruments. He wore eccentric clothes, decorated with ribbons, and was popularly known as 'Klondyke'.

He died in 1890 aged 72 in Stafford Lodging House.

E. Warrilow, *A Sociological History of the City of Stoke on Trent.*

EMBERTON, Thomas Isaac (1836-81), *earthenware manufacturer,* Tunstall.

TIE was baptised at Audley on 4 December 1836, the son of Wiliam Emberton (q.v.) and his wife Hannah, née Dean, When WE died in 1867 his sons Thomas and James carried on the business at Highgate Pottery, Brownhills until 1882. They produced the usual kinds of ware and also specialised in pottery for the Indian and Far Eastern markets. In 1871 the factory employed 47 men, 22 boys, 27 women and 27 girls.

TIE, by his wife Jane (born about 1837 in Smallthorne), had three children. In 1871 he and his family were living in 47 Princess Street. His wife had died by 1881 when TIE and his family lived in 30 Princess Street, with two servants living in. TIE was a member of the Tunstall Local Board of Health from 1855 and chairman in 1878/9. On his death his brother James (born 1839) carried on the business alone, and continued the firm until his death on 18 January 1885.

TIE died on 18 May 1881.

Census 1871; Dir. 1872; IGI Staffs; Jewitt; *National Index to Wills and Administrations; Tunstall Board of Health Annual Reports.*

EMBERTON, William (died 1867), *earthenware manufacturer,* Tunstall.

WE bought Highgate Pottery, Brownhills, in 1846, and manufactured both for the home and India market. He served on the Tunstall Board of Health from 1856 to 1867, and as chairman 1865-6. He was a treasurer of Wesley Place Sunday School from 1863 to 1866. He married Hannah Dean before 1836 and had two sons, Thomas Isaac Emberton (q.v.). and James Emberton, who carried on the business after his death. He lived in Sneyd Street in 1851. He died on 19 July 1867.

Dir. 1851; Jewitt; *Tunstall Board of Health Annual Reports; Wesley Place Centenary Souvenir 1799-1899.*

EMBREY, Godwin (c. 1832-90), *baker,* Fenton.

GE was born in Fenton about 1832. In 1881 he was in business at 2 Queen Street, Fenton, as a blacksmith, employing five men. Soon after he changed his occupation to that of baker, owning a bakery in Queen Street until 1892. He had a second bakery at 29 King Street.

GE died on 1 July 1890 and his son, Godwin Embrey, continued the business. By 1924 the two branches of the business had separated; G. Embrey was postmaster at East Fenton post office and was a wholesale baker, also in King Street. In 1953 the bakery moved to Liverpool Road, Newcastle under Lyme. The old bakery had become the By-Rite showroom by 1984.

Census 1881; Dir. 1892, 1896, 1926; *National Index to Wills and Administrations.*

EMERY, Francis (c. 1792-1857), *colour manufacturer,* Burslem.

FE was born in Cobridge about 1792. He had founded a colour manufacturing business in Cobridge by 1845, which after his death was carried on by his sons, Joseph (q.v.) and Robert Emery. The brothers parted about 1877. Robert built a new works in Waterloo Road to produce colours for sale in the Potteries and Joseph remained in the old works in Grange Street, producing colours for export outside the Potteries and overseas.

By his wife Mary, FE had at least six children, including F. J. Emery (q.v.). He was a lifelong friend of Joseph Andrew Blackwell, an agent for Lord Palmerston in central and eastern Europe. Blackwell, son of John Blackwell, pottery manufacturer of Cobridge Road, Burslem, wrote many letters to Emery. These were the subject of a special exhibition at the Gladstone Pottery Museum, Longton, whose colour gallery contains many samples from the Grange Street works.

Census 1851; *Evening Sentinel* 15 September 1982; *The Guardian* 17 September 1982.

EMERY, Francis J. (c. 1830-97), *earthenware manufacturer,* Burslem.

FJE (Francis G. in 1861 census) was the eldest son of Francis Emery (q.v.), colour manufacturer, and was born about 1830 in Cobridge. In 1859 while working for Furnivals of Cobridge he took out a patent for a method of decorating unglazed ware with ceramic crayons, and a second patent followed in 1865. FJE was in partnership with Edward Clerke, who bought Davenport's Lower Bridge works at Longport. FJE later manufactured at the Churchyard works, and took Bleak Hill works in 1879. By 1884 he was in financial difficulties and was bankrupt in 1894.

He was elected to Burslem council in 1879 and in 1890. He died at 143 Waterloo Road, Burslem, on 10 November 1897.

Jewitt; *National Index to Wills and Administrations; Oldham; Staffs. Advertiser* 14 April 1894.

EMERY, John (c. 1826-99), *musical instrument seller,* Hanley.

JE was born about 1826, the eldest son of John Emery, portrait artist and his wife Susan. By 1871 he was in business as a vendor of musical instruments and a professor of music in Broad Street, Hanley.

He was elected councillor for Hanley North Ward in 1870 and served as mayor in 1882. He was appointed a justice of the peace in 1884. He was a Roman Catholic and was forbidden by his church to continue his membership of the Menturia Lodge of freemasons. He married and had four children. He gave a statue of St. Joseph to Jasper Street R.C. church, Hanley.

He died at his home in Broad Street, Hanley, on 17 March 1899.

Huntbach; *Hanley Jubilee Souvenir 1857-1907; Staffs. Advertiser* 18 March 1899.

EMERY, Joseph Peter (born c. 1834), *colour manufacturer,* Burslem.

JPE, the son of Francis Emery (q.v.) and his wife Mary, was born in Cobridge about 1834, He and his brother Robert continued the colour manufacturing business founded by their father in Grange Street, Cobridge, in 1845. They ended the partnership about 1877, Robert built a new works in Waterloo Road while JPE remained in Grange Street. They agreed not to compete, JPE confining his sales to areas outside the Potteries and overseas markets. The firm continued until recent years, eventually becoming incorporated in the Fenton business of James M. Brown Ltd.

JPE was elected to the Burslem Board of Health in 1873, representing Rushton Grange. He attended a local Roman Catholic church. He lived in Edge Fields, Norton, in 1881 and at Beaconsfield House, Porthill, in 1892.

Census 1871; Dir. 1880; *Burslem Board of Health Annual Reports; Men of the Period* (HRL).

EVANS, William (1816-87), *trade unionist,* Hanley.

WE was born in Abergavenny. He came to Hanley and served an apprenticeship as a gilder, completing his term of years in time to be involved in the potters' strike of 1836.He was active locally in the Chartist movement but later became an outspoken opponent of Chartism. In 1843 Evans was instrumental in founding the United Branches of the Operative Potters a union which he claimed had about 2,000 members, and which consisted largely of hollow ware pressers. The union launched its own newspaper originally named *The Potters' Examiner and Workman's Advocate,* with Evans as editor. The paper helped to expose and thus to end the evils of truck in the pottery industry. Evans believed in emigration as a solution to the pottery workers' problems and used the newspaper to found the Potters' Joint Stock Emigration Society, registered on 15 May 1844. In 1845 there was a split in the Hollow Ware Pressers branch of the union over the use of union funds for emigration, and Evans came into conflict with Chartists who advocated home colonisation. The Society had acquired land in Wisconsin, U.S.A., and adopted the name Pottersville for the area. There was not much emigration from the Potteries, and the Society, beset by financial problems, administrative difficulties and legal disputes in the U.S.A., collapsed in 1851, and Evans' newspaper with it. Evans temporarily went back to Wales but returned to the Potteries in 1854. He was destitute and was given £20, presented in a silk purse, at the Swan Inn, Burslem. In 1864 Evans became editor of *The Potteries Examiner,* again financed by the Hollow Ware Pressers. He was replaced as editor in 1867 after controversy over his political views. Little is known about him after this date. He died, aged 71, in Accrington, in 1887.

R. Boston, 'William Evans and the Potters' Emigration Society' (Univ. of Keele thesis 1974); F. Burchill and R. Ross, *A History of the Potters' Union;* W. Evans, 'The Life and Death of a Working Potter' and 'The Art and History of the Potting Business' (with foreword by S. Hobson) in *Journal of Ceramic History* No. 3 (1970); H. Owen, *The Staffordshire Potter;* W. M. Warburton, *The History of Trade Union Organisation in the North Staffordshire Potteries.*

EYRE, George (c. 1816-87), *pottery artist,* Stoke upon Trent.

GE was born in Leicester about 1816. He trained at Stoke School of Art and at Somerset House, London, 1845-7 and was employed in the tile department of Minton's. In 1854 he moved to Samuel Alcock's works in Burslem, and later became art director at Copeland's. His reputation is for spirited figure drawing on various earthenware bodies.

By his wife Betsy, born in Kent, he had at least four children, of whom Peter became a potter's engraver and John was employed at Doulton's. In 1861 the family was living at Albion Place, Albion Street, Hanley. GE died in 1887 at The Villas, Stoke.

Census 1861, 1871; M and H; Turner.

FARADAY, Samuel Bayliss (1797-1844), *pottery manufacturer,* Fenton.

SBF was born in Birmingham on 17 December 1797, the son of the Revd. William Faraday, a minister of the Swedenborgian church. About 1825 SBF became a traveller for Charles J. Mason (q.v.), and was Mason's partner from about 1840. In 1827 SBF was convicted at Oxford of selling goods without a hawker's licence.

He married Anne Adkins in 1825. He helped to found the Fenton Athenaeum in 1839. He died in 1844 and his death is said to have contributed to the decline of Mason's fortunes.

R. Haggar and E. Adams, *Mason's Porcelain and China; M and H; VCH viii.*

FARAM, Henry Charles (1841-94), *ironmonger,* Stoke upon Trent.

HCF was born in Church Lawton, Cheshire, on 13 June 1841. His father became postmaster at Etruria and HCF was apprenticed to William Holdgate, ironmonger, of Church Street, Stoke upon Trent. For some years he lived in Chelmsford and Watford but by 1867 was established in business as an ironmonger in Glebe Street, Stoke upon Trent. From at least 1882 he was in premises in Church Street, the building still, in 1984, showing the initials HCF and the date 1882. In 1869 he was an agent for the French velocipede.

HCF was elected to Stoke upon Trent council in 1875, was alderman in 1886 and mayor 1892-4. He is stated to have initiated soup kitchens in the town. He was also important as a sports administrator. He competed in the first bicycle race at Stoke Victoria Athletic Club Sports in 1869, was the secretary of Stoke Victoria Athletic and Cricket Club, replacing J. W. Thomas, from 1877 to 1890. He attended the inaugural meeting of the Amateur Athletic Association at Oxford, in 1880.

He married twice, (1) a Miss Harris and (2) Elizabeth Garton Baldock, and had two children. In politics he was a Conservative.

He died at The Cliffe, Hartshill, on 5 December 1894.

Census 1871; Dir. 1872; H. P. Mawdesley, 'The Development of Athletics in the Potteries 1850-1900' (Univ. of Manchester dissertation, 1977).

FARMER, Florence A. (1873-1958), *teacher,* Longton.

FAF was born in 1873 the daughter of George Edward Farmer (q.v.). She trained as a teacher and became headmistress of Uttoxeter Road School, Longton, for nine years, before leaving the profession to join her brother, G. E. Farmer, in founding the Phoenix Steam Laundry and Dry Cleaning Works, Longton. She became a senior partner in the firm in 1927.

FAF was a lifelong socialist, and held a number of positions in the Stoke on Trent Labour Party, including that of president. Her interest in public affairs began in 1916 when she was appointed to the Stoke on Trent Board of Guardians. She was first elected to the council in 1919 and served continuously until 1945. She was created an alderman in 1928 and was elected lord mayor in 1931. Her chief interests were educational and she served on numerous bodies; she was vice-chairman of the governors of secondary schools and Hanchurch Open Air School, chairman of the Libraries and Museums Committee and supported voluntary organizations such as the Workers' Educational Association. She was a member and later secretary of the Stoke on Trent Ethical Society, secretary of the police court mission and a licensing justice. She was the first woman to be elected to the city council and the first woman magistrate in Longton. She was trustee of the Longton Unitarian church and of the Old Meeting House, Newcastle under Lyme.

She died at Blythe Bridge on 26 June 1958.

Evening Sentinel 9 November 1931, 28 June, 2 July and 4 July 1958.

FARMER, George Edward (1837-1915), *printer and stationer,* Longton.

GEF was born in Bewdley on 23 January 1837. He came to Longton in 1859, and established a business as a printer and stationer. For 25 years, until about 1889, he published a yearly almanac. One of his first activities in Longton was to help in forming a ratepayers' association. He took a leading part in the establishment of a People's Penny Library, which later was amalgamated with the Longton Athenaeum and was successfully carried on until the adoption of the Free Libraries Act. He was appointed registrar of births and deaths for Longton district in 1870. In 1875 he was elected chairman of the Sanitary and Fire Brigade Committee and later appointed a captain in the Longton Fire Brigade. He was connected with the arrangements that led to the opening of Queen's Park, and was chairman of several educational and other bodies. For several years he was a governor of the Longton Endowed School (later Longton High School). In 1870 he was elected to the council and in 1894 became mayor. He was appointed justice of the peace in 1896. In 1868 and 1880 he was secretary of the Longton section of the local Liberal party, and he acted as election agent for W. L. Bright in the election of 1885.

Unitarian in religion GEF inaugurated the fund for the erection of a Unitarian chapel in Stoke Road, Longton. He was a member of the Royal Victoria Lodge, Longton, of the R.A.O.B. for about 40 years, served as knight, Past Worthy Grand and Past Grand Secretary of the Order. The George E. Farmer Lodge in Macclesfield was named in his honour.

He married and had three sons and four daughters. One of the daughters was Florence Farmer (q.v.), later lord mayor of Stoke on Trent.

GEF died on 31 August 1915 at Stone Road, Longton, and was buried in Longton cemetery.

Dir. 1872; *Staffordshire County Biographies; Staffs. Sentinel* 2 September 1915.

FENN, Joseph G. (born 1850), *printer,* Stoke upon Trent.

JGF was born in London in 1850. In 1871 he rented premises at 10 Glebe Street, Stoke upon Trent, selling stationery, dress patterns, newspapers and printed dance tickets amongst other items. By 1877 he had a printing press and for a short time produced a newspaper *The Stoke on Trent News Sheet,* which had a circulation of about 5,000. JGF wrote editorials on local affairs. About 1886 he took over publication of Woolley's *Stoke Borough Almanac,* retitling it *Fenn's Almanack.*

He married Mary E. Hayward, born in Stoke in 1854 an assistant school mistress at Cross Street school. They had one son, Burt, who for a time helped in the family business but later joined the Indian Army and was killed on the Khyber Pass. JGF lived over his shop, and was recalled as a colourful character who would come out in a red smoking cap and velvet jacket to enjoy the morning sun. In 1885 JGF was elected president of the Angling Society.

He left his printing business to J. E. Boulton, whom he had taken on as an apprentice about 1877. Boulton's descendants still continue the business today (1985).

Census 1881; R and S.

FENTON, Elijah (1683-1730), *poet,* Hanley.

EF, son of John Fenton (died 1694), an attorney and coroner, was born on 20 May 1683 at Shelton Old Hall (destroyed by fire 1853). The youngest of eleven children he was educated at Newcastle under Lyme Grammar School and at Jesus College, Cambridge (B.A. 1704, M.A. 1706). Refusing to take the oath of allegiance to the Hanoverian monarchy he was thereby debarred from public or church office. He earned a precarious living as a schoolmaster, tutor and writer, helped by various patrons but hindered by his own habitual or constitutional indolence. His original poems were few : *An Ode to the Sun for the New Year* is perhaps the most celebrated. He published his first volume of poetry in 1717 and his tragedy *Mariamne* ran successfully in London for some time. Dr. Johnson, who judged him 'an excellent versifier and a good poet' also said of him that he liked to lie in bed and be fed with a spoon. Fenton was employed by Alexander Pope to help in the translation of the *Odyssey* into blank verse, and was responsible for Books I, IV, XIX and XXII. He produced editions of Milton's *Paradise Lost* and of the poems of Edmund Waller with a prefatory biography in each case.

He died on 16 July 1730 at the home of his patroness, Lady Trumbull, in Easthampstead, and was buried in the churchyard there. Alexander Pope wrote the epitaph inscribed on the tomb. Part of the inscription runs:

> Foe to loud Praise, and Friend to learned Ease,
> Content with Science in the Vale of Peace,
> Calmly he look'd on either Life, and here
> Saw nothing to regret, or there to fear;
> From Nature's temp'rate feast rose satisfy'd,
> Thank'd Heav'n that he had liv'd, and that he dy'd.

DNB: E. Harlan, *Elijah Fenton;* S. Johnson, *Lives of the Poets;* VCH VIII; Ward.

FERNEYHOUGH, Revd. William (born 1754), *minister of religion (Church of England),* Stoke upon Trent.

WF was born in Great Fenton in 1754, the son of a clergyman, the Revd. William Ferneyhough. He graduated B.A. from Balliol College, Oxford, in 1774. From 1775 to 1805 he was curate of Stoke upon Trent, parish church. He was appointed vicar of Aspatria Church, Cumberland, in 1793, and held this post until 1815, but was non-resident, preferring to remain in North Staffordshire.

He wrote poetry, including *Poems on Several Occasions* (1814). In one of these dated pieces WF is seen with friends dining at the Trentham Inn, eating local 'pig-pudding' and drinking Staffordshire ale. The poem *Trentham Park,* composed about 1789, is perhaps his moment of highest inspiration.

Carlisle Castle archives; information from Revd. R. A. Cason and Revd. G. G. Douglas; R. Nichols, *History of Stoke Church;* Simms.

FIELDING, Abraham (1854/5-1932), *pottery manufacturer,* Stoke upon Trent.

AF was born in Middleton, Lancs., the son of Simon Fielding (died 1906), an authority on dogs and poultry, who came to Trentham to work for the Duke of Sutherland. AF was educated at St. Peter's School, Stoke upon Trent, and at Thomas Hemming's school in Copeland Street, where, in 1870, he passed the Cambridge Local Examination. He served an apprenticeship as a colour maker at Blythe Colour Works, Cresswell, later becoming a partner in this firm. Their productions included majolica argenta. AF's father lent money to three potters to set up in business at the Railway Pottery, Sutherland Street. The business ran into financial difficulties and Abraham Fielding took it over in 1878, and expanded its operations.

AF became president of the Ceramic Society, and was a freemason. As a young man he had been an athlete, cyclist, swimmer and footballer and served as secretary of the Victoria Cycling Club, often travelling from his home in Cresswell to work on a penny-farthing bicycle. He was president of the North Staffordshire Harriers, and for some years was chairman of Stoke Football Club. He continued to ride to hounds, often three times a week, until an advanced age.

His only son, Alec Ross Fielding, played football professionally for Stoke F.C., Nottingham Forest and West Bromwich Albion. One anecdote told of him concerns West Bromwich club officials who came to the house to sign him up. They were received by the butler who informed them that Master Ross was out riding to hounds.

AF died on 23 March 1932 at Mill House, Blurton.

Information from D. J. Benning; Jewitt.

FINNEY, Samuel (1857-1935), *miner and Member of Parliament,* Hanley.

SF was born on 22 April 1857 at Audley, the son of Francis Finney and his wife Martha née Humphreys. He attended the local Primitive Methodist day school and at the age of ten began work at Talke-o'-the-Hill colliery, going underground at 12 years of age. He was involved in the trade union movement while still a young man and by 1888 had worked his way up to become president of the North Staffordshire Miners' Federation. In 1912 he succeeded Enoch Edwards as secretary and agent of the Midland Federation. In the same year he unsuccessfully contested the parliamentary election for Hanley as the Labour candidate, but in 1916 was returned unopposed as Labour member for North-West Staffordshire. After the boundary re-arrangements of 1918 he was returned as member for the Burslem division of Stoke on Trent. He retired from the House of Commons just before the general election of 1922.

In 1884 he married a Miss Bagnall and had four daughters. He was elected to the local magistrates' bench. He was an active Primitive methodist all his life, a local preacher in the circuit and as a young man had seriously considered training for the Methodist ministry. He died at Codnor on 14 April 1935.

Dictionary of Labour Biography. vol. 1; S and L.

FITTON, Samuel (born 1812/13), *flour miller,* Burslem.

SF was born in Cheshire about 1812. By 1851 he was living in Newport Road, Burslem. He operated the Port Vale corn mill in 1848. The firm of Fitton and Pidduck were still working the mill in 1924. A Macclesfield firm, Fitton and Son, probably related to Samuel Fitton, marketed Hovis bread about 1890.

SF was a Liberal in politics, serving on the Burslem Board of Health from 1850 to 1854. He may have been the Samuel Fitton who retired to Evesham and was living there in 1875.

The corn mill stood beside the canal at Bridge (late Milvale) Street, Middleport, and is dated 1844. By the 1960s most of the building, of five storeys, was derelict.

Census 1851; Oldham; VCH viii.

FLEET, George (1836-1908), *draper and furnisher,* Stoke upon Trent.

GF was born on 21 April 1836, the son of John and Hannah Fleet. He attended William Bridgman's Academy in Newcastle under Lyme. At the age of 14 he was apprenticed to Cotton's, drapers, of Crewe, and later gained further experience of the trade in London. In 1863 he set up in partnership with his brother, William, trading as Fleet Brothers, 22 High Street, Stoke upon Trent. About 1873 they moved to 44/5 High Street, adding a furnishing department to their shop. The partnership with William was dissolved in 1880, two sons, George and Herbert William, joined the firm in 1883 and became partners in 1896, and a third son, Sydney, was later also taken into partnership. The firm gained a reputation for the supply of high quality furnishings, and catered for the 'carriage trade'. It is recalled that male assistants wore black frock coats and were not allowed to leave the shop without their silk top hats. By 1900 the firm was responsible for the decorations for balls and assemblies at Stoke town hall, and were also arranging funerals.

GF was a member of the Church of England and of the Portland Lodge of freemasons. He also served as a poor law guardian. Fleet Brothers were agents for the articles produced by the Cripples' Guild of Handicrafts founded by Millicent Duchess of Sutherland (q.v.). GF supported the request to the Local Government Board for a loan to build an electricity works (opened in 1904) and he pressed for improved tram and road communications.

In 1863 GF married Elizabeth Poulson and by her had nine children. He died on 3 October 1908 at his home in Field House, Stoke upon Trent, and was buried in Hartshill cemetery. The flags on the town hall and parish church were flown at half mast on the occasion of his funeral.

Census 1881; Dir. 1851, 1873/4, 1889; *Staffs. Sentinel* 4 and 11 October 1908; *Stoke on Trent Electricity Supply Company 1910-39;* information from Mrs. M. Creyke, great granddaughter, and family papers.

FOLKER, Herbert Henry (1864-after 1923), *ophthalmic surgeon,* Hanley.

HHF was born at Hanley on 16 July 1864, the son of William Henry Folker, FRCS, and his wife Ellen Jane née Fourdrinier. He gained his MRCS and LRCP in 1889, studying at Charing Cross Hospital. Part of his training was as assistant house surgeon at the North Staffs. Royal Infirmary. Returning to Staffs. he became, first, assistant ophthalmic, then ophthalmic surgeon to the North Staffs. Blind and Deaf Asylum, and specialist referee (ophthalmic) to County Court Circuit 26. He was also certifying factory surgeon for Hanley district. He was a member of the British Medical Association and served as chairman of the North Staffs. Division of that organisation. He published 'Notes on 5 Cases of Toxic Amblyopia (lead)' in *Transactions of the Ophthalmic Society of Great Britain* 1899, and 'Nodular Opacities of the Cornea in Three Generations', *loc. cit.* 1909.

He married Eliza Georgina Ashworth by whom he had at least one child. He served as captain in the 1st Volunteer Battalion, North Staffs. Regiment, and was a member of Gordon Lodge freemasons. He lived 1890-3 at Bedford House, Hanley, 1894-1902 at 11 Havelock Place, Hanley and 1911-20 at Bedford House, Shelton. Entries in the archives of the Royal College of Surgeons of England cease after 1923. He had been awarded the O.B.E. for his services in the First World War.

C. Penn, *Staffordshire at the Opening of the Twentieth Century;* information from Miss J. M. Aspden, Library Secretary, Royal College of Surgeons of England.

FORD, Charles (1810/11-77), *engineer,* Hanley.

CF was born in Shropshire, about 1810, the son of Derby Ford, an agent. By 1840 he was in the Potteries, having built a factory in Hanley to manufacture stilts by means of metal dies controlled by a steam hammer. He took out several patents. In 1851 he was living in Mill Street, Hanley.

He married twice, possibly three times. By his second wife, Selena, he had a daughter Elizabeth. When he married again, in 1874 or 1875, he made a new will, benefiting his latest wife. Later he tried to revoke this will by codicil, but in 1877 his widow went to court and the original probate of that year was ruled invalid. GF also left instructions in his will that Robert Mansell, his works manager, was to continue at a salary of £300 per annum and to have a pension of £100 at his retirement.

Census 1841, 1851; Dir. 1851; *National Index to Wills and Administrations:* VCH ii.

FORD, George Beardmore (1833/4-1902), *architect and surveyor,* Burslem.

GBF was baptised at St. John's church, Burslem, on 26 January 1834, the son of William Ford (q.v.), builder, and his wife Emma. GBF may have been named after George Beardmore, architect, of Hanover Street, Burslem. He was articled to Henry Ward of Hanley. In his career GBF designed a number of the Burslem Board Schools, the Clowes Memorial Church (1878) and the Haywood Hospital (1887). He was valuer to the Wolstanton and Burslem Board of Guardians and surveyor to Wolstanton District Council. He was preparing plans to oppose Wolstanton's annexation by Newcastle under Lyme at the time of his death.

GBF was a member of Burslem council from 1877 to 1901, and an alderman from 1888. He served for two years as mayor.

He died unmarried, at Sidmouth House, Sidmouth Avenue, Newcastle under Lyme, on 10 December 1902.

Oldham; *Staffs. Sentinel* 11 December 1902 (obit.).

FORD, William (born 1810/11), *builder,* Burslem.

WF was born about 1810. In 1851 he was a builder, living at 50 Navigation Road, Burslem. By 1853 he was described as a brickmaker and by 1860 as a coalowner and ironmaster.

WF was elected to the Burslem Board of Health in 1859 and became chief bailiff in 1861. He built the Wesleyan Day and Sunday Schools at Swan Bank, Burslem, in 1850. By his wife Emma, whom he married by 1833, he had a son George Beardmore Ford (q.v.). In 1881 he was living at 200 Waterloo Road, Burslem.

Census 1851; Dir. 1853, 1860; Oldham.

FORSYTH, Gordon Mitchell (1879-1952), *pottery designer,* Stoke upon Trent.

GMF was born in Fraserburgh, Scotland, in 1879 and educated at Robert Gordon's College, Aberdeen, and the Royal College of Art, London. He was appointed art director of Minton's in 1903. He moved to Pilkington's Tile and Pottery Co., in 1906, also as art director. From 1916 to 1919 he worked for the Royal Flying Corps, then returned briefly to Pilkington's and from 1920 until his retirement in 1944/5 he was principal of Stoke on Trent Schools of Art. After retiring he worked part-time for Grimwades Pottery, Stoke on Trent.

His designs include five large vases, shown at the Franco-British Exhibition of 1908. His published works include *The Art and Craft of the Potter* (1934) and *Twentieth Century Ceramics* (1936). His daughter Maura, also an artist and a designer in stained glass, painted the murals in St. Joseph's R.C. Church, Burslem.

The Collector's Encyclopaedia; R. Haggar, *A Century of Art Education in the Potteries.*

FORSYTH, John Curphey (c. 1815-79), *railway engineer,* Stoke upon Trent.

JCF was born in Pembrokeshire about 1815. He became assistant engineer in 1845 during the building of the North Staffordshire Railway, engineer in 1845, general manager 1853-63 and consulting engineer until his death. His salary, after an increase on 1 July 1853, was £850 per annum. He died on 15 February 1879 at Marsh House, Newcastle under Lyme.

His younger brother, Joseph, designed Hartshill cemetery.

R. Christiansen and R. W. Miller, *The North Staffordshire Railway; National Index to Wills and Administrations.*

FOURDRINIER, George Henry (1766-1854), *paper manufacturer,* Hanley.

GHF was born in Lombard Street, London, on 11 February 1766 of a family of French Protestant extraction. The Fourdrinier family brought a French paper-making machine to England, erected a factory in Hertfordshire and after improvements established a factory at Ivy House Paper Mill, Hanley, in 1827. The firm made the tissue paper used by potters in printing copper-plate engravings and other coarser papers for wrapping etc. The factory was powered by steam. GHF's father patented a machine for producing paper from pulp in a few minutes in wide sheets and capable of endless extension. Competitors infringed his patent rights and brought him near financial ruin. He petitioned Parliament and eventually received £7,000 compensation, an amount considered inadequate in view of the benefit in reduced prices that his invention had produced. The firm also made paper-making machinery, which was exported all over the world, at their iron foundry at Eastwood Mill. In 1846 GHF patented an improved printing press, using steam, hot air or water, a paper-cutting machine, potters' steam presses and slip softeners. The family also made a small boat for use on the canal. Ivy House Mill was taken over by Thomas Brittain in 1855, after GHF's death.

GHF married and had a number of children. He died in Mavesyn Ridware, Rugeley, on 3 September 1854.

Huntbach; *Sentinel Summer Number* 1907; VCH ii and viii; Ward.

FRANKS (FRANCKS), Abraham (1781-1848), *optician,* Hanley.

AF, a member of a Jewish family, was born in 1781, the son of Isaac Franks, a Dutch hawker of lenses. Isaac Franks came to England in 1760 and helped to establish a Jewish congregation in Manchester. AF opened an optician's shop in Newcastle under Lyme in 1825, an important step in the establishment of a settled Jewish community in North Staffordshire. Hitherto Jews had been itinerant tradesmen. By 1836 AF was listed as optician, umbrella maker and clothes dealer, of 34 Hick Street.

AF died in 1848 and his son Henry transferred the business to Hanley. Abraham's brother, Jacob, who ran the Manchester branch of the shop, had 24 children, eight of the eleven sons becoming opticians. Jacob's grandson, Benn, was probably the Jewish child attending the British school in Newcastle and mentioned in G. C. Coode's *Report on the State of Popular Education 1861,* in spite of the requirement of attending at prayers, because his parents were impressed by the high standard of education at the school.

I. Down, 'A Modern History of Jewish Settlement in the Potteries' (Univ. of Keele, B.A. dissertation, 1984).

GARLICK, George William (c. 1836-1915), *bank manager,* Burslem.

GWG was born at Ryecroft, Aston under Lyme in 1836, the son of Joseph Garlick, a cotton mill manager. He entered banking with the Manchester and Liverpool District Bank at Oldham. He was appointed manager of Alcock's Bank, Market Place, Burslem, but returned to the Manchester and Liverpool when they took over Alcock's in 1865. He was branch manager 1871-98.

He acted as treasurer to Burslem corporation, Burslem and Wolstanton Board of Guardians, Haywood Hospital and Wolstanton Urban District Council. He was chairman of Kidsgrove Gas Co., and of the Aerograph Co. of Hanley and London. A Congregationalist he was instrumental in founding churches in Alsager and Wolstanton. A close friend of William Woodall (q.v.), he laid the foundation stone of the Woodall Memorial church in Moorland Road, Burslem.

In 1871 he was living over the bank, at 26 Market Place, Burslem, with his wife Anne, by whom he had three children. He died on 21 December 1915.

Oldham; *Staffs. Sentinel* 21 December 1915 (obit.).

GARNER, James (c. 1851-1905), *pottery worker,* Hanley.

JG, born about 1851, was for many years employed as a potter in J. and G. Meakin's Eastwood Vale Works, Hanley. He became a member of the brass band established by the Meakins, learning to play the cornet and clarinet. At the age of 12 he learned tonic sol-fa in the juvenile choir run by J. Powell (q.v.) in Burslem, and later learned to play the harmonium. He became organist and choirmaster at the Baptist chapel, Eastwood Vale, Hanley. He entered the chapel choir in the competitions run in Longton by a Welsh Congregational minister, and they won the competition in 1881 at their third attempt. The choir formed the nucleus of the Hanley Glee and Madrigal Society, which JG founded in 1882. JG was the first English conductor to win the principal prize at the Welsh National Eisteddfod. He was choirmaster of Bethesda chapel, Hanley, for over 21 years. By his wife Sarah Ann, he had five children.

He died at Franklin Street, Hanley, on 27 August 1905. A concert was held to his memory in the Victoria Hall, Hanley, on 21 September 1905.

R. Nettell, *Music in the Five Towns; Staffs. Sentinel Summer Number,* 1911.

GARNER, Robert (1808-c. 1890), *medical practitioner,* Stoke upon Trent.

RG was born at the Foley, Longton, in 1808, the ninth child of Robert Garner an earthenware manufacturer and his wife, née Middlemore. He received an early medical training at the North Staffordshire Infirmary and was the first student to enrol at the new University College, London, in 1828. After qualifying he went to Paris from June to October 1830, treating the persons wounded in the troubles of that year at La Charité. He practised in London for a short time, then in 1831 was house surgeon at St. Mary's Dispensary, Nottingham. In 1834 he returned to Stoke, where he set up a practice, being joined in 1852 by Michael Ashwell. He was a physician and consultant surgeon to the North Staffs. Infirmary in 1851-64 and also attended at the union workhouse.

He published numerous medical articles and books, the most important of which was *Eutherapeia* (1855). His main hobby was local history. His *Natural History of the County of Stafford* was published in 1844, with a supplement in 1860. He helped to found Stoke upon Trent Museum, various local libraries and other institutions and the North Staffordshire Naturalists Field Club (1865), the words 'and Archaeological Society' being added to the title in 1877, and the whole shortened to the North Staffordshire Field Club in 1897.

He married (1) Lucy Cotterill, daughter of the Revd. T. Cotterill, vicar of Longton and (2) a Miss Bishop, of Shelton Hall. His daughter Lucy, married Charles Lynam (q.v.). The family was living at Glebe Street, Stoke upon Trent, in 1837, at Brook Street in 1847 and 1851 and at Winton Villa, Shelton in 1859. RG died, aged 82, in 1890, at The Quarry, Hartshill, Stoke upon Trent.

M. W. Greenslade, *The Staffordshire Historians;* Simms; *Staffs. Advertiser* Aug. Sep. 1890; *Transactions of the North Staffs. Field Club* 1886.

GARNHAM, George (1816-73), *police superintendent,* Longton.

GG was born in Ipswich in 1816. He first worked as a labourer then served for six years in the Ipswich police and a further three years in the Suffolk police. He was appointed to the Staffordshire constabulary on 1 February 1846 and was promoted to the rank of superintendent in 1857. He retired on pension on 1 July 1869 but obtained further employment as a sanitary inspector for Longton in 1870 and as machinist, living in Vauxhall Street, Longton, in 1871.

He died on 23 November 1873..

Census 1871; Dir. 1870, 1871; Staffs. Constabulary Force Book. (SRO); *St. James' Church, Longton, Memorial Inscriptions.*

GEEN, Frederick (1858-1915), *accountant,* Stoke upon Trent.

FG was born at Audlem, in 1858, the son of William Henry Geen, a gardener, later registrar of Stoke (Hartshill) cemetery, and his wife, Elizabeth. The family moved to Stoke upon Trent in 1865 where FG attended St. Peter's (National) School. On leaving school he joined the audit department of the North Staffordshire Railway, then worked in several pottery firms before setting up as an accountant in 1884. In 1896 he became a Fellow of the Institute of Chartered Accountants. About that time the firm moved to premises in Liverpool Road, where it is still located.

Geen's first venture into public life was in February 1889 when at the request of the local ratepayers' association he challenged in election the sitting borough auditors, Broady and Stringer, who had been returned unopposed since the borough was incorporated in 1874. Geen replaced Broady. He stood for election to the council in the following year in a by-election, was defeated but won in 1891, when he stood as a candidate opposed to the scheme to erect a new gas works. His contention that alteration and extension would prove more profitable and reduce the rates was vindicated. He was mayor three times in succession, from 1897 to 1899. In 1903 he made proposals for the federation of Stoke upon Trent, Fenton and Longton but the idea came to nothing. He supported a second similar scheme in 1907, which eventually helped to bring about federation of the six towns when it was extended, though FG disliked the extension as he feared it would be a take-over by Hanley. He thus became a bitter anti-federationist, carrying the majority of Stoke upon Trent council with him. He carried his opposition to federation right through to the end. When he was defeated and federation was accepted FG ensured that Stoke upon Trent obtained the best deal possible and secured the erection of new municipal buildings which became the headquarters of the new county borough council. His opposition to federation cost him the mayoralty of the county borough but he was appointed deputy mayor and given the freedom of Stoke upon Trent. In 1913 he entertained King George V and Queen Mary to lunch in his home Cliffe Ville, prior to the formal opening of the King's Hall, in effect Geen's monument.

Politically Conservative he opposed any extension of municipal trading, defeating proposals to municipalise the water and tramway utilities, and thereby incurred the hostility of the Labour members of the council. He was twice asked to stand for Parliament but declined because of his many commitments, which were so many that one of his clerks worked full-time on them. For 25 years he was secretary to the North Staffordshire Miners' Relief Fund. It was this involvement that led to the final controversy in his life. During his mayoralty in 1913 when a serious coal strike occurred, he set up a national fund. He continued to operate the fund after his term of office was over, and some of the money was spent on improving Stoke upon Trent churchyard. Labour members demanded an explanation and FG was about to reply when he collapsed in the council chamber on 28th January 1915 and died.

In 1882 he married Jane Austin and had four daughters.

Staffs. Sentinel 9 November 1911 and 29 January 1915 (obit.); VCH viii; Victoria Theatre, Stoke on Trent, programme of play *Six into One*.

GIMSON, Joseph (1817/18-1900), *pottery manufacturer,* Fenton.

JG was born in Leicester about 1817. He came to the Potteries at the age of 18 to join his uncle, Abraham Kay Holmes), in the firm of W. Baker and Co. He founded his own business, Joseph Gimson and Co., potters, in 1861. He also had business connections with Wallis Gimson and Co., and Glebe Colliery.

JG was elected chief bailiff of Fenton 1865-7, and was an improvement commissioner 1862-73. He was first chairman of the Board of Health in 1873, and a member of Stoke School Board in 1874. A churchwarden in the local Anglican church he was also a superintendent and manager of the Sunday school for 30 years. He married Jane Pratt in 1855. By 1881 he was living at Great Fenton Hall, a widower. In 1892 he moved to Llandudno and died there on 29 December 1899.

Staffs. Advertiser 6 January 1900; VCH ii.

GITANA, Gertie (ASTBURY, Gertrude) (1888-1957), *music hall artist,* Hanley.

GG, daughter of William Astbury a pottery works foreman and his wife Lavinia, a teacher at St. Peter's R.C. School, Cobridge, was born in 1888 at 7 Shirley Street, Longport. At the age of three she moved to Frederick Street, Hanley, renamed Gitana Street in 1957 in her honour, where her mother kept a shop. By the time she was four she was a child prodigy, working with Tomlinson's Royal Gypsy Choir as a male impersonator. Her music hall debut as Little Gitana is said to have been at the Tivoli, Barrow in Furness, in 1896, when she was eight or at the Argyle Theatre, Birkenhead, when she was ten. She first sang 'Nellie Dean', the song for which she is chiefly remembered, when she was 16. She was one of the few variety artistes to succeed at the Lyceum Theatre, London, playing there in 1905-6, and then at the Royal Holborn Empire. Her repertoire of songs, including 'Silver Bell,' 'When the Harvest Moon is Shining,' 'Sweet Caroline' and 'Never Mind' made her popular, and the sale of her picture postcards raised several thousand pounds for comforts for wounded soldiers during the First World War. In 1926 she scored another great success in the musical *Dear Louise,* singing 'Let Me Call You Sweetheart.' In 1928 she married Donald Ross, the juvenile male lead in *Dear Louise.* She retired in 1938 but returned to the stage in 1948 to appear in a revival of old-time music hall *Thanks for the Memory,* presented by her husband. The show ran for three years and the company performed at the Royal Variety Performance at the London Palladium in November 1948. She died at her London home, in Haverstock Hill, on 5 January 1957.

R. Busby, *British Music Hall;* G. J. Mellor, *The Northern Music Hall; Staffs. Weekly Sentinel,* 11 January 1957, obit.

GLEAVES, Samuel (born c. 1834), *boot and shoe maker,* Burslem.

SG was born in Burslem about 1834. He was in business as a cordwainer at 47 Market Place, Burslem, in 1861 and was still there by 1880. By his wife Ann, born in Scotland, he had five children.

Census 1861, 1871; Dir. 1861, 1880.

GLOVER, James (c. 1797-1869), *brewer,* Longton.

JG, of a family from Mancetter, Warwickshire, was born in Hanford, Stoke upon Trent, about 1797. He was working a brewery in Sutherland Road, Longton, by 1829, described as an 'extensive ale and porter brewery'. In 1851 the business was listed as Jas. Glover and Sons. It had closed by the 1890s. JG also later owned a colliery, and the brewery and colliery together amounted to about one eighth of the total rate income of Longton.

JG was chief bailiff of Longton during the Chartist riots of 1842. He was elected mayor following the town's incorporation as a borough in 1865. He was Liberal in politics but withdrew from the Liberal party following an argument with the parliamentary election candidates over electoral expenses.

He married Catherine Cliffe on 3 December 1817 at Trentham church, and by her had at least six children. The family lived at Sutherland Place, Longton, in 1841 and at Sideway Villa, Longton, by 1851. He died in 1869. His sons, James and Alfred, were partners in the flint grinding business at Longton Old Mill and Upper and Lower Goms Mills. They were also partners in Longton Hall colliery and Longton Hall ironworks. Subsequently both served as mayors of Longton. JG's daughter, Catherine Lydia, married Michael Hoole Ashwell (q.v.).

Anderton; Census 1841, 1851; VCH viii.

GODDARD, John Hackett (1820-83), *colliery owner and pottery exporter,* Longton.

JHG, son of Thomas Goddard (q.v.), was born about 1820. He founded the firm of Goddard and Burgess of Longton, exporting white granite ware and other earthenware and china on a large scale to the associated company of Burgess and Goddard, of New York, U.S.A. Later he inherited the Glebe Colliery and an ironworks from his father and engaged in pottery manufacture as well as export. About 1880 he suffered heavy financial losses but was still able to leave £100,000 to be shared equally between his five sons.

JHG was a population census enumerator in 1851. He was one of Fenton improvement commissioners, mayor of Longton 1869-70 and for some years president of the Longton Liberal Club. He married Mary Anne Shaw, of Hulme, Longton, at Caverswall church on 15 January 1852, and had five sons, Henry Hesketh, John Shaw (q.v.), William Shallcross, Bertram Edward and Thomas Arthur. He was living in Park Hall in 1852 and in Stone Road, Longton, in 1867. In 1872 he leased Longton Hall from the Heathcote family. He died in 1883 at Southport.

Census 1861; Diary of John Hackett Goddard (by courtesy of Mr. J. Goddard); *Staffs. Sentinel* 9 November 1915.

GODDARD, John Shaw (1857-1939), *pottery manufacturer,* Hanley.

JSG was born at Park Hall, Longton, on 15 July 1857, the son of John Hackett Goddard (q.v.). He was educated at Uttoxeter Grammar School, Shrewsbury School and Owen's College Manchester. He learned potting from his uncle by marriage James Frederick Wileman. About 1881 his father bought him the business of George L. Ashworth and Brothers, earthenware manufacturers, Hanley.

JSG was elected to Fenton Urban District Council in 1895, serving as chairman from 1900 to 1903. He was instrumental in obtaining a gift of land from W. M. Baker (q.v.) for the building of a public library and fire station, and a gift of £5,000 from Andrew Carnegie for the library. He was president of the North Staffordshire Chamber of Commerce 1900 to 1904, a county justice of the peace from 1903 and a justice for Stoke on Trent from 1911.

At first he supported federation, but became opposed on the grounds that the draft order creating the new borough penalised Fenton financially, raising its rate from the lowest to the highest of the six towns. After federation he represented Fenton on the new county borough council, served as mayor 1915-17 and as alderman 1912-28.

He married Anne, daughter of John Basford, of Oundle, Northants., and by her had seven surviving children. The family lived in 1910 at Glebe House, Fenton, and in 1915 at Stoneyfields, Newcastle under Lyme. JSG died at Llandudno in 1939.

Diary of John Hackett Goddard (by courtesy of Mr. J. Goddard); Federation Newscuttings (HRL): *Pottery and Glass Record*, xxi, 1939; *Staffs. Sentinel* 9 November 1915.

GODDARD, Thomas (c. 1791-1872), *medical practitioner and pottery manufacturer,* Longton.

TG was born about 1791 in New Mills, Derbyshire, of a family believed to have originally been Huguenots evicted from France after the Revocation of the Edict of Nantes in 1685. TG and his brother Samuel were educated as doctors at the expense of their uncle Hesketh Goddard, of Stanislands, Alderley Edge. They set up in practice in Longton in 1814. TG later acquired interests in a pottery factory, an iron works and a colliery in Lane End (Longton). He acted as registrar for births, marriages and deaths, and as medical officer of health for Stoke upon Trent and Fenton. He was elected chief bailiff of Longton from 1851 to 1854 but declined an invitation to become mayor of the town after its incorporation in 1865. He was a borough and county magistrate, a director of Stoke and Fenton Gas Company and a trustee of the Newcastle under Lyme-Blythe March Turnpike.

TG married Elizabeth Palmer, of a family of timber merchants who were related to the Turners, the 18th century potters. He and his wife had four sons and four daughters. The family lived for some time at Bank House, Foley, but by 1861 had leased Park Hall from the Parker-Jervis family. In that year TG was living with his son William, a civil engineer born about 1832 who was involved in the construction of the Leek branch of the North Staffordshire Railway, and a grandson John Shaw Goddard (q.v.). Another son, Thomas, became curate of St. Mary's church, Stafford, and rector of Kingsley, Staffs. A third son, Samuel Palmer Goddard (died 1866), was medical officer of health for Burslem from c. 1850 to 1872. A fourth son, John Hackett Goddard (q.v.), became mayor of Longton.

TG died in 1872 and was buried in Caverswall cemetery.

Census 1861; Diary of John Hackett Goddard (by courtesy of Mr. J. Goddard); *Staffs. Sentinel* 9 November 1915.

GOODALL, Jeremiah (1811-70), *publican and coalmaster,* Tunstall.

JG was baptised on 3 November 1811, the son of John and Martha Goodall. John Goodall (died 1836) was the licensee of the Lamb Inn, Tunstall, and Jeremiah became the licensee himself in due course. By 1861 he also had an interest in Bank Top colliery.

JG served on the Burslem local Board of Health 1860-3. He died on 25 December 1969 and was buried in Newchapel churchyard.

F. Harper, *Bygone Tunstall;* IGI Staffs.; Oldham.

GOODALL, Samuel Alfred (1843/4-1917), *surveyor,* Fenton.

SAG was born in Nottingham about 1843. He came to the Potteries in 1867 on his appointment as assistant to J. W. Higginbotham, surveyor to the Fenton improvement commissioners, and he himself was appointed surveyor in 1874. He also acted as inspector of nuisances. When Fenton was constituted an urban district council in 1894 SAG retained his post. During his tenure of office Fenton cemetery (1887) and the sewerage works (1883-6, 1905-8), were opened. He also supervised the erection of the town hall and free library. He retired in 1910.

He married in February 1873, his wife Frances bearing him five children. He died at his home in Raglan Street, Fenton, on 19 February 1917.

Census 1871, 1881; *National Index to Wills and Administrations; Staffs. Sentinel* 24 March 1917; VCH viii.

GOODSON, James (1838-1911), *shoe manufacturer,* Hanley.

JG was born on 13 December 1838 at Armley, Leeds. His first job was in the tanning trade, then he worked for Seale, boot manufacturer. He came to Hanley to manage the firm's shop, in Market Square in 1868. He opened his own business in Parliament Square in 1891, later moving to larger premises in Tontine Square. He was elected to Hanley council in 1891 and served until his defeat, by only seven votes, in the 1904 election. He was also a member of Hanley School Board and Board of Guardians.

He attended Charles Street Wesleyan Methodist chapel and was associated also with Mill Street mission and Stockton Brook chapel. He was chairman of the Hanley Glee and Madrigal Society. By his wife Lydia, née Seanor, he had four sons and one daughter. Two of his sons continued the business after his death on 4 November 1911, and the firm continues today (1985).

Census 1871; *Staffs. Sentinel* 6 November 1911 (obit.).

GOODWIN, Benjamin (born c. 1863), *pottery worker,* Longton.

BG was born in Upper Hill Street, Longton, about 1863. He was the second but eldest legitimate child of seven children of Benjamin Goodwin and Caroline, née Cartlidge. The area in Longton in which the family lived contained some of the worst slums in the Potteries. Upper Hill Street had only two taps and two privies for 14 houses. In the immediate vicinity were eight public houses and two off-licences, which were open from six in the morning to eleven at night. There were also four pawnshops nearby. BG left school at the age of 11 to work as a moulder runner at Chapman's Pottery, earning 2s. 6d. for a 55-hour week. At the age of 14 he became an apprentice presser. In 1884, 'out of his time', he was dismissed so that he should not have to be paid at a journeyman's rate. He obtained another job, which he held for three years, only to be dismissed just at the time his wife was pregnant. Eventually he managed to find work in the growing sanitary ware trade in a factory in Stoke upon Trent, four miles away from his home in Longton. He had to catch a train at 6.23 a.m. and one back at 6.31 p.m. with a mile to walk to and from the station at each end. The weekly fare was one shilling.

To supplement his income BG became a part-time collector for the Royal Oak Society and also for a local doctor's dispensary. He combined all these jobs with that of secretary of the Pleasant Sunday Afternoon, organised by the Caroline Street Congregational church, Longton. He was also sick visitor for the North Stafford Provident Society.

BG's son, Albert Goodwin, born in 1890, became assistant general secretary of the Society of Pottery Workers in 1947. In his unpublished memoirs written in 1961 he describes his parents as 'obnoxious' and from whom he expected no kind treatment, but excuses this as a product of their trying to fit him for harsh poverty-stricken life.

J. Burnett, *Destiny Obscure* (1982); ex. inf. F. L. Harris.

GOSS, William Henry (1833-1906), *potter,* Stoke upon Trent.

WHG was born in London on 30 July 1833, the son of Richard Goss and Sophia, née Mann. He studied at the School of Design, Somerset House, London, then in 1857 came to W. T. Copeland as chief artist. A disagreement led to his setting up in business on his own in 1858. Initially he specialised in ivory porcelain and was awarded a medal at the 1852 International Exhibition. He perfected a method of improving the finish of jewelled porcelain and invented the body and enamels for the heraldic china by which he is best known today. He transferred his factory from the Cock Works, Leese Street, Stoke upon Trent, to the Falcon Works, Kirkham Street, about 1870. His sons later joined him in the business and he gradually retired from active management. He gave the vases for the terrace in Hanley Park.

WHG was an improvement commissioner in 1866. He wrote a number of books and articles and was vice-president of the North Staffordshire Field Club. He was a friend and the biographer of Llewellyn Jewitt (q.v.), a fellow of the Geographical Society and of the Royal Meteorological Society. His article on Stoke Wakes sports, entitled 'English Olympic Games', was published in the *Pottery and Glass Trades Review* in 1878.

He married Georgiana Goldswain in 1854 and had seven children. He died in Stoke upon Trent on 4 January 1906.

N. Emery, *W. H. Goss and Goss Heraldic China;* E. A. Goss, *Fragments from the Life and Writings of William Henry Goss;* J. D. Magee, *Goss for Collectors.*

GRAHAM, Venerable John Malcolm (1851-1931), *minster of religion (Church of England),* Burslem.

JMG was born on 1 May 1851 in Margate, Kent, the son of Prebendary John Graham, rector of St. Chad's, Stowe, Lichfield, for 40 years. JMG was educated at Rossall School and Brazenose College, Oxford, where he won an athletics blue. He graduated B.A. in 1875 and was awarded an M.A. in 1878. In the same year he became curate of St. George's church, Newcastle under Lyme, and in 1882 vicar of St. Paul's, Burslem. He built up a large congregation by his enthusiastic evangelising and with the assistance of his curate, Henry Venn Stuart (q.v.) who was placed in charge of a mission church. JMG was an advocate of open air services.

His health was affected by his work and in1901 he left Burslem to become vicar of Shrewton, Wiltshire. After seven years he returned to North Staffordshire as vicar of Trentham. He was appointed archdeacon of Stoke on Trent in 1908 and a prebendary of Lichfield Cathedral in 1909.

JMG continued to participate in sporting activities until shortly before his death. He held an exhibition of his own watercolour paintings at Hanley Museum in 1929, the proceeds being given to the North Staffs. Royal Infirmary. He wrote *Cup and Saucer Land,* which was published in 1908. He had served as a member of Burslem School Board from 1886-9.

He married Florence Louisa Coghill, daughter of Henry Coghill and there were three sons and a daughter of the marriage. He died on 2 December 1931.

Foster; Oldham; *Evening Sentinel* 3 December 1931.

GREATBATCH, Daniel (1780/1-1864), *engraver,* Stoke upon Trent

DG was born in Penkhull about 1780. He is listed in the directory of 1851 as an engraver, and appears in the section on Gentry, Clergy, Partners and Firms and Others, rather than under the heading Trades and Professions, and this suggests that by this date he was a man of some substance.

By his wife Anne he had four children, the eldest of whom was born about 1810. DG died on 9 July 1864, aged 84.

Census 1851; *National Index to Wills and Administrations;* Parliamentary Election Poll Book 1862.

GREATBATCH, Ernest Venables (c. 1840-1910), *potter's merchant,* Hanley.

EVG was born in Porthill about 1840. His early life was spent in Runcorn. He returned to the Potteries and set up in business as a potter's merchant, probably in Jasper Street, Hanley, about 1871.

His importance lay in his work as a pioneer in the education of the blind and the deaf. He and A. J. Story, headmaster of the Mount School, were largely responsible for new legislation making opthalmia neonatorium a compulsorily notifiable disease. He was chairman of the governors of the North Staffordshire Workshops for the Blind, which he had pioneered, chairman of the committee for Workshops for the Blind, Victoria Road, Shelton, and vice-president of the National Association of Teachers of the Deaf.

EVG was prominent in local politics as a Conservative, a member of Stoke upon Trent council and later of the county council where he sat on the education committee. He was a member of the Werrington Industrial School committee and one of the governors of the Potteries Pupil Teachers' Centre.

He was initiated into the freemasons in 1876, became a master of Menturia Lodge and of St. Michael's Lodge, Stone, and was appointed a provincial senior grand warden, together with various other posts.

EVG was a supporter of federation, and the first to submit the question of federation to the North Staffordshire Chamber of Commerce, of which he was president for four years, from 1898 to 1902.

Married, with one son, R. E. Greatbatch, he died at Jasper House, Jasper Street, Hanley, on 15 February 1910.

Staffs. Advertiser 18 February 1911 (obit.).

GREEN, Thomas (1798-1859), *pottery manufacturer,* Fenton.

TG was born in 1798 at Churchyard Works, Burslem, where his father Thomas was potting. The elder Thomas was judged bankrupt in 1811 and removed to Somerset, where Thomas junior worked as a traveller. He returned to the Potteries in 1822 to learn how to make bone china, working for Minton's and Copeland's. He became tenant of the Minerva Works in Fenton in 1833, in partnership with Richard Hassell and then with his brother-in-law, William Richards. The partnership with Richards continued until 1847. Four of TG's eight sons entered their father's business, two as travellers, one as an artist and one as a production and technical manager.

TG died on 12 January 1859 and his widow, Margaret, née Richards, continued the business as M. Green and Co., in partnership with the four sons. The freehold of the works was bought from the Broade family in 1863. The second son, Spencer, was in effective control of the firm and on his mother's death in 1877 he ran the business alone until joined by his two eldest sons, Alfred and Samuel. Spencer Green died in 1903. He had served as a Fenton commissioner in 1872 and as chairman of the local board of health in 1879.

From 1859 to 1876 the firm traded as Green and Co., from 1876 to 1889 as T. A. and S. Green, from 1889 to 1948 as Crown Staffordshire Porcelain and Co., and then as The Crown Staffordshire China Co. Ltd.

British Bulletin of Commerce 1954; Jewitt.

GRENFELL, Henry Riversdale (1824-1902), *Member of Parliament,* Stoke upon Trent

HRG was born in London in 1824, the second son of Charles Pascoe Grenfell and Lady Georgiana Isabella, eldest daughter of 2nd earl of Sefton. HRG was educated at Harrow and Christ Church, Oxford. He became a partner in the firm of Pascoe,

Grenfell and Sons, copper smelters and manufacturers. He was private secretary to Lord Panmure during the Crimean War and to Sir Charles Wood at the India Office. As a Liberal he was in favour of an extension of the franchise, a redistribution of seats and secret ballot. He unsuccessfully contested elections at Chester (1857) and Lymington (1860) before succeeding at Stoke upon Trent in August 1862. He was re-elected in 1865, retiring in 1868.

Later he became a banker in the firm of Morgan, Grenfell and Co., and in 1881 was appointed a governor of the Bank of England. He died unmarried on 11 September 1902.

Anderton; V and S.

GRIFFITHS, Alfred Vavasour (1847/8-1905), *medical practitioner,* Fenton.

AVG was born in Stone, Staffs., about 1847, the son of Samuel Griffiths, a draper, by his wife, Mary. He qualified as M.R.C.S. and L.S.A. and after working in Newcastle, Lichfield and West Bromwich he was appointed Medical Officer of Health for Fenton Local Board of Health in 1875, and to the Fenton Urban District Council when it was created in 1894, serving in this post until 1904.

He was vice-president of Fenton Conservative Club. His other interests included photography—he was president of Fenton Photographic Society —and he was a member of the North Staffordshire Field Club.

He married Deborah Thacker about 1875, and lived at The Limes, Glebedale Road, Fenton, where his initials AVG may be seen over the side door.

Dir. 1882, 1900; *Staffordshire Advertiser* January 1905 (obit.).

GRIMWADE, Leonard Lumsden (c. 1863-1931), *pottery manufacturer,* Stoke upon Trent.

LLG was born in Ipswich about 1863, the son of Richard Grimwade. He began his business life with his uncle as a dry salter in Ipswich. He came to the Potteries as a modeller but quickly moved to manufacturing. He was joined by his brother, Sydney, by 1886, and worked the Winton Pottery. The style became Grimwade's Ltd. about 1890. LLG went for a time to Australia but returned to the Potteries. In association with Brittain's, of Cheddleton, he devised a thin printing tissue with a detachable backing, known as 'Duplex' paper, which facilitated the handling of lithographic sheets. The invention helped to make the litho process commercially viable. He is also credited with installing the first continuous process kiln, in 1901. In this process, known as the Climax kiln, the ware was packed into iron cages on wheels. A serious fire at the Winton factory in 1916 led to LLG's proposing that Stoke on Trent should have at least three motor fire engines.

A Liberal free-trader LLG was elected to Stoke upon Trent council and was also appointed to the local magistrates' bench. He was secretary of the Potteries Association for the Promotion of Federation, founded in 1907, and published 160 favourable replies to a circular letter to leaders of trade and industry in his *Book of Opinions*. Questioned by counsel for Fenton during the passage of the federation bill through Parliament and asked where he lived LLG replied 'I sleep in Wolstanton but I live in the Potteries'. He unsuccessfully contested the parliamentary election in Hanley as a Liberal in 1918. He was a member of King Street, Newcastle, Congregational church.

He modified his free-trade views to some extent during the First World War, by which time his five factories employed 1,000 people. In December 1917 he printed a message from the prime minister asking for economy in consumption of food on reduced sized butter dishes, milk jugs and plates, which sold at one shilling each.

He married twice and had two sons and two daughters. His first wife, Marion, was elected to the Stoke Board of Guardians in 1897. He was killed in a road accident on 26 January 1931 and was buried in Hartshill cemetery.

Pottery Gazette 2 March 1931; VCH ii.

GRINDLEY, William Harry (c. 1867-1926), *pottery manufacturer,* Tunstall.

WHG was born in Stafford about 1867 and entered the pottery trade under Turner of Chell. He took over Newfield Pottery from William Adams and in 1891 acquired and rebuilt the Woodland Pottery. In 1908 he set up the Grindley Hotelware Company in newly-built works, in partnership with, first Alfred Meakin, and later with Sir James Fleming of Glasgow. His youngest son, Harry, and Fleming's son, both captains in the North Staffordshire Regiment, were killed in the 5th Battalion's attack on the Hohenzollern Redoubt in October 1915. WHG retired from business in 1921.

He was opposed to federation on grounds of the great dissimilarity of Longton and Tunstall; Tunstall men, he asserted, would never go to Longton to live.

He died on 8 March 1926 at The Cedars, Stone.

Federation Newscuttings (HRL); *Staffs. Sentinel* 9 March 1926 (obit.).

GROSE, William Marshall (baptised 1815-1890), *china clay merchant,* Stoke upon Trent.

WMG, son of John Grose, was born in Lanivet, Cornwall, in 1815, being baptised on 31 December of that year. He moved to the Potteries after 1843 and was in business as a china clay merchant in Wheatley Place, Hanley, by 1851

He was a Stoke upon Trent improvement commissioner in 1861 and later a member of the Board of Guardians and the Stoke upon Trent School Board. He was a member of London Road Baptist chapel, president of the North Staffordshire Baptist Association 1886-90 and he gave the site for and £1,300 towards the cost of, Fenton Baptist Church.

He married Deborah probably née Simpson and had two children. His daughter Mary married A. D. Stocker of the firm of Grose and Stocker. The family lived at 31 Glebe Street, Stoke upon Trent in 1872 and at 21 The Villas, Stoke upon Trent, in 1884. WMG died in 1890.

Census 1851, 1861, 1881; Diary of J. H. Goddard (by courtesy of Mr. J. Goddard), Dir. 1872.

HALES, Harold Keates (1868-1942), *shipowner and Member of Parliament,* Burslem.

HKH was born on 22 April 1868 the son of Lewis George Hales. He attended Chorlton High School, Manchester, and when the family moved to Burslem to take over a drapery business he went to Burslem Endowed School and later studied at the Wedgwood Memorial Institute where he met Arnold Bennett (q.v.). He was apprenticed to an earthenware manufacturer and at the age of 21 became a commercial traveller. In 1893 he travelled to North America and on his return set up in business in Burslem Market Place as a cycle dealer. The law requiring a motor car to be preceded by a man carrying a red flag was repealed in 1896 and a year later HKH bought his first car, a 2 horsepower Benz and opened his own motor agency, holding shows in the Drill Hall, Burslem. He also built a garage, reputedly the first in the Potteries. He opened a music shop selling pianos in the premises adjoining his cycle depot. In 1908 he acquired a disused pottery works in Waterloo Road and opened it as a roller skating rink, and in 1914 he bought the Coliseum Theatre, Burslem.

Among his many interests was ballooning and on one occasion he flew from Hanley to Manchester. He also bought an aeroplane in 1910 for £150. Occasionally he wrote articles for the *Staffordshire Sentinel* on ballooning and motoring. He had been elected to Stoke on Trent council after federation.

On the outbreak of the First World War he joined the army as an armoured car driver and machine gunner, giving his age as 39, and saw service in Gallipoli, Alexandria and elsewhere in the Middle East. In 1916 in India he met Gandhi and became his personal friend. He remarked of the Taj Mahal in Agra that it was a beautiful building 'but so is Burslem town hall if seen from the right angle'. Further travel took him to the Philippines, Hong Kong and Singapore before he returned to Burslem in 1923. He renewed his acquaintance with Arnold Bennett, claimed to be the original of Bennett's *The Card,* and asked for royalties. Bennett replied that Hales should pay him for the free publicity he had enjoyed. In 1929 HKH founded Hales Brothers Shipping House. In 1931 he was elected in the Conservative interest for the Hanley parliamentary division of Stoke upon Trent but was defeated by the Labour candidate at the next election, in 1935. In Parliament he spoke frequently on diverse topics including India, the car industry, herrings, profane language, flogging, Palestine and Japanese competition. As an M.P. he was instrumental in effecting the repeal of the law that forbade car owners to lock the car or to carry goods in a private vehicle. He commented that 'It was due partly to me that you can take your wife's shopping home with you in your car'. He also opposed the imposition of a speed limit. He presented a Blue Riband trophy — made by H. Pidduck (q.v.) for the fastest liner crossing of the Atlantic. He died in a boating accident on the Thames on 7 November 1942.

Staffs. Sentinel 31 March 1910; *Evening Sentinel* 8/9 Nov. 1942; H. K. Hales, *Road to Westminster,* and *Hales' Travels.*

HALES, Ralph (1819-75), *surveyor,* Burslem.

RH was born in Cobridge in 1819, the son of Lewis George Hales and Mary née Sale. He was appointed surveyor to Burslem Local Board of Health in 1850, and to Tunstall in 1853. He was also surveyor to Lawton and Newcastle Turnpike Trust. He was the surveyor for the Burslem tithe map of 1848. With his brother, William H. Hales, he occupied an iron foundry at Cobridge and was criticised by William Lee of the General Board of Health in 1849 for diverting the Waterloo Road sewer for use in his foundry boiler, blocking the sewer and causing an explosion of the boiler in August 1848 which killed two workmen.

He lived at Cobridge Cottage, Elder Road, with a housekeeper, Sarah Bull. He was a member of the Church of England and a Conservative in politics. He died, aged 56, on 12 August 1875.

Census 1871; *Daily Sentinel* 12 August 1875; Dir. 1875; Oldham; *Staffs. Advertiser* 19 and 26 August 1848.

HAMMERSLEY, Edwin John (c. 1839-1903), *accountant,* Hanley.

EJH was born about 1839, and established a business as an accountant in Hanley. He was elected to Hanley town council in 1871, was appointed alderman in 1886 and again in 1892 and 1898, and served as mayor from 1892 to 1894. He was active on a number of committees and helped to secure a court of quarter sessions for the borough. He was secretary of the North Staffs. Provident Association, and donated money for a public park and a fountain. He was one of the founders of the Gilbert Charity. He served as president of Hanley Chess Club and was a member of Hanley Bowling Club. He was made a freeman of the borough in 1898. He died unmarried on 17 October 1903.

Huntbach; *Staffs. Advertiser* 24 October 1903.

HAMMERSLEY, Ralph (c. 1830-82), *earthenware manufacturer,* Burslem.

RH was born in Burslem about 1830, the son of Ralph Hammersley and his wife Mary. Ralph Hammersley senior was a wheelwright in 1841, living in Woodland Street, Tunstall. RH became a manufacturer's clerk, probably working at the factory of Edward Challinor (q.v.). Later he operated Church Bank Pottery, Tunstall, then took over the rebuilt Overhouse Works, Wedgwood Place, from Edward Challinor, in 1870. He had a large export trade to the United States of America, Canada and Sweden.

He was a member of Tunstall Board of Health from 1864 and served as chairman 1879-81. By his wife Susanna he had two sons who joined him in the business, which traded as Ralph Hammersley and Sons until 1905. RH and his family lived in Rathbone Street, Tunstall, in 1851 and at Field House, Brownhills, in 1880. He died on 21 December 1882.

Census 1841, 1851; Dir. 1872; Jewitt; Oldham; *Tunstall Board of Health Annual Reports;* memorial inscription Wolstanton churchyard.

HAMPTON, Thomas (1836-1921), *brick manufacturer.* Hanley.

TH, the son of Enoch Hampton, was born on 15 December 1836 in Burslem. His family moved to Hanley when he was a child, and later he studied at Hanley Art School. He worked as a modeller for Livesley Powell and Co., until, in 1866, following medical advice, he started outdoor work in his father's business of E. Hampton and Sons, brick, quarry and potter's marl merchants, Eastwood and Mousecroft Works. He retired in 1905.

In November 1871 he was elected to Hanley council for the South Ward. He served twice as mayor, in November 1878, when he initiated the Hanley Charity Organisation Society and in November 1906, when his period of office coincided with the town's jubilee celebrations (1857-1907). He was a justice of the peace in 1880, an alderman in 1888 and an honorary freeman on 14 October 1902. He was chairman of the conference of local authorities which considered the issue of federation, and on the governing body of Birmingham University. He founded science classes at the Mechanics' Institute, gave money to enlarge the art school, persuaded Louis Jahn (q.v.) to become Hanley Museum's curator, and pushed through the building of the sewage disposal works, the outfall works being opened on 23 May 1907 while he was mayor.

His hobby was fly fishing which he took up at the suggestion of his friend J. I. Harris (q.v.). He was also a member of the North Staffs. Field Club. By 1881 he was living at 34 Lichfield Street, Hanley, with his wife Caroline and their daughter, Anne, who acted as his mayoress in 1906-7. Later he lived at Walton, near Stone and at Park House, Sandon Road, Stone where he died on 10 September 1921. He was buried in Christ Church, Stone.

Census 1881; Dir. 1879; Huntbach; *Souvenir of Celebration of Jubilee of Hanley Borough* 1907; *Staffs. Sentinel* 9 November 1906 and 12 September 1921.

HANCOCK, Jabez J. (c. 1825-76), *pottery manufacturer.* Tunstall.

JJH was born about 1825, probably the son of Sampson Hancock and Hannah née Nixon. He was in business as a pottery manufacturer, Tunstall, in 1871.

He was a member of the Tunstall Board of Health from 1855 and served as chairman in 1865-6. He was associated with Wesley Place Sunday School, of which he was a superintendent in 1860-1. He lived in Bank House, Church Street, Tunstall, in 1867. He died, aged 57, on 14 November 1876

Dir. 1871; *Tunstall Board of Health Annual Reports; Wesley Place Centenary Souvenir 1799-1899;* gravestone in Tunstall cemetery.

HANCOCK, William (born c. 1804), *brass and iron founder,* Fenton.

WH was baptised on 28 January 1804 in Stoke upon Trent, the son of William and Elizabeth Hancock. In 1851 he or his father was an ironfounder employing 52 men at High Street works, Fenton. The firm supplied lamp posts to the Fenton commissioners about 1855. William Hancock junior appears in the poll book in 1862. In 1863-4 the firm had a contract to supply the Stoke upon Trent commissioners with cast-iron lamp posts and it was reported that there was a long delay in delivery. In 1877 WH was living with his brother-in-law John Lockett at Great Fenton Hall, and was listed as a hot water engineer.

By his wife Elizabeth, whom he married about 1830, WH had at least three sons and one daughter. One of his sons, John W. Hancock, was secretary of the Fenton Athenaeum in 1862 and a commissioner in 1865.

Census 1851, 1871; Dir. 1851, 1867; Fenton Improvement Commissioners' Minutes; Poll Books 1862 and 1865.

HANDLEY, Ralph (born 1799/1800, died before 1862), *coal and iron master,* Fenton.

RH was born at Harriseahead, Staffs., about 1799. In 1851 he was living in Duke Street, Fenton, and listed as coalmaster, Railway Colliery, Fenton. By 1853 he also worked Wetley Colliery, Caverswall.

By his wife, Martha, RH had a son, William, born about 1833. RH had died by 1862 when his affairs were in the hands of executors. William was described in 1871 as of independent means, his income derived from coalmines.

Census 1851, 1871; Dir. 1851.

HARBER, Arthur Landon (1867-1926), *printer and stationer,* Longton.

ALH was born on 20 May 1867 at Longton, the son of Thomas Harber and his wife Sarah née Landon. He was educated at Dresden Grammar School, leaving at the age of 14 to be apprenticed to Wright, a Longton printer. He began in business on his own account in 1888, in partnership with Stephen Hughes, in Stafford Street, Longton. After Hughes' death in 1890 ALH continued the business, trading as Hughes and Harber, and published Hughes and Harber's *Longton Borough Almanack* from 1890 to 1913. He transferred his business to Market Street in 1897, and there published a magazine *East Asia.* In 1897 he became a printer to the Prince of Wales and in 1907 a printer to H.M. King Edward VII. He produced the *Souvenir of the Trade Union Congress 1905* when that body visited the Potteries. The business was turned into a limited company in 1907. Alec Webberley was a director of the firm before setting up on his own in Hanley in 1913.

ALH was elected mayor of Longton in 1906 although he was not a member of the council. He opposed federation and led the Longton delegation of traders at the inquiry by the Local Government Board in February 1907. His antipathy to the idea of federation did not prevent his printing the pro-federation *Book of Opinions* for Leonard Grimwade (q.v.).

He married Mary Webberley, daughter of John Webberley, a Longton pottery manufacturer. He served as president of Longton Cricket Club. He died at Rosslyn, Forsbrook, on 9 March 1926.

R and S; *Staffs. Sentinel* 9 November 1906; Programme of Victoria Theatre's production *Six into One,* 1968.

HARLEY, Thomas (1778-1832), *pottery manufacturer,* Longton.

TH was born in 1778. He was in partnership with John, George, and William Weston, 1799-1801, but from 1801 he worked on his own as an enameller, black printer and earthenware manufacturer. He was in partnership with Seckerson in 1818. He owned a potworks in St. Helens and a shop in Dublin.

In 1814 he was involved in a meeting which called for the abolition of the slave trade, and in 1815 was on a committee which protested against the window tax. He died in August 1832 at St. Helens, Lancs.

M and H.

HARRIS, John Thomas (1845-1908), *industrial porcelain manufacturer,* Hanley.

JTH was born in Berkshire on 1 November 1845. He became assistant to William Wentworth Buller, founder of Bullers Ltd., Joiners Square, Hanley and by 1906 he was managing director of the firm. He was Liberal in politics, and a Congregationalist by religious denomination, and was involved in the building of Tabernacle church, Hanley, in 1883. He provided most of the cost of installing electric light in the North Staffordshire Royal Infirmary about 1907, and was president of the hospital committee and of the Hanley Nursing Society. In 1897 he was appointed to the county bench of justices of the peace. He served as president of the Hanley Glee and Madrigal Society.

He had two sons, John Waugh and Gilbert Harvey. He died at The Redfords, Stone, on 8 December 1908.

Huntbach; *National Index to Wills and Administrations; Staffs. Sentinel* 8 December 1908 (obit.); VCH viii.

HARRISON, Thomas William (c. 1843-1909), *colour manufacturer,* Hanley.

TWH was born in Chelmsford, Essex about 1843. He was employed in Ipswich by the uncle of Leonard Grimwade (q.v.) before coming to the Potteries at the age of twenty. He later invited Sydney Grimwade, brother of Leonard, to work for him in Hanley. TWH worked for, and later owned the business of, John Gerrard in Bath Street, Hanley, manufacturing colours and glazes.

He became a member of the Hanley School Board in 1888 and as a member of the non-sectarian group he was elected chairman in 1893, at a time when the question of the provision of a Higher Grade School was in the balance. He overcame the objections of other board members including E. Duncan Boothman, rector of Shelton, and the school was built in 1894 in Birch Terrace on part of what is now Hanley Bus Station and later developed into Hanley High School.

In 1902, he proposed the construction of tenements as a means of providing better accommodation for the very poor and ridding the town of its slums. His idea was to build flats several storeys high around a central courtyard, which could be made into a communal garden. TWH was a Liberal in politics and president of Hanley Liberal Association. He belonged to the Congregational Church and was president and secretary of the Staffs. Congregational Union and a member of the national executive of that body. His religious views led him to become a passive resister to the payment of rates to aid church schools and although a magistrate, he submitted to a summons for non-payment of rates.

He married Marianne Green (possibly a member of the family which controlled Crown Staffs. China) and there were at least two sons of the marriage, Sydney Thomas and Arthur Cecil. The family lived at The Hollies, Northwood. TWH retired to Bournemouth, where he died on 20 September 1909.

Hanley School Board minutes; Local pamphlets vol. 38: *Municipal dwellings for the very poor — a scheme for dealing with the slum districts of Hanley (1902); Staffs. Sentinel* 20 September 1909, 21 November 1918.

HARTLEY, John William (1845-1942), *engineer,* Fenton.

JWH was born in Wentworth, near Rotherham, Yorks., in 1845. He was educated at King Edward's School, Sheffield. His father was borough surveyor of Rotherham and JWH worked with him for two and a half years before being apprenticed to Dodds and Sons, Engineers, of Rotherham. Afterwards JWH worked in Sheffield as a draughtsman. In 1870 he was appointed chief locomotive draughtsman of the North Staffordshire Railway, at the time that T. W. Dodds (of Dodds and Sons) was engineer. Dodds resigned in 1874 and JWH probably left about the same time. In the same year he started the California Works, Fenton, in partnership with Arnoux and Fanning as potters' engineers. He maintained a close relationship with the North Staffordshire Railway, supplying nearly all the rail chairs for the company. In 1886 he designed and built a gas holder one hundred feet in diameter for Fenton gas works. In 1891 he was building locomotives for the Glasgow firm of Kerr Stuart. He sold the California Works to that firm in 1892, and they continued there until 1930.

He left the Potteries for some time but returned in 1895 as works manager for Kerr Stuart before branching out once more on his own as an environmental engineer. In 1904 he patented a rectangular sewage distributor, an improved version of which was later installed at Strongford works, and elsewhere. In 1916 with his son Cyril he opened a new works at Etruria for the manufacture of railway chairs. This works later specialised in equipment for the sewage industry, and continues today as Simon Hartley. In 1913 JWH was involved in another company, Hartley, Causton and Richmond. A continuous kiln made by his company was installed at Empire Porcelain in Stoke upon Trent. JWH was a member of the Institute of Mechanical Engineers.

In 1881 JWH was living in Blurton Road, Fenton, with his wife, Teresa, and his three sons, Ernest, Philip and Cyril. There were also two daughters of the marriage. JWH had formed a cricket club in Rotherham, played football for Stoke and was president of Trentham and Stone Golf Clubs.

He died, aged 96, at Drysdale House, Stone, Staffs., on 11 May 1942.

Census 1881; *Evening Sentinel* 11 May 1942.

HARVEY, Charles (1779-1860), *banker and pottery manufacturer,* Longton.

CH was born in Longton in 1779. By 1799 he had a pottery factory in Stafford Street, Longton. He opened Harvey's Bank, Longton, in 1827. In 1851 he was living in No. 2 Longton Hall Lodge. He married and had a son William Kenwright Harvey. CH died in 1860.

In 1866 the bank failed and WKH fled to America. The failure set in train a string of local bankruptcies, including Bullocks, china manufacturers, and a number of other organisations lost money.

Briggs; Dir. 1867; *Staffs. Advertiser* 29 June 1860.

HASLAM, Edward Young (born 1812/13), *schoolmaster,* Hanley.

EYH was born in Newcastle upon Tyne about 1812. He came to the Potteries and took over a school formerly run by Revd. A. Smith in Albion Street, Hanley. He moved the school to Eastwood Cottage, Hanley, in 1836 and to Ivy House, Hanley, formerly the residence of Mountford Baddeley, in 1841. One of the assistants at the school was Charles Alfieri (q.v.). EYH owned property in Miles Bank and Great York Street, his name appearing in the rate books from about 1864 to 1874.

He was elected chief bailiff of Hanley in 1852 but declined to serve for a second term. By his wife Jane he had two children, Edward and Agnes.

Census 1851, 1861; Hanley Improvement Commissioners' Minutes; Hanley rate books; *Potteries Mercury* 20 March 1841; *Staffs. Advertiser* 8 October 1836; Townley.

HATTON, William (1835-c.87), *pottery worker,* Longton.

WH, born in 1835, learned the trade of a hollow-ware presser. At the age of 19 he enlisted in the Royal Artillery and was drafted to Corfu. From there his unit was sent to the Crimea where he fought at Balaclava and Sebastopol, and served until the end of the war unscathed. His unit returned to England and was later sent to India where WH fought in the Indian Mutiny. His experiences affected him so much that he took to drink and was discharged from the army. On his return to England he found work as a miner in Yorkshire for three years, then, back in the Potteries, became a looker to ware. In 1873 he married a widow with one child. By 1887, affected by bronchitis, he was in the workhouse, and died not long after.

Farmer's New Borough Almanack, 1887.

HAWES, Robert (1817-80), *minister of religion (Church of England),* Tunstall

RH was born on 12 January 1817 at Portsea, Hants., the son of John Hawes, shipwright, and his wife Mary. RH studied for the ministry and served at Jainpur, India, from 1841-9, as a missionary and chaplain. He returned to England and became curate at Walsall 1849-53 and vicar of Tunstall 1853-80. He was admitted sizar at St. John's College, Cambridge, in 1855, and was awarded the degrees of B.D. in 1865 and D.D. in 1875.

He acted as chaplain to the Earl of Shrewsbury. He married and had a daughter Margaret Markland Hawes. He died on 30 April 1880.

F. Harper, *Bygone Tunstall;* Venn.

HAWLEY, Felix Hulme (1819-91), *pottery manufacturer and colliery owner,* Longton.

FHH was born in Longton on 9 September 1819, the eldest son of John Hawley and Frances née Hulme. He later owned Mossfields and Bentilee Colliery Company and with his brother Robert operated Foley Potteries, Fenton, established in 1842, making earthenware.

In 1864 he was elected chief bailiff of Longton and later was created an alderman. He belonged to Bethesda Methodist New Connexion chapel. By his wife Charity née Barker, whom he married in Stone in 1844, he had six children. The family lived in Summer Row, Trentham Park, from at least 1861. FHH was one of the enumerators of the 1861 population census of Longton.

He died on 10 January 1891 and was buried in Longton cemetery.

Census 1861; Dir. 1882; IGI Staffs; Jewitt; memorial inscription in Longton cemetery.

HAWLEY, George Hulme (1839-90), *town clerk,* Longton.

GHH was born in 1839, the youngest son of John Hawley and Frances née Hulme. He trained as a solicitor and became a partner in the firm of Clarke and Hawley, solicitors. He acted as clerk to the Longton borough magistrates, to the burial board and to the commissioners to administer oaths. From about 1873 he was town clerk of Longton, a post he held for 18 years. He was also clerk to the governors of Longton Endowed Schools (Browne's Charity) and solicitor to the County of Staffordshire Permanent Benefit Building Society. His offices were in Portland Chambers, Church Street. He lived at Hawley House, Blythe Bridge, by 1873.

His main leisure interest was music. He played the euphonium and founded Longton's brass band, called the Borough Prize Band. He organised competitions which attracted the best bands from the north of England. Havergal Brian (q.v.) called him 'the musical town clerk'.

By his wife Elizabeth he had three sons, Cuthbert, George and Ernest. George, born in 1867, became clerk to the borough magistrates, a post he held from 1890 for the next 55 years. Like his father, George was musical, played the trumpet, and formed an orchestra of which Havergal Brian was the pianist and musical arranger for ten years. George was still alive in 1949 his interest in music unabated, and at the age of 82 playing the banjo.

Census 1861, 1881; Dir. 1872; H. Brian, 'The Faraway Years' in *Musical Opinion* January 1949; *Report of an Inquiry into the case of Cecil Basil Whelan June 4, 1945* (HRL).

HAWLEY, Robert Hulme (baptised 1831-90), *pottery manufacturer and colliery proprietor,* Longton.

RHH was baptised on 6 November 1831 at Longton Methodist New Connexion church, the third son of John Hawley and Frances née Hulme. He managed the Foley Works which he owned with his brother Felix, and had a share in the Hawley and Bridgwood colliery.

In 1871 he was elected a councillor for St. John's Ward, Longton, was appointed alderman for St. Paul's ward in 1875 and served as mayor in 1876. He was appointed chief magistrate in the borough in 1875.

He married and had four children. He was Anglican by religion and Conservative in politics, serving as president of the local Conservative Association. He died of gout on 3 July 1890 at the home of his son at Tower Bridge, London.

Census 1861; Dir. 1872; IGI Staffs; Jewitt; *Staffs. Sentinel* 5 July 1890.

HAWLEY, Thomas (1842-1928), *grocer,* Longton.

TH was born in Fenton in 1842. His father died when TH was two years old, leaving his mother to bring up eight children. TH was educated at Methodist Sunday schools at Mount Tabor, Fenton, and Mount Zion, Longton. He went to work in a pottery factory before he was eight years old, and was employed at various factories, spending the longest time at Shufflebotham's.

In 1862 he married Mary Walker. She had a grocery shop in Carlisle Street, Dresden, which became the family home for many years. TH left the pottery industry and joined his wife in keeping the shop. They had 15 children of whom nine survived.

He was elected to the Dresden Local Board of Health and on that body's annexation by Longton in 1884 TH was elected to Longton borough council, on which he served for twelve years. He was a supporter of the temperance movement and founded the first Band of Hope in Longton. In religion TH had become a Unitarian, and wrote a pamphlet for his children entitled *An Open Letter to my Children on how I became and why I remain a Unitarian.* He published his reminiscences of life in Fenton and Longton in 1908. A generous character with a dry sense of humour he was always to be found in his shop wearing an embroidered cap.

He died in November 1928 and was buried in Longton cemetery.

T. Hawley, *Sketches of Pottery Life and Character* (reprinted in 1979 by Stafford County Library with an introduction and biographical note by D. Beard); *Staffs. Sentinel* 28 November 1928.

HAYNES, W. B. (died about 1941), *minister of religion (Baptist),* Stoke upon Trent.

WBH was minister at London Road Baptist church from 1903 to 1914, having previously served at Stafford for 16 years. He was imprisoned in 1904 for refusing to pay the education element in the rate as a protest against the Education Act of 1902, which, some nonconformists claimed, would subsidise Anglican and Roman Catholic schools and teaching from the rates. WBH was released fromn prison on 6 December 1904, one of a small number of persons in the area who suffered similarly for their convictions.

London Road Baptist Chapel 1841-1941; Staffs. Advertiser various issues in December 1904; J. H. Y. Briggs, *A Hundred Years and More: Baptists in Newcastle under Lyme;* VCH viii.

HAYWARD, (Sir) Frederick (1876-1944), *Co-operative Society official,* Burslem.

FH was born in Burslem in February 1876, the second child of James Hayward, a potter and a prominent member of the Pottery Workers' Society. FH was educated at the Central Board School, under C. F. Gregory. He started work as a jigger turner at the age of ten, then worked in a clothing shop and eventually was apprenticed to a biscuit placer. He followed the last occupation until 1904, soon after which he became full-time secretary of Burslem Co-operative Society. He had helped to found the Society in 1901 and was its honorary secretary 1902-5 and managing secretary 1920-35. He was a member of the National Executive of the Co-operative Union and chairman of the Co-operative Congress in 1919.

FH was elected to the Wolstanton and Burslem Board of Guardians in 1904 and was chiefly instrumental in securing the adoption of the Sheffield Scattered Home System, whereby workhouse children were transferred to small homes in the care of a foster-mother. A supporter of federation he was elected to the new Stoke upon Trent council in 1910, was created alderman in 1913 and served as mayor in 1926. In politics he supported the Labour party and favoured parliamentary representation for the co-operative movement.

He was knighted in 1931. He died on 19 December 1944.

Evening Sentinel 22 December 1944: Oldham.

HAYWOOD, Howard (c. 1791-1874), *brick and tile manufacturer,* Burslem.

HH was born about 1791, the son of Daniel and Sarah Haywood. He and his brother, Richard Howard Haywood, operated a brick and tile factory in Brownhills for some years before 1843. The smoke from this factory prompted Ward's criticism in his *History of the Borough of Stoke upon Trent.*

HH by his will proved in 1875 left £30,000 to be applied to the sick poor of Burslem and immediate neighbourhood, and the Howard and Richard Haywood Hospital was built in Moorlands Road, Burslem, in 1886-7. This building was replaced in 1927-30, and by 1963 was used for the care of chronic invalids.

The brothers built Brownhills Villa in the late 1830s and HH died there, unmarried, in 1874 or early 1875.

G. E. Lowndes, *Haywood Hospital 1880-1948;* IGI Staffs.; VCH viii; Ward; E. Warrilow, *A Sociological History of the City of Stoke on Trent.*

HEAP, Charles Swinnerton (1847-1900), *musician,* Hanley.

CSH was born in Birmingham on 10 April 1847 and educated at the King Edward Grammar School, Birmingham. From an early age he was trained by his father to be a musician and played the violin professionally at the age of 12. He won the Mendelssohn scholarship in 1865 and studied piano, organ, composition and solo singing in Leipzig. On his return to England he studied with Dr. Best, the organist, at Liverpool. CSH was awarded a B.Mus. in 1871 and a D.Mus. (Cambridge) in 1872. He conducted the Birmingham Philharmonic Union for 19 years and was involved in the formation of a number of other similar societies in the Midlands. In October 1876 a public meeting under the chairmanship of R. Minton Taylor decided to form a Stoke Philharmonic Society and CSH was invited to become its conductor. He hired a room in Medina's music shop near Stoke church from which he organised the society. The first of a regular series of concerts was held in Stoke Town Hall on 17 April 1877. One of the many items performed by the society was Heap's own composition, Fair Rosamund.

Under CSH the North Staffordshire Triennial Music Festivals assumed a national as well as local importance. The first festival was held in the Victoria Hall, Hanley in 1888, and there were five festivals in all. There were two first performances during the festivals: in 1896 Elgar conducted his oratorio *King Olaf,* and in 1899 Coleridge Taylor conducted *The Death of Minnehaha.*

An Illustrated Souvenir of Hanley Borough Jubilee; R. Nettel, *Music in the Five Towns; North Staffordshire Music—a social experiment;* and *The Englishman makes Music.*

HEATH, Arthur Howard (1856-1930), *Member of Parliament,* Hanley.

AHH was born in 1856, the second son of Robert Heath (q.v.) and Anne née Beech. Robert Heath was the owner of Biddulph Valley collieries, and AHH and his two brothers, Robert (q.v.) and James (q.v.) inherited the business as joint partners in 1893. He was chairman of Birchenwood Colliery Co. Ltd. in 1925.

AHH was educated at Clifton College and at Brasenose College, Oxford. As a young man he was prominent as a cricketer. He played for Trentham C.C. and Norton C.C. in 1883, for Staffs. County from 1883 and was captain from 1885. He played for England v. Australia at the County Grounds, Stoke upon Trent, in 1886. He was first president of the North Staffs. Cricket League in 1889, secretary of Staffs. County C.C. 1887-9 and 1893, and treasurer in 1898.

In 1892 AHH contested the Hanley parliamentary constituency as a Conservative but was defeated by W. Woodall, and suffered a similar reverse at his hands in 1895. He won the seat against Enoch Edwards, however, in 1900 but was defeated by Edwards in 1906. He was returned for the Leek division in 1910 but retired from politics in that year.

AHH served as president of the North Staffs. Royal Infirmary 1909-12 and was also president of the North Staffs. Institute of Mining Engineers and the Staffordshire Beekeepers' Association. He was chairman of Newcastle Endowed Schools and president of the Biddulph Conservative Club.

Married, with one son and one daughter, he died in London on 21 April 1930.

Staffs Advertiser 26 April 1930; *Staffs. Sentinel* numerous issues 1883-98; V and S.

HEATH, Charles (born 1824), *pottery manager,* Hanley.

CH was baptised at Bethesda Methodist New Connexion chapel on 1 August 1824, the son of William Heath and Nancy née Melkin. In 1851 his occupation was described as potter's presser and in 1871 as potter's foreman.

CH was elected clerk to Shelton Highways Board about 1850. He opposed the establishment of a local board of health in Hanley on the grounds that it would cause an increase in the rates which working men could not afford. Similarly he was opposed to the institution of a free library in Hanley in 1864, arguing that he had been a Sunday school teacher for 20 years, had built up his own collection of books, and that others could do likewise or join the Mechanics' Institute. Nor did he approve the idea of municipal help to the School of Art, stating that this would help only pottery manufacturers. He was elected to Hanley council in November 1868 and served until he was defeated in the election of 1871.

CH married twice, by his first wife, Ann Green, having four children, and marrying his second wife, Annie Finney, on 13 April 1873. He lived in 1851 in Hope Street and in 1871 in Great York Street, Hanley, in which road he owned four houses between 1862 and 1894. His name does not appear in the local rate books after 1894.

Census 1871; Hanley Rate Books; Townley.

HEATH, Robert (1816-93), *iron and coal master, Member of Parliament,* Tunstall.

RH was born in Sneyd House, Burslem, in August 1816, the son of Robert Heath and Jane née Plant. He was educated at Dr. Magnus' School, Etruria Hall. He succeeded his father as manager of Kinnersley's Clough Hall Ironworks and Colliery. From 1854 to 1856 he was in partnership with Francis Stanier at Silverdale Ironworks. In 1857 he leased the Childerplay coalmines at Biddulph (now Victoria Pit), from John Bateman, and an estate at Newchapel owned by John Kent. He sank ironstone pits at Packmoor, and by 1870 had acquired the Goldendale and Ravensdale Ironworks, and was also working Brownhills and Grange Collieries. By 1873 his extensive holdings included 28 coal and ironstone pits, eight blast furnaces, 154 puddling and ball furnaces and 14 rolling mills. He was involved with his workpeople in industrial disputes on a number of occasions. He retired from business in 1886 and was succeeded by his four surviving sons. In August 1928 the company was put in the hands of receivers.

RH was president of Newcastle under Lyme Conservative Club from its inception in 1867. He stood successfully as a Conservative in the parliamentary election for Stoke upon Trent in 1874 but was defeated at the general election of 1880. From 1869 he was a county magistrate, from 1874 a deputy lieutenant and he served as high sheriff of Staffordshire in 1885. Later he represented Biddulph on Staffordshire county council. He had served as chief bailiff of Tunstall in 1871 and on the Tunstall Board of Health from 1871 to 1875.

He married Anne Beech, daughter of James Beech, earthenware manufacturer, of Sandyford, on 30 November 1843, and by her had five sons and four daughters. The family lived first at Brampton Hill, Newcastle under Lyme and then at Biddulph Grange, which RH bought in April 1873. He died in Harrogate, Yorkshire, on 7 November 1893, leaving £320,045 in his will. There are memorials to him in Biddulph and Knypersley churches.

Adams, *Notes;* Dir. 1872; *Guide to the Iron Trade of Great Britain 1873; Staffs. Advertiser* 14 October 1893 (obit.).

HEATH, William (1827-1903), *colliery owner,* Burslem.

WH was born in Talke-o'-the-Hill in 1827 and began working in a local mine at the age of seven. In 1842 he moved to Congleton where his parents had a small farm. Some time later he returned to the Potteries and after working at Bank Top colliery, Jackfield, he became manager and later part-owner of Stanfield Colliery. In 1875 Charles May (q.v.) and his brother Joshua, were declared bankrupt, and WH took over their mine at Sneyd, making it eventually one of the most prosperous in North Staffordshire. He ended the butty system of small contractors and improved working conditions generally. Shortly before his death he became company chairman. His firm also owned a brickworks and produced at one time 10,000 glazed bricks a day.

WH was a member of Burslem council and of the local Congregational church. He served as president of the North Staffordshire Institute of Mining. He died on 30 March 1903 at his home, Edgefields, Stockton Brook, leaving a widow, four sons and three daughters. He was buried in Burslem cemetery.

Men of the Period; (HRL); *Staffs. Advertiser* 4 April 1903 (obit.); *Staffs. Sentinel* 26 April 1890; VCH viii.

HEATH, William (1856/7-1915), *company secretary,* Hanley.

WH was born about 1856 in Hanley. He was apprenticed to George Ellis, a builder, of Hanley, and later worked for his uncle also a builder, in Southport. On his return to Hanley he continued in the building trade and also ran a hotel. He was secretary of the North Staffordshire Billposting Co. at the time of his death.

WH became a leading sports official locally. He started as a football referee and also reported on matches for the *Staffordshire Sentinel.* In 1886 he persuaded the Staffs. Football Association to start a Staffordshire junior cup competition. He was secretary of the Staffs. F.A. from 1892 to his death. Through his efforts three F.A. cup semi-finals were staged at Stoke. He helped establish Stoke and Port Vale as limited companies. He proposed that a maximum wage of £4 per week be paid, and that F.A. cup matches gate money be shared.

He died early in February 1915, aged 58, at his home in Eastwood Place, Hanley, leaving a widow, Lavinia.

Staffs. Sentinel 20 February 1915; gravestone in Hanley cemetery.

HEATHCOTE, Richard Edensor (1780-1850), *member of Parliament,* Stoke upon Trent.

REH was born at Longton Hall in 1780. He was the eldest of ten children of Sir John Edensor Heathcote by Anne née Gresley. He was educated at Christ Church, Oxford, B.A. 1803 and M.A. 1805. He was member of Parliament for Coventry 1826-30. He contested Stoke upon Trent unsuccessfully in 1832, but was returned in the uncontested election of 1835. He accepted the Chiltern Hundreds in January 1836. A Liberal in politics, he favoured Catholic emancipation.

He married three times (1) in 1808 Emma Sophia Gresley (died 1813), by whom he had four children; (2) in 1815 Lady Elizabeth Keith Lindsay (died 1825) by whom he had three children and (3) Susanna Cooper, by whom he had three children. He and his family lived at Longton Hall (extensively altered in 1777/8), where it is believed that the stable block occupied the site of a former porcelain factory. REH remodelled Longton Hall at a cost of over £5,000 in 1824-7. The family ceased to live there by about 1840 and in 1847 REH leased the hall to Charles Harvey, banker, from Longton. From 1853 it was sub-let to a number of other tenants and in 1872 leased for 14 years to John Hackett Goddard (q.v.). On J. H. E. Heathcote's death in 1928 the hall was sold to Messrs J. and F. Wotton, and was demolished in 1939.

REH died at Geneva on 3 May 1850.

Anderton; E. D. Heathcote, *The Family of Heathcote;* Stenton; VCH viii.

HEBERT, Charles (died 1890), *minister of religion (Church of England),* Burslem

CH graduated B.A. from Trinity Coll., Cambridge, 1831, M.A. 1834, B.D. 1872, D.D. 1874. He was appointed vicar of Lechdale 1844-51, rector of St. John's church Burslem 1850-8, rector of Lowestoft 1862-72 and Vicar of Ambleside 1875-8. He wrote a number of articles on theological and other matters. He died at 1 Marine Terrace, Silleth, Cumberland, on 23 June 1890.

F. Boase, *Modern English Biography;* VCH viii.

HEMMINGS, Theophilus (born 1840/1), *schoolmaster,* Stoke upon Trent.

TH was born in Wilton, Wilts. about 1840, the son of Theophilus Hemmings. He began teaching in 1860 on leaving college, and came to St. Peter's school, Stoke upon Trent, in 1866. He was appointed master in 1867 when J. W. Thomas went to Penkhull. In 1870 he started a private school in Copeland Street, moving in the following year to London Road where he taught up to 100 boys. He lost 30 boys when the Roman Catholic school opened in 1875, and his school suffered further losses as other secondary schools opened.

By his wife Jane who had died by 1881, he had three children. He was organist of Stoke parish church 1879-86, and was a Fellow of the Royal College of Organists and a B.Mus. (Oxford). He was living in Shepherd Street by 1872.

Foster; *Staffs. Sentinel* 13 November 1919.

HENSHALL, Hugh (1734-1817), *engineer,* Tunstall.

HH was born in Newchapel in 1734, the son of John Henshall, partner of James Brindley (q.v.) and whose daughter Brindley married. HH became Brindley's assistant or junior partner, and when Brindley died in 1772 HH succeeded him as engineer to the Chesterfield Canal and also completed the Trent and Mersey Canal, practising as Hugh Henshall and Co.

HH lived first at Trubshaw Cross and later at Bank House, Etruria, built originally for Thomas Bentley, Wedgwood's partner but never lived in by Bentley. HH died unmarried in 1817, and was buried at Newchapel beside the grave of James Brindley. HH left his estate to his nephew Hugh Henshall Williamson (q.v.).

C. T. G. Boucher, *James Brindley, Engineer 1716-1772.*

HICKS, Richard (1765-1844), *pottery manufacturer,* Hanley.

RH, son of Richard Hicks, was born in Shrewsbury in 1765. He served an apprenticeship to Thomas Turner of Caughley, Shropshire. He set up his own pottery works in partnership with Joseph Boon, as Boon and Hicks, Broad Street, Shelton 1805-8, then with Job Meigh, as Hicks and Meigh, 1810-35. The latter partnership was joined by Johnson in 1822. Hicks, Meigh and Johnson became one of the most successful firms in the Potteries, producing good quality 'stone china', earthenware and china. RH married Lydia Meigh in 1801. He died aged 79 (according to the Bethesda chapel register, although the gravestone states 74 and the obituary in the *Staffs. Advertiser* states 76) on 2 March 1844.

Jewitt; M and H; Dir. 1818: *Staffs. Advertiser* 9 March 1844.

HIGGINBOTHAM, John (1805/6-72), *surveyor and auctioneer,* Fenton.

JH was born in Cappoquin, Ireland about 1805. In 1851 he was the licensee of the Cock Inn, Foley, and also was in business as an auctioneer and surveyor. In 1861 his business was located in Foley Place.

He was a Fenton Improvement Commissioner in 1858 and served as chief baliff 1863-5. In 1869 he acted as surveyor to the Fenton Board of Guardians. By his wife Elizabeth, whom he married about 1834, he had at least five children. His eldest son, Joseph W. Higginbotham continued in his father's profession and was surveyor to the commissioners 1863-73 and in business as Butlers and Higginbotham, Caroline Street, Longton, in 1887.

JH died on 15 November 1872.

Dir. 1851; Census 1861; Fenton Improvement Commissioners' Minutes; *National Index to Wills and Aministrations.*

HINDE, Thomas Rawlinson (1822-1894), *rope maker/theatre proprietor,* Hanley.

TRH was born in Bury, Lancs., in 1822. He began a rope making works in Mill Street (Etruria Road), Shelton, in 1851, which by 1876 he had moved to Mousecroft. This lay in the area between Cannon Street and Regent Road (part of which is now the Hinde Street car park, deriving its name from TRH). The rope walk is shown on a map of 1900 at the rear of Raymond Street. Hinde continued this business into the 1880's, but by 1884 he was renting the premises to Arthur Thomas Robson, who later transferred the works to the present day Robson Street off Broad Street, where it remained until recently.

In 1850 he was associated with others, mostly working men, in the establishment of a People's Hall in a former chapel in Brunswick Street, Shelton. It was hoped that this would become a centre of radical politics but it lacked support and closed within a year. Following that failure TRH and more than 20 others converted the premises into a theatre with the help of James Rodgers (q.v.) who had leased the Theatre Royal at Newcastle about 1844. The venture became known as the Royal Pottery Theatre, but faced much initial opposition from both magistrates and Hanley Commissioners who thought it would encourage young people to drink and mix with low company. The theatre eventually succeeded and the original building proving too small, was demolished and a New Theatre and Opera House, designed by TRH, was built in 1871.

TRH was elected to Hanley Council in 1866 and served until 1875. At the date of his election he kept a beer shop in Bethesda Street and probably worked a pottery in Ranelegh Street. In 1871 he lived in Adventure Place with his wife Elizabeth and daughter Madeline, aged 13. His wife had died by 1881 when he was living in Houghton Street and employing three men and a boy at his rope walk.

He died at Myrtle Villa, Clive Street, (Parkhouse Street), off Havelock Place, Shelton, on 1 June 1894 and was buried in Hanley cemetery.

Census 1871, 1881; Dir. 1860, 1867, 1876, 1884; Hanley Rate Books, 1873/4, 1880/1, 1884/5; Jewitt; *Sentinel Summer Number* June 1906; Theatre Royal, contents of glass bottle discovered in foundations 1887 (HRL); VCH viii; information from Mr. R. Downie. Robson-Barnett Ltd., Burslem.

HITCHINGS, James, (c. 1840-1935), *printer,* Hanley.

JH was born in West Bromwich about 1840, where he was apprenticed to a printer. He moved to Walsall as a journeyman printer and helped to found a local newspaper. In 1868 he came to Hanley as a compositor-reporter for the *Staffordshire Sentinel.* He set up in business on his own account as a newsagent and stationer in Hope Street, Hanley, in 1870, and later added a printing business. He traded as James Hitchings and Sons, Ltd., Excelsior Printing Works. The business was later transferred to Lamb Street and then to Market Street.

In July 1870 JH married Margaret Colclough, of Hanley and had at least two sons. He was a member of and held several official positions in the Charles Street Wesleyan Methodist church, Hanley. He died at Breedon, Lower Oxford Street, Basford, on 13 January 1935.

Evening Sentinel 15 January 1935; *Staffs. Advertiser* 19 January 1935.

HOLLAND, James (1799-1870), *artist,* Burslem.

JH was born in Burslem on 18 October 1799, and baptised on Christmas Day 1805 in Burslem church. His mother married again after her first husband's death, and JH lived with his step-father, Timothy Edge, and his mother, on a farm situated between Burslem and Wolstanton. JH's grandfather, Thomas Holland, was a potter at Hill Top Pottery, and his mother and grandmother were both pottery artists. In 1812 JH was apprenticed to John Davenport of Longport. At the end of his apprenticeship he went to London, where he earned his living teaching drawing. He became successful enough to be asked to give drawing lessons to Queen Victoria. He lived at 3 Union Place, Blackheath, and in 1823 exhibited a painting 'London from Blackheath'. He travelled widely at home and in Europe, painting in water colours and in oils. He exhibited at the Royal Academy, the Society of British Artists, the British Institution and the Water Colour Society. He died on 12 February 1870. His half-brother Thomas Holland, also became an artist. JH's portrait, a water colour by W. H. Hunt, is in the Victoria and Albert Museum, and there is a copy in Hanley Art Gallery.

DNB; *Dictionary of British Landscape Painters;* Simms; *Trans. of the Greenwich and Lewisham Antiquarian Society,* vol. 7, no. 6, 1972.

HOLLINS, Arthur (1876-1962), *trade unionist, Member of Parliament,* Burslem.

AH was born on 19 September 1876, the son of William and Caroline Hollins. He was educated at St. Paul's Church School, Burslem and attended classes at the Wedgwood Memorial Institute, but went to work in a pottery factory before the age of ten. He worked as a handler for 20 years, in the meantime working his way up as a trade union officer. He was secretary of the Jet and Rockingham Workers Society in 1899, a delegate to the National Society of Pottery Workers from 1906 and general secretary of this organisation from 1910 until his retirement in 1947. A local magistrate, he was elected to the Stoke on Trent council, became an alderman and in 1933/4 served as lord mayor of the city. He was created a freeman of the city. In the general election of 1928 he was elected as Labour candidate for Hanley, was defeated in 1931 and re-elected in 1935, then serving until he retired from the seat in 1945. He was awarded the C.B.E. in 1949. He married a Miss Sturgess on 4 August 1900 and had one son and one daughter. He lived at Eastbourne Villa, 2 Eastbourne Road, Hanley, dying on 22 April 1962.

F. Burchill and R. Ross, *A History of the Potters' Union;* S and L; *Who was Who* 1961-70.

HOLLINS, Michael Daintry (1815-98), *pottery and tile manufacturer,* Stoke upon Trent.

MDH was born in Manchester in 1815, the fourth son of Thomas Hollins. He qualified as a doctor and became a member of the Royal College of Surgeons, but never practised his profession. He was a nephew by marriage of Herbert Minton (q.v.) and he joined Minton's in 1839 and took charge of the commercial department. He became a partner in 1845 in the tile department, then trading as a separate business under the title of Minton, Hollins and Co. On Herbert Minton's death Hollins and Colin Minton Campbell continued in partnership until 1868, after which Hollins took over the encaustic tile department which he transferred to a new factory in Cliff Vale.

In August 1868 MDH became president of the Staffordshire Potteries Board of Arbitration and Conciliation which he and William Owen (q.v.) had taken a leading role in founding. In 1872 Minton's introduced the system of payment 'good from hand' which replaced 'good from oven' in which the employee was paid only for wares perfect after firing. It was not, however, until 1919, that 'good from oven' was generally abolished and not until 1964 that its last traces disappeared.

MDH became a justice of the peace in March 1861. He was a Stoke upon Trent improvement commissioner and served as chief bailiff in 1866. He represented Stoke division on the Staffordshire county council from the first formation of that body in 1888, retiring after three years. He was the first chairman of the local chamber of Commerce, a position he held for over 20 years, a period characterised by peaceful relations between the potters and the masters.

MDH married Elizabeth McKenzie on 2 June 1844 and by her had four sons and five daughters. The family lived from 1846 at Fenton Hall, which MDH had leased from George Whieldon, later at Springfield Hall, Chorlton, and later still at Whitmore Hall, formerly the seat of the Mainwaring family. MDH rose to the rank of colonel in the local volunteers. He contributed to the retiling of numerous churches and chapels in the area, including St. Giles, Newcastle under Lyme, where he paid £600 for retiling the floor with tiles based on the design of medieval tiles found during the rebuilding of church in 1873.

MDH died at Whitmore Hall in 1898.

Anderton; F. Burchill and R. Ross, *History of the Potters' Union; Staffs. Sentinel* 12 February 1898; VCH viii.

HOLLINS, Samuel (1748/9-1820), *pottery manufacturer,* Hanley.

SH, born about 1748, was the son of Richard Hollins and the grandfather of Michael Daintry Hollins (q.v.). He became a partner in the New Hall Company formed in 1781 to work the patent for the manufacturer of hard-paste porcelain from china clay and stone, and trading as Hollins, Warburton and Company. He also had a factory at Vale Pleasant, beside the Caldon Canal at Shelton and inherited a share in mines at Birches Head and Rowhurst.

By his first wife Nancy née Daintry SH had six children. He married twice more. In 1787 he contributed to the building of St. John's church, Hanley, and in 1813 to the parsonage house. He was mayor of the social club 'the ancient corporation of Hanley' in 1796.

He died at Shelton on 5 November 1820 aged 71.

IGI Staffs; Jewitt; VCH viii.

HOLLIS, Frederick William (born c. 1830), *chemist and druggist,* Stoke upon Trent.

FWH, son of James Hollis, was born in Wolverhampton about 1830. On 7 February 1852 he married Jane Gething, daughter of Thomas Gething, publican, of Market Street, Fenton. Some time later he was sentenced to ten years' penal servitude for procuring an abortion. He served 7½ years then was released on ticket of leave. In December 1877 and July 1882 he was sued by local tradespeople for non-payment of goods supplied to his wife and children while he was in prison. Judgment was given for Hollis. On 10 November 1882 he was sentenced to death for the murder of Mary Ann Wood, housekeeper to Hugh Bennett, a butcher of Liverpool Road. He was almost immediately reprieved but found guilty of murder while performing a surgical operation (abortion).

Staffs. Sentinel 15 July and 11 November 1882; M. J. Stanley, 'A History of Stafford Gaol' (typescript in WSL).

HOLTOM, William Fifield (1863/4-1919), *solicitor and magistrates' clerk,* Stoke upon Trent.

WFH was born about 1863, the son of Charles Holtom, a surgeon. After being articled to a firm of solicitors he was admitted as a solicitor in September 1885. He became clerk to the magistrates on 12 December 1900 and clerk to the licensing justices of the county borough of Stoke upon Trent.

He married a Miss Bill in 1890, becoming a Roman Catholic in order to do so, and had two sons and three daughters. Conservative in his politics he acted as agent for S. Joyce Thomas in his unsuccessful contest in December 1910 against John Ward. He committed suicide by prussic acid poisoning at his office in Church Street, Stoke upon Trent, on 24 November 1919.

Staffs. Sentinel 24, 25 and 27 November 1919 (obit. notices).

HOMER, Charles James Horatio (1837-93), *mining engineer,* Hanley.

CJHH was born on 17 August 1837 probably in Hanley. In 1841 he was living in the household of a relative, Joseph Homer, in Broom Street, Hanley. After Joseph Homer's death in 1864 Charles Homer inherited the former's 35 properties in Hanley. He speculated successfully and amassed considerable wealth, owning houses, shops, a limekiln and wharf, beer houses and Northwood colliery, together with about 60 acres of land in Hanley. His business address was 24 Broom Street, and he is variously described as land surveyor, mining surveyor etc. In 1864 he became managing director and mining engineer of the Chatterley Ironstone Company, founded on land leased from Ralph Sneyd of Keele Hall. This company bought the Whitfield colliery estate in 1871 in order to improve its coal supplies. The colliery became part of Chatterley Ironstone Company but the estate was Homer's personal property, and in 1882 he successfully sued the Whitfield company for loss of royalties from the non-working of coal under his estate. Chatterley Whitfield continued to expand and in addition in 1871 Homer had bought two collieries near Oswestry, and was also involved in the building of the Longton-Adderley Green railway. In the depression of the mid-1870s CJH continued to advocate expansion, his fellow directors disagreed and he resigned. With the Duke of Sutherland, John Pender, M.P. and John Bourne, in 1874 he launched the Stafford Colliery and Ironworks at Great Fenton. He owned Hanley Colliery Company and Northwood Colliery and at the time of his death was planning to re-open the collieries on his Turnhurst estate.

In 1859 he married Sarah, a daughter of John Weatherby, deceased, formerly a farmer of Sheildscroft, Brown Edge. The Weatherbys farmed in the area around Norton-in-the-Moors and Brown Edge. The Homer family moved to The Fens, Stockton Brook. There were three children from this marriage, Laura, born in 1860, Frederick born in 1865 and Joseph Edward, born in 1871. In 1875, however, Homer had left his family and was living at Caverswall Castle with his mistress, Mary Ann Rixon, by whom he had four children, two sons and two daughters. On his death his estate was shared between Mary Ann Rixon and three sons (the eldest son, Frederick, not being mentioned in the will and his wife Sarah mentioned only in confirmation of the marriage settlement made in 1859.

Charles Homer's public office holding was concentrated into the mid 1870s; he was a member of the Tunstall Local Board of Health in 1873-4 and chief bailiff in 1874-5. He was a freemason, a founder member of the North Staffordshire Institute of Mining Engineers and its president from 1874 to 1876. He was a director of the Staffordshire Potteries Water Board and of the North Staffordshire Newspaper Company. Conservative in politics he became president of the Hanley Conservative Association.

He died at Ivy House, Hanley, on 4 November 1893.

Staffs. Sentinel 11 November 1893 (obit.); W. Jack, *Short History of the Whitfield Colliery;* Diaries of C. J. Homer.

HOOD, George (*floruit* 1831), *pottery manufacturer,* Tunstall.

GH was in business in Tunstall as a pottery manufacturer from about 1822. He built Highgate Pottery, Brownhills, in 1831 and took over Walton's figure and toy factory in

Navigation Road, Burslem, in 1835. In January 1841 the warehouse of the Walton factory, holding about ten tons of ware, collapsed, and three of the 20 women workers below were seriously injured. GH sold the Highgate Pottery in 1841. He started up in business again in a works on Bourne's Bank, making figures and dogs.

It is generally accepted that George Hood is the 'George H.' referred to in Charles Shaw's *When I was a Child.* Shaw provides a vivid and fairly sympathetic portrait of him, stout, cheery despite his financial misfortunes, employing only a dozen people in his toy manufactory instead of the scores he had previously employed, in a broken-down works which produced mostly figures of Napoleon.

IGI Staffs; M and H; VCH viii.

HOPKINSON, Robert (born c. 1801), *newspaper editor,* Hanley.

RH was born in Nottingham about 1801. He was a printer's compositor by trade and came to the Potteries about 1850. At that date he was the secretary of the People's Hall in Brunswick Street, Shelton at which politically radical lectures were given. He began a newspaper *The Lever* in January 1851 but it failed in October through lack of support. RH complained that even at ½d. a copy insufficient interest was shown. Although there were over seven thousand possible subscribers only sixty people were prepared to back the paper, which maintained a radical, temperance and anti-clerical stance. The Hall later became the Royal Pottery Theatre.

He was elected as Surveyor of the Shelton Highways Board during its period of control by working class members. In June 1855 after a disputed election and meeting had produced two rival boards, RH was convicted of refusing to hand over his books of account. In July 1856 he gave up his books and numerous errors were uncovered. Although there was evidence that fraud may have occurred, this could not be proved and RH was not prosecuted.

In 1851 he was living in Old Hall Terrace with his wife Elizabeth and son Thomas, both born in Birmingham.

Census 1851; *Staffs. Advertiser* 6 April 1855; *Staffs. Advertiser* 4 June 1855; *The Lever* (HRL- RS 107): Townley.

HORDLEY, Ralph (c. 1826-1908), *hospital secretary,* Stoke upon Trent.

RH was baptised at Tabernacle Independent chapel, Hanley on 6 August 1826, the son of Thomas Hordley and Mary Clinton née Slaney. He was employed as secretary of the North Staffordshire Infirmary, and wrote a history of that institution entitled *A History of the North Staffordshire Infirmary and Eye Hospital 1802-1902.* He was a shareholder in the Potteries Street Railway in 1879.

By his wife Ellen née Brooks he had a son Edward Ralph, born about 1858.

Census 1861; IGI Staffs; VCH viii.

HORRY, William Frederick (1843-72), *publican,* Burslem.

WFH was born on 17 November 1843 at Boston, Lincs., the son of William Horry of the Red Cow Inn, a successful brewer. WFH spent much of his father's money. He was given £800 to buy the George Hotel, Burslem, about 1866. In 1867 WFH married Jane Wright, a barmaid at the hotel. The couple had three children, but WFH believed, rightly or wrongly, that his wife had been unfaithful with several of Burslem's prominent inhabitants. He himself was often drunk and suffered from *delirium tremens,* but was popular in the town.

The couple separated in March 1871 and WFH sold the business in May. His father gave a home to Mrs. Horry and the children. WFH spent the remainder of the year in a round of dissolution, dividing his time between the Potteries and Nottingham where his lavender kid gloves and fashionable attire, and the presence of his 'gaily-dressed inamorata' attracted much attention. He filed for a divorce, naming five correspondents.

In January 1872, having spent a week in a Hanley brothel, he returned to Nottingham where he bought a revolver. He went on to a hotel in Boston, Lincs., where he treated the customers to drinks telling them of his desire for a reconciliation with his wife. He persuaded his father to allow him a last meeting with his wife, promising to leave England for ever. He met her on 15 January 1872 and shot her dead.

He was found guilty of murder at Lincoln Assizes in March with no recommendation for mercy. Petitions were circulated in Burslem, where a fund for his defence was well subscribed, in Boston and in Lincoln, where the mayor headed the list of signatories. His wife's brother also pleaded for mercy, but he was executed at Lincoln Castle on Easter Monday, 2 April 1872. Shop keepers in Burslem drew their blinds on that day.

In a statement made before his death he thanked his 'dear friends of the Potteries' for their sympathy and pecuniary assistance. He felt he had been deeply sinned against and wronged, but pardoned those who had done so.

On the following Sunday, funeral cards were distributed in Burslem depicting him as a Christian and a martyr. Hundreds of people attended a service in St. John's church where the Rev. Alfred Watton (q.v.) preached on a text from Proverbs 13, 22.

There was little condemnation of the activities of Horry's friends locally, but the *Saturday Review* carried an attack upon them and upon the Rev. Alfred Watton. WFH's friends erected a memorial to his and his wife's memory in St. John's churchyard.

Staffs. Sentinel 20 Jan, 6 Apr, 13 Apr, 20 Apr, 6 May 1872.

HOWSON, George (1818-96), *sanitary ware manufacturer,* Hanley.

GH, son of Richard and Jane Howson, was born in Burslem on 2 March 1818. He had radical political opinions and because of his Chartist sympathies found difficulty in obtaining work. By 1865 he had raised sufficient capital to set up his own business at Eastwood Works, Hanley, manufacturing sanitary ware. With the growing public concern for hygiene the business prospered and by 1881 Howson was employing 50 people. His sons carried on the business after his death. The factory was sold to Armitage-Shanks in 1966.

GH was associated with J. W. Powell (q.v.) in the development of music in the area. He founded a scholarship for North Staffordshire students in the Tonic Sol-Fa College, London. He himself travelled on foot to outlying villages to teach this system of musical notation. He was president of the Hanley Glee and Madrigal Society. Among his local benefactions was the bandstand in Hanley Park. He was one of the first persons to receive the freedom of the borough of Hanley. He was a Methodist.

By his wife, Eliza née Taylor, whom he married about 1864, he had five children. He lived at 27 Clifford Street, Hanley, in 1881, and later in Stoke Road, Shelton, where he died on 11 April 1896.

British Bulletin of Commerce Survey, 1955, part 2; Census 1881; *Country Life* 6 May 1976. Huntbach; IGI Staffs; R. Nettell, *Music in the Five Towns* and *North Staffordshire Music: a social experiment;Staffs. Advertiser* 11 April 1896.

HULME, Thomas (1808-84), *draper,* Burslem.

TH was born in Burslem in 1808, the son of Thomas and Mary Hulme. He was of sufficient means to be able to devote much of his time to local government affairs. He was elected to the Burslem Board of Health, where he proposed incorporation but was defeated by the anti-incorporation candidate in 1870. He was re-elected in 1873 and served as the last chief bailiff of the town before its incorporation as a borough in 1878, a development for which he had been largely responsible. He was elected to the new council and immediately created an alderman, serving as first mayor of the borough and again serving in this office in 1882.

TH was a Liberal in politics. He married and had a son, W. B. Hulme. From about 1873 he lived at Dunwood Hall, Burslem, where he died on 5 March 1884.

Staffs. Sentinel 5 and 8 March 1884.

HULME, Thomas (1830-1905), *earthenware manufacturer,* Burslem.

TH was born on 15 August 1830. He began work as a clerk for John Wedgwood's Woodland Street Works, Tunstall. He then obtained employment in the offices of James MacIntyre and Co. Ltd., Washington Works, Burslem, of which he became one of the owners and a partner of William Woodall (q.v.). He retired from business in 1880.

He was elected to Burslem School Board and served as chairman for ten years. He was twice mayor of Burslem, in 1882 and in 1905, and represented the town on Staffordshire county council. He served as president of the Burslem Tonic Sol-Fa Society and was organist at Hill Top Methodist Sunday School for 40 years. He was one of the compilers of the Methodist Free Church Tune Book in 1893. In 1894, on the occasion of the visit of Princess Louise and her husband, the Marquess of Lorne, to Burslem, TH gave to the town his collection of Old Wedgwood ware (now in the City Museum). Princess Louise unveiled his portrait, painted by William Mainwaring Palin, who had been trained in the Burslem School of Art. The portrait is now in the City Museum. In 1904 TH gave the site for a new school of art, next to the Wedgwood Memorial Institute, at a cost of £5,000.

He lived at The Mount, Knutton Lane, Wolstanton, and for a few years before his death, at Woodleigh, Porthill Bank, Longport. He died, unmarried, on 26 August 1905.

Oldham; *Staffs. Advertiser* 20 October 1894; *Staffs. Sentinel* 10 October 1907.

HULSE, Joseph (1818-91), *colliery proprietor,* Longton.

JH was born in 1818. He first earned his living as a schoolmaster in Caroline Street and then in the Wesleyan Day School in King Street. He went into business as a general commission agent and on the death of his uncle, Thomas Pye, of the firm Stirrup and Pye, in 1855, became the owner of Adderley Green Colliery.

He was an improvement commissioner for Longton, was elected to the council on the incorporation of the borough in 1865, and became an alderman. He served as mayor in 1867. He was a member and later vice-chairman of the first Longton School Board, and before Dresden became part of Longton he was chairman of the Dresden Board of Health. He became a trustee of Longton Cottage Hospital and the Hulse Ward was named after him. He died on 3 May 1891.

Staffs. Sentinel 4 May 1891 (obit.).

HUNTBACH, Alfred (1866-1950), *author,* Hanley.

AH was born in 1866. In 1910, on the eve of federation, he published *Hanley, Stoke upon Trent,* a history of the town from the 13th to the 20th centuries. He served as a magistrate from 1912 and was chairman of the Stone bench. He was elected chairman of the North Staffs. Field Club.

Staffordshire Life Vol I, No. 3; H. Stickels, 'The Contribution of John Ridgway and the Methodist New Connexion to the urban development of Hanley' (Univ. of Keele B.A. dissertation, 1971).

HUNTBACH, Michael (1837-1910), *draper,* Hanley.

MH was born on 4 November 1837 at Whitehouse Farm, Pipe Gate, the son of Robert and Mary Huntbach. He was apprenticed at Easter 1852 to Thomas Swift, draper, of Upper Market Square, Hanley, and remained there until 1861. Then, having been refused an increase in salary, he opened his own shop in Lamb Street, in premises previously occupied by Hans Ringland. His original staff consisted of his wife and two of his sisters, one of whom later married Benjamin Riseley (q.v.). In 1876 he acquired the shop owned by Charles Vyse, paying £2,000 for the property, the highest price for any property at that time within the borough limits. The shop was bought at an auction, MH bidding against Thomas Rogers of the Lamb Inn, on the other side of Vyse's shop. Rogers later sued Huntbach, claiming that the latter's alterations had damaged his property, but the case was settled out of court. On Roger's death, some years later, MH paid £4,000 for the Lamb Inn. He sold the licence for £250, an action which upset his fellow temperance supporters although he gave the proceeds to the Library Committee.

MH's next purchase was Robinson's, drapers, on the corner of Swan Passage, and Jones, chemist, next door. He also acquired a four storey building on the opposite side of Lamb Street called Little Huntbach. Between his two large blocks of property stood a small shop owned by William Jackson, known as 'The Blacking Shop'. Huntbach's attempts to acquire this property form the basis of Arnold Bennett's story 'The Feud' in his *Tales of the Five Towns.* MH (Ezra Brunt in the story) was advised to take legal action against Bennett but did not do so. Family tradition states that Michael Huntbach offered to cover the floor of Jackson's shop with sovereigns to buy the property. He did obtain possession, a short time before his death, and the 'thorn' was demolished. By the time of his death Huntbach had increased his frontage from 30 to 200 feet and employed 300 persons on 20,000 square feet of shop floor.

MH was elected to Hanley council in 1871, served for three years but then did not rejoin the council until 1890, during his period as mayor 1889-91. He served as mayor a second time in 1904. He was made a freeman of the borough in 1898. He gave £1,000 towards the cost of making Hanley Park and cut the first sod there in 1894. As chairman of the markets committee he endeavoured unsuccessfully to move the annual wakes fair from the Market Square. He was associated with Bethesda Methodist New Connexion church and served as superintendent of the upper girls' school and as treasurer to the trustees.

He married Elizabeth Kirkby, daughter of a secretary to the Duke of Sutherland and there were four children. The family lived in King Street in 1871 and at The Hill, Barlaston, by 1880. There were two further homes, at Mere House, Alsager, and finally at Methven, Church Walk, Llandudno, where MH died on 22 February 1910. He was buried in Hanley cemetery.

Census 1871; Dir. 1875, 1910; Huntbach; *Staffs. Sentinel* 26 February 1910; information from Mr. S. Huntbach, great-grandson.

HÜRTEN, Charles Ferdinand (1818-1901), *pottery artist,* Stoke upon Trent.

CFH was born in Cologne in 1818. After working for various decorating establishments and specialising in floral painting he was employed on special commissions for the Sèvres factory. Examples of his work at the Paris Exhibition in 1858 were noticed by Copeland's, who engaged him in 1859. He remained with the firm until his retirement in 1897. Paintings taken direct from nature or gouache studies were made at Trentham and Chatsworth. Examples of his work are found in many national museums all over Europe. In 1873 he was living in Winton Terrace and in 1892 at 24 Shepherd Street.

Dir. 1873, 1892; G. Godden, 'Four Victorian Ceramic Artists' in *Apollo,* 1961.

JAHN, Louis, (1840-1911), *pottery artist and museum curator,* Stoke upon Trent.

LJ was born in Oberweisbach, Thuringia, Germany, in 1840. He came to the Potteries in 1862 as an artist at Minton's. He became art director at William Brownfield and Sons, Cobridge, and designed the Brownfield China Vase for the 1879 Crystal Palace Exhibition. Later he returned to Minton's as art director.

He married a Miss Henk in 1863, and had three children, Henrietta, Albert and Francis. He was widowed by the age of 41, living at 15 Church Street, Hanley.

He joined the North Staffs. Field Club in 1871, becoming an authority on lepidoptera and coleoptera. He often spent his afternoon off hunting beetles in Dovedale. His interest in natural history increased after his retirement from work, and he also collected old pottery. In September 1904 he was appointed curator of Hanley Museum, which at that time housed the Field Club's natural history collection and also collections of pottery made by Cartlich, Goss (q.v.) and Solon (q.v.). He was elected vice-president of the Field Club in 1908 and in the following year received the Garner medal for his studies of coleoptera in North Staffordshire. He was a member of the Menturia Lodge of Freemasons.

He died on 20 April 1911 and was buried in Hanley cemetery.

Census 1881; F. Freeth, 'A Glance round Hanley Museum' in *The Connoisseur* vol. 16, 1906; *Staffs. Sentinel* 21 April and 23 May 1911.

JEWITT, Llewellyn (1816-86), *publisher and author,* Stoke upon Trent.

LJ was born at Kimberworth, Yorks, on 24 November 1816, the 17th and last child of Arthur Jewitt and Martha née Sheldon. In 1838 he went to London to work as an illustrator. He executed nearly all the illustrations for *London Interiors* and contributed to *Pictorial Times* and *Illustrated London News.* About 1846 with his brother Thomas he worked on Parker's *Glossary of Architecture* and *Domestic Architecture.* From 1849-53 he was chief librarian at Plymouth Public Library. In 1853 he began the *Derby Telegraph* and acted as the paper's editor until 1868. He established the antiquarian magazine *The Reliquary* in 1860. Among his many books of particular interest and importance to the Potteries are, *The Wedgwoods* (1865) and *The Ceramic Art of Great Britain* (1878, 2 vols. revised edition 1883). By his wife, Elizabeth née Sage, he had two sons.

Llewellyn Jewitt, F.S.A., died at Duffield, Derbyshire, on 4th March 1886.

G. A. Godden, *Jewitt's Ceramic Art of Great Britain 1800-1900;* D.N.B.: W. H. Goss, *The Life and Death of Llewellyn Jewitt;* Simms.

JOHNSON, Harry (c. 1880-1957), *tile manufacturer,* Tunstall.

HJ was the son of a pottery manufacturer, Robert Lewis Johnson. On leaving school he entered the family business. His father acquired the Crystal Porcelain Works in Cobridge, and here, in 1901, the firm, trading as H. and R. Johnson, began producing glazed tiles. The firm's output rose to 200,000 per week. In 1907 the company took over the Highgate factory of Alfred Meakin at Tunstall and in 1911 the Eastwood Tile Works of Sherwin and Cotton. The Cobridge factory closed during the First World War and never re-opened under the name of H. and R. Johnson. Production was concentrated at the Highgate and Eastwood factories. HJ became president of the British Pottery Manufacturers' Federation and chairman of the British Ceramic Research Association. By the time of his death in 1957 the weekly output had risen to three million. In 1960 the firm owned four factories in Stoke upon Trent, another in Hereford and three overseas.

HJ died in August 1957.

Ceramics 1959, vol 10; *Pottery and Glass* vol. 33, 1955; VCH ii.

JONES, Alfred Bailey (1851-1940), *pottery manufacturer,* Longton.

ABJ was born in Longton in June 1851, the son of William Jones, a former customs and excise officer, of Caroline Street. He was educated at the Zion and Wesleyan Schools, Longton. He began work at Aynsley's Pottery, Longton, at the age of ten. By 1876 he had established his own business as a pottery factor. He built the Grafton Works, Longton, in 1900, making all kinds of ware, and trading as Alfred B. Jones and Sons.

In 1900 he was appointed a justice of the peace, and in November 1905 he was elected mayor, although he was not then a member of the council. He served as mayor again in 1910 and was in this office at the time of federation, of which he was a supporter. He attended the Methodist New Connexion church, and was treasurer and president of the local branch of the British and Foreign Bible Society. He acted as joint secretary of the Methodist New Connexion Conference, and represented the Longton circuit at Conference on a number of occasions. He was also a trustee of Mount Tabor church, Fenton. In politics he was a Liberal.

He married (1) Annie Howson by whom he had six children and (2) Sarah Poole. He was living at 7 Carlisle Street, Longton, in 1889 and at Spring Garden Road, Longton, in 1907. He died at Bank House, Trentham Road, Oakhill, on 6 January 1940.

Evening Sentinel 8 January 1940; C. Penn, *Staffordshire at the Opening of the 20th Century; Pottery and Glass* July-December 1956.

JONES, Elijah (1802-68), *auctioneer and valuer,* Hanley.

EJ was born in Hanley, where he was baptised on 25th April 1802, the son of Thomas and Dorothy Jones. From about 1831 to 1840 he was in partnership with Thomas Hughes at the Villa Pottery, Hot Lane, Cobridge, then until 1843 with Edward Walley (q.v.). By 1851 EJ was living in Lichfield Street, Hanley, and in business as a colour merchant with premises in Mill Street (Etruria Road). Later he became an auctioneer and potter's valuer. In 1860 he offered a prize of £10 for the design of an improved drying oven for potters. In 1861 he persuaded a meeting of Hanley ratepayers to reject the council's proposal to provide the town with sewers.

EJ was an advocate of the temperance movement. When in 1857 he was defeated in the Hanley council elections he denounced the combination of 'spirit tap and beer barrel' which he claimed had undue influence on the council. In January 1859 he became editor of *The Beacon,* the monthly journal of the North Staffs. Temperance Association. He claimed success when Hanley council granted only one new liquor licence from 13 applications in that year. He was also accused of intimidating traders and shopkeepers during the parliamentary election campaign in the same year in his endeavours to gain support for the temperance candidate, Samuel Pope (see also James Bebbington).

In 1861 he was living in Lichfield Cottage, Lichfield Street, Hanley, with a wife Harriet and six children. He had possibly been married previously, to Nannie Walley, in 1826. He died on 26 December 1868. One of the executors of his will was J. E. Keates (q.v.), another leader of the local temperance movement.

Census 1861; Dir. 1851, 1860, 1867; IGI Staffs.; *Staffs. Advertiser* 14 January 1860, 11 May 1861; M. J. Wilson, 'The Temperance Movement in the Potteries 1840-60', (Univ. of Keele M.A. thesis 1972); information from Mr. J. W. Bentley, Lytham St. Annes.

JONES, John (1805-91), *manufacturing chemist,* Stoke upon Trent.

JJ, son of John and Elizabeth Jones, was born in Broadway, Worcestershire in 1805. He was established in business in High Street, Stoke upon Trent, from at least 1834, and acquired a reputation as a leading authority on chemicals and minerals used in the pottery industry. He was one of the first to break the European monopoly of the manufacturer of borax by importing borax from California. His factory was on the corner of Hartshill Road and Shelton Old Road in 1900.

In 1841 JJ was living at Knowl Lodge, Cliff Bank with his wife Charlotte and his mother, Elizabeth (probably widowed). His father may have been the John Jones of March Parade, Newcastle under Lyme, in partnership with Birch as a manufacturer of copperas (vitriol) at Shelton.

JJ qualified as a commissioner for Stoke in 1842. He died at Knowl Lodge, Stoke upon Trent, on 18 January 1891.

Staffs. Sentinel 26 January 1891 (obit.).

KEARY, William (1815/16-1886), *solicitor,* Stoke upon Trent.

WK was born in 1815/16 in Stockton, Yorkshire, the son of the Revd. H. W. Keary and Lucy, daughter of Hall Plumer, of Bilton Hall, Yorks. WK's father was an Irishman from Tuarn Galway who had served in the British army during the Peninsular war and whose fortune had been adversely affected by land ownership problems. He took holy orders and among other preferments became rector of Nunnington, Yorks. His son, WK, entered the legal profession and from about 1840 was practising in Stoke upon Trent as a solicitor, in partnership with, successively, Frederick Tomlinson, J. H. Sheppard and Marshall. In 1840 WK became a Stoke upon Trent improvement commissioner, was cheif bailiff in 1846 and 1858, and the first mayor of the borough on its incorporation in 1874. He acted as solicitor to the North Staffordshire Railway from 1845, was a director of the Staffordshire Potteries Waterworks Company, and a governor of the North Staffordshire Royal Infirmary. He became Conservative party agent for north-west Staffordshire in 1883-4.

He married (1) on 4th March 1841, Ann Archer, by whom he had three sons, William Plumer, Charles Francis and henry Mee. Ann died c. 1847 and WK's sister, Annie Keary, came to live with the family at the Hollies, Trent Vale, to look after the three children. She was later a noted novelist and writer of children's stories, many of which originated when she entertained her nephews. WK's second son, Charles Francis, became Keeper of the British Museum, and wrote a number of books under the pseudonym H. Ogam Matuce. WK later married Mary Peyton Sparkes, by whom he had three daughters, Mary, Alice and Helen.

WK died on 23 November 1886. His family arms, originally derived from Adam de Keary, c. 1200, of Castle Cary, Somerset — on a bend sable three roses of the field seeded proper — were included in the arms of the borough of Stoke upon Trent.

DNB; E. Keary, *Annie Keary, a memoir; Staffs. Advertiser* 27 November 1886.

KEATES, James Edward (1817-1913), *draper and tailor,* Burslem.

JEK was born in Cheadle, Staffs., on 22 August 1817, the son of Thomas Keates (died 1872) and Elizabeth (died 1868). He was educated at Marton Bank Academy, Macclesfield, Cheshire. He was apprenticed to a tailor in Sheffield, and then worked in Preston, Lancs., where he became a total abstainer, lodging with Joseph Livesey, an early leader of the temperance movement. JEK moved to Burslem in 1840, where he was in business as a tailor and draper, in premises variously located as 7, 9 and 11 St. John's Square.

In 1859 JEK was editor of the *Beacon,* the Potteries temperance journal, published by his brother John Keates (q.v.). JEK also wrote for the *Alliance News,* the national temperance journal. He served as treasurer of the North Staffordshire Temperance Association and spoke on behalf of Samual Pope, the Liberal temperance candidate, in the parliamentary election of 1859. JEK visited America three times, studying the temperance movement there. He is believed to have started the first Band of Hope in the Potteries. He was attached to the Wesleyan Methodist church.

JEK's other great interest was music. He was a bass singer and played the violin and flute. He was connected with the Tonic Sol-Fa Choir.

In 1880 he married Sarah Tipper (died 1880), and by her had two sons, James and Thomas, and two daughters. After his retirement in 1893 he lived at Rosette Cottage, Hereford, then in Leek, until finally coming to live with his daughter and his grandson, Harold K. Hales (q.v.) in Watlands Avenue, Wolstanton, where he died in February 1913.

Alliance Weekly News, March 1857; *Beacon,* April, June, July 1859; Dir. 1854, 1864; *Potteries Examiner,* January 1875; Simms; *Staffs. Sentinel* 7 February 1913 (obit.).

KEATES, John (1819/20-93), *printer and publisher,* Hanley.

JK, son of Thomas and Elizabeth Keates, was born in Cheadle about 1819. He moved to the Potteries and after a period as a schoolmaster he set up as a printer, about 1842, at 38-40 Cheapside, Hanley. His works, on the corner of Brunswick Street, was later the site of the Hanley Economic Building Society. JK was the original publisher of the *Gazetteer of the Staffordshire Potteries and Newcastle* from 1876 to 1893, of a series of directories, published every four years or so between 1865 and 1893, of an annual trade directory from 1865 to 1868, and in 1888 of an *Illustrated Household Almanac.* He was associated with the *Staffordshire Sentinel,* whose offices were next door to his in Cheapside, and from 1860 the firm of Keates printed the *Sentinel.* JK also published various books and a newspaper, *The Beacon,* edited by his brother James Edward Keates (q.v.).

By his wife, Elizabeth, he had, by 1861, nine children, and in that year he was living at 12 Albion Place, Albion Street, Hanley. He had moved, by 1881, to The Hollies, Etruria Vale, Hanley. For more than 50 years he was a member of Bethesda New Connexion church and was a local preacher in the circuit. He died in Sheffield, at the house of one of his daughters on 1 December 1893.

Census 1861; Dir. 1872; R and S; *Rendezvous with the Past: Sentinel Centenary* 1854-1954; *The Sentinel Story; Staffs. Advertiser* 9 December 1893.

KEELING, Anthony (1738-1815), *pottery manufacturer,* Tunstall.

AK is first documented as a partner in Hollins, Warburton and Co., which had been formed to exploit the patent for hard-paste porcelain taken out by William Cookworthy of Plymouth in 1765. Richard Champion of Bristol acquired the patent rights in 1774 and in 1781 began production in Keeling's works in Tunstall. In the following year, however, the company broke up, Champion lost interest in manufacturing and Keeling and his partner Turner concentrated on other types of pottery.

In the late 1770s AK took over Phoenix Works belonging to his father-in-law, Enoch Booth, and rebuilt the works. He made Queen's ware, blue-painted ware and enamelled Egyptian black. The firm prospered and AK built Calver House, in Well Street, for his residence and by 1802 had a second pottery works in Tunstall. By the end of the 18th century his was the most important works in the town. During the Napoleonic wars the firm underwent some decline. About 1810 AK retired to Liverpool, where he died in 1815. The Phoenix Pottery, after passing through several hands, was pulled down soon after 1877.

AK married Ann, daughter of Enoch Booth, on 22 August 1760. For many years he was the principal supporter of a small religious denomination, the Sandemanians. Their meeting house, which he owned and which adjoined his house, was registered for worship in 1812 by AK and eight others including his partner Enoch Keeling. The group had ceased to meet by about 1838.

Jewitt; M and H; SHC 4 ser. iii; VCH viii; Ward.

KEELING, James (c. 1762-1837), *earthenware manufacturer,* Hanley.

JK was born about 1762. He is recorded as an earthenware manufacturer of New Street, Hanley, from 1795 to about 1830. He is not listed as a potter in the 1834 directory but is given under his private address as a gentleman and may by then have retired. His firm produced dinner and teaware in transfer-printed underglaze. In 1828 he produced a service with views from Buckingham's *Travels in Mesopotamia.* He patented a number of improvements in decorative processes, and, in conjunction with Valentine Close, some improvements in pottery ovens.

JK married twice. His first wife, Sarah, died on 26th December 1785 aged 23, and he married again, his first child being born in October 1796. In 1816 JK was a member of a committee under the chairmanship of Josiah Wedgwood II for the establishment of a new school in Hanley, and in 1830 he was one of 86 signatories to a petition against the Truck Acts.

He died at South Terrace, Hanley, on 8th August 1837.

S. Shaw, *History of the Staffordshire Potteries; Morley College Ceramic Circle Bulletin* 1978, vol. 1, no. 1; D. Rodney Halson, *The Revd. R. W. Newland and the Tabernacle Independent Chapel,* Hanley.

KENEALY, Edward Vaughan Hyde (1819-80), *barrister, publisher, Member of Parliament,* Stoke upon Trent.

EVHK was born in Cork on 2 July 1819, the son of William Kenealy, a well-to-do merchant. He was educated at Trinity College, Cambridge, B.A. 1840, LL.B. 1846 and LL.D. 1850. He was called to the bar in 1847, joining the Oxford circuit. In 1850 he was sentenced to one month's imprisonment for punishing his son with undue severity Kenealy was junior defence counsel in the trial of William Palmer, the Rugeley poisoner, in 1856. He and his senior were not successful and Palmer was found guilty and hanged outside Stafford goal. The local railway company ran special excursion trains from London to Stafford for the event. Kenealy was also advocate for William Orton, the bogus claimant in the Tichborne case in 1873. During the trial he was censured by the jury for the language he employed. His advocacy, however vehemently expressed, failed, Orton was found guilty on 17 August 1874 and Kenealy was disbarred for his behaviour and indiscretions. The attendant publicity helped Kenealy in his campaign for the Stoke upon Trent parliamentary election of 18 February 1874. He had failed to get elected for Wednesbury in the election of 1868, but in the Stoke election, standing as an independent, he successfully broke the monopoly of Conservative and Liberal representation for the borough. When he took his seat in the House of Commons no member could be found to introduce him, and on the motion of Benjamin Disraeli, the ceremony was dispensed with.

During the campaign Kenealy had been opposed by the Liberal editor-proprietor of the *Staffordshire Sentinel,* Thomas Andrews Potter (q.v.). After the election Kenealy started his own newspaper in the Potteries, the *Staffordshire News and Trade Advertiser,* which was edited by his son, A. J. Kenealy. The first issue contained an attack on the pottery manufacturers, Copeland and Minton, for burning bones. kenealy likened the experience of local residents to his own journeys on the River Ganges in India, when 'the indescribable odour of roasted Hundu wafter to us on the morning breeze from the funeral pyres'.

EVHK's political success was short-lived. In the general election of 1880 he stood as candidate again but came bottom of the poll. He was a voluminous writer, his published works including three volumes of poetry, 1875-9. He married Elizabeth Nicklin of Tipton, Staffs., and by her had eleven children. He died on 16 April 1880 at hangleton, Sussex.

Anderton; DNB: *The Sentinel Story 1873-1973;* V and S.

KENNEDY, William Sadler (fl. 1851), *pottery manufacturer,* Burslem.

WSK began in business in King Street, Burslem, producing palettes for artists in 1838. He moved to Bourne's Bank where he operated Washington Works from 1847-54, being joined by his brother-in-law, James MacIntyre, in 1852. The factory made door furniture and handles. In 1854 he left for London and James MacIntyre took over the business.

He was a member of the Burslem Board of Health 1850-3 and chief bailiff 1849-54. He was critical of the more vulgar aspects of the annaul wakes and suggested that a more cultural Wedgwood Festival should take their place.

He lived in Camoys Terrace, Burslem, in 1851.

D. R. Beard, *Burslem Commissioners* (Univ. of Keele, Dept. of Adult Education local history certificate essay); Dir. 1851; Jewitt; Oldham; *Staffs. Advertiser* 9 September 1852; VCH ii.

KENT, George, C. (1853-1926), *town clerk,* Longton.

GCK was born at Lane End on 30 October 1853, the son of John Kent, china and earthenware manufacturer, and his wife, Sarah. In 1868 he was articled to E. Young, solicitor, Longton, and then to a firm in London. He qualified in 1875 and in 1877 was appointed clerk to Longton School Board. He was elected to Longton borough council but resigned on his appointment as town clerk in January 1890. He retained this office until federation, of which he was a supporter, giving evidence in favour of the scheme to the House of Commons and House of Lords committees. On 3 September 1908 he was given an honorarium of 300 guineas for his services to the federation movement.

GCK was chairman of Taylor Tunnicliffe, Ltd., potters, of Eastwood Vale, Hanley. He served as Deputy Provincial Grand Master of Staffordshire Freemasons in 1919. From about 1910 he lived at Stone and became a member of Stone council. He died on 5 January 1926 at Radford Cottage, The Avenue, Stone.

Federation Newscuttings (HRL); IGI Staffs; *Staffs. Sentinel* 6 January 1926; memorial inscription in Blurton churchyard.

KENT, James Aloysius (c. 1864-1953), *pottery manufacturer,* Fenton.

JAK was born about 1864, the son of Charles Kent, draper. At the age of 13 he was apprenticed to his brother-in law, John Tams (q.v.) By 1888 he was senior partner in the firm of Barker and Kent. The partnership was dissolved in 1897 when JAK took over the Old Foley Pottery, in King Street, Fenton, the scene of John Wesley's visit to the Potteries in 1790. JAK's art designer was Septimus Bennett, brother of Arnold Bennett (q.v.). In 1900 JAK acquired the Manor Mills in Fenton, premises which included a 21 oven factory.

JAK was one of the founders of the Pottery Trade Fair held in the King's Hall, Stoke upon Trent. He served as president of the Pottery Manufacturers' Association in 1910.

He married Margaret Aston, and had eight children. He lived in Stone for many years and became the oldest parishioner of St. Dominic's church. He was still governing director of James Kent, Ltd., at the time of his death, which occurred on 31 May 1953 at The Mount, Stone.

Evening Sentinel 1 June 1953 (obit.); Jewitt; VCH viii.

KIPLING, John Lockwood (1837-1911), *architectural sculptor/illustrator,* Burslem.

The eldest son of the Revd. Joseph Kipling, a Wesleyan Methodist minister, who died at Skipton in 1862, JLK was born in 1837. He was educated at Woodhouse Grove Methodist School, Bradford. An excursion to London to see the Great Exhibition of 1851 turned his attention towards art and he became a student of Sir Philip Cunliffe-

Owen. He worked as an artist in London and it is believed he was involved in the decoration of the South Kensington (later Victoria and Albert) Museum, carrying out modelling from the designs of his employer, Godfrey Sykes. He came to the Potteries to work for Pinder Bournes of Burslem, designing dinner plates. In 1863 he and Robert Edgar were awarded joint first prize in the competition for the design of the facade and elevation of the Wedgwood Memorial Institute in Burslem. He used terra-cotta rather than brick because of the former's grime-resisting qualities.

It is traditionally accepted that JLK became engaged to his future wife, Alice Macdonald, daughter of the Revd. George Browne Macdonald, on a picnic at Rudyard Lake, and their son Rudyard Kipling the novelist, was accordingly given this name. JLK and his wife left for Bombay in 1865 where he was appointed an architectural sculptor at the school of art in that city, where Rudyard Kipling was born. There was another child, Alice, born in 1868. In 1875 JLK was appointed curator of the Central Museum and Head of the School of Industrial Arts at Lahore, and remained in this post until his retirement in 1893.

JLK illustrated many of his son's books. The character Strickland in *Kim* and other works is supposed to be based on the author's father. JLK himself wrote, his publications including *Beast and Man in India,* published in 1891. He died on 26 January 1911 at The Gables, Tisbury, Wiltshire.

Alice Macdonald was one of four sisters whose husbands or children became well known public figures: Georgiana (1840-1920) married the painter Sir Edward Burne-Jones; Louise married Alfred Baldwin, M.P. and was the mother of the statesman Stanley Baldwin; Agnes married the painter Sir Edward John Poynter.

A. W. Baldwin, *The Macdonald Sisters* (1960); J. Craig 'John Lockwood Kipling: the Formative Years' in *The Kipling Papers* (1980); E. Rowley, *Origins and Influence of the Wedgwood Memorial Institute, Burslem* (typescript, HRL).

KIRK, George, (bap. 1809), *iron founder and engineer,* Hanley.

GK was baptised in Burslem on 30th April 1809. He was the sone of Christopher Kirk of Etruria and Margaret his wife. His father, also an engineer from c. 1822 to c. 1853, supplied a steam engine to Minton's in 1819. GK had established his headquarters at Etruria Inn by 1850, and is listed as an engineer in a directory of 1860. In 1871 he was employing 60 men at his Etruria Grove foundry. He supplied much of the machinery for Hatton water pumping station, and his business included servicing boilers at nearby factories, one of which was Shirley's bone mill. CK invested £2,000 in the ill-fated Whitfield Colliery Company in 1871, but survived its liquidation in 1875. His business is listed in the 1880 directory but not in 1884.

He married, and had two children by his wife, Sarah. He lived in Belmont Road, Hanley. A man of some eccentric character he had his coffin made of oak and delivered to his works where he kept it until he died.

Census 1871; J. Thomas, *The Rise of the Staffordshire Potteries;* E. J. Warrilow, *The History of Etruria.*

KIRKHAM, George (c. 1818-49), *Sunday school teacher,* Tunstall.

George Kirkham was a leader and Sunday school teacher at Mount Tabor Methodist New Connexion church, Tunstall. The church fell into disruption following the expulsion of the Revd. Joseph Barker (q.v.) in 1841 and Kirkham helped to revive it. He is mentioned in Charles Shaw's *When I was a Child* as an important influence in the latter's life. He died on 21 September 1849.

C. Shaw, *When I was a Child;* J. Young, *After One Hundred Years: a history of Burslem Bethel Circuit;* Schedule of headstones in Christ Church churchyard, Tunstall.

KIRKHAM, William (1829-1913), *pottery manufacturer,* Stoke upon Trent.

WK was born on January 19th or February 2nd 1829 at Radwood, Staffordshire, the son of Samuel Kirkham. His wife, Mary Ann, born in Wellington, Shropshire, bore him four daughters and two sons. In 1859 he bought a pottery factory in London Road, Stoke upon Trent, and began manufacturing hospital and laboratory ware, school and artists' requisites, chemists' receptacles and a wide range of components for industry. In 1881 he employed 33 men, 18 women, 16 boys and 5 girls. He was active in local government, serving as mayor of Stoke upon Trent from 1890-3 and acting as chairman of the committee appointed to implement the Technical Education Acts in the borough. He was a member of the Stoke upon Trent school board, was elected to Staffordshire county council and was county justice of the peace. He also belonged to the Duke of Sutherland's Lodge of Ancient Shepherds. During his period of office as mayor he was presented by his workpeople with a portrait of himself painted by Lucien Boullemier (q.v.). After his death, which occurred on 13th April 1913, his sons took over the business.

British Bulletin of Commerce, 1955; Dir. 1872-1907; Woolley (or Fenn) Almanacks for 1872-1903; C. Penn *Staffordshire at the Opening of the 20th Century* (photograph on p. 63).

KNIGHT, John King (1788/9-1856), *earthenware manufacturer,* Fenton.

JKK was born at Thringstone, Leicestershire, in 1788/9. He married Elizabeth Elkin at Bucknall on 25th January 1813, and by her had two children, John King Wood and Hannah. He worked the Foley Potteries, Fenton (built by John Smith about 1820), in partnership with the Elkin brothers and John Bridgewood, producing blue-printed earthenware including the Willow and Broseley patterns. He was joined by Henry Wileman of London in 1853 who continued alone after JKK retired in 1856. He lived at Golden Hill in 1851, and is listed in that year as potter, coal master and farmer of 220 acres. He owned Ubberley Colliery in 1854. He was chief bailiff for Great Fenton in 1841.

He died at Golden Hill on 15th May 1856.

Jewitt; VCH viii.

LAMB, Revd. William D. (born c. 1815), *minister of religion (Church of England),* Burslem.

WDL, born in Yorkshire in 1815 or 1816, was the incumbent of Christ Church, Cobridge, from 1846 to 1871. He served on the Burslem Local Board of Health from 1850 to 1856, representing Rushton Grange. He held strong Conservative political opinions. In 1851 he was living at Cobridge Villa with his wife and a new-born baby.

Census 1851; Dir. 1851, 1867; Oldham.

LAKE, Thomas (1788/9-1872), *upholsterer and cabinet maker,* Stoke upon Trent.

TL was born in 1788 or 1789 at Draycott, Staffordshire. He earned his living as an upholsterer and cabinet maker but posterity remembers him as parish clerk of Stoke upon Trent for 50 years. It was written of him that 'His face was disciplined into a becoming gravity and he was properly conscious of his dignity as a licensed parish clerk.' He was listed in the 1851 census as married with two children, Samuel and Thomas. He qualified as an improvement commissioner in 1857. He died at 1 Glebe Street, Stoke upon Trent, on 2 February 1872 and was buried in Stoke churchyard, where his gravestone was still surviving in 1984.

R. A. Cason, *Time and the Place;* Census 1851; Dir. 1851, 1872.

LAWTON, Spencer (c. 1828-1901), *commission agent,* Burslem.

SL was born about 1828. He established a business as a commission agent and lived in 1876 in Waterloo Road, Burslem. He was elected to the Burslem Board of Health in that year and served as mayor in 1886, 1893 and 1894. He died at Elm House, Burslem, on 17 August 1901, and was buried in Burslem cemetery.

Census 1881; Dir. 1912; gravestone in Burslem cemetery.

LEADBEATER, Edward James (1837-1911), *pottery manufacturer,* Stoke upon Trent.

EJL was born in Hanley in 1837. He was apprenticed to Thomas Worthington, of Hanley, earthenware and stoneware manufacturer at the Brook Street Works, Hanley. In 1865 he and Frederick Robinson bought the Glebe Street Parian ware factory, with the moulds, begun in 1858 by Giovanni Meli (q.v.). In 1870 the partners also acquired the Wharf Street Works. The two factories specialised in the production of Parian ware (a semi-transparent highly vitrified form of bisque porcelain) and became one of the largest manufacturers of this type of ware in the district. They produced a variety of forms — figures, groups and busts. Their busts included representations of many Victorian celebrities, and for the American market, to which most of their output was sent, they produced busts of such personalities as Lincoln and Longfellow. The firm continued into the 20th century and continued to trade under the name of Robinson and Leadbeater, although Robinson set up a business of his own in 1905.

EJL was elected to the Stoke upon Trent council and served as mayor 1899-1900, at which period he was living at Myrtle Villa, James Street, Stoke upon Trent. By his wife Emily he had three sons and five daughters. He died at Sheppard Street, Stoke upon Trent, on 22 March 1911.

Census 1871; C. and D. Shinn, *The Illustrated Guide to Victorian Parian China; Staffs. Sentinel* 23 March 1911; headstone in Hartshill cemetery.

LEAK, Joseph (1833-1909), *schoolmaster,* Longton.

Joseph Leak, a native of Burslem, taught for many years at Idle, Yorks. He married a Miss Fernyhough, daughter of a Longton china manufacturer and returned to the Potteries about 1870 as a partner with his father-in-law. He was in another partnership with F. Cartlidge and Son.

He organised the opposition to the annexation of Florence and Dresden by Longton in 1884 but withdrew his opposition when separate rating was agreed. He was elected to Longton council representing Florence ward in 1884, and to the School Board. He was chairman of the education committee from 1902. He served as mayor of Longton 1892-3, was in favour of federation and chairman of the Longton council federation committee. His politics were Liberal and his religious views nonconformist. He died on 23 November 1909.

Hughes and Harber Almanack 1904; *Staffs. Sentinel* 24 November 1909.

LEASON, George (1841-1911), *pottery manager,* Stoke upon Trent.

GL, the son of George and Prudence Leason, was born in Hartshill on 25th August 1841. His father worked for Minton and helped with experiments on encaustic tiles c. 1835-45. George junior was educated in Newcastle under Lyme until the age of 10 when he became a messenger boy. His father apprenticed him to Minton's when he was 13, and in time he became a journeyman and then a foreman. In 1868 he was appointed manager of the china works and in 1883 became a director. He left Minton's in 1900 to work for the firm of Guillaume, Frans and Mahlem in Germany, and stayed with that company for five years.

His wife Emma, née Griffiths, bore him two children, George Griffith and William. He was elected a councillor for the borough of Stoke upon Trent in 1875 and was mayor for three consecutive years, 1884-5, 1885-6 and 1886-7. He died on3 April 1911.

Staffs. Sentinel 5 April 1911 (obit.).

LEICESTER, Thomas (1811/12-98), *chemist,* Burslem.

TL was born about 1811, possibly in Cheshire. He was in business from at least 1851 to 1882 at 38 Market Place, Burslem. In 1861 he is shown as chemist, with a wife, Ada, and two children, an assistant, a servant and a nursemaid. He served on the Burslem Board of Health 1868-9. In 1876 he lived at The Limes, Waterloo Road, Burslem. He died on 4 April 1898, leaving a legacy to set up a convalescent fund and another for an annual scholarship at Newcastle High School.

Census 1861; Oldham; inf. from Miss M. F. Mackenzie, Pharmaceutical Soc. of Great Britain.

LEIGH, Edmund, (1854-1924), *pottery manufacturer,* Burslem.

EL was born at Tunstall on 26 March 1854, the son of William Leigh, who with his partner Burgess, controlled the Hill Pottery at Burslem. Edmund was educated at the Wesleyn Day School, Burslem and at the age of 13 began to work for his father. In 1872 he became the firm's representative in London and later visited Australia, America, South Africa and Germany. His father died during the building of the firm's new factory beside the canal at Middleport, completed in 1888, the first commission for A. R. Wood (q.v.), and EL became partner in his father's place.

In politics he was a Liberal, and was an original member of the National Liberal Club in 1883. He supported Irish Home Rule and was offered the nomination of a seat, but he did not actively consider a national political career. He played the principal part in launching Enoch Edwards on his political career. Edwards subsequently switched to the Labour party. In 1922 EL openly supported Andrew McLaren, the Labour candidate, against Sydney Malkin, the Liberal Unionist, and his intervention was believed to be decisive in McLaren's narrow victory by only 40 votes.

EL was a member of Burslem borough council, serving as chairman of the gas committee. He was a supporter of federation. In December 1909 he persuaded Arnold Bennett (q.v.) to write a political manifesto for the district. He became a member of Stoke on Trent council after federation, and was chairman of the licensing and compensation committee. He also represented Kidsgrove on Stafford county council.

By his wife Jane he had three sons and a daughter. The family lived in Emberton Street, Wolstanton, in 1881, by 1896 at The Oaks, Wolstanton and later at Mansion House, Stone. EL died at Radford House, Stone, on 1 January 1924.

N. Flower (edit.), *Journals of Arnold Bennett,* vol. 1; *Staffs. Sentinel* 2 January 1924 (obit.).

LEVESON-GOWER, Hon. Edward Frederick (1819-1907), *Member of Parliament,* Stoke upon Trent.

EFL-G was born in London on 3 May 1819, the son of 1 Earl Granville by Henrietta Elizabeth Cavendish, daughter of 5 duke of Devonshire. He was educated at Christ Church, Oxford, where he took his M.A. in 1844. He was called to the bar, at the Inner Temple, in 1845. He served for a few months in the Foreign Office as a précis writer in 1851-2. He was elected M.P. for Derby in 1847 but at the by-election in that year his election was declared void. He sat for Stoke upon Trent from 1852 to 1857, when he was defeated, and for Bodmin from 1859 to 1885. He was a Liberal in politics.

He married Lady Margaret Compton, daughter of the 2 marquess of Northampton, on 1 June 1853 and by her had a son, George Granville. He died on 30 May 1907.

Burke's *Peerage;* S and L.

LEVESON-GOWER, Granville George, 2 Earl Granville (1815-91). *colliery owner,* Hanley.

GGL-G was born at Great Stanhope Street, London on 11 May 1815, the son of 1 Earl Granville by his second wife, Lady Henrietta Cavendish, daughter of the 5 duke of Devonshire. He was educated at Eton and Christ Church Oxford. GGL-G entered Parliament, sitting for Morpeth, in 1836 and for Lichfield in 1841. He attained high office under a number of Liberal governments. He became lord president of the council 1852-8 and 1859-66; was secretary of state for the colonies 1868, foreign secretary 1870-4 and 1880-5, and again secretary of state for the colonies in 1886. He was created Knight of the Garter in 1857.

In the Potteries he owned Shelton collieries and was the principal owner of Etruria Iron Works. His properties in Hanley paid nearly one third of the rates of the town. He supported the local school of art, founded Granville schools at Cobridge in 1854, and in the mid-1850s built two model rows of cottages for his workers at the southern end of Waterloo Road.

His decision, in July 1842, at a time of trade depression, to give notice of a reduction of 6d. a day in miners' wages, precipitated a miners' strike, which was an element in the background to the Chartist riots of August 1842.

He married twice, (1) in 1840, Marie Louise Acton, daughter of the Duc de Dalbert and widow of Sir F. R. E. Acton and (2) in 1865 Castalia Rosalind Campbell. He died at South Audley Street, London, on 31 March 1891 and was buried in St. Michael's churchyard, Stone, Staffs.

Burke's *Peerage;* J. Epstein and D. Thompson, *The Chartist Experience;* Local Pamphlets Vol. 37 (HRL); VCH viii.

LEWIS, Joseph (born 1827/8), *newsagent and billposter,* Fenton.

JL was born about 1828 in Whitchurch, Salop. From about 1872 to about 1900 he was in business at 127 High Street, East. The words 'J Lewis, Bill Poster, Fenton'; are painted on the wall of Medina and Knobes premises in Glebe Street, Stoke upon Trent. He was also listed as a bookseller in 1881. He acted as town crier for Fenton until at least 1892, and was an unsuccessful candidate for election to the Fenton Urban District Council in 1894.

By his wife, Rachel, he had at least one child, Daniel.

Census 1881; Dir. 1872-1900

LITTLER, William (baptised 1724-84), *pottery manufacturer,* Longton.

WL was baptised in Burslem on 1 December 1724. He was the son of William Littler of Bourne Meadow and Sarah née Shaw. In 1751 he joined in partnership with William Jenkinson of Longton who was producing what has been claimed as the first Staffordshire porcelain.

WL continued the venture with various other partners but it was not a commercial success. His last partner, the Rev. Robert Charlesworth, of Bakewell, Derbyshire, seized and sold most of the company's stock in 1760. WL. with his wife, Jane, a paintress, whom he had married in 1753, was engaged to run a small pottery in West Pans, Musselburgh, Scotland. He was made an honorary burgess of Musselburgh in 1764. It is believed that most of the ware sold by the West Pans factory was Longton Hall ware decorated in Scotland. Although one of WL's customers was the duke of Atholl, by 1777 the business had failed. WL returned to Burslem where he died in October 1784, a poor man.

English Ceramic Circle Trans. vols. 5 and 6; VCH viii; B. Watney, *Longton Hall Porcelain.*

LLEWELLYN, Arthur Price (1852-1926), *solicitor,* Tunstall.

APL was born at Chell House, Tunstall, in 1852. He was the son of Thomas Llewellyn, who had founded a solicitor's practice in Tunstall in 1835 and became American consul for the Potteries, the first non-American so chosen. APL entered his father's practice in 1869 and qualified as a solicitor in 1874. APL went into practice with Henry Ackrill and became deputy clerk to Tunstall Local Board of Health, under Ackrill, in 1874. In 1876 he became secretary to the Staffordshire Pottery Manufacturers' Association and continued as secretary to the successor body, the British Pottery Manufacturers' Federation from its creation in 1919. From 1886 APL was secretary of the North Staffordshire Chamber of Trade. He became clerk to the Tunstall Local Board of Health in 1883 and continued as clerk to the Urban District Council from 1894 to federation. He was awarded 100 guineas by the council for his work during the negotiations leading up to federation, although he himself had been in favour of Tunstall's continued independence. He was also responsible with A. R. Wood (q.v.) and J. N. Peake (q.v.) for the construction of Victoria Road and the park, against much opposition.

He married Marie Hammack, daughter of an English businessman resident in Chile, and there were five sons and three daughters of the marriage. APL's son, Rupert Arthur Llewellyn became clerk to the Stoke magistrates after the suicide of William Holtom (q.v.). The family lived for many years at Seabridge Hall, Clayton, and latterly at Cathkin, Barlaston. APL died at his son Rupert's home, Aston Hall, Stoke on 12 November 1926, and was buried in Barlaston churchyard.

Federation News Cuttings (HRL); *Staffs. Sentinel* 2 January 1920 and 13 November 1926.

LOBLEY, Joseph (1841/2-1919), *borough surveyor,* Stoke upon Trent.

JL was born in Liverpool about 1841. Little is known about his early life, but in 1871 he was appointed surveyor and engineer of Hanley, a position he held until federation in 1910. His two main contributions to the town were the design of the Victoria Hall, built 1887/8 as an extension to the town hall, and whose good acoustic properties ensured its position as the musical centre of the Potteries, and 1909/10, with R. Scrivener and Sons, the council chamber of Hanley town hall.

He died in July 1919, aged 77, at Richmond Terrace, Shelton.

R. Malkin, *A Grand Tour; Staffs. Sentinel* 28 July and 2 August 1919; VCH viii.

LOCKETT, Harry (born c. 1855/6), *printer and stationer,* Hanley.

HL was born in Derby about 1855. In 1881 he was in business as a stationer at 27 Harley Street, Hanley. He was probably the Lockett who played for Stoke 2nd XI against Leek in the match reported in the *Staffordshire Daily Sentinel* on 31 October 1877. He participated in hare and hounds events on 3 and 14 October 1878, was an umpire with Hanley Rangers Football Club and secretary of Stoke F.C. in July 1884 on the retirement of Walter Cox. He was appointed honorary secretary of the Football League whose first meeting was held at the Anderton Hotel, London, on 22 March 1888, and served as secretary from 1890 to 1902. He was also secretary to Stoke Baseball Club. In 1908 when the Swifts fell into financial difficulties HL found guarantors for the club's liabilities and this enabled Stoke Football Club to be saved. He became a director.

He was not so successful in managing his own business affairs. In 1897 he formed the New Press Printing Company (Hanley), Ltd., whose publications included the *Staffordshire Catholic Chronicle.* In 1910 he was declared bankrupt. The business was eventually sold to Sherwin and Co.

Evening Sentinel Centenary Edition 16 April 1973; R. Speake, *One Hundred Years of County Football; Staffs. Daily Sentinel* 21 April 1878.

LODGE, (Sir) Oliver (1851-1940), *scientist,* Stoke upon Trent.

OL was born on 12 June 1851 at The Views, Penkhull, Stoke upon Trent, the eldest son of Oliver Lodge and Grace née Heath. His father, a clerk with the North Staffordshire Railway, later set up his own business selling clays and glazes. Oliver went to a dame school in Penkhull, then to Newport Grammar School, and eventually received private tuition from the rector of Combs, Suffolk. The family moved to Moreton House, Wolstanton, and later to the Watlands, Wolstanton. OL left school in 1865 to help his father in the business. He was invited by an aunt to stay in London, where he was excited by lectures which he attended at London University and the Royal Institute. Back in the Potteries he studied at the Athenaeum, Stoke upon Trent and at the Wedgwood Institute, Burslem. In 1874 he went to University College, London, and was awarded the degree of Doctor of Science in 1877. He taught at University College for some time, then in 1881 he was appointed professor of physics and mathematics at the newly-established University College of Liverpool. In 1900 he became the first principal of Birmingham University. He was knighted in 1902 and retired in 1919.

OL was forestalled by Hertz in the discovery of electromagnetic waves, but was the first man to transmit a message by radio telegraphy. This was at a British Association meeting in Oxford, on 14 August 1894. Lodge himself wrote, 'I signalled from another building in Oxford into the Museum where the lecture was given'. He also invented the method of electrical spark ignition for the internal combustion engine, and later two of his sons developed his ideas and founded the Lodge Plug Company. OL's many honours included a Fellowship of the Royal Society (1877), presidency of the British Association (1913) and dozens of honorary degrees from universities all over the world.

He was a popular lecturer, was concerned with social conditions and had radical views on a number of subjects, including student participation in the running of universities and female emancipation. At Liverpool he developed an interest in psychic phenomena, and came to believe that it was possible to communicate with the dead.

On 22 August 1877 he married Mary Marshall, of Brampton House, Newcastle under Lyme, and by her had six sons and six daughters. One son, Raymond, was killed in the First World War, and Lodge believed that he had established contact with Raymond's spirit.

He returned to Normanton House, near Salisbury, in 1920, and died there on 22 August 1940. His portrait by Sir George Reid, is in Birmingham University and a bust, by C. J. Allen, in Liverpool University Library.

The Lodge family often returned to North Staffordshire. Sir Oliver was made a freeman of the city of Stoke on Trent and an honorary member of the North Staffordshire Field Club. When the Penkhull area was redeveloped, his birthplace, The Views, built about 1780 was saved from demolition by the efforts of Deaconess B. I. Smee. At the 1967 public inquiry her witnesses cited the Oliver Lodge connection and the house was preserved for its historic and architectural interest. OL's parents are buried in Penkhull churchyard.

V. G. Aston, *The History of Penkhull;* W. P. Jolly, *Sir Oliver Lodge;* O. Lodge, *Past Years, an autobiography;* City of Stoke on Trent Housing Compulsory Purchase Order 1967 (Rothwell Street).

LONGBOTTOM, Luke (c. 1826-1902), *locomotive engineer,* Stoke upon Trent.

LL, born about 1825, came from a family of engineers. He served an apprenticeship in Leeds and worked for various firms until he became superintendent of the North Western Railway. In 1852 he was appointed locomotive superintendent of the Kendal and Windermere Railway and on that railway's amalgamation with the London and North Western Railway he became district locomotive foreman at Tebay and then Preston. He came to the Potteries in 1882 as locomotive and carriage and wagon supervisor of the North Staffordshire Railway on the death of Charles Clare. He achieved a much needed standardisation of boilers, cylinders and other locomotive fittings. He retired in 1902.

By his wife, Martha, he had two daughters, Sarah and Susannah. The family lived at Fenton Villa, where LL died on 12 February 1902, aged 76.

G. Dow, *North Staffordshire Album;* R. Christiansen and R. W. Miller, *The North Staffordshire Railway.*

LOWE, William (1833/4-1913), *ironfounder,* Stoke upon Trent.

WL, born about 1833, was a partner in the firm of Dean, Lowe and Machin which in 1868 took over the old foundry business in Cross (now Epworth) Street, Stoke upon Trent, formerly worked by Bostocks. Later these premises, comprising workshops and an old Georgian house, became George Fleet and Co., furnishers. About 1873 the firm moved to Railway Foundry, Fenton, and later they had premises in Welch Street, which the firm continued to use until about 1980.

WL by his wife, Emma, had four sons. He was a member of the North Staffordshire Institute of Mining Engineers.

He died on 23 June 1913 at The Laurels, Quarry Avenue, Stoke on Trent.

Cox's Pottery Annual 1926; *Staffs. Sentinel* 24 June 1913.

LYNAM, Charles (1829-1921), *architect,* Stoke upon Trent.

CL was born on 9 February 1829 at Colwich, Staffs., the son of George and Hannah Lynam. Not long after this event his father set up an architect's and surveyor's practice in Glebe Street, Stoke upon Trent. CL was educated at Christ's Hospital School, London, worked for two years with his father then was articled to a London architect. He joined his father's business in 1850, and in that year, through the influence of Herbert Minton, was appointed architect for the Stokeville Building Society, and designed 24 'superior' houses – 'The Villas' – for the Society. This district had the distinction of being the first designated conservation area in Stoke on Trent. CL was taken into partnership in 1853 by his father, who died later in that year. CL's official appointments included serving as surveyor to the Stoke upon Trent improvement commissioners (1860) and to the highways board, and he became surveyor to the borough of Stoke upon Trent on its incorporation in 1874. He resigned from his appointments on his election to the borough council. He was elected an alderman in 1877 but retired from local government affairs from pressure of work.

Lynam built up a large private practice and designed numerous public buildings, including the Stoke upon Trent Free Library and Baths (1877-8), the Stoke upon Trent new market complex (1883) and with another architect, Nicholl, the North Staffordshire Infirmary when it moved from Etruria to Hartshill. He was responsible for the design of a number of new churches and many restorations of old churches within and outside the county. Pevsner considers Christ Church, Fenton, to be Lynam's *magnum opus.* CL was elected a Fellow of the Royal Institute of British Architects in 1882. He was re-elected to Stoke upon Trent borough council in 1897, and served until 1903, when he was elected mayor, although he was no longer a member of the corporation. He also served as a Stoke magistrate for many years.

In 1857 CL married Lucy, daughter of Dr Robert Garner, the local historian. She bore him 14 children, the family living, for all Lynam's adult life, in the Penkhull area.

Lynam's main interest, outside his work and local government, was archaeology. He joined the North Staffordshire Field Club in the year of its inauguration, 1865, and set up its archaeology section. He was president of the Club in 1874, was awarded the Garner medal in 1894, and was again president in 1894. He became vice-president of the Archaeological Institute and was elected a Fellow of the Society of Antiquaries in 1895. Among his archaeological achievements were the elucidation of the ground plans of Croxden Abbey, near Uttoxeter, and Hulton Abbey, Stoke. His work on the later was used 50 years later to prevent the erection of a housing estate over the hidden foundations of the abbey. He undertook excavation work on the bath-house at the Roman site of Wall, near Lichfield. The old parish church of Stoke upon Trent had been demolished in 1830 and some of its stone used to form the bed of a watercourse serving Boothen Mill. Lynam discovered these in 1881 and used them to reconstruct two arches and other features of the old church, set up on the site of the old church. He acted as surveyor for Lichfield diocese for many years, and became a leading authority on local churches.

He published numerous articles in the *Transactions of the North Staffordshire Field Club* and in national archaeological journals. He wrote the articles on ancient earthworks for volume 1 of the *Victoria County History of Stafford* (1908) and helped with the chapter on Romano-British Staffordshire. His work on Croxden Abbey is contained in his book *The Abbey of St. Mary, Croxden, Staffordshire* (1911) and he published a monograph *The Inscriptions on the Ancient Church Bells of the County* in 1889.

He died at Cliff Bank House, Stoke on Trent, on 21 February 1921.

M. W. Greenslade, *The Staffordshire Historians;* T. W. Lancaster, *Hulton Abbey;* N. Pevsner, *The Buildings of England: Staffordshire; Transactions of the North Staffs. Field Club,* vol. lv; Turner; *Staffs. Sentinel* 24 November 1903; *Staffs. Advertiser* 26 February 1921; VCH viii.

MACDONALD, Revd. Frederick W. (1842-1928), *minister of religion (Wesleyan Methodist),* Burslem.

FWM was born on 25 February 1842 in Leeds, the son of the Revd. George Brown Macdonald (died 1868) and Hannah. He was educated at a private school in Buckinghamshire, St. Peter's Collegiate School, London, and Owens College, Manchester. In 1853 FWM's father became superintendent of Sloane Terrace Chapel, Chelsea. FWM trained as an accountant for two years but then studied for the Methodist church and began work as a minister in the Burslem circuit in 1862. In his autobiography he claimed that he helped to smooth the way for the operation of the 1864 Factory Extension Act, which regulated the labour of children and women in the pottery industry. His book is a chatty, informative account of his work among potters, miners and canal navvies, giving a picture of working class life and of the experiences of a young minister learning his job. William Owen (q.v.) the trade unionist, stated that he had been converted to Methodism by Macdonald during a public debate on the

American Civil War in 1862. FWM left Burslem for Liverpool in 1865 and later travelled to America, Australia and New Zealand. He became president of the Methodist Conference in 1899. He married Mary Cork.

His sister Georgiana married Edward Burne-Jones the artist, in 1860. Another sister, Louisa, married Alfred Baldwin, father of Stanley Baldwin, later prime minister, and a third sister, Alice married John Lockwood Kipling, (q.v.) father of the poet and novelist Rudyard Kipling.

FWM died in 1928.

A. W. Baldwin, *The Macdonald Sisters;* F. W. Macdonald, *Reminiscences of my Early Ministry; As a Tale that is Told; Proceedings of the Wesley Hist. Society* vol. xxi, 'The Macdonald family'.

MACINTYRE, James (1803-68), *pottery manufacturer.* Burslem.

JM was born in 1803 in Glasgow. Early in life he went to Liverpool and there became a shipowner. He came to Burslem in 1832 as a clerk to the canal company, Alexander Bell and Co. The Macintyre family formed the Anderton Carrying Co., and JM returned to Liverpool to supervise the business until 1848 when it was bought by the Bridgwater Trustees. JM now went back to Burslem to manage the Potteries branch of this company. He gave evidence at numerous government enquiries on inland waterways. In 1854 he took over the business of his brother-in-law William Sadler Kennedy. Kennedy had started manufacturing palettes and other articles in King Street about 1838, moved to Bourne's Bank and in conjunction with William Maddock made improvements in the manufacture of door handles etc. The business moved, about 1847, to Washington Works. Under James Macintyre's ownership the firm's production of porcelain specialities increased. JM patented methods of producing oval and other forms by the lathe, and his 'Ivory China' gained a high reputation. He took his manager, Thomas Hulme (q.v.) and his son-in-law, William Woodall (q.v.) into the business.

JM was a member of the Burslem Local Board of Health from 1855 to 1867, a poor law union guardian, and was elected chief bailiff on three occasions. Liberal in politics he was a frequent speaker at reform meetings. He was interested in education and engaged in local philanthropic activities. He was the first honorary secretary of the Wedgwood Institute Committee. He protested against the action of the Revd. J. E. Armstrong (q.v.) in helping to found the Burslem Rifle Corps, describing it as 'an unseemly perversion of a peaceful calling'.

He married Ellen Kennedy (died 1874) and had a daughter, Evelyn, who married William Woodall (q.v.) and another daughter who married Dr. Craig of Shelton House, Hanley. The family lived next door to the Washington Works, but later moved to Grange Cottage, Burslem, where JM died on 19 December 1868. He was buried in Hanley cemetery.

Jewitt; Oldham; Anderton; *Staffordshire Sentinel* 26 December 1868 and 5 August; Wedgwood Institute Scrapbook (HRL).

MADDOCK, John (c. 1807-77), *pottery manufacturer,* Burslem.

JM the son of John and Sarah Maddock, was baptised on 19 July 1807; (another JM, son of Charles and Elizabeth Maddock, was baptised on 9 February 1812). The firm of John Maddock and Sons was founded about 1830 in premises in Newcastle Street, Burslem. JM was in partnership with Seddon from 1839 to 1842. The firm made granite ware for the American market. JM required all his employees to join a sick club. He retired from the business in the 1870s.

JM was a member of Burslem Board of Health from 1850 to 1868, and was chairman and chief bailiff 1852-3 and 1854-5. When the Baths and Washhouses Act was not adopted in Burslem in 1852 JM offered to build public baths at his own expense if he could be guaranteed £50 p.a. in subscriptions. He was a member of the British Anti-State Church Association. He married Martha née Knowles and his children included James Maddock. He died in 1877. His widow presented the mayoral chain of Burslem in his memory in 1880.

IGI Staffs; Jewitt; *Staffs. Sentinel* 8 July 1916; VCH viii.

MALKIN, Ralph (c. 1805-86), *pottery manufacturer,* Fenton.

RM, son of Elijah Malkin and his wife Thirza, was baptised at Stoke upon Trent on 5 March 1805. He manufactured earthenware at Park Works, Market (later King) Street, Fenton from about 1865 to 1894.

He was a commissioner for Fenton in 1874, chief bailiff and a poor law guardian in 1879 and served on the school board for Stoke upon Trent (which included Fenton) in 1874. By his wife Ann, whom he married c. 1830, he had three sons and three daughters. He lived at Market Street, (then Duke Street), Fenton, from 1851 to 1879 at least and died at Argyle House, Newcastle under Lyme on 5 May 1886.

Census 1871; Dir. 1879-96; IGI Staffs; Jewitt.

MALKIN, Sydney (1865-1953), *Tile manufacturer,* Burslem.

SM was born at The Mount, Penkhull, on 31 August 1865, the son of James Malkin and Annie, daughter of Joseph Edge (q.v.). He was educated at Osmond's Academy, Richmond Terrace, Shelton, and from 1879 to 1881 at Newcastle High School. He then joined his father, who was connected with two businesses, Edge, Malkin and Co., earthenware manufacturers, and Malkin, Edge and Co., tile manufacturers. In partnership with his brother Elijah SM set up in his own business, as a tile maker, at Newport Lane, Middleport, in 1894. The firm became a limited company in 1900.

SM was elected to the Burslem School Board in 1898 and to the Burslem council in 1900. He was created alderman in 1906 and served as mayor in 1907. In favour of federation he resigned from the federation committee of the council because of its anti-federation majority. He became an alderman of the new federated county borough but resigned from this position in protest at what he called the dictatorship of Frederick Geen (q.v.) over the issue of the purchase of the Staffs. Potteries Waterworks Company. He had pushed through the building of a new town hall in Burslem in 1909-10 against opposition and the building, later the Queen's Theatre, was called by some 'Malkin's Folly'.

In 1922 SM stood as National Liberal candidate for the Burslem parliamentary constituency but was defeated, owing it was alleged to the influence of Edward Leigh (q.v.). He was chairman of the North Staffordshire Cripples Aid Society founded by Millicent Duchess of Sutherland (q.v.) and a governor of Haywood Hospital. He was a local preacher and held other offices for Swan Bank Wesleyan Methodist church. In 1904 he was summonsed for refusing to pay the education portion of the local rate, but he rejected any connection with the Passive Resistance League. For many years he was chairman of the justices' probation committee and opened a boys' club near his factory in Middleport.

By his first wife, Edith Jordan née Stormer, he had four sons. She died in 1941 and he married Doris Eshelby. After his death his widow gave their house, Penrhyn, Waterloo Road, Cobridge, to Burslem Old People's Housing Society and it was renamed Sydney Malkin House. The family also lived at The Limes, First Avenue, Porthill and at Westfield, Endon.

SM died on 30 January 1953.

Evening Sentinel 30 January 1953 (obit.); Federation Newscuttings (HRL), 1907-8; Oldham; information from Mr. D. J. Malkin (grandson).

MALLAN, Thomas Hill (died 1875), *dentist,* Stoke upon Trent.

THM son of Thomas Hill Mallan, had established a dental practice in Newcastle under Lyme by 1839. The business moved to Stoke upon Trent then back to Newcastle then again to Stoke, where by December 1850 it was established at 19 Liverpool Road.

In 1862 THM was charged with attacking his wife, Mary Ann née Bird, (married at Stoke upon Trent 10 October 1852), when he returned home drunk one night. He was bound over in the sum of £40 for six months. He died early in February 1875.

Census 1861; Dir. 1851, 1867; *Staffs. Advertiser* 8 August 1862 and 20 February 1875; Stoke upon Trent parish registers.

MASON, Charles James (1791-1856), *pottery manufacturer,* Fenton.

CJM was born on 14 July 1791, the third son of Miles Mason (q.v.) and Ruth née Farrar. He and his brother George Miles Mason (q.v.) took over their father's business at the Minerva Works, Fenton, in June 1813. On 31 July of that year CJM patented Mason's Ironstone China. The brothers later acquired a larger factory, Fenton Stone Works, which was demolished between the two world wars for new housing. CJM was unpopular with other pottery manufacturers for his sharp business methods which included selling wares by auction. He was accused by his employees of depreciating wages and they also opposed his introduction of a machine for making flat and hollow ware patented by George Wall in 1843. Their opposition, and defects in the ware produced, caused the withdrawal of this machine in 1845. In 1842 CJM's house in Fenton, Heron Cottage, had been one of the targets for attack by Chartist rioters. CJM filed a bankruptcy petition on 17 February 1848 and from 1848 to 1854 worked at Daisy Bank, Longton.

He married, firstly, on 31 August 1815, Sarah Spoke, grand-daughter of Josiah Spoke I (q.v.) and by her and two children. He married, secondly, in 1852, Miss Asbury, of Longton, by whom he had a daughter.

CJM died on 5 February 1856 and was buried in Barlaston churchyard.

J. Epstein and D. Thompson, *The Chartist Experience;* R. Hagger, *The Masons of Lane Delph;* Jewitt; A. Lamb, 'Mechanisation and the Application of Steam Power in the North Staffordshire Pottery Industry' in *North Staffs. Journal of Field Studies* vol. 17, 1977; VCH ii and viii.

MASON, George Heming (1818-72), *artist,* Fenton.

GHM, the son of George Miles Mason (q.v.) and Eliza née Heming, was born on 11 March 1818 at Fenton Park. He was educated at Anderton's School, Brampton, Newcastle under Lyme, and in 1834 was articled to W. R. Watts, a Birmingham surgeon, but the articles were cancelled. GHM left England with his brother in 1843 and travelled on foot through France, Switzerland and Italy, arriving at Rome in 1845. There he took a studio and earned his living by painting portraits of visiting English people, their dogs and their horses. He often painted the landscape of the Campagna. During the siege of Rome in 1849 when French forces crushed the newly-established Roman Republic, GHM was arrested as a spy and only narrowly escaped death. In 1858 he returned to England, married Mary Emma Wood on 5 August 1858 and settled in a corner of the family mansion at Wetley Abbey. There were two sons and five daughters by the marriage. In 1864 he moved to Westbourne House, Shaftesbury Road, Hammersmith, London. He was elected A.R.A. in 1869, moved to 6 Theresa Terrace, Hammersmith, and died there on 22 October 1872. He was buried in Brompton cemetery. He has been described as 'the greatest of idyllic painters of England'.

DNB.

MASON, George Miles (1789-1859), *pottery manufacturer,* Fenton.

GMM was one of the three sons of Miles Mason (q.v.). When his father retired in 1813 GMM with his brother Charles James Mason (q.v.) took over the Minerva Works, Park Street, Fenton. They moved to a works in what is now Victoria Place in 1815 when the lease held by Josiah Spode expired. There they began their manufacture of patent ironstone china. George retired from business about 1829. He unsuccessfully contested the Stoke upon Trent parliamentary election as a Liberal in 1832. Later he devoted himself to literature and painting, adopting the life style of a country gentleman at Wetley Abbey, where he moved in 1848.

GMM married Eliza Heming in 1814 and there were four children including George Heming Mason (q.v.). He died at Wetley on 31 August 1859.

Anderton: VCH viii.

MASON, Miles (1752-1822), *pottery manufacturer,* Fenton.

MM was born at Dent, Yorks., in December 1752. the son of William Mason and Ann née Bailey. After a successful career in London as a glass manufacturer and china dealer he began about 1796 to make pottery first at Liverpool and then about 1800 in Staffordshire. By 1805 he had moved to the Minerva Works, Fenton. In June 1813 he handed over the business to his sons George Miles Mason (q.v.) and Charles James Mason (q.v.). The eldest son, William, was in partnership with his father about 1806, trading as M. Mason and Son, and remained in business until 1824. The business relationship between William and his two other brothers is unclear.

MM married Ruth Farrar, daughter of Richard Farrar, a London glass merchant and had a daughter, Ann Ruth and the three sons mentioned above. He died in 1822.

G. Godden, *The Illustrated Guide to Mason's Patent Ironstone China;* R. Haggar, *The Masons of Lane Delph;* VCH viii.

MASSINGHAM, John Deacon (c. 1827-82), *minister of religion (Church of England),* Burslem.

JDM was born about 1827 and educated at Trinity College, Dublin, B.A. 1851, M.A. 1854, LL.B and LL.D 1867, B.D. and D.D. 1869. He was appointed curate of All Souls, Derby in 1851, vicar of St. Paul's Derby 1853, vicar of St. Paul's Warrington 1863 and vicar of St. Paul's, Longport, 1872, where he remained until his death on 20 June 1882.

Dir. 1882; F. Boase, *Modern English Biography.*

MASSEY, Thomas (born c. 1780), *gentleman,* Burslem.

TM was born in Staffs. about 1780. He is shown as a proprietor of houses in the 1851 census, living at 107 Moorland Road, Burslem. He was a member of the Burslem Local Board of Health 1850-5 and of Liberal political opinions.

Census 1851; Oldham.

MATTHIAS, Revd. T. D. (fl. 1875-81), *newspaper editor,* Hanley.

TDM succeeded William Owen (q.v.) as editor of the *Potteries Examiner* in 1875. He made the paper less of a union journal and more middle class in opinion.

He was living in 54 Great York Street in 1871 and in 17 St. Clare Street in 1881.

Anderton; Census 1871, 1881; *The Sentinel Story 1873-1973.*

MAY, Charles Bower (born c. 1820), *colliery owner,* Burslem.

CBM was baptised on 9 June 1820 at Whittington, Derbyshire, the son of Charles Hughes May and Anne Elizabeth née Bower. He was in partnership with Joshua May as coal and ironstone masters, Sneyd Colliery, 1862. He was bankrupt about 1875 and the business was taken over by William Heath (q.v.) as Sneyd Colliery Co.

He was a member of the Burslem Local Board of Health 1850-1, 1854-5, 1868-71. His political views were Conservative and he was Church of England in religious denomination. In 1871 he lived with his wife Harriet at Sneyd Farm, Burslem.

Census 1871; Dir. 1862, 1872, 1876; IGI Staffs.

MAYER, Elijah (1750-1813), *pottery manufacturer,* Hanley.

EM, the son of Elijah Mayer and his wife Elizabeth, was born in 1750. In his youth he was an enameller and travelled abroad as the agent of Jacob Warburton (q.v.) of Cobridge and the Chatterley brothers of Shelton. He was described as an enameller in 1787 and produced enamelled cream ware at the Cobden Works, High Street (Town Road), Hanley. He also manufactured cane ware with relief figures and black basalt of the finest quality. He took his sons Elijah junior and Joseph into partnership. His son Joseph was later in partnership at the Cobden Works with Leonard Abington (q.v.) and William Ridgeway and at his death in 1860 left an immense amount of money which was the subject of many legal proceedings and is still sometimes though to be available to the correct claimant.

EM married a cousin, Jane Mayer, on 5 March 1774, when he was described as a merchant.

He died on 9 January 1813 and his tomb still stands in St. John's Churchyard, Hanley.

Adams; Jewitt; M and H; *Staffs. Advertiser* 16 January 1813; VCH ii and viii.

MAYER, Thomas (1800-55), *pottery manufacturer,* Burslem.

TM, second son of Samuel Mayer (d.1838) of Newcastle under Lyme, was born in 1800. He was educated at Newcastle under Lyme Grammar School and at Wood and Pullen's School, Chester. After leaving school he was employed by Wilson & Breeze, of Hanley. From at least 1826 to c. 1837 he leased Cliff Bank Works, Stoke upon Trent. In 1841 it was stated he employed 500 people. About 1843, with his brothers John and Joseph, he operated Dale Hall Works, Burslem, trading as Mayer Brothers and Elliot (Liddle Elliot, q.v.). The firm produced a large earthenware table described as the chef-d'oeuvre of the potter's art, and introduced many improvements in manufacture, especially in polychromatic bisque printing. They won a medal at the Great Exhibition in 1851.

TM married Charlotte Adams and had a daughter Mary. In 1851 his house was at Dale Hall, where he died on 12 October 1855.

Census 1851: *Gentleman's Magazine,* 12 October 1855; Jewitt; VCH viii.

MAYER, William (floruit 1871-8), *pottery worker,* Longton.

WM worked at Daisy Bank as a turner. In 1868 he became secretary of the Longton branch of the Reform Union. He was also a member of the Labour Representation League and William Woodall M.P. (q.v.), thought he might stand for election to Parliament in 1871. He was a member of Longton School Board 1871-8. In religion he was a member of the local Methodist New Connexion church.

Anderton.

McILROY, Clarke (1857-1935), *department store owner,* Hanley.

CM was born on 5 March 1857 at Aghadowey, Co. Londonderry, and was educated at Coleraine Normal school. One of eleven children of a farmer, he joined one of his brothers in business in Reading in 1874. CM came to Hanley in 1883 and took over the business of Boulton and Thomas in Lamb Street. He took his nephew, James Clarke, into the business in 1908 and sent him to America to study the methods of Wanamaker of New York, owner of the largest store in the world. The original business employed six assistants but by 1921 there were 200 employees in 24 departments, and was one of the largest stores in the area. In 1935 the number of employees was 350. CM remained in sole control until October 1928 when the business was incorporated, CM serving as chairman and managing director. A large rebuilding scheme began in the 1930s. The City Arcade, on the north side of Lamb Street, and occupying the site of Bishp and Stonier's pottery, was opened in December 1933, with the new main store scheduled to open in September 1935. McIlroy's store was the Bostocks of Arnold Bennett's novels. He wrote that 'their advertisements attack you at every railway staion', and that because of its frontages on three streets it might be called 'the shop of the one hundred windows'.

McIlroy's was eventually bought by Lewis's; the original store was demolished in 1964 with the opening of Lewis's new premises.

CM was originally a Presbyterian but after moving to Stone, Staffs., he became a Congregationalist. He married twice, firstly to Augusta Gordon Long, who died in 1914, and secondly to a Miss Brown. He lived at The Brooms, Stone.

He died while on a visit to Newbury on 2 June 1935 and was buried in Stone cemetery.

Evening Sentinel 3 June 1935 (obit.); *Staffs. Advertiser* 15 January 1921; E. J. D. Warrilow, *Arnold Bennett and Stoke-on-Trent.*

MEDINA, Rolfe (c. 1827-76), *musical instrument maker and music teacher,* Stoke upon Trent.

RM was born in Geissen, Duchy of Hesse Darmstadt, Germany (see denisation certificate, though 1861 census states Frankfurt), about 1827. He came to England about 1842 and was living in Stoke upon Trent from 1854. In 1861 he was living at 31 Liverpool Road, and made, imported and sold musical instruments. He was in partnership with Herr Knobes, who managed the factory in Saxony from which RM imported his instruments. RM also gave tuition in piano, harp, guitar and zither. The business was later transferred to Glebe Street where a large painted advertisement for Medina and Knobes was still surviving on the side of the building in 1984.

By his wife, Elizabeth, also German-born, RM had two daughters, Clara and Arabella. On 7 November 1864 he was granted a certificate of naturalisation, which enabled him to purchase property. He became a Stoke improvement commissioner from 1872 to 1874. He died on 17 September 1876. His widow continued the business for some years, and it later came into the hands of William Sherratt (q.v.).

Census 1861; Dir. 1860, 1876; Home Office Certificate of Denisation HO 1. 118, Cert. No. 455B; Stoke upon Trent parish registers, (burials); Stoke upon Trent Improvement Commissioners' Minutes.

MEIGH, Job (1784-1862), *pottery manufacturer,* Hanley.

JM, son of Job Meigh, a pottery manufacturer, was born in 1784. Job Meigh senior rebuilt the Old Hall Works, Hanley, in 1790, and JM continued his father's business, in partnership with Richard Hicks 1810-35. The firm was awarded a gold medal by the Society of Arts for producing a leadless glaze for red earthenware. JM had apparently retired by 1851 when his son Charles was running the works. Charles founded the Old

Hall Earthenware Company Ltd., the first limited company in pottery manufacture, in 1862, after his father's death. The company was replaced by the Old Hall Porcelain Works Co., which ran the pottery from 1887 until it closed in 1902.

JM died at Ash Hall on 30 January 1862.

Dir. 1851; Jewitt; M and H; VCH viii.

MELI, Giovanni (born c. 1815), *pottery modeller,* Stoke upon Trent.

GM was born about 1815 in Palermo, Sicily. He came to England in 1838 and worked in London. He attracted attention in art circles and Samuel Alcock (q.v.), invited him to Burslem about 1840. Meli quarrelled with Alcock and moved to Stoke upon Trent where he set up in business as a free-lance modeller, working for Copeland Garratt and other firms. About 1852 (some sources suggest 1858) he established a business in Rome Street and Glebe Street, although during the 1860s he did some modelling for James Duke and Nephews. In 1865 he sold his business to Robinson and Leadbeater (see Edward James Leadbeater) and returned to Italy with the intention of manufacturing terra-cotta ware. Unable to find suitable clays he emigrated to the United States of America and established a factory in Chicago. He exhibited at the 1862 Exhibition, his work including Parian statuettes, vases etc. His models for Adams and Sons included the Spanish Brigand, the Italian Fruit Girl and Abraham offering up Isaac.

In 1850 GM became an original member of the Stokeville Building Society, though he never lived at The Villas and sold his share in 1853. In order to accept the conveyance of a house he took out British naturalisation papers. In 1861 he lived at West Bank, Penkhull. He voted for Beresford Hope, the Conservative candidate, in the election of 1865. By his wife Jane he had a number of children, including Edward John Salvatore, Vincent, Leopoldo, and one other. Edward John Salvatore probably accompanied his father to Chicago but had returned to Stoke upon Trent by 1877 when he was in business in Liverpool Road as a music teacher.

M. Ashford 'The Alcocks and Hill Top Pottery' (Univ. of Keele Adult Education Department local history certificate essay 1972); Census 1851, 1861, 1881; Dir. 1851, 1861, 1879; Jewitt; PRO HO/1/45, certificate no. 1438; C. and D. Shinn, *The Illustrated Guide to Victorian Parian China;* Turner.

MELLOR, Joseph (1869-1938), *scientist,* Stoke upon Trent.

JM was born in Huddersfield in 1869, son of Job Mellor, a woollen-mill worker who emigrated with his family to New Zealand in 1879. Joseph worked in a boot factory, attended evening classes, and eventually went to Otago University, where he obtained a first class honours degree in chemistry in 1899. He married Emma Cranwell Bates in that year, and taught for some months in an agricultural college before taking up a research scholarship at Owens College, Manchester. He produced eight research papers on organic and inorganic chemistry; he was awarded the degree of doctor of science by the University of New Zealand in 1902. He was appointed chemistry teacher at Newcastle under Lyme High School in 1902 became interested in the technical problems of pottery manufacture and was appointed lecturer at the Pottery School, Tunstall, in 1904. He became a member of the North Staffordshire (later British) Ceramic Society in 1905 and was later appointed secretary. He was largely responsible for the transformation of this body into an international institution. He published over 100 papers in the society's transactions, some in collaboration with Bernard Moore (q.v.) who became a life-long friend. JM realised the importance of high temperature-resistant refractory furnace linings for the pottery industry, and was instrumental in the formation of the British Refractories Research Association under the Department of Scientific and Industrial Research, and set up its laboratories in Shelton in 1919. He became its first director of research and held that office until 1937. His 16 volume encyclopaedia *A Comprehensive Treatise on Inorganic and Theoretical Chemistry,* was published from 1921 to 1937. His work on ceramics led to his election to a Fellowship of the Royal Society in 1927, a distinction only once before conferred on a worker in this field, Josiah Wedgwood (q.v.). He published seven other textbooks on chemical subjects, a book on mathematics and a book of cartoons reflecting his sense of humour. He was an accomplished chess-player. He lived in the Villas, Stoke upon Trent. In 1938 he was made a Companion of the British Empire. He died on 24th May 1938.

Obituary Notices of the Royal Society of London, No. 7, vol. 2 (1939); *Refractories Journal, 1957; Transactions of British Ceramic Society, vol. 38* (April 1939).

MELLY, George (1830-94), *shipowner and Member of Parliament,* Stoke upon Trent.

GM, the son of Andre Melly, a Liverpool merchant and Ellen née Gregg, was born in Liverpool in 1830. He was educated at Rugby School, then joined the family firm of Melly, Forset and Co., merchants and shipowners. He served as a justice of the peace in Liverpool and on the Mersey Docks and Harbour Board. In politics a Liberal he unsuccessfully contested Preston in 1862 and Stoke upon Trent in 1865. He succeeded in gaining election for Stoke upon Trent at the by-election of 20 February 1868 and was returned again, with a fellow Liberal, W. S. Roden (q.v.), in the uncontested election of 16 November 1868. He was returned a third time on 7 February 1874 but retired immediately to manage the family business.

In 1852 he married Sarah Mesnard, daughter of Samuel Bright, a Liverpool merchant. He served as a major in the 4th Lancashire Artillery Volunteers 1859-67. He was a prolific traveller and writer, his books including *Khartoum and the Blue and White Niles* (2 vols.). He wrote pamphlets on various topics including education, Italy, prison discipline etc. He died on 27 September 1894.

Anderton; Simms; Stenton; V and S.

METEYARD, Eliza (1816-79), *authoress,* Burslem.

EM was born in Liverpool on 21 June 1816. She began writing in her late teens, and contributed to various periodicals, either stories or articles on social topics. Her first novel was written in 1840 for *Tait's Magazine* and was republished in 1845 under the title *Struggles for Fame.* Her most popular novels were *Mainstone's Housekeeper* (1860) and *Lady Herbert's Gentlewomen* (1862). Between 1850 and 1878 she wrote a series of seven or eight stories for children. Her two volume biography *The Life of Josiah Wedgwood* was published in 1865-6. In the publication of this biography she was helped by Joseph Mayer, a Liverpool jeweller and goldsmith who was a native of Newcastle under Lyme. She gave permission for 500 copies of the chapter in the book dealing with the Wedgwood Memorial Institute, Burslem, to be reprinted and sold at 6d. (2½p) each to provide extra income for the building. Her other works on Wedgwood were *A Group of Englishmen* (1871), *Memorials of Wedgwood (1874), The Wedgwood Handbook* (1875), and *A Catalogue of Wedgwood Manufactures* (1879).

EM died in South Lambeth, London in 1879.

DNB; M. W. Greenslade, *The Staffordshire Historians* (SHC 4 ser. vol. 11); E. Rowley, 'The Origins and Influences of the Wedgwood Memorial Institute, Burslem' (1978); Simms.

MIDDLETON, Revd. John (1714-1802), *minister of religion (Church of England),* Hanley.

JM was baptised on 3 May 1714, the son of John Middleton of Shelton, potter and his wife Felicia. After graduating from Oxford he was appointed curate in charge of the first Anglican chapel in Hanley, a post he retained until his death. His other preferments were to the rectory of Walkington, Yorkshire and to the perpetual curacy of Stone, Staffs. It is stated that he was given the latter post in recognition of his success in preventing a mob from marching on Trentham Hall in the troubled years of the 1780s.

He was secret partner of Warner Edwards in the Bell Bank Works, Shelton. A considerable classical scholar he was for some time secretary to Archbishop Potter, the editor of *Archaeologia.* During the 1745 rebellion of the Young Pretender he was captured near Leek by the rebels and held for two days until he was released.

He married Lydia Heath and by her had at least three children. JM had quarrelled with and been disowned by his father and he in turn disowned his son John. Among his numerous eccentricities was a dislike of the organ in church. Ward writes that, more than once, 'as the organ played the congregation into church it played him out of it; when his flock, after waiting some time in vain for the return of their shepherd, retired to their respective homes'.

JM died in 1802, aged about 88.

Adams; Foster; Huntbach; Ward.

MINKS, Thomas (1825-1898), *builder,* Fenton.

TM was born at Cawood in Yorks. in 1825. A carpenter by trade, in 1851 he was living in High Street, Fenton and later in Temple Street. He was in partnership with John Oakley by 1867 and in 1875 built the Church Schools at Fenton Low. By 1881 he was employing 29 men as joiners, bricklayers and labourers. In 1894 he stood unsuccessfully for election to the first Fenton Urban District Council. By his wife Elizabeth Jackson, a widow whom he married about 1849, he had three sons and five daughters. He died at his home in Temple Street on 8 February 1898 leaving an estate worth £17,000.

Census 1851, 1881; Dir. 1851, 1867; *National Index to Wills and Administrations.*

MINTON, Arthur (1805-39), *independent means,* Stoke upon Trent.

AM fourth and youngest son of Thomas Minton (q.v.) was born in Stoke upon Trent on 19 March 1805. He worked in his father's factory from c. 1818 to 1826 when he sustained an accident during riding and thereafter was often ill. About 1832-3 he built a small church and later a school at Oakhill for 100 boys and girls; he was a member of Stoke upon Trent parish church select vestry, and in 1833 the people's churchwarden. In July 1834 he became treasurer of the Stoke upon Trent Building Society. In this year he was living in Oakhill Cottage. In January 1828 he married Elizabeth, daughter of Colin Minton Campbell (q.v.). He died at Grappenhall, near Warrington, on 2 June 1839.

Dir. 1834; Jewitt; Minton Archives, No. 277; R. Nicholls, *History of Stoke Parish Church; Staffs. Advertiser* 5 January 1828, 23 March 1833, 20 April 1833, 12 July 1834 and 8 June 1838; *Staffs. Mercury* 22 March 1826.

MINTON, Herbert (1793-1858), *pottery manufacturer,* Stoke upon Trent.

HM, second son of Thomas Minton (q.v.) and Sarah née Webb, was born on 4 February 1793. He entered his father's pottery works at the age of 13, and in 1817, together with his elder brother Thomas, became a partner in the business. Thomas withdrew from the partnership in 1823 and Herbert in 1828 but on his father's death in 1836 Herbert assumed full control of the business. From 1836 to 1841 he was in partnership with John Boyle, trading as Minton and Boyle. In 1842 he took into partnership his wife's nephew, Michael Daintry Hollins and from 1849 his own nephew, Colin Minton Campbell (q.v.). Minton's became internationally famous, winning medals at exhibitions in 1851 at the Great Exhibition, London, in New York in 1853 and in Paris in 1855. Minton was the first manufacturer to introduce foreign artists into the area. These included Leon Arnoux (q.v.), Emile Jeannest, Albert Carrier and Hugues Protat. HM also employed A. W. N. Pugin, reviving the production of encaustic floor tiles and adapting medieval techniques of tile manufacture to modern mechanical processes. In the 1850s Minton floor tiles were used for public and private buildings all over the world. Amongst the many buildings where they are found are Lichfield cathedral and the Houses of Parliament. In 1846 the firm introduced parian porcelain, a matt white modelling material that proved very popular. A Sèvres-style porcelain was also produced. Under Léon Arnoux, art director from 1849, Minton's reproduced many 16th and 17th century ceramics. Coloured glazes, known as majolicas, were displayed at the Great Exhibition in 1851.

By 1851 there were four large Minton factories in Stoke upon Trent, each specialising in a particular form of ware. By 1858 the firm employed over 1,500 people, who enjoyed working conditions which by the standards of the time were good. HM built workers' houses at Hartshill. He himself lived at Longfield Cottage, not far from Holy Trinity Church, Hartshill, which was built at his expense in 1842. HM married (1) on 1 September 1819, Anne Hollins, daughter of Samuel Hollins, potter of Shelton; (2) in 1844, Mary, daughter of John Webb of Lee Hall, Staffs., and widow of Thomas Browne; (3) in the 1850s, Mrs. Fraser, née Leekie. There were no children from any of these marriages.

HM became a local justice of the peace and served as a deputy lieutenant for Staffordshire. He helped with the establishment of schools of design in the Potteries, and at his instigation the Soulanges collection of bronzes and majolica was bought for the nation. He retired in 1855 to Torquay, where he died on 1 April 1858. He was buried beneath the chancel in Holy Trinity church, Hartshill. The baths (recently demolished) in London Road, Stoke upon Trent, were opened in 1860 as part of the Herbert Minton Memorial Buildings.

His nephew Colin Minton Campbell, succeeded to the ownership of the business.

P. Atterbury, *The Story of Minton;* Jewitt; M and H; VCH viii.

MINTON, Thomas (1765-1836), *pottery manufacturer,* Stoke upon Trent.

TM was born in Wyle Cop, Shrewsbury, Shropshire, in 1765, and educated at Shrewsbury Grammar School. He was apprenticed to an engraver at Thomas Turner's Caughley China Works, Broseley. On completion of his apprenticeship he moved to London, where he engraved some patterns for Josiah Spode II (q.v.). He returned to Stoke upon Trent in 1789 and set up as an engraver and designer at Bridge House, Stoke upon Trent. His designs for Josiah Spode I (q.v.) included the popular Willow Pattern. In 1793 he bought land on which he began to build a pottery works known later as Eldon Place Pottery. He began to produce ware in 1796 in partnership with Joseph Poulson and William Pownall of Liverpool, concentrating at first on blue-printed earthenwares. He made a number of trips to Cornwall in search of regular supplies of Cornish clay and became one of the proprietors of the Hendra Company from 1800 to 1820 for the supply of china clay. From about 1798 the firm began to produce cream-coloured earthenware and bone china, the business prospered and by 1810 the partners were marketing a wide range of wares. For reasons not known the production of bone china was abandoned in 1816 and not resumed until 1824. During this early period Minton's made mostly table, tea and dessert wares, though some chimney ornaments and figures were produced. From about 1824 however the firm increased its trade in the decorative and luxury market. TM had become sole owner in 1808, and took his sons Thomas Webb Minton (q.v) and Herbert Minton (q.v.) into the business with him, as partners, in.1817. Thomas ceased to be a partner in 1823, and Herbert ceased in 1828, only to return to take over the business on his father's death.

He married Sarah Webb on 1 January 1789 and had four sons and six daughters. He was a churchwarden of Stoke upon Trent parish church in 1806-7 and 1820-1. He acted as returning officer for Stoke upon Trent in the parliamentary election of December 1832. He lived at Bridge House in 1789, near the Eldon Place Works after 1796, on Talbot Bank (now Hill Street, on the corner of Commerce Street) and in High Street, Penkhull, by 1832. He died on 29 May 1836.

P. Atterbury, *The Story of Minton;* Dir. 1822-3, 1834; Jewitt; R. Nicholls, *History of Stoke Parish Church;* Simms; VCH ii and viii; Ward; list of electors, Stoke upon Trent December 1832.

MINTON, Thomas Webb (1791-1870), *minister of religion (Church of England),* Stoke upon Trent.

TWM was born in Stoke upon Trent on 25 December 1791, the eldest son of Thomas Minton, pottery manufacturer of Stoke upon Trent (q.v.). He was educated at Audlem Grammar School under the Rev. Nicholas Breakspear. In 1817 he became a partner, with his father and brother Herbert Minton (q.v.) in the Eldon Place pottery works in Stoke upon Trent, but in 1821 he left the firm to enter the church. This move was opposed by his father and the partnership was dissolved on 4 January 1823. He was ordained in 1825, and served as curate in Chesterfield, in St. Cuthbert's Darlington and in St. John's Weardale. He was vicar of Birmingham, Derbyshire 1832-46, then of Holy Trinity, Darlington, 1846-65. TWM was the chief beneficiary under his father's will in 1836 and surrendered £23,000 for the benefit of his brothers and sisters. In 1842 he contributed at least £2,500 towards the cost of the erection and endowment of St. Thomas's church, Penkhull, Stoke upon Trent, of which he was also patron of the living. He gave £5,000 towards the cost of building the church (and the school) in Coalville, Leicestershire, of which he was patron. He married (1) Jane Hoskins, and (2) Elanor Senhouse (d.1854), by whom he had a son, Samuel Minton-Senhouse (q.v.). He died in Darlington on 15 March 1870.

Jewitt; Simms; *Staffs. Sentinel* 26 March 1870; VCH viii.

MINTON-SENHOUSE, Samuel (1820-94), *minister of religion, (Church of England),* Stoke upon Trent.

SM-S was born on 16 March 1820, the son of Rev. Thomas Webb Minton (q.v.) and Eleanor, probably née Senhouse. He was educated at a private school in Lancaster, at Rugby and was a scholar at Worcester College, Oxford in 1838, B.A. 1842, M.A. 1844. He married on 20 April 1843, Cecil Mary Rosser, daughter of W. H. Rosser, barrister, and had six sons and four daughters. He was priest-in-charge at St. Thomas's church, Penkhull, 1844-49; St. Silas, Liverpool, 1851-57; minister of Percy Chapel, London, 1857-60; Eaton chapel, London, 1864-74; curate in Brighton in 1874. He succeeded his father to the right of appointing the incumbent of St. Thomas's church, Penkhull, from 1870 to about 1883. He assumed the final name Senhouse when he came into possession of Calder Abbey, Cumberland, in 1884. He was one of the first ministers of religion to preach in connection with theatre services, one example of which was at the Victoria Theatre, Hanley on 8 January 1860. He also preached occasionally in non-conformist chapels. SM-S was the author of numerous theological works.

He died in Putney, London and was buried at Wandsworth cemetery on 28 March 1894.

Hutchinson *The Archdeaconry of Stoke on Trent;* Simms; *Staffs. Sentinel* 22 November 1884 and 29 March 1894.

MITCHESON, George (c. 1795-1850), *colliery agent,* Fenton.

GM was born in Long Benton, Northumberland and baptised there on 14 February 1796, the son of John and Mary Mitcheson née Greener. As a youth he worked with George Stephenson at Killingworth Colliery and was recommended by him as agent to the Lane End Ironworks and Foley Collieries, at Fenton, c. 1828. He and his wife Ann had lived in North Staffordshire for several years previous to that date, and a daughter Ann was born at Wolstanton c. 1824, the first of at least 11 children. The sons included George John Mitcheson (q.v.), and William Summersides Mitcheson, who followed his father as agent at Lane End and Foley, was a partner of John Hackett Goddard (q.v.) at Goldenhill Colliery, Fenton from 1854 to c. 1858 and sometime borough surveyor of Longton, and Market Inspector.

GM was well known as a valuer of mining and other property, the latter on behalf of the Longton Building Society founded in 1838. He was consulting agent to John Ashwell (q.v.) in a compensation case against the North Staffs. Railway in August 1848.

He died, after a short illness, at The Foley on 24 December 1850.

Census 1841, 1851; IGI Northumberland; *Institute of Mechanical Engineers, Proceedings 1952-53* re J. Cecil Mitcheson (great grandson); *Staffs. Advertiser* 28 December 1850; Letters from W. H. Sparrow to G. Mitchson, 1861-7 (SRO, D/321).

MITCHESON, George Arthur (1868/9-1934), *mining engineer,* Longton.

GAM was born in Dresden, Longton, about 1868, the son of George John Mitcheson (q.v.). He succeeded his father as manager of Meir Hay Colliery, Longton, and Turnhurst Colliery, Tunstall. Later he had an extensive practice as a mining engineer, with the North Staffordshire Railway, the Duke of Sutherland, Captain Edward Heathcote and Sir Francis Boughey among his clients. He held other posts as mining engineer at Berry Hill Collieries, director of Mossfield Colleries, general manager of Stafford Iron and Coal Co., Fenton, and general manager of Florence Colliery. He had an office in Stafford Street, Longton, in 1900, and in Market Street, Longton in 1912.

For nearly 50 years he was an examiner of colliery managers for the Home Office, and his experience was used in rescue and recovery operations after the disasters at Mossfield in 1891 and Diglake in 1895. He pioneered many mining improvements: he installed the first steam turbine engine in the country at Florence Colliery, and was an early advocate of the use of electricity in mines. He was elected Fellow of the Geological Society and was a member of the Institute of Mining Engineers. He left the Potteries about 1918 to become mining engineer at Birch Coppice Collieries, Tamworth.

As a young man GAM was an amateur racing cyclist, a long distance runner and a member of Stoke Victoria Athletic Club. He married Sarah Bardsley and had three sons and three daughters. In 1912 the family lived at Hem Heath. One son, James Cecil Mitcheson, became president of the Institute of Mining Engineers and professor of mining at Imperial College, London.

GAM died at Hall End Hall, Tamworth, on 22 February 1934.

Dir. 1884-1921; *Staffs. Advertiser* 24 February 1934; *Trans. North Staffs. Institute of Mining Engineers 1933-4.*

MITCHESON, George John (1834-80), *colliery manager,* Longton.

GJM was baptised on 23 March 1834 at Longton, son of George Mitcheson and his wife Ann. He became agent for Foley Colliery Co. in 1851. He succeeded his brother William Summersides Mitcheson as manager of W. H. Sparrow's mines and ironworks at Lane End, Longton, about 1860, and served in this position until 1867 when Sparrow sold out to Thomas Goddard and Son. GJM then became manager of Meir Hay Colliery, Longton, until his death. He was a founder member of the North Staffordshire Institute of Mining Engineers in 1872 and served as a member of the Institute's council from 1873. He had at least three children, including a son George Arthur Mitcheson (q.v.). He died at Florence Villa, Normacott, near Longton on 20 August 1880.

Diary of John Hackett Goddard 1865-7 (in possession of Mr. J. Goddard); Diaries of George John Mitcheson 1865-67, and Letters from W. H. & Arthur Sparrow to members of Mitchson family about colliery business, (SRO D/321).

MOLLART, Owen (c. 1884-1912), *miner,* Tunstall.

OM was born at 9 Samuel Street, Packmoor, about 1884. He earned his living as a miner, but his chief interest was, and his importance lay in, music. At the age of eight he joined the choir of St James's church, Newchapel, and eventually became organist and choirmaster. He was to a large extent self-taught. He was also a member of a vocal quartet, the Packmoor Apollo Glee Singers. He was secretary of the church Bible class, which had a membership of about 100, mostly miners from the local collieries. OM was killed in an accident at Newchapel colliery on 16 January 1912, in the same coal seam in which his father had been injured in an accident in 1885.

Staffs. Sentinel 22 January 1912.

MOLLOY, William (c. 1815-90), *minister of religion (Roman Catholic),* Hanley.

WM was born in Limerick about 1815, and educated at the English College, Rome. After his ordination he worked in Madeley, Shropshire. In February 1860 he became the first resident priest for the church of St. Mary and St. Patrick, in Lower Foundry Street, Hanley, where he remained for the rest of his life. Though the congregation increased to about 1,000 during his period of office, it was one of the poorest in the area and the building of a new and larger church, which had always been intended, was delayed until 1889-91. WM saw the laying of the foundation stone of the new church, the Sacred Heart, by Bishop Ilsley of Birmingham, in July 1889, but he died on 21 January 1890, before the new church was completed.

M. W. Greenslade, *A Brief History of the Catholic Church in Stoke-on-Trent* (1960); *Staffs. Sentinel* 25 January 1890.

MOODY, Arthur Rowley (1861-1919), *medical practitioner,* Hanley.

ARM was born on 6 January 1861, the son of William Moody of Newcastle under Lyme. He attended the Endowed Schools at Newcastle, and studied medicine at Edinburgh University, obtaining the degrees of M.B. and C.M. He came to Hanley to practise medicine and lived in Richmond House, Snow Hill, Shelton. He invented and patented a respirator for medical use, and was local medical referee for the Miners' Federation. He was elected president of Hanley Liberal Club in 1907. After his death early in December 1919, the Liberal Club premises in Percy Street, Hanley were reconstructed and dedicated to his memory on 11 January 1921.

C. Penn *Staffordshire at the Opening of the 20th Century; Staffs. Sentinel* 9 December 1919.

MOORCROFT, William (1872-1945), *potter,* Burslem.

WM was born in Burslem on 27 March 1872, the son of Thomas Moorcroft, an artist and designer, who died about 1884. WM was educated locally at Longport Hall School and at the Wedgwood Institute in Burslem, and later studied at South Kensington and in Paris. He was awarded an Art Master's Certificate in 1897.

In the same year he was invited to open a studio within the Washington Works of James Macintyre and Co. in Burslem, manufacturers of general earthenware and electrical porcelain. Here he evolved Florian ware and began his experiments with colours, which became a feature of his work. His productions at Macintyres were distributed by Liberty in London and Tiffany in New York.

He set up his own pottery, W. Moorcroft Ltd., at Cobridge in 1913, made his own colours and glazes and increased the range of underglaze colours. He produced Blue tableware in 1913 and Flambé in 1919. He was appointed Potter to Queen Mary.

He married (1) Florence Lovibond and (2) Marian Lasenby, and had three children, Walter, John and Beatrice. He died at his home at Trentham on 14 October 1945.

Evening Sentinel 15 October 1945; Beatrice Moorcroft, *William Moorcroft 1872-1945; programme notes for centennial exhibition.*

MOORE, Bernard (1850-1935), *pottery designer,* Longton and Stoke upon Trent.

BM was born on 13 January 1850, the eldest son of Samuel Moore of Moore and Hamilton, St. Mary's works, Longton. Bernard grew up at The Cottage, Normacot, and attended St. Mary's Convent School, Chesterfield. On leaving school he joined the family firm and became interested in the chemistry of glazes. He took over the firm on his father's death in 1867. He was joined by his brother Samuel Vincent Moore in 1870 and they traded as Moore Brothers. The factory produced high quality china tableware and ornamental pottery with a range of glaze effects based on Far and Near Eastern styles. BM's best-known achievements were the reproduction of the ruby-red Chinese glaze known as sang-de-boeuf and his flambé ware. In association with Doulton and consultant and using Doulton's Burslem laboratories, he engaged, in collaboration with Cuthbert Bailey, son of Doulton's factory manager, in the large-scale production of rouge-flambé.

In 1905 the Longton works were sold to T. C. Wild, and BM took over premises in Wolfe Street (now Kingsway), Stoke upon Trent, specialising as an experimental studio potter and consultant. His son Bernard Joseph joined him as a consultant in 1906. The firm won numerous international awards. A fire at the Brussels exhibition of 1910 destroyed many examples of Moore's work.

In collaboration with Dr. J. W. Mellor, F.R.S. (q.v.) BM wrote technical articles for the *Transactions of the British Ceramic Society,* of which he served as president 1902-3. He was a member of the American Ceramic Society and of the Research, Inventions and Designs Committee of the National Council for the Pottery Industry.

BM was associated with St. Mary's Roman Catholic church, Cresswell, and commanded the Longton company of Volunteers. He died at his home, The Grange, Draycott-in-the-Moors, on 3 April 1935 and was buried in Cresswell cemetery. His son was responsible, with Arthur J. Campbell, for the installation of the first successful electrical kiln in the pottery industry.

A. Dawson, *Bernard Moore, Master Potter, 1850-1935;* D. Eyles, *Royal Doulton 1815-1965; Evening Sentinel* 4 April 1935; *Pottery and Glass* April 1935; *Pottery Gazette* May 1935; *Trans of the British Ceramic Society* (various issues 1902-32); VCH ii.

MOORE, William (c. 1822-66), *pottery manufacturer,* Hanley.

WM, born about 1822, began work in a factory owned by John Ridgway (q.v.), and worked his way up to become general manager of the firm. He eventually became a partner in the firm of Bates, Brown-Westhead and Moore which took over from Ridgway's in 1859.

Like many of Ridgway's employees WM attended Bethesda Methodist New Connexion chapel in Hanley, becoming a class leader, trustee and circuit steward. His political opinions were Liberal. He was elected mayor of Hanley in 1865, but died, aged 44, before the end of his year of office, leaving two sons.

Huntbach; Jewitt; VCH ii and viii.

MORLEY, Francis (died 1883), *pottery manufacturer,* Hanley.

FM, son of Richard Morley, founder of the hosiery firm of J. and R. Morley, was born in Sneinton Hall, Nottinghamshire. By 1840 he was a partner in the pottery firm of Ridgway, Morley, Wear and Co., Broad Street, Shelton, experimenting with the application of lithography to pottery. He became sole proprietor in 1845. The firm traded as Morley and Co. from 1850 to 1858 and as Morley and Ashworth from 1858 to 1862. In 1848 FM bought the designs of C. J. Mason (q.v.).

He married Emma, daughter of William Ridgway (q.v.), on 2 September 1835. He retired to Breadsall Priory, Derbyshire, in 1862, and died there on 23 January 1883.

R. G. Haggar and E. Adams, *Mason Porcelain and Ironstone; IGI Staffs.; National Index to Wills and Administrations;* M and H; VCH ii.

MORRIS, Rowland James (c. 1847-1909), *ceramic sculptor,* Longton.

RJM was born about 1847. He studied at Hanley School of Art under Hugues Protat and was awarded a national scholarship to the South Kensington School of Art. He sculpted the figures on the panels Labour of the Months and Processes of the Pottery Industry on the facade of the Wedgwood Memorial Institute, Burslem (1865-73), and modelled the dragons by the fountains in Hanley park. He worked for Bernard Moore (q.v.), at St. Mary's Works, Mount Pleasant, Uttoxeter Road, Longton, from about 1885 to 1890. He died in 1909.

R. Haggar, *A Century of Art Education in the Potteries;* M and H; E. Rowley, 'The Origins and Influences of the Wedgwood Memorial Institute, Burslem' (HRL).

MOUNTFORD, David Harding (born 1847), *theatre proprietor,* Stoke upon Trent.

DHM was born in 1847, the son of Samuel Mountford. In 1889 he was employed as a brewer's agent, in 1892 he was licensee of the Royal Oak public house, Fenton and in 1896 of the Regent Hotel in Whieldon Road. Later he took over the Bee Hotel in Stoke upon Trent, renaming it the Gordon Hotel. DHM moved into the theatre business in 1899 when he bought out a Mr. Carlton, proprietor of the Crown Theatre in Wolfe Street (now Kingsway), Stoke upon Trent. He demolished the old wooden theatre and built the Gordon Theatre on the site at a cost of £15,000. The theatre opened in March 1900, but DHM was forced to close it in the face of competition from the Hanley theatres. The Gordon Theatre was then leased to Pat Collins, the fairground proprietor, who renamed it the Hippodrome and ran it for two years. It was leased again, in 1907, to T. Allan Edwards, who bought it about 1910. By 1924 the theatre had been converted into the present Gaumont Cinema.

DHM was living in Campbell Road, Stoke upon Trent, in 1888. His first wife, Harriet, died in that year, and in 1889 he married Eleanor Stone. His children were named Frank, David, Gordon and Dorothy Christina Rossetti. DHM was living at 31 Church Street, Stoke upon Trent, in 1909. He was a member of Stoke upon Trent borough council 1900-2.

Fenn's Stoke Borough Almanack 1910; VCH viii.

MOUNTFORD, Elizabeth Wright (1863-1958), *local benefactress,* Hanley.

EWM was born in 1863, the daughter of Henry Dutton of Sunny Bank House, Northwood. She married (1) in 1890, John Bentley, borough surveyor of Hanley, and (2) in 1909, Samuel Mountford. After her second husband's death she gave much of her income away to a variety of charitable causes and cultural institutions in the Potteries area, including the North Staffordshire Infirmary, the North Staffordshire District Choral Society, the University College of North Staffs. (later the University of Keele), the Lifeboat Guild, the R. J. Mitchell Fund, the Red Cross, and many other bodies and organisations. She was awarded the O.B.E. in 1953. She died on 29 December 1958.

Evening Sentinel 29 December 1958.

MOUNTFORD, Frederick (1847-1911), *colliery secretary,* Hanley.

FM was born in 1847, the son of Elijah Mountford, choirmaster of Bethesda Methodist New Connexion chapel, Hanley. He was first employed in the offices of Stanyer and Company, Silverdale, Newcastle under Lyme, and later became secretary of Taylor, Tunnicliffe and Company, Hanley, porcelain insulator manufacturers.

FM displayed a talent for music very early in life. He studied the flute under Thomas Haywood and the piano under John Emery. As a boy soprano he sang alto in a performance of the Messiah in Shelton church in 1852. He bacame a member of the Hanley and Shelton Choral Society, organist in Shelton church 1857-61 and Silverdale church 1861-90. He was also a member of the male voice choir formed by Dr. Barry, the organist of Stoke upon Trent parish church and a member of the choir of St. Giles's church, Newcastle under Lyme. Eventually he became choirmaster of Shelton parish church, conductor of the North Staffordshire Choral Society and the Hanley Philharmonic Society. In 1888 he was appointed chorus master of the Triennial Music Festival, and held this position during the whole period of the festival's existence. He was a prolific composer, his many works including chants and band arrangements.

FM was a member of a freemason's lodge. He died at 17 Havelock Place, Shelton, on 30 October 1911.

County Borough of Hanley Jubilee Souvenir 1857-1907; Dir. 1907; Staffs. Sentinel 6 September 1890 and 31 October 1911.

MOUNTFORD, John (1817-1906), *pottery modeller,* Stoke upon Trent.

JM was born at Back Sytch, Burslem, on 13 January 1817. His family moved to Derby in the same year and his father worked as an enamel fireman in Nottingham Road. JM was apprenticed as an ornamental potter. On completing his apprenticeship JM came to Stoke upon Trent and worked for Copeland and Garratt as a figure maker. An order from Art Union of London for 50 copies of Gibson's Narcissus led to the development of Parian ware, which JM claimed as his invention. The first figure was completed on Christmas Day 1845.

JM left Copeland and Garratt and went into partnership with Samuel Keys, who had migrated from Derby about 1830. They made Parian ware at a factory in John (now Leese) Street, Stoke upon Trent, and exhibited at the Crystal Palace in 1851. The partnership proved unsuccessful and JM returned to Derby where he worked at the Crown Derby works until his retirement, at the age of 81, in 1901. He died in June 1906.

F. A. Barratt and A.L. Thorpe, *Old Derby Porcelain;* Jewitt; M and H; C. and D. Shinn, *The Illustrated Guide to Victorian Parian China; Staffs. Sentinel* 6 June 1906.

MULOCK, Dinah Maria (Mrs. Craik) (1826-87), *authoress,* Stoke upon Trent and Newcastle.

DMM, better known as Mrs. Craik, was born in Longfield Cottage, Hartshill, Stoke upon Trent, on 20 April 1826. Her mother, Dinah née Mellard, came from a family of tannery owners in Newcastle. Her uncle by marriage was William Parker, a former chief bailiff of Hanley and a justice of the peace, whose residence, Albion House, was burnt down during the Chartist riots of 1842. Dinah's father, Thomas Samuel Mulock, was an eccentric Irishman with a literary bent and the author of numerous pamphlets on religious subjects. He had been a barrister but had become a Baptist minister by the time he came to Stoke upon Trent about 1822. Thomas Mulock preached in the upper room of a china factory but later a chapel was built in Thomas (later Aquinas) Street. TSM gave up the ministry in the 1830s and the building eventually passed into the hands of the Society of Friends. TM lodged with the gardener in a cottage in the grounds of Longfield and in 1825 married Dinah Mellard. Dinah Mulock was the first of three children of the marriage. The Mulock family moved to Newcastle under Lyme about 1831 and Dinah attended the Brampton House Academy in Queen Street. Her mother later ran a private school in Newcastle and Dinah helped with the teaching. The Mulocks moved to London in 1840, helped financially by a Mellard family trust fund. When Dinah's mother died in 1845 Dinah had to care for her two younger brothers, Thomas and Benjamin, as her father was unwilling or incapable of looking after them. She began to write children's books, finding a patron in Robert Chambers, publisher of *The Journal.* Eventually the trust fund gave her financial security and she was able to concentrate on writing full-length novels. These included *The Ogilvies* (3 vols., 1849), *Olive* (1851), *The Head of the Family* (1851), *Agatha's Husband* (1853), and her best known work, *John Halifax Gentleman* (1857). The last novel is supposedly set in Tewkesbury, Glos., but has names from the Hartshill and Newcastle localities. DMM wrote altogether 19 novels and 20 other works and collections of poetry.

In 1864 she married George Lillie Craik, who became a partner in Macmillans, the publishers. The family lived at The Corner House, Shortlands, near Bromley, Kent. Dinah kept in touch with North Staffordshire and visited the area later in life. She dedicated a window in St. Giles' church, Newcastle, to the Mellard family. She died at Shortlands on 12 October 1887.

DNB; D. G. Harnaman, *A Brief Account of the Life and Writings of Dinah Mulock;* T. Pape, 'The Birth Centenary of the author of John Halifax, Gentleman' in *Trans. North Staffs. Field Club, 1925-6; Staffs. Advertiser* 15 October 1887; D. G. Stuart, 'The Burial Grounds of Society of the Friends in Staffordshire' in *South Staffordshire Archaeological and Historical Society Transactions,* 1970-72, vol. xii.

NAYLOR, John Henry (1859-1932), *potter's thrower,* Tunstall.

JHN was born on 19 November 1859, son of William Naylor, of Leeds, a potter's thrower. About 1893 JHN and his brother Thomas came to the Potteries. Thomas settled in Hanley, and became a nationally-known exhibition thrower. JHN lived in Tunstall. His output at the wheel was too great for one pottery manufacturer to employ him full time and he worked for several factories, attending one to two days at each. These included Wedgwood and Co. (Tunstall), Lingard, Webster and Co., Hollishead and Kirkham and Lancaster and Co. (Etruria). Visitors to Tunstall were frequently taken to see him working. He also acted as a sort of unofficial shop steward for pottery workers, negotiating with the employers for more work, if it seemed to them at the beginning of the week that they were unlikely to earn enough to keep their families.

JHN married Hannah Morley, and had five sons and two daughters. He was vice-president of Tunstall Brotherhood for 20 years, a body which organized Pleasant Sunday Afternoons in Tunstall Town Hall. Average attendance at these gatherings was 500 and guest speakers later included Sir Oswald and Lady Cynthia Mosley and Philip Snowden. JHN was also on the committee of the Tunstall and District Assurance Collecting Society, was a member of the Salvation Army and later of Wesley Place Methodist church. He was a committee member of the old Tunstall Cricket Club, whose ground stood opposite Brownhills High School.

He died on 18 December 1932, and was buried in Tunstall cemetery.

Dir. 1912; *Pottery and Glass Record,* New Series, vol. 15, No. 1. Jan. 1933; *Staffordshire Weekly Sentinel,* 24 December 1932.

NEALE, James (1740-1814), *pottery manufacturer,* Hanley.

JN was born in 1740. He began his career about 1760 as a merchant of St. John's, Wapping, London. In 1767 he was described as living in St. Paul's Churchyard. He acted as agent for several Staffordshire potters, including Josiah Wedgwood. He was also the agent and secret partner of Humphrey Palmer who about 1760 built the Church Works, in High Street, Hanley. Palmer produced Egyptian black and other ware in imitation of Wedgwood and was eventually sued for infringement of the patent covering Etruscan painted vases. Palmer's business failed in 1778 and JN took over control. With various partners he produced a variety of wares, some still in imitation of Wedgwood, although business relationships between the two firms continued. James Wilson, JN's partner since 1786, succeeded as sole owner in the early 1790s. Church Works passed through several hands including the Ridgways. The building was demolished about 1948.

While in London JN was an active member of the London Missionary Society. He married Elizabeth Simpson and had a son, Cornelius. He died on 8 February 1814.

The Connoisseur, vol. cxx July-December 1947; M and H; VCH viii.

NEWLAND, Ridgway William (*floruit* **1816-61**), *minister of religion (Congregationalist)*, Hanley.

RWN, born in the later 18th century, was educated at Hoxton Academy, London. He came as pastor to Hanley Tabernacle (opened 1784) on 29 September 1816 and served until 1839 when he emigrated to Victor Harbor, South Australia, taking with him 16 other men and women. He founded a church at Victor Harbor later called the Newland Memorial church. During his pastorate in Hanley, Tabernacle church was enlarged and new schools erected. RWN was associated with the establishment of the Potteries Mechanics' Institute.

He married (1) by 1820 Sophia, died 6 November 1825 and (2) about 1826 Martha. There were children by both marriages. RWN's eldest son, Simpson, became a member of the South Australia parliament.

D. Rodney Halson, *The Rev. R. W. Newland and the Tabernacle Independent Chapel, Hanley;* A. G. Matthews, *Congregational Churches of Staffordshire; North Staffs. News,* 10 May 1984 quoting J. Cameron, *A Book of Pioneers;* VCH viii.

NICHOLLS, Robert (born 1864), *timber merchant,* Stoke upon Trent.

RN was born on 21 November 1864, the son of Benjamin Nicholls, a pottery warehouseman and his wife Martha. He was educated at Penkhull School and the science schools in Stoke upon Trent and Hanley. He probably worked first in the timber business owned by his uncle, Richard Nicholls, in Wharf Street, Stoke upon Trent. He lived at 42 Havelock Street, Stoke upon Trent and later 22 Victoria Place (now St. Thomas's Place), Penkhull. He was one of the beneficiaries of his uncle's will in 1899 and bought Hartshill Hall. He owned his own timber business, but in 1903 was declared bankrupt. About 1910 he was employed in Stoke upon Trent Labour Exchange, and later as a book keeper at Birks and Rawlins, potters, of Boothen.

His main interest was local history, his published works including *The History of Penkhull cum Boothen* (1929) and *A History of Madeley* (1935). He married Rachel Charlotte née Blake, who died in 1910, and secondly, Gladys May née Benson.

R. Talbot, *Penkhull Remembered Again; Staffs. Sentinel* 21 September 1907.

NORTHCOTE, Revd. James Spencer (1821-1907), *minister of religion (R.C.),* Stoke upon Trent.

JSN was born on 26 May 1821 at Feniton, near Honiton, Devon. He was educated at King Edward's Grammar School, Ilminster and Corpus Christi, Oxford, graduated B.A. 1841, M.A. 1844. Ordained a deacon in 1844 he was appointed supernumary curate at Ilfracombe. In 1846 he followed his wife into the Roman Catholic church, writing a pamphlet *Four Fold Difficulties of Anglicanism.* He visited Rome 1847-50. His wife died in 1853 and in 1856 he was ordained at St. Dominic's Priory, Stone, Staffs. In the following year he was appointed to the Catholic Mission in Back Glebe Street (now Cranmer Street), Stoke upon Trent. He supervised the building of the new church of Our Lady of the Angels and St. Peter in Chains in 1857, giving £1,000 towards the cost. He was appointed canon of St. Chad's cathedral, Birmingham and president of Oscott Theological College, Birmingham in 1860. In 1866 he was charged with technical assault on one of the boys of the College whom he had locked, for troublesome behaviour, in a room awaiting the arrival of his father. He resigned from Oscott in 1877 and took charge of a mission in Stone. He returned as priest-in-charge to Stoke upon Trent, holding this post until his death in 1907.

In 1842 he married his cousin Susannah Spencer Rushcombe-Poole (died 1853). He was an acknowledged authority on Roman catacombs, his published works including *A Visit to the Roman Catacombs* (1877). He served on Stoke upon Trent School Board until illness forced his resignation.

He died in Stoke upon Trent on 3 March 1907 and was buried at Oscott. His memory is perpetuated in Northcote Hall at Oscott College.

J. J. Coyne, *Oscott College (St. Mary's), a brief history;* Simms; *Staffs. Sentinel* 5 March 1907 (obit.).

OLIVER, Thomas Milward (1769/70-97), *surgeon/apothecary,* Burslem.

TMO was born about 1769 in Oldswinford, near Stourbridge. He was apprenticed to a surgeon/apothecary in Stourbridge, gained further medical experience in London and eventually became a partner to a surgeon in Rugby. About 1792 he moved to Burslem as partner to Dr. Hickman. Professional attendance on the wife of John Wood, potter, of Brownfields House, led to friendship with the family, and TMO fell in love with John Wood's daughter, Maria. John Wood objected and forbade TMO to make further visits to the house. A chance meeting about a year later between Oliver and Maria was observed by John Wood, an argument ensued and blows were struck. Thereafter Oliver neglected his practice and took to drinking at The Turk's Head public house in Burslem. He decided to commit suicide, borrowed a pair of pistols and on 27 January 1797 went to Wood's house to shoot himself in Wood's presence. After an exchange of words he shot Wood instead.

At his trial at Stafford assizes a plea of temporary insanity was entered, doctors arguing that an hereditary derangement of mind was prompted by disappointed love. Another witness, however, Theophilus Smith, a potter of Smithfield (q.v.), gave evidence that on the evening before the shooting Oliver did not appear to be insane, and Oliver was found guilty. He was hanged on 28 August 1797.

An Account of the Life and Trial of T. M. Oliver (HRL): *A Report of the Trial of T. Milward Oliver at Stafford Summer Assizes before the Honourable Baron Penryn.*

OULSNAM, William Emmerson (1826/7-82), *tobacco dealer/earthenware manufacturer,* Burslem.

WEO was born in Stanley, Leek, about 1826. He had moved from Penkridge, Staffs. (where his son George was born) to Burslem by 1847 where he was in business with Obadiah Williams (possibly his brother-in-law), as a tobacco dealer in Port Vale Street. In 1860 he was in business as an earthenware manufacturer in High Street, Tunstall, trading as Oulsnam and Holdcroft, and he was also a cratemaker at Greenfield. In 1880 he was in partnership with his son at Furlong, making earthenware.

He was a member of the Tunstall Board of Health and served as chief bailiff in 1869. He was on the Burslem Board of Health 1875-6 and 1877-8. From at least 1861 he lived at 4 Newport Street, Burslem.

By his wife Mary WEO had four sons. He died in Southport on 1 March 1882.

National Index to Wills and Administrations; Burslem Board of Health Annual Reports; Census 1861, 1881; Dir. 1867; *Tunstall Board of Health Annual Reports.*

OUTRIM, George (1806/7-78), *accountant/agent,* Stoke upon Trent.

GO was born in Stoke upon Trent, where he was baptised on 8 March 1807, the son of William Outrim and Elizabeth née Cheadle. He became secretary/accountant to W. T. Copeland and Sons. He was also appointed clerk to the Stoke upon Trent improvement commissioners in 1859, defeating Oliver Lodge (q.v.) by 17 to 13 votes, and having to find security of £500. In 1862 he became clerk to the Fenton commissioners.

He was an original member of Stokeville Building Society in 1850. By his wife Ellen he had three daughters. The family lived in Upper Cliff Bank in 1851 and in Liverpool Road in 1861.

He died in Toronto, Canada, on 17 September 1878.

Census 1861; Dir. 1851; *Fenton Improvement Commissioners Minutes; National Index to Wills and Administrations;* Turner.

OWEN, Harold (1872-1930), *journalist/author,* Burslem.

HO was born in Burslem on 3 May 1872, the son of William Owen (q.v.). He trained as a journalist in London and held various editorial posts in his life. Subsequently he gave up journalism to become a writer on sociological and political subjects. His books include *The Staffordshire Potter* (1901), *Woman Adrift* (1912), *Disloyalty the Blight of Pacifism* (1918), *Unpopular Opinions* (1922) etc. He also wrote a number of plays one of which *Loyalty* was given a command performance in 1918.

He died on 10 May 1930.

Who was Who 1929-40.

OWEN, William (1844-1912), *journalist/printer,* Burslem.

WO was born in Burslem on 5 December 1844, the son of John Owen, a potter's printer. His grandfather was a soldier from Newton Montgomery, said to have been drafted to the Potteries during some riots, and possibly distantly related to Robert Owen, the socialist and philanthropist, although William Owen never claimed any relationship. WO became an apprentice turner at Pinder's pottery, Burslem (the site of which is now occupied by the Royal Doulton works). Here the stories he heard from his fellow workers about the hardships of their life and work made a deep impression on his mind. Nothing is known about his education, but on 27 July 1867 he was appointed editor of the *Potteries Examiner,* a trade union newspaper.

Owen was primarily responsible for the establishment of the Potteries Board of Arbitration and Conciliation in 1868 which lasted, with one serious break, until 1891. In June 1871 the *Potteries Examiner* was taken over by the Co-operative and General Printing Company, which Owen, with the help of local unions, had set up. He now expanded the coverage of the newspaper, seeking to make it a rival of the *Staffordshire Sentinel.* In 1874 he was elected to the Trades Union Congress Parliamentary Committee where he promoted the candidature of Alfred Walton for the Stoke upon Trent constituency. Walton was unsuccessful in the election of February 1874. Owen had moved in the previous year to Wolverhampton where he hoped to improve the circulation of another trade union newspaper. He returned to the Potteries in 1879, resumed control of the *Potteries Examiner* and published several other newspapers and magazines, including the *Staffordshire Knot* and the *Daily Mail,* but without much commercial success.

WO served on the Burslem School Board in 1874 and later on Burslem council. In 1886 he stood unsuccessfully as Liberal candidate for Newcastle under Lyme, and later that year, again unsuccessfully, in Sheffield. Originally attached to the Church of England he later became a Wesleyan Methodist and a Sunday school teacher. He married and had a son, Harold Owen (q.v.). His last appearance in public was as a speaker at the third triennial conference of the International Federation of Pottery Workers. His reputation and influence extended far beyond the Potteries. From 1893-7 he was president of the North Staffordshire Trades and Labour Council.

He died at his home in Longport, Burslem, on 11 October 1912.

Anderton; F. Burchill and R. Ross, *History of the Potters' Union;* H. Owen, *The Staffordshire Potter; Staffs. Advertiser* 19 October 1912; *Staffs. Sentinel* 14 October 1912 (obit.).

PALMER, Henry (died 1902), *brickmaker and timber merchant,* Hanley.

HP was a borough magistrate and councillor in Hanley and also acted as registrar of births, marriages and deaths. He was mayor of the borough for two years, 1887 and 1888. He rose to the rank of colonel in the local volunteers.

He died in 1902.

Dir. 1880; Huntbach.

PALMER, Humphrey (died 1786), *pottery manufacturer,* Hanley.

HP was descendant of John Palmer of Bagnall, who is said to have discovered salt-glazing in 1680. Humphrey Palmer built Church Works, High Street, Hanley, in the mid-18th century, and produced Egyptian black and other wares in imitation of Josiah Wedgwood (q.v) from about 1760. The rivalry increased when in 1769 Palmer employed John Voyez (q.v), after the latter had quarrelled with Wedgwood. Palmer's business failed in 1778 and James Neale, his London agent and secret partner, took over. One of Palmer's apprentices was Enoch Wood (q.v), who claimed to have been the first person to use bone in the manufacture of earthenware while he was at Palmer's factory.

HP married three times. His first wife was Ann, daughter of John Adams of Birches Head, and HP is said to have discoverd clay suitable for making black basalts on his father-in-law's land. His second wife was a daughter of Thomas Heath, of Lane Delph. She managed the business while HP concentrated on potting. About 1763 Josiah Wedgwood accused her of stealing the secrets of his blue-necked vases. One historian has argued that it is unfair to remember HP only as a robber of Wedgwood's ideas. HP's third wife was Hannah Ashwin.

Adams; M. H. Grant, *The Makers of Black Basalts;* Jewitt; M and H; S. Shaw, *History of the Staffordshire Potteries;* VCH ii and viii.

PARKER, Henry (c. 1825-85), *brewer,* Burslem.

HP was born in Wales about 1825. Early in life he joined a regiment of dragoons and rose to the rank of sergeant. By 1865-6 he had established a brewery in Regent Street East (later Zion Street), Burslem. He took William Warrington Dobson into partnership in 1881, and in the following year they began to buy licensed houses as these came on the market. By 1899 the firm owned more than 400 licensed houses in the area. HP died a wealthy man, his estate being valued at £93,000. The firm merged with Ind Coope and Allsopp in 1949, the brewery being used thereafter as offices and a depot.

For several years HP commanded a detachment of volunteers in Burslem. He was a member of the Wolstanton and Burslem Board of Guardians and in 1872 was elected to the Burslem Board of Health. He served as treasurer of the Sutherland Lodge of Freemasons and in 1872 was president of the Burslem Association for the Prosecution of Felons.

He married three times. By his second wife, Emma née Bradshaw (died 1879), he had a son Harry Victor, to whom there is a memorial window in St. John's church, Burslem. HP lived at Bleak House, 183 Waterloo Road, Burslem in 1872, and by 1876 at The Hollies, Brampton, Newcastle under Lyme, where he died on 3 August 1885. He was buried in St. John's churchyard.

Dir. 1865-6; *National Index to Wills and Administrations;* Oldham; *Staffs. Advertiser* 8 August 1885 (obit.); VCH viii.

PARKER, Myles Harper (1864-1929), *trade union officer and Member of Parliament,* Hanley.

MHP was born on 6 May 1864 in Bold Street, Northwood, Hanley, the son of Henry Parker, a miner who became a colliery manager, of Madeley, Shropshire. MHP was educated at Northwood National School, the local Roman Catholic school and Charles Street Wesleyan school. He began work at the age of 12 as a door opener at Slippery Lane pit, Shelton, where his father was then under-manager. For three years from the age of 15 he tended the boilers at the Racecourse pit, afterwards becoming an engineman, first at the Etruria Hall collieries and then at Shelton colliery.

His trade union career began in 1885 when he joined the Enginemen's Union, of which he eventually became president. He led the union into mergers with other associated unions to form the National Amalgamated Union of Enginemen, Firemen,

Mechanics, Motormen and Electrical Workers. In 1900 he refused a paid union post, preferring to continue as an engineman and as unpaid district secretary, but in 1907 accepted the post of agent for the Midlands and South Wales.

His political career began in 1910 when he was elected to the council of the new federation, and was made an alderman. He served on the council until 1922, resigning shortly before becoming Labour M.P. for Hanley. He was again elected in 1923 but by this time his health had collapsed. He resigned his seat in 1924.

He married Prudence Flackett in 1888. The family lived at 2 Hill Street, Sneyd Green, where he was a supporter of the allotments movement. He died at his home on 14 January 1929.

S and L; *Staffs. Sentinel* 14 January 1929 (obit.).

PARKER, Ralph (1819-95), *commission agent,* Burslem.

RP was born in Burslem on 26 March 1819. He was in business as a commission agent from about 1855, and was also manager of the County of Stafford Loan and Discount Company, Ltd., 14 Waterloo Road, Burslem.

RP was Liberal in his political views. He was elected to the borough council in 1878 and was created alderman in 1895. He was associated with St. John's church, Burslem, and served as a manager of the church schools. For 30 years he was a trustee and later treasurer of the North Staffs. District of the Ancient Order of Foresters. He was also connected with the Independent Order of Foresters, the Independent Order of Oddfellows (M.U.), the Order of Shepherds, the Freemasons and the Free Gardeners.

He was twice married, with four sons and two daughters. One son, Ralph, became organist at St. John's church, Burslem, and another, Robert, organist at St. Paul's Burslem.

Dir. 1892; *Staffs. Sentinel* 11 July and 16 November 1895.

PARKES, Noah (1859-1940), *trade union official,* Burslem.

NP was born at Burslem in 1859, the son of John Parkes, a publican of Bond Street. He was general secretary of the Printers' and Transferrers' Union until its amalgamation with the National Society of Pottery Workers, when he became an organiser for the combined Union.

He became secretary of the North Staffs. Trades and Labour Council and placed that organisation's support behind federation, although he attracted criticism in doing so. He resigned from his union posts in 1910 to become manager of the Stoke on Trent Labour Exchange a post which he held until his retirement in 1924.

He was elected to Burslem Council in 1903 and was a member of the Education Committee from 1906. After federation he became a Labour member of Stoke on Trent Council until ill health forced his retirement in 1937.

By his wife Rose Ann he had two daughters. By 1912 the family had a grocery shop at 93 Slater Street, Middleport, where NP died on 2 March 1940. He was buried in Burslem cemetery.

Evening Sentinel 2 March 1940; Oldham; Potteries and Newcastle Directory 1912; *Staffs. Sentinel* 11 July 1907.

PARKES, Samuel (1761-1825), *chemist,* Stoke upon Trent.

SP was born on 26 May 1761 in Stourbridge, Worcestershire, the son of Samuel Parkes and Hannah née Mence. He came to Stoke upon Trent about 1793 to start a soap-boiling factory, a business in which his great grandfather had made money. He set up his works in the area of the present Michelin factory, off London Road, Stoke upon Trent.

He was the author of *A Chemical Catechism* (which ran into 12 editions between 1803 and 1826) in which he contrasted the health of Staffordshire potters unfavourably with those of the Continent, drawing attention to the dangers of glazes made with lead. He was a member of numerous learned British and foreign societies.

He married Sarah Twamley on 23 September 1794 and had a daughter, Sarah. SP was a Unitarian, and conducted services in his own home. He built a house in Hartshill Road which later became the Registrar's Office. He moved to London in 1803 and died in Mecklenburgh Square, London, on 23 December 1825.

DNB; *Evening Sentinel* 13 June 1964; R. D. Woodall, *Midland Unitarianism and its Story.*

PARKIN, Frederick (born c. 1884), *pottery worker,* Burslem.

FP was born about 1884. He was apprenticed to Lovatt and Lovatt, Langley Mill, Derbyshire, where he first came into contact with trade unionists. Dismissed from his employment as a turner he moved to Burslem in 1905 where he worked for Wood and Capper, Longport. He was in the employment of Gibson and Sons, Burslem, when he took the chair at a union meeting held in the Clowes Memorial Hall, and was given notice to quit. He was later re-engaged by Gibson's and stayed there for several years. He acted as secretary of the local branch of the Independent Labour Party for six years, was a member, then president, of the management committee of the Burslem Co-operative Society, and a member of the local education authority. He was unemployed for some years in the 1930s, was reduced to poverty and advised to seek public assistance. He took out a pedlar's licence, earned money from part-time gardening, and eked out a meagre existence until his death, some time after 1939.

F. Parkin, *Autobiography of a Pottery Trade Unionist and Reminiscences of 45 Years.*

PARTINGTON, William (1850-1912), *medical officer of health,* Tunstall.

WP was born in Lennoxtown, Stirlingshire, on 15 January 1850, the son of William and Margaret Partington. He was educated at Lennoxtown New Subscription School and at Glasgow University. He came to the Potteries as house surgeon in the North Staffordshire Infirmary. In 1887 he bought the practice of Dr. Brady in Rathbone Street, Tunstall. He acted as medical officer of health to Tunstall and as police surgeon and medical officer to Burslem and Wolstanton Poor Law Union.

He married Alice Maude Woodroffe and had a son and daughter. He built Lennox House, High Street, Tunstall, where he lived for some years, later moving to Congleton and then to Brampton Vale, Newcastle under Lyme, where he died on 13 July 1912.

C. Penn, *Staffordshire at the Opening of the 20th Century; Staffs. Sentinel* 15 July 1912; headstone in Tunstall cemetery.

PATZER, Frederick Robert (1842-1922), *hotelier,* Stoke upon Trent.

FRP was born in Erselben, Saxony, Germany, on 16 February 1842. He came to Scotland and was associated with the Queen's Hotel, Glasgow 1864-9 and the Royal Hotel, Edinburgh, 1869-72. He applied for naturalisation as a British subject when he was living at 1 St. George's Villas, Cricketfield Road, Clapham, London, and was granted denisation on 5 November 1872. From about 1873 he became proprietor of the North Stafford Hotel, retiring in 1910 as chairman of the company which owned the hotel. The lease ran out in 1918 and it was subsequently taken over by Trust Houses.

He married Francis Legate and died at Clatyton Lodge, Newcastle under Lyme on 10 September 1922.

Public Record Office, HO.1. Denisation (HO4S/9319/16589); *Staffs. Sentinel* 10 September 1922 (obit.).

PEAKE, John Nash (1837-1905), *tile manufacturer,* Tunstall.

JNP was born in Tunstall on 3 April 1837, the son of Thomas Peake (q.v) and his wife Harriet. JNP went to the North London Collegiate School and attended classes at the Royal Academy. About 1858 he joined his father's tile making business in Tunstall, taking over as manager on his father's death in 1861. He successfully expanded the firm, which produced vases, urns, ornamental garden pots etc. as well as tiles. The factory became one of the largest in the country, having 35 ovens and kilns. JNP also owned Rosemary Hill Colliery, SIlverdale, Newcastle under Lyme. He was sharply criticised by George Smith, author of *The Cry of the Children from the Brickyards of England* (1871) about working conditions of children in tileyards. Smith, a native of Tunstall, also campaigned about over-crowding and living conditions on canal boats.

JNP was chairman of the Stoke upon Trent Liberal Association and was active in all elections from 1857. He was elected to the Tunstall Board of Health in 1863, serving as chief bailiff 1884-5. He became a member of the Tunstall Urban District Council after 1894. He was opposed to federation and it was on his resolution in September 1902 that Tunstall council decided to have nothing to do with the project. JNP served as a Stafford county magistrate from about 1897.

JNP was an amateur artist, painting mostly portraits and landscapes. He had studied at the Royal Academy under Millais, and one of his portraits was accepted by the Royal Academy in 1855. His many portraits of local Potteries people included Smith Child (q.v), William Adams (q.v) and others. He was commissioned lieutenant in the 1st Battalion Rifle Volunteers from its inception in 1859.

He married Eleanor Bull, of Bloomfield, and had two children. In 1880 he was living in Belvedere House, Congleton, where he died on 29 April 1905. In his will, proved in 1905, he left the interest on £500 to be distributed among the poor of Tunstall at the discretion of his executors and the chief bailiff of Tunstall. The charity was known as the Nash Peake Fund.

Dir. 1882, 1892; *Men of the Period;* Staffs. County Council Education Committee Local History Source Book G25, *Canal Boat People; Staffs. Sentinel* 1 May 1905 (obit.); *Tunstall Board of Health Annual Reports; VCH viii.*

PEAKE, Thomas (1798-1881), *tile manufactuer,* Tunstall.

TP was born in Wolstanton in 1798. He was in business in Watergate Street by the late 1820s, producing bricks, tiles, pipes and ornamental garden pottery in a factory equipped with steam-driven machinery. In 1856 he was working a coal and ironstone mine at his tileries. His son, John Nash Peake (q.v), took over the business at his father's death.

TP contributed to the building of Tunstall's first church, Christ Church (1831-2). He was elected to the local Board of Health and served as chief bailiff three times, in 1858, 1859 and 1860. He was also a member of the Board of Guardians of the Burslem and Wolstanton Poor Law Union. He retired from the Board of Health in 1863 and from active business some years before his death. He lived at Brampton Lodge, Newcastle under Lyme and latterly at Great Malvern, where he died on 22 April 1881. He was buried in Great Malvern cemetery.

Dir. 1828, 1851, 1876; *Staffs. Advertiser* 30 April 1881; *Tunstall Local Board of Health Annual Reports; VCH viii.*

PEARSON, Edward (1812/13-75), *pottery manufacturer,* Burslem.

EP was born about 1812 and was established as a master grocer and earthenware manufacturer in Liverpool Road by 1851. From at least 1853 he operated the Abbey Works, Cobridge, which is said to have been established as early as 1703. EP occupied the factory to 1873. He was succeeded by H. Meakin until 1879, and this firm was succeeded by Wood and Hawthorne to 1887 who in turn were replaced by Sant and Vodrey to 1893.

In 1851 EP was living in Waterloo Road with his wife Charlotte and four children, Charlotte Louise, Mary Ann, Emma and Edward. In 1862 he lived in Sneyd Green. He served on the Burslem Local Board of Health 1856-64. He died at Trentham on 10 November 1875.

Census; Jewitt; *National Index to Wills and Administrations;* Oldham.

PHILLIPPS, William Douglas (1839-1933), *railway manager,* Stoke upon Trent.

WDP was born in 1839, the son of the Revd. Thomas Phillipps. After attending Hereford College School he was apprenticed to Scott Russell who was then building the SS Great Eastern. WDP was a nephew of the chairman of the Llanelli Railway Company, who employed him. He became manager of the line at the age of 21. He moved later to Swansea as the district goods manager of the London and North Western Railway. In 1882 he was appointed manager of the North Staffordshire Railway, holding this post until his retirement in 1917 when he joined the board of directors. The N.S.R. was opposed to federation on the grounds that the company would be adversely affected by any rise in Fenton's rates, and WDP gave evidence to the House of Commons' committee on the company's behalf.

While at Llanelli WDP was captain and secretary of Llanelli Cricket Club. He was chairman of Stoke upon Trent Conservative Association and a member of the school board 1898-1901 and 1901-4. He married Alice Alcock, daughter of Joseph Locker Alcock fo Burslem, and had two children. After his retirement he lived at Cresswell Manor, Stafford. He died at Eccleshall, Staffs., in 1933.

R. Christiansen and R. W. Miller, *The North Staffordshire Railway;* G. Dew, *North Staffordshire Album;* Manifold, *The Leek and Manifold Light Railway.*

PIDDUCK, Henry (1813-73), *clockmaker and jeweller,* Hanley.

HP was born in Shrewsbury in 1813. He was apprenticed to Thomas Joyce, clockmaker of Whitchurch, in 1827 and became a master clockmaker in 1833. In 1841 he established a watchmaker's and jeweller's shop in Market Square, Hanley. After his death his two younger sons, Frederick James and Edward John, carried on the business, and their sons, Eric William and Norman Andrew, in turn succeeded. In 1935 the Pidducks made the Hales Silver Trophy (see Harold Hales), and they also supplied much of the civic silverware.

Henry Pidduck was elected to the Hanley borough council in 1857 and was elected mayor in 1864. By his wife Hannah, born in Middlesex, he had four sons and at least four daughters. He carefully set down in a notebook all childhood illnesses of his children and grandchildren.

In 1854, he advertised a Permanent Clock and Watch Society, through which customers could buy goods on the instalment system, e.g. three shillings a fortnight for a year for a silver verge watch. In 1861, living at 1 Grove Place, Shelton, he employed three men and two boys. He died in 1873.

His sons Frederick James (born 1852) and Edward John (born 1857), were members of Hanley Tabernacle church and both town and county magistrates. A grandson, Norman, was killed at the Battle of the Somme in July 1916 and another grandson Eric William, wounded. The latter served as a magistrate from 1942, and retired to Sidmouth in 1963.

Census 1861; *Hanley Jubilee Souvenir 1857-1907; Magistrates' Year Book; Staffordshire Sentinel Souvenir* (Jubilee of Federation); *Pidduck 125: the story of Pidducks;* information from Mr. Neale Harrison (great grandson of Henry Pidduck).

PIDDUCK, John (died 1886), *ironmonger,* Burslem.

JP was established as an ironmonger in Market Place, Burslem, by 1851, living on Bleak Hill. He was opposed to the payment of church rates. He had the distinction of possessing the only water closet in Cobridge in 1849, but he was unable to use it because the sewer had been blocked, probably by Hales' Foundry diverting it for boiler water. He served as president of the Burslem Association for the Prosecution of Felons in 1857 and 1858.

Dir. 1851; Oldham; *National Index to Wills and Administrations.*

PINDER, Thomas (died 1867), *earthenware manufacturer,* Burslem.

TP was born in the early 19th century. He succeeded his uncle, James Cormine, at the Nile Street works, and traded as Pinder, Bourne and Co. The firm won medals at the exhibitions in London and Paris in 1851, 1855 and 1867. They patented improvements in ovens and in steam printing presses, but the latter attracted the hostility of rioters in 1842 and were abandoned. After TP's death his great-nephew Shadford Pinder took over the works, in partnership from 1877 with Doulton and Co., who assumed control when Shadford Pinder retired in 1881. They added a new wing to the factory in 1884 for the manufacture of bone china. Large scale modernisation after the Second World War made Royal Doulton into one of the largest pottery works in the world.

TP served on the Burslem local Board of Health 1866-7. He died on 25 June 1867.

Dir. 1851; Jewitt; Oldham; VCH viii.

POOLE, Thomas (died 1938), *pottery manufacturer,* Longton.

TP was born about 1860, or 1880 according to one authority, the son of Thomas Poole of Bridge Pottery, Heathcote Road, Longton, in 1846 and Cobden Works in 1870.

He started work at the age of ten at Spode-Copeland's in Stoke upon Trent, as an apprentice thrower. He moved to Ashworth Pottery, Hanley, for four years, then he and his brother Albert James Poole joined their father in the Cobden Works. TP took complete charge in 1883. The firm continued as Thomas Poole until about 1925 when the name was changed to Thomas Poole (Longton) Ltd.

TP became a Stoke on Trent city councillor and a justice of the peace. He was succeeded in the business by his sons James and Horace.

Dir. 1882, 1887; Jewitt; *Pottery and Glass* 1947.

POPE, Samuel (1826-1901), *barrister,* Stoke upon Trent.

SP was born in 1826 in Manchester, the son of Samuel Pope, a merchant. He was educated at London University and qualified as a barrister by 1858. He practised in Manchester until 1865 when he moved to London, and was made a Queen's Counsel.

He was secretary of the United Kingdom Alliance and unsuccessfully contested the parliamentary election at Stoke upon Trent as a temperance candidate in 1859. He also failed to get elected at Bolton in 1865 and 1868. He was appointed recorder of Bolton in 1869. He died in 1901.
Anderton; S and L.

POTTER, Thomas Andrews (1824-80), *newspaper editor,* Hanley.

TAP was born in 1824. He came from a Congregationalist family in Tewkesbury, where he was educated and apprenticed to a printer. He became sub-editor of the *Bradford Observer,* then in 1860 moved to the Potteries as editor/proprietor of the *Staffordshire Sentinel,* whose first issue was on 7 January 1854. It was a weekly newspaper but TAP raised its circulation to 5,000 and on 15 April 1873 launched a daily edition, the first daily in the Potteries. The paper's offices in Cheapside, Hanley, were now too small and on 24 July 1874 TAP moved to a new site in Foundry Street, Hanley, where the *Staffordshire Daily Sentinel* was produced as well as the weekly edition being continued.

TAP, a Liberal in politics, employed a number of Nonconformists as leader writers, including the Revd. Thomas Mills, a Methodist New Connexion minister and the Revd. John Mills, pastor of Caroline Street Congregational church, Dresden. Mills succeeded TAP as editor. When the American Civil War broke out in 1861, the *Sentinel,* unlike many newspapers in industrial England did not support the South. The editorial of 14 December 1861 stated that 'the slave states of America are contending for the maintenance of an institution the foulest and most detestable that the world has ever known'.

By his wife, Mary, TAP had a son and two daughters. In 1861 the family lived in Mollart Street, Hanley, and in 1871 in Bagnall Street. They moved later to Oulton Hall, Stone, where TAP died on 18 April 1880.
Census 1861, 1871; *The Sentinel Story 1873-1973.*

POULSON, Joseph (1749-1808), *pottery manufacturer,* Stoke upon Trent.

JP was baptised on 3 December 1749, the son of Joseph and Hannah Poulson whose family had held the post of sacrists in Stoke parish church for generations. JP and his brother Samuel owned the Stone Works in Stoke upon Trent, although JP was reputedly manager of Spode's pottery in 1790. In 1793 Thomas Minton (q.v) formed a partnership with JP and William Pownall, of Liverpool. They opened a pot works in Eldon Place, Stoke upon Trent in 1796, making at first only white, cream and blue-printed ware, though porcelain was later added to their products. Thomas Minton became sole owner on JP's death.

JP married and had a son, John. He died on 30 November 1808.

G. Godden, *Minton Pottery and Porcelain of the First Period; Holden's Triennial Directory* 1805-7, 1809-11; Minton Mss. 180; G. W. and F. A. Rhead, *Staffordshire Pots and Potters;* Stoke upon Trent parish registers; family papers in possession of Mrs. Creyke; gravestone in Stoke upon Trent churchyard.

POVEY, Thomas (born 1813), *police superintendent,* Burslem.

TP was born at Overton-on-Dee, Cheshire in 1813. He served with the Manchester police force, then came to Trentham and on the recommendation of the Duke of Sutherland was appointed to the Staffordshire police on 1 March 1843. He was promoted to the rank of superintendent in 1845. He retired with a pension on 16 April 1871. In addition to his police duties in Burslem he was superintendent of the fire brigade, market inspector and inspector of nuisances for the Burslem Commissioners. In 1851 the police station was in Market Place. It was replaced by a station in Jackson Street in 1939.

By his wife Alethea whom he had married by c. 1844 he had five sons and two daughters.
Census 1861; Dir. 1851, 1860; Staffs. Constabulary Force Book (Staffs Record Office); VCH viii.

POWELL, Edwin (1827-90), *earthenware manufacturer,* Hanley.

EP was born on 16 January 1827, the son of George Powell, for some years registrar of births and deaths in Burslem, and his wife Mary. On leaving school EP served an apprenticeship with J. Dimmock and Co. Afterwards he joined the firm of Livesley, Powell and Co., manufacturers of parian and other ware, in Old Hall Street, later Stafford Street, Hanley. He became a partner in the firm of Livesley, Bishop and made visits to America where they marketed much of their production. In 1866 Livesley left and the style of the firm became Powell and Bishop, and in 1878 Powell, Bishop and Stonier. The firm owned two other factories, Church Works and Waterloo Works. At Stafford Street only earthenware was produced, including a ware called Oriental Ivory. The firm won medals at the Exhibition of 1862. Powell, Bishop and Stonier continued until 1891 when they were succeeded by Bishop and Stonier, who continued to the 1930s.

In 1871 EP served as mayor of Hanley, in 1872 he was appointed a borough magistrate and in 1877 he was elected alderman. He was for many years a member of Charles Street Wesleyan Methodist church, a local preacher and circuit steward. In 1849 he married a Miss Baines and had two sons and four daughters. He died at Colwyn Bay in June 1890. He was the younger brother of J. W. Powell (q.v).

Dir. 1880; Huntbach; Jewitt.

POWELL, Josiah Wolstancroft (1820-91), *town clerk,* Burslem.

JWP, son of George and Mary Powell was born in Market Drayton and baptised at St. John's church, Burslem, on 24 March 1820. George Powell was master of Burslem Free School and also registrar of births, marriages and deaths in Burslem. JWP was educated by his father and by the local Baptist minister. He began work in the warehouse of Enoch Wood, Fountain Place Works, Burslem, left to go into the office of Harding, solicitor and coroner for North Staffordshire, and at the age of 18 took over the running of Burslem Free School from his father and also became Burslem registrar. He was master from 1838 to 1845, when he was succeeded by Philip Brabazon Ellis. JWP then became clerk to the Burslem Board of Health and to the Highways Board. On the establishment of the borough in 1878 JWP became town clerk. He also served as clerk to the governors of the Haywood Hospital Charity, was secretary to the Star Mutual Building Society, and acted as a correspondent of the *Staffordshire Advertiser.*

JWP's chief interest and importance lies in his contribution to the musical development of the Potteries. He was attached to Burslem Wesleyan Methodist church and his attempt to form a choir led to his search for a method of sight reading suitable for less educated people. He qualified as a teacher of the tonic sol-fa system publicised by J. Curwen, formed his Burslem tonic sol-fa choir in 1855 and established a class in 1858. The system spread through the Potteries and surrounding towns and Powell and his life-long collaborator, George Howson (q.v), gained the description 'fathers of vocal music in the Potteries'. The Staffordshire Potteries Choir gained 3rd prize at the national competition organised by Curwen at the Crystal Palace in 1860, 2nd prize in 1861 and 1st prize in 1862. Some of Powell's pupils, e.g. James Garner (q.v), became conductors of successful choirs. Powell and Howson's last joint effort was to send 1,000 singers to the festival marking the jubilee of tonic sol-fa in 1891.

On 31 May 1842 JWP married Mary Anne Babb, daughter of John Babb of Castle Donington, Leics. In 1851, described as registrar and agent, he was living at 31 King Street, Burslem. He died at Wolstanton on 22 May 1891, leaving a widow, four daughters and three sons, the youngest of whom, Frank Curwen Powell succeeded his father as registrar of Burslem. JWP was buried in Burslem cemetery. His brother Edwin Powell (q.v) was mayor of Hanley.

Census 1851; R. Nettell, *Music in the Five Towns;* J. W. Powell, 'History of the Burslem Tonic Sol-fa Choir' (unpublished ms. HRL); *Staffs. Advertiser* 23 May 1891.

PRATT, Charles O'Neil (1812-72), *minister of religion (C. of E.),* Burslem.

COP was born in County Antrim the son of the Revd. William Henry Pratt and Maria née Corry. He was educated at Enniskillen School, and Trinity College, Dublin, becoming B.A. 1835, and M.A. 1842. He was ordained deacon in 1836 and priest in 1837. He served as curate in his father's parish in County Monaghan. He came to England as curate with sole charge of Christ Church, Macclesfield, and in 1862 was appointed vicar of St. Paul's, Burslem. His unsuccessful attempts to get the Burslem Board of Health to repair the road near the church and vicarage prompted him to verse:

> When a railway crosses the Irish Sea
> When laziness leads to wealth,
> Then Ellgrave Street will complete be
> By Burslem Board of Health.

He did succeed, however, in rebuilding the parsonage of St. Paul's in 1869. The building now belongs to Heath Filtration Ltd.

COP was the author of numerous books. He published *Twenty Sermons on Various Subjects* (1847), A *Metrical Translation of the Ars Poetica* (1850) and later *Holy Scripture, the true rule of Faith* and *Last Standard of Appeal, the right of private judgment vindicated.*

He married Elizabeth Court, and died on 24 May 1872.

S. A. Allibone, *Dictionary of British and American Authors* (1859); Dir. 1873; W. J. Harper, *Bygone Tunstall;* VCH viii.

PRATT, Felix Edward (1813-95), *pottery manufacturer,* Fenton.

FEP, son of Felix Edward Pratt, (1780-1859) was born in Fenton in 1813. He entered the family business of F. and R. Pratt at the age of 15. By 1846 he was the driving force in the business and his brother Thomas, the works manager, was overshadowed. About this time he came into contact with Jesse Austin (q.v), who recognised his abilities and the two collaborated in the production of multi-colour printing on pottery, particularly 'pot lids'. The firm received a special mention at the Great Exhibition of 1851. Two Etruscan-style vases, the largest hitherto made, were also exhibited and were bought by Prince Albert. The firm continued into the 20th century. It was worked as Rialto Pottery between about 1920 to 1926 and later became part of Cauldon Potteries. The works, sited on the north side of what is now City Road, was demolished by 1934. By 1960 workshops of the blind occupied the site.

FEP was chairman of the trustees of the new town hall in Stoke upon Trent in 1851. By 1841 he had married Marianne Baker, by whom he had a son, James, and was living in Brook Street, Stoke upon Trent.

He died on 17 February 1895 and was buried in Hartshill cemetery.

Census 1841; Dir. 1851; Jewitt; VCH viii; C. William-Wood, *Staffordshire Pot Lids and their Potters.*

PRATT, Henry Lark (1805-73), *pottery artist,* Stoke upon Trent.

HLP was born at Derby in 1805 and trained as an artist at Derby porcelain factory. He came to the Potteries in 1830 and was employed at Minton works. In 1844/5 he was commissioned by Chapman and Hall of London to make sketches of the baronial halls of Staffordshire, Cheshire and Derbyshire. He moved to Derby about 1845, but had returned to the Potteries by 1861. He painted landscapes and portraits in his spare time and three of his oil paintings are in Derby Art Gallery, with others in public and private collections. His View of Stoke from Penkhull, c. 1832-1845 is in the City of Stoke on Trent museum.

HLP married and had nine children.

Census 1841, 1851, 1861; Dir. 1873, 1875; G. Godden, *British Pottery and Porcelain 1780-1850; Staffs. Sentinel* 8 March 1873 (obit.).

PRINCE, Arthur George (1837-1904), *chemist,* Longton.

AGP was born in Ipstones, Staffs., on 19 June 1837, and was educated in Cheadle, Staffs. He established a chemist's business in Market Street, Longton, in 1871. In 1875 he was elected to the borough council, served as mayor 1881-2 and was created alderman in 1890. He sat for No. 3 electoral district of Longton on Stafford county council from 1898.

He married twice, (1) Elizabeth Johnson of Denstone and (2) Isobell Ann Upton of Burton upon Trent, but left no children. He was a freeman of the borough, justice of the peace and for 12 years chairman of Longton Cottage Hospital committee. He died at Spratslade House, Dresden, on 17 February 1904.

The County of Stafford and its Families; F. Ludlow (edit.), *County Biographies, Staffordshire; Staffs. Sentinel* 18 February 1904 (obit.).

PYE, Thomas (1775/6-1855), *colliery owner,* Longton.

TP was born about 1775. He started work as a collier but by 1851 was a partner in a business, Stirrup and Pye, Chapel Street, Longton, as a coalmaster and merchant. They also worked a colliery at Adderley Green, where TP had his residence.

Dir. 1851; Memorial inscription in St. John's church, Longton.

QUINTON, Rowland (born 1847), *museum curator,* Tunstall.

RQ was baptised on 11 July 1847 in Newcastle under Lyme, the son of George and Sarah Quinton. George Quinton was licensee of the Waggon and Horses public house, Tontine Street, Hanley, in 1861. RQ was apprenticed to a pawnbroker, Charles Butters (q.v), of Marsh Street, Hanley. By 1881 he was in business as a draper and clothier at 74 High Street, Tunstall, and was married to Alice Ann, with a daughter aged 5 and a son aged 1, both born in Longton, and a second son, an infant born in Tunstall. By 1900 RQ was employed as curator of the museum (opened 1897) in Victoria Institute, Tunstall. The museum was transferred to the City Museum, Hanley, Stoke on Trent, after 1956.

RQ was hon. secretary of the Early Closing Association in 1872.

Census 1861, 1881; Dir. 1900, 1907; IGI Staffs.; *Staffs. Sentinel* 18 May 1872; VCH viii.

RAY, George (1811-65), *pottery modeller,* Longton.

GR was born in 1811. He worked as a modeller for Turner Brothers, Lane End, and by some authorities is credited with the bust of William Turner, now in the City Museum, Hanley, Stoke on Trent.

In 1834 he was living in Liverpool Road, Stoke upon Trent, and from 1860-64 at Normacot Road, Longton.

Dir. 1834, 1864; B. Hillier, *Master Potters of the Industrial Revolution—the Turners of Lane End* (1965).

RENSHAW, William Robert (1845-1923), *engineer,* Stoke upon Trent.

WRR was born at Handforth, Cheshire in 1845. He was apprenticed at the Kidsgrove foundry of Barker & Cope, and by 1880 he was in his own business at the Victoria Works, Tunstall, between Rathbone Street and the Railway Station, producing equipment for collieries, forges and mills. In 1881 he and his Tunstall-born wife Rachel were living at 19 Rathbone Street, Kidsgrove. Before 1884 he had taken over the premises of his former employers, Union Foundry, Kidsgrove, and traded as Renshaw, King & Co.

About 1890 he moved to the Phoenix Works at Cliffe Vale, south of Etruria railway station where at first he manufactured equipment for the infant electricity industry but then concentrated on building railway rolling stock. About 1897 he built 67 special carriages and waggons for Barnum and Bailey's Circus to whom he rented winter quarters in Garner Street, Cliffe Vale. In addition he constructed in six weeks a special iron safety curtain for the Circus's performances at Olympia in London, without which the show could not have gone on. The business later ran into difficulties and Renshaw was adjudged bankrupt in November 1909 with liabilities of £18,000 and assets of £1,000, the deficit being caused by his attempts to keep the business operating. The reversal led him to cease manufacturing and he latterly concentrated on consultancy work.

He and his wife Rachel had several sons; William John, Arthur Ernest and Arnold Davies all attended Newcastle High School. By 1892 he was living at Winton Square, opposite Stoke railway station and by 1900 in Cemetery Road, Shelton. At the date of his bankruptcy he was living in Newport Road, Stafford. He died on 19 February 1923 at Northcote House, Hartshill Road, Stoke on Trent.

Census 1881; Dir. 1880, 1884, 1892, 1900; *Staffs. Sentinel* 30 November 1909, 21 February 1923; Newcastle High School registers (Newcastle Ref. Library).

REYMOND, Karen Marie Elisabeth (1853-1926), *music teacher,* Burslem.

KMER, daughter of Frederick Holst, a master cooper, was born in Copenhagen, Denmark, in 1853. She studied music under various noted teachers, including Niels Gade. She and her father came to Burslem in 1887, and lived first at Beethoven House, Moorland Road, where she taught singing, pianoforte and violin. She sent one of her pupils, John Cope (q.v) to Munich to study the organ under Rheinburger. She founded the Potteries Orchestra and served as its business manager, with John Cope acting as its conductor. Financial difficulties caused the dispersal of the orchestra in 1919.

Madam Marie Reymond, as she was known locally, died on 27 December 1926 and was buried in Hanley cemetery. She is mentioned in Arnold Bennett's novel *These Twain* as 'twenty three years, tall, slim and blonder than any girl ever seen in the Five Towns'.

Madam Marie Reymond (HRL); R. Nettell, *Music in the Five Towns; Staffs. Sentinel* 28 December 1926.

RHEAD, Charlotte (1885-1947), *pottery artist,* Burslem.

CR was born in Burslem on 19 October 1885, the fourth child of Frederick Rhead. She worked as an artist for T. and R. Boote, Crown Pottery, Wood and Sons and Burgess and Leigh, Burslem. At Burgess and Leigh's she trained a team of artists in tube lining technique, in which the decoration is applied to the ware by squeezing a rubber bag attached to a fine glass nozzle. One of her designs for this firm was Florentine, still to be found in quantity. She joined A. J. Richardson in 1931, her designs for that firm including Byzantine, Foxglove and Wisteria. She became a director of Wood and Sons, a post which her father had held, in 1943. She died on 6 November 1947.

B. Bumpus, 'Pottery designed by Charlotte Rhead', in *Antique Collector,* January 1983; G. A. Godden, *Victorian Porcelain.*

RHEAD, George Woolliscroft (born 1832), *pottery artist,* Burslem.

GWR was baptised at Bucknall-cum-Bagnall on 12 May 1832, the son of George and Mary Rhead. His father, born about 1803, was a modeller and potter in 1851, living at Bleak Hill, Burslem. He was one of the earliest pupils at Stoke upon Trent School of Design in the 1840s, and transferred to the Newcastle under Lyme School of Art about 1853. Between 1857 and 1862 he won several national medals. He was appointed assistant to J. P. Bacon at Newcastle in 1869 but resigned in 1879 to teach at Longton School of Art. He began the Fenton School of Art in 1889.

By his wife Fanny, whom he had married by 1855, he had four sons and one daughter. His sons George Woolliscroft Rhead and Frederick Alfred Rhead wrote *Staffordshire Pots and Potters* (1906). GWR was a brother-in-law of Frederick Hürten (q.v).

Census 1851; R. Haggar, *A Century of Art Education in the Potteries;* IGI Staffs.

RHODES, John Harold (1891-1917), *miner,* Tunstall.

JHR was born in Mellor Street, Packmoor, Staffs., on 17 May 1891, the son of Ernest Rhodes, an ex-soldier. He went to school in Newchapel and after leaving school worked as a miner. About 1910 he joined the Grenadier Guards and served for three years. He returned to the Potteries and worked at Chatterley Whitfield Colliery. On the outbreak of the First World War in 1914 JHR was recalled to the forces as a reservist. He won the Distinguished Conduct Medal on 17 May 1915 and three months later was awarded a bar to this medal. He returned to England to recover from a wound and in December 1915 married Elizabeth Meir of Pittshill. There was one son, John, born in May 1917, whom JHR never saw. He returned to the front and on 9 October 1917 won the Victoria Cross for storming an enemy pill-box and capturing nine prisoners single handed. He was also awarded the Croix de Guerre for this action. He was wounded in action on 27 November 1917 and subsequently died of his injuries.

Memorial services were held in Newchapel parish church on 16 December 1917, in Packmoor Primitive Methodist Chapel on 23 December 1917 and at Pittshill Primitive Methodist Chapel on 30 December 1917. A memorial plaque was unveiled at Chatterley Whitfield Mining Museum on 20 April 1984.

Evening Sentinel 7 February 1983; *Staffs. Sentinel* 27 November, 6 December, 17 December and 31 December 1917.

RICARDO, John Lewis (1812-62), *railway company director,* Stoke upon Trent.

JLR was born in 1812, the son of Jacob Ricardo and a nephew of David Ricardo the economist. On the death of his father JLR entered the family financial business. He became chairman of the North Staffordshire Railway in 1846 and continued in this post, with a break of five months in 1855 when he resigned because of a failure to amalgamate with the London and North Western Railway, until 1862. He was also a director of the London and Westminster Bank and associated with railway construction in Norway and Denmark. Until 1856 he was also chairman of the Electric Telegraph Company, having been active in its formation in 1846.

In politics he adopted a respectable radicalism. He was elected as Liberal Member of Parliament for Stoke upon Trent in 1841, and remained a representative of the borough until his death, winning elections in 1847, 1852, 1857 and 1859. A free-trader he was instrumental in obtaining the repeat of the Navigation Acts in 1849. He disappointed local Liberals in Hanley by remaining neutral on the question of Hanley's becoming a local board of health.

He married Katherine Duff, daughter of General Sir A. Duff, in 1841, and had one son, Augustus Lewis. He died in London on 20 August 1862.

Anderton; F. Boase, *Modern English Biography;* R. Christiansen and R. W. Miller, *The North Staffordshire Railway;* DNB; *Staffs. Advertiser* 23 August 1862; Townley; V and S.

RICHARDS, John (1792-c.1851), *shoemaker,* Hanley.

JR was born about 1792. He earned a living as a shoemaker. From 1818 he was active in a variety of local radical movements and was elected as Potteries delegate to the Chartist National Convention in 1838. After the Chartist riots in the Potteries on 15 and 16 August 1842 JR was arrested, tried for incitement and sentenced at Stafford in October 1842 to one year's imprisonment. He served his sentence in Stafford gaol. After his release he continued to campaign for Chartism until about 1850.

Burchill and Ross; J. Epstein and D. Thompson, *The Chartist Experience.*

RIDGWAY, Edward John (1814-96), *pottery manufacturer,* Hanley.

EJR, son of William Ridgway, potter, of Bell Works, Shelton, and Church Works, Hanley, was born in Hanley in 1814. He was officially in partnership with his father from c. 1838, the firm trading as William Ridgway, Son and Co., until 1845. EJR was also in partnership with Leonard John Abington (q.v) from about 1835-60. In 1866 production was transferred from the Church Works to the newly-built Bedford Road Works, Vale Road, Shelton. Church Works passed to Powell and Bishop and the buildings had been demolished by about 1948. In 1870 EJR took his son John into partnership. He retired in 1872 leaving the business to his sons John and Edward Ackroyd Ridgway, who were later joined by Joseph Sparks. The firm continued trading into the 20th century trading under various titles. In 1955 it was styled Ridgway Potteries, Ltd., and was a subsidiary of Allied English Potteries, Ltd.

One of the specialised products of the firm in the mid-19th century was jet ware, decorated in raised enamel in the Limoges style, and another was relief decoration on various stoneware bodies.

In August 1838 EJR married Mary Ackroyd, of Halifax, Yorks., and had three sons and two daughters. He was elected chief bailiff of Hanley in 1841, alderman in 1857, mayor in 1859, and was granted the freedom of the borough in 1893. He retired from the council in 1871. He was justice of the peace for the county from 1858 and for Hanley from 1859. He rose to the rank of captain in the 2nd Hanley company, Rifle Volunteers, and then to major in the 1st Administrative Battalion. In 1863 he played cricket for Hanley Cricket Club.

He lived for some time at Bank House, Hanley and later at Rownall Hall, Werrington, where he died on 11 May 1896.

G. A. Godden, *The Illustrated Guide to Ridgway Porcelains;* Jewitt; *Staffs. Advertiser* 16 May 1896; VCH viii.

RIDGWAY, George (1822-99), *miller,* Hanley.

GR the son of Job Ridgway (q.v) was born at Northwood House, Hanley on 30 July 1822. He was educated privately. He started work as a potter's printer but by 1843 was established in business as a flour miller, at Cliffe Vale, Hanley. He married Elizabeth Ellen Coulter (1823-1906) and had five sons of whom the eldest, George Ridgway (q.v) succeeded him in the business.

GR was elected to Hanley council on the town's incorporation in 1857, served as mayor 1868-9, was created alderman 1871 and given the freedom of the borough 1895. His portrait, presented for 40 years' public service, hangs in Hanley town hall. He was a member of Bethesda Methodist New Connexion church, where there is a memorial tablet to him, and served as trustee and circuit treasurer.

He died on 18 February 1899 at Rownall Hall, Werrington. His sons George Ridgway (q.v) and Edwin Charles Ridgway (of The Woodlands, Stone, died 1910), succeeded him in the business.

C. Penn, *Staffordshire at the Opening of the 20th Century; VCH viii.*

RIDGWAY, George (1847-1913), *miller,* Hanley.

GR the eldest son of George Ridgway (q.v) was born on 29 September 1847. He became the senior partner in George Ridgway and Sons, corn millers, of Cliffe Vale, Hanley, with an interest in a grocery business in Swan Walk, Hanley, run by his brothers Ralph and Alfred John. Like his father he was a member of Bethesda New Connexion church, and served as treasurer and trustee. He was a local justice of the peace. For ten years he was treasurer and secretary of Prince Albert Friendly Society.

He lived at Northwood House, Hanley, then at Rownall Hall, Werrington, where he died on 26 November 1913. He left a widow, two sons, Joseph, who took over the family business in Cliffe Vale, George, who became a corn factor in Liverpool, and a daughter.

Dir. 1875-6; *Staffs. Sentinel* 26 November 1913.

RIDGWAY, Job (1759-1814), *pottery manufacturer,* Hanley.

JR was born at Chell, Burslem, in 1759, the son of Ralph Ridgway a potter. His father moved to Swansea in search of work and Job was apprenticed to a potter in that town. He returned to Staffordshire about 1780 but failing to find work moved to Leeds for about two years. He came back to Hanley and about 1782 with his brother George (c. 1758-1823), took over the Bell Works, Shelton. The partnership ended in 1802 by which date Job had built Cauldon Place Pottery, where he produced blue-printed ware and a type of procelain similar to that which he had known in Swansea. He was a partner in the Bellevue Pottery, Hull, from 1802 to 1804 and again with his brother George from 1806.

After a period of spiritual self-searching JR joined a Methodist society in Leeds. On his return to Hanley, then part of the Macclesfield circuit, he became a class leader. He was one of the founder members of the Methodist New Connexion in Hanley in 1797 who met temporarily in a coach house in Albion Street until Bethesda chapel was built on the site in 1798.

JR married Elizabeth (died 1809) daughter of Elijah Mayer, potter, on 25 March 1785, in the church at Newcastle under Lyme. He had three sons, John (q.v), William and Joseph (died in infancy). John and William received an equal share in the family business in 1808, the year in which the manufacture of porcelain was begun in Cauldon Place Pottery. He married again, a Miss Cadman, of Sheffield, in January 1813. He died in 1814.

Simplified Ridgway Family Tree
*(subjects of biographies denoted by *)*

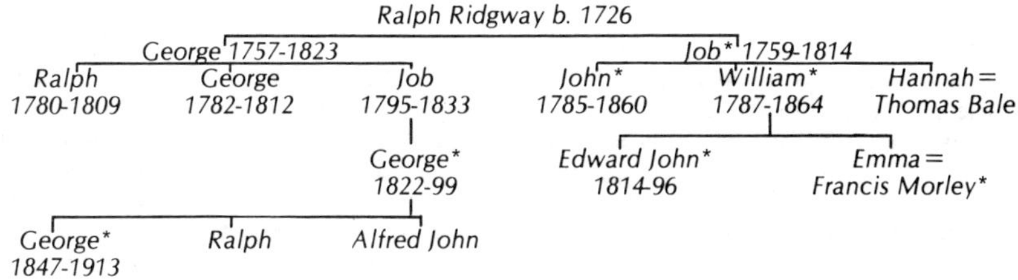

Memoir of Mr. Job Ridgway, New Methodist Magazine Sept.-Dec. 1814 (reproduced in G. Godden, *The Illustrated Guide to Ridgway Porcelains);* Jewitt; H. Smith and A. Beard, *Bethesda Chapel, Hanley* (WSL); VCH viii.

RIDGWAY, John (1785-1860), *pottery manufacturer,* Hanley.

JR was born on 1 February 1785, the eldest son of Job Ridgway (q.v) and his wife Elizabeth née Mayer. He was educated at Burslem and privately by the Revd. Mr. Trueman, a Baptist minister. On the death of his father in 1814 he, with his brother William, carried on the family business at Cauldon Place, Hanley. JR visited America in 1822 and subsequently the firm produced much ware for the American market, including the series The Beauties of America. In 1830 the brothers inherited the Bell Works, Hanley from their uncle, George Ridgway. Their partnership now ended, William taking the Bell Works and John retaining Cauldon Place. By 1850 the latter was one of the largest factories in the Potteries employing 500 people. Ridgway's stand at the Great Exhibition of 1851 showed 400 pieces of ware. Ridgway was appointed potter to Queen Victoria and made liberal use of his right to display the royal arms on his wares. Ridgway porcelains, especially the floral encrusted ware, won a high reputation. The firm also pioneered several new decorative processes, including the application of photography, and in 1840 JR took out the first patent for a machine which actually made pottery. From 1830 to 1855 John Ridgway traded, with various partners, as John Ridgway and Company. From 1854 JR's partners were Thomas Sanders Ball, Thomas Richard Sanders and Frederick George Sanders of the Architectural Pottery Company, Poole, Dorset. From 1856 to JR's retirement in 1858 the firm was styled John Ridgway, Bates and Co. This company was succeeded by Bates, Brown-Westhead and Co., in 1858-61, which was replaced by Brown-Westhead Moore and Co. in 1862. By 1906 the style was Cauldon Ltd., and from 1920-62 Cauldon Potteries Ltd. In 1962 the earthenware side of the firm was acquired by Pountneys of Bristol and the porcelain side by E. W. Brain and Co. Ltd., later Coalport China Ltd.

John Ridgway had a controlling interest in six other factories in the area and four businesses; he owned shares in a coal mining company, was chairman of the Staffordshire Potteries Waterworks Company and was a director of the North Staffordshire Railway.

He was an enlightened if paternalistic employer. Conditions of work at Cauldon Place were good for the time: no children under 12 were employed and a compulsory sick benefit scheme operated. A row of cottages which JR built was rented to his workers at £10 a year per cottage and received a favourable mention in a report made to the Board of Health in 1850.

JR and his brother William held progressive political opinions. They were described, in a hostile newspaper article, as 'the radical saints of Hanley'. The author of the article, James Amphlett, made libellous charges about the brothers for which he was successfully sued in the courts. JR supported the anti-slavery movement, repeal of the corn laws and though not a Chartist favoured universal suffrage at the national level. In local government, however, he advocated a high property qualification. For many years he devoted much if not most of his time to local government affairs. He was a founder member of the Hanley Watching and Lighting Commissioners in 1825 and chief bailiff in 1827. He was elected a Hanley market trustee in 1830, a body whose membership was dominated by his friends, relations or associates in Bethesda chapel.

He supported the idea of incorporation and in 1857 was elected first mayor of the newly-created borough of Hanley. He was appointed to the justices' bench in 1853 and also served as a deputy lieutenant for Staffordshire. The camel on the coat of arms of the city of Stoke on Trent comes from the Ridgway crest. JR was offered, but refused, a knighthood. He was opposed to the creation of a park, arguing that a cemetery must come first.

He married Sophia Bale of Bristol in 1810. There were no children of the marriage. Like his father JR was a leading member of Bethesda Methodist New Connexion church and was the driving force behind the expansion of the New Connexion denomination locally in the first half of the 19th century. He contributed to the building of MNC chapels in Tunstall, Bethal (Burslem), Mount Tabor (Fenton) and elsewhere. There is a mural tablet to his memory in Bethesda chapel.

He died at his home in Cauldon Place, Hanley, on 8 December 1860.

G. Godden, *The Illustrated Guide to Ridgway Porcelains;* H. Stickels, 'The Contribution of John Ridgway and the Methodist New Connexion to the urban development of Hanley' (Univ. of Keele, B.A. dissertation, 1971); A. Lamb, 'Mechanisation and the application of steam power in the North Staffordshire pottery industry' in *North Staffordshire Journal of Field Studies,* vol. 17, 1977; plan of J. Ridgway's property, Howard Place, Hanley 1865 (HRL).

RIDGWAY, William (1788-1864), *pottery manufacturer,* Hanley.

WR was born in 1788, the son of Job Ridgway (q.v). With his brother John (q.v) he became a partner in the Cauldon Place Works in 1808, having joined the business in 1802 when the factory was built. After the death of their father in 1813, the brothers continued in partnership at Cauldon Place and also had the Bell Bank works (on the site of the present Museum), formerly occupied by their uncle George Ridgway.

The partnership ended in November 1830 and WR took the Bell Bank Works. Alone, with his son Edward John (q.v), and with partners such as Francis Morley (q.v), his son-in-law, Leonard Abington (q.v) and William Wear, he came to operate six factories in Hanley. These included, in the vicinity of Hanley parish church, the Cobden Works, the High Street Works and the Church Bank Works once held by Humphrey Palmer. WR also held the Broad Street Works (now Mason's Ironstone). He retired in 1854, apparently in some financial difficulty, said to have been caused by problems in the American trade which accounted for much of his production and by his own lack of caution.

He lived at Prospect Place, Northwood and there built several houses as well as almshouses for poor widows and a school for poor children. WR was credited with "converting a rude and demoralised part of Hanley into a well ordered hamlet". He was chief bailiff of Hanley in 1830. WR married Ann Sharp and there were several children including Edward John, William Henry, Emma, who married Francis Morley (q.v), and Helen Maria, who may have been the music teacher at Allbut's School for Young Ladies at the The Mount, Penkhull in 1851.

WR was a member of Bethesda Methodist New Connexion Church and was buried in the family vault there. He died at Clayton on 29 March 1864.

G. A. Godden: *Illustrated Guide to Ridgway Porcelains* (1972); S. Shaw: *A History of the Staffordshire Potteries* (1829); *Staffs. Advertiser* 9 April 1864; *National Index to Wills and Administrations.*

RILEY, Thomas (c. 1846-1933), *schoolmaster,* Stoke upon Trent.

TR was born in Newton Regis near Tamworth about 1846. After qualifying as a teacher at Saltley College he was appointed assistant master at St. Peter's church school, Stoke upon Trent in 1869 and headmaster in 1872. He retired in 1913 when his son became headmaster in his place, but returned to teach full time during the First World War. After the war he continued as gardening instructor until 1929.

He was churchwarden of St. Peter's church, a Sunday school superintendent and a member of the choir 1870-1913. He formed Stoke St. Peter's School football team, who achieved a record score of 44-0 against Bucknall St. Mary's, in February 1888. He married Mira Greenhill, an infants' school teacher at St. John's school, Hanley, on 8 August 1876, and had a son, William Martin Riley and two daughters. He died on 16 October 1933 at his home in Sheppard Street, Stoke on Trent and was buried in Hartshill cemetery. A memorial to him was erected in the parish church.

F. W. Wright, *Schools of the Parish of St. Peter ad Vincula; Evening Sentinel* 16 October 1933.

RINGLAND, William Hans (1839/40-85), *draper and house furnisher,* Hanley.

WHR was born about 1839, the son of Hans Ringland, a native of County Down, woollen draper of Hanley. WHR succeeded his father in the business some time after 1861. He was elected to Hanley borough council in 1882 and served as mayor in 1883. On 17 December 1883 he opened a new branch post office in Percy Street. By his wife Rosa, whom he married on 17 December 1867 he had at least four daughters. The family lived in Birch Terrace in 1871 and at Brunswick House, Newcastle under Lyme in 1881, where WHR died on 6 February 1885.

Census 1861; Dir. 1872, 1883; Huntbach; IGI Staffs.; memorial in Hanley cemetery.

RISELEY, Benjamin Thomas (born 1846), *grocer,* Hanley.

BTR was born in Macclesfield on 26 November 1846, the son of Robert Riseley, a publican and later a baker. He was educated at Christ Church School, Macclesfield, but later moved to Hanley where he set up in business as a grocer. He became chairman of the North Staff. Sugar Association and also of Hanley Grocers' Association.

He was elected to Hanley council in 1883 and served as mayor in 1905. He was made an alderman of the federated borough in 1910. He was a member of Bethesda Methodist New Connexion church for over 25 years, filling many of the offices connected with the church. He married a sister of Michael Huntbach (q.v), a draper's assistant of Lamb Street, Hanley, on 28 December 1871, and had four sons and three daughters. The family lived at 25 New Parliament Row in 1881.

BTR served on the bench of the local justices of the peace. Like John Ridgway (q.v) he was opposed to the creation of a park in Hanley before the establishment of a cemetery: 'The town must prepare for the dead and let the living take care of themselves', he argued.

Bethesda Methodist New Connexion church registers; Census 1881; Dir. 1880; Huntbach; C. Penn, *Staffordshire at the Opening of the 20th century.*

ROBERTS, Ellis (1860-1930), *artist,* Burslem.

ER, the second son of Thomas Roberts, pottery works manager of Longport, Burslem, was born on 27 October 1860. He was educated at Ellison's Grammar School, Burslem, then apprenticed to Minton's Pottery, Stoke upon Trent, as a china painter. He studied at Minton's Art School 1874-82, from where he was awarded a two years' scholarship to the South Kensington Art Training School. From there he won a travelling scholarship to Italy for six months. He also went to Paris where he lived in poverty while studying at Atelier Julien. Back in England he found his first patron in Joseph Shaw of Derby, mineral manager of the Midland Railway. ER's portrait of Lord Bury, exhibited at the Grosvenor Gallery, marked a turn in his fortunes. He was elected to the Society of British Pastelists in 1889, in which year he exhibited a pastel portrait of Lady Hilda Keppel also at the Grosvenor Gallery. The Keppel family's associations with Edward, as Prince of Wales and as king, brought Roberts success. He became the most sought-after portrait painter of the time, the peak of his fame being reached when King Edward visited his studio in 1902. He painted portraits of many society beauties and members of the aristocracy and gentry, some with Potteries associations, including Millicent Duchess of Sutherland (q.v) and Sir Henry Doulton. Ellis Roberts had the knack of making plain women into pretty ones and pretty ones into visions of incredible beauty. He was electd an A.R.C.A. and to membership of the Royal Society of Portrait Painters. There was much contemporary criticism of his work as well as popular acclaim, including George Moore's article in *The Year's Art for 1896*. He married Eliza Glover. He died at 12 Wexford Road, Wandsworth Common, London, on 24 September 1930.

Art Journal 1899; *The Book of Beauty* (Hutchinson c. 1896); *Evening Sentinel* 13 October 1960; *The Lady's Realm* 1898; *Staffs. Sentinel* 25 April 1896; *Who was Who* 1929-40.

ROBEY, Thomas (born 1800/1), *schoolmaster,* Stoke upon Trent.

TR, possibly the younger brother of William Robey (q.v) was born about 1800 in Warrington, Cheshire. In 1822 he was running the Commercial Academy, Church Street, Hanley. From 1841 he rented a room in the Wesleyan Methodist schoolroom in Market Street, Stoke upon Trent, where he ran a private school. He claimed in an advertisement in 1850 that his was the largest voluntary school in the county. In 1868, however, he was evicted from the premises he occupied because of his failure to pay the rent.

By his first wife, Abigail (died 1858), he had a daughter, Elizabeth Hannah Robey, who died in infancy in 1842 in Cross Heath Street, Stoke upon Trent. In 1851 he was living in Princess Street. He was still living there in 1861, with his wife Mary and his stepsons.

Census 1861; *Cross Street Chapel 1799-1949;* Dir. 1841, 1851; Stoke upon Trent parish registers.

ROBEY, William (1785-1863), *schoolmaster,* Longton.

WR was born in Warrington on 11 April 1785. By 1818 he was running an academy at Vauxhall, Lane End, in a building which later became part of the Longton Athenaeum. By 1851 his academy was in Gower Street, but the Misses Robey, possibly his daughters, were also running a school in Vauxhall. By 1860 the school was under Leonard Austin, son of Jesse Austin (q.v.).

WR was one of the founders of Longton Building Society in 1838 and Longton New Building Society in 1850. He married Elizabeth Mayer at Stoke upon Trent on 2 February 1806 and had ten children. One of his sons, Ralph Mayer Robey, in partnership with William Ridgway in 1838, emigrated in 1841 to New South Wales, Australia, where he became a member of the State legislature.

WR died at Gower Street, Longton, on 1 January 1863.

Briggs: *Dictionary of Australian Biography; Index to Births, Marriages and Deaths, Staffs. Advertiser* (Staffs. Record Society, 1968); *Staffs. Advertiser* December 1850; memorial in St. John's church, Longton; tomb of R. M. Robey, Hanley cemetery.

ROBINSON, Herbert Minton (died 1923), *pottery director,* Stoke upon Trent

HMR, son of John Robinson of Westwood Hall, Leek, was the adopted son of Herbert Minton-Senhouse. He joined Minton's as managing director and company secretary when the firm was formed into a limited liability company about 1883. He held this position until his death.

HMR married on 5 October 1887. He was patron for some years of the local composer Havergal Brian (q.v.). He died at Beechfield, Queen's Road, Penkhull, in December 1923.

Cox's Potteries Annual and Year Book 1925; Minton's Archives, 54.

ROBINSON, Samuel (1807-69), *pottery worker,* Hanley.

SR was born in 1807 and by the 1840s was employed as a china painter, He was a supporter of the temperance movement, a member of the Reform Union and the Reform League, and became a Chartist. He is reported to have spoken against the monarchy and the Duke of Sutherland at a meeting held in Trentham village hall in 1842. He also supported the miners' strike. He was arrested after the Chartist riots of 14-15 August 1842 and was sentenced to imprisonment for conspiracy. He died in 1869.

Anderton; J. Epstein and D. Thompson, *The Chartist Experience; Staffs. Sentinel* 20 September 1842.

ROBINSON, Samuel (1871-1955), *wholesale newsagent,* Burslem.

SR was born in Smallthorne in 1871, the son of Levi Robinson, a newsagent. From the age of five he helped his father, selling and delivering newspapers. He realised his ambition of becoming a wholesale newsagent in 1902, intially handling one thousand copies of publications a week. Fifty years later the business handled one million copies a week. SR's first premises were The Shed, Moorland Road, Burslem, then in Reginald Street and finally in Hamil Road, where the firm of S. Robinson is situated today (1985). It became a limited company in 1927.

SR was opposed to federation and wrote a number of letters on the subject to the *Staffs. Sentinel* in 1907. He argued with another correspondent "Fairplay to Hanley" about the rates in their respective towns and the amount of property unlet as a result. He believed that Hanley's high rates were forcing traders there out of business and that federation would be Hanley's means of reducing its rates burden at the expense of the other towns. He attempted to show the great expense which would ensue from federation by producing lists of staff numbers and costs in other towns throughout the country. He so monopolised the correspondence column of the *Staffs. Sentinel* that the editor was forced to ration SR's future letters, particularly as he thought the comparisons little to the point. In 1920 SR wrote to oppose the proposed boundary extension of Stoke on Trent, saying that the inhabitants of those areas to be taken in (of which he was one) should not be forced in against their will.

SR lived at Milton for some years and founded the Milton Brotherhood of which he was president. He was noted as a hymn writer especially for Sunday school anniversaries. He married Florence Sarah Millington and there were two children, Richard and Betty. He died on 23 March 1955 at his home, Sunny Croft, Stockton Brook.

Evening Sentinel 23 March 1955; information from Mr. P. Robinson, S. Robinson and Co. Ltd., Burslem (grandson); *Staffs. Sentinel* 17 May, 5 July, 9 July, 11 July, 15 July, 14 October 1907; 19 January 1920.

RODEN, William Serjeant (1829-82), *ironmaster and Member of Parliament,* Hanley.

WSR was born in Wolverhampton in 1829 and educated in Bristol. He was first placed with his uncle, Thomas Brown, an ironmaster of South Wales, then, in 1857, he joined Shelton Bar Iron Co., and became managing director.

Soon after his arrival he was elected to the local Board of Guardians and in 1863 to Hanley council. He served as mayor of Hanley 1866-8. He was created alderman in 1873. He founded the Hanley Rifle Volunteer Company, formed the Staffs. Artillery Volunteer Corps and became honorary colonel when the Staffs. corps was merged with the Shropshire Artillery Volunteers.

Liberal in politics WSR developed ambitions for a political career. He was nominated, together with the sitting member, George Melly, as Liberal candidate, for the election of November 1868. His nomination was not without difficulty; his rival for the candidature, Robert Hartwell, claimed that during the recession of 1864 in the iron industry, Roden had reduced wages and that he also had a black list of strikers in the 1865 dispute. Hartwell argued that Roden was not the man to represent those members of the working class enfranchised by the 1867 Reform Act. Roden got the nomination and in the event he and Melly were returned without a contest. In the 1874 election, however, there was a third Liberal candidate, and though Melly was returned the voters were split and Roden was defeated by the Conservative candidate, Robert Heath.

WSR married Theodora Butler in 1860. She died in 1867 and he on 28 April 1882.

Anderton; *Staffs. Advertiser* 29 April 1882; V. and S.

RODGERS, James (1814-90), *theatre proprietor,* Hanley

JR was born in 1814 at Ashted Barracks, Birmingham, the son of an officer in the Royal Scots Greys. His father wished him to follow a military career, but to avoid this JR ran away at the age of seventeen and joined a theatrical company. His acting career progressed and he played second lead to both Charles Kean (son of Edmund) and Charles Macready, the foremost actors of the day. He became an actor manager and leased the theatre in Nelson Place, Newcastle under Lyme, but is seems that the venture was not successful. In the early 1850's he became licensee of the Saracen's Head in Piccadilly, Hanley and was asked to become the lessee of a theatre to be opened in the premises of the former People's Hall in Brunswick Street, Hanley.

JR's name and reputation persuaded the magistrates to grant a licence which they had refused before. He was, however, required to put up a bond of £500 and two other securities of £50 and to "maintain proper order and decorum during performances". He ran the Royal Pottery Theatre for two years until November 1854. After a period probably spent in Liverpool, where his daughter Onoria was born in 1855, he returned to the Potteries and was again lessee of the theatre by 1859. He continued to accept acting engagements elsewhere and it is possible that he may have created the pantomime dame with the role of Widow Twankey in *Aladdin*. He may have found the idea in the Liverpool expression current at the time for those women whose husbands were lost from ships known as Twankays which sailed to China.

JR purchased the Prince of Wales Theatre in Birmingham in 1866 and gave up the Royal Pottery Theatre (by then the Theatre Royal) about 1873. While in Hanley he was a member of the Menturia Lodge of Freemasons and in 1862 was living in High Street (Town Road).

He died on 6 January 1890 at 28 Calthorpe Road, Edgbaston, Birmingham, a widower with three children

Birmingham Faces and Places vol. ii (Birmingham Reference Library—Local Studies); inf. from Channel 4 Television programme 1982 on Pantomime Dames; Hanley Commissioners' minutes; *Staffs. Advertiser* 14 February 1852, 24 September 1852, 3 December 1853, 4 November 1854; *Sunday People* 9 December 1984; *Staffs. Sentinel* 6 January 1890.

ROSE, Thomas Bailey (1805-78), *stipendiary magistrate,* Stoke upon Trent

TBR, the son of J. Rose, an attorney of Gray's Inn, London, was born in Kentish Town, Middlesex, in 1805. He was educated at St. Paul's school, and was called to the bar on 27 June 1827. In 1831 he became conveyancer and equity draftsman for the Aylesbury session in the Norfolk circuit. By 1833 he was living in Betley, Staffs., where he married. In June 1839 Parliament sanctioned the appointment of a stipendiary magistrate for the Potteries area. TBR obtained this post and held it until June 1864. His duties required him to travel around the six towns presiding over the various police courts. He earned the reputation for severity and for inflicting punishments designed to deter rather than to do justice. At Lane End (Longton) he is reported to have threatened to 'make the people so dread breaking the law that I shall be able to hang my watch in the Market Square overnight and go the next morning and find it there'. His house in Penkhull was one of those attacked during the Chartist riots of August 1842, and Rose was formally censured by the Home Secretary for abandoning the Potteries to the mob during the night of 15/16 August. He sat on the special commission set up at Stafford to deal with the many people subsequently arrested. In June 1864 he was appointed to the Stafford and Shrewsbury sessions of the Oxford circuit.

On 27 April 1833 TBR married Arabella Short, daughter of Charles Short of Betley. There were six children, Thomas, George and Arabella, born in Betley, and Rosalind, Charles and Gertrude, born in Penkhull. The family lived at Grove House, Penkhull, from 1839 to 1852, in Stoke Lodge from 1852 to 1857, in Brook Street in 1859 and at 16 Stokeville (The Villas) from 1859 to his retirement, when he moved to 56 Southbank Road, Southport.

TBR was a strong Tory in his political views, blaming Liberals for encouraging the working classes in their subversive ideas. He was also a staunch supporter of the established Church of England. In the 'No Popery' agitation that followed the re-establishment of the Roman Catholic hierarchy in England he spoke at a meeting in Stoke upon Trent on 30 November 1850 in which he stated that he had 'no sympathy with the system of Popery, which, serpent-like, coiled itself in secret to dart at its prey'.

He died in Southport on 26 June 1878.

Aston, V. G. *History of Penkhull;* Epstein, J. and Thompson, D., *The Chartist Experience;* Hawley, T., *Pottery Life and Character;* Greenslade, M. W. 'Staffordshire 'No-Popery' 1850-1' in *Staffordshire Catholic History* No. 21, 1982; 'How they Polled', HRL Local Pamphlet Vol. 30; *Southport Visitor,* 29 June 1878; *Staffs. Advertiser* 27 April 1839, 20 and 27 August 1842, 7 February 1857, and June 1864; censuses 1841 and 1861.

ROWLEY, William (fl. 1884-95), *footballer (goalkeeper),* Stoke upon Trent

WR was born in Hanley and educated at St Thomas's Roman Catholic School, Stoke. He was playing for Port Vale in 1887 and was sued by them and an injunction awarded against him to prevent him from playing for Stoke. He did however play for Stoke in the first Football League season in 1888-89.

He was capped by England twice, both times against Northern Ireland, in 1889 at Everton (Anfield) when England won 6-1 and in 1892 in Belfast when England won 2-0. On the latter occasion the full-backs were his Stoke club colleagues, Clare and Underwood. WR played fourteen consecutive matches for Staffordshire between 1884 and 1890. When his playing career ended in 1895 he became the secretary of Stoke football club, but the financial circumstances required him to use his own money to pay transfer fees. On one occasion he had to rely on the Football League to force the directors to reimburse him for the transfer of Hislop from Sunderland.

WR later became a publican before emigrating to America.

P. Buxton *Stoke City F.C. 1863-1963;* information from Mr. E. Hawley, Smallthorne.

RYAN, Revd. Patrick Joseph (1866-1951), *minister of religion (Roman Catholic),* Tunstall.

PJR was born in Cappawhite, Co. Tipperary, in March 1866, and educated at St. Patrick's College, Thurles, and Oscott College. He was ordained priest on 24 February 1894, served as curate in Newcastle on Tyne to 1897 and then in St. Anne's Birmingham. He was appointed parish priest at the Church of the Sacred Heart, Tunstall, in 1899. A new church was built between 1922 and 1930, employing only unemployed men. The original architect was J. S. Brockleby.

PJR served on the local Board of Guardians for eight years. He became a recognised authority on housing and was a director of Stoke Building Society. He,died early in February 1951. A building in the Boulevard was acquired for use as a parish hall and named Ryan Hall in his memory.

Evening Sentinel 9 February 1951; M. W. Greenslade, *A Brief History of the Catholic Church in Stoke on Trent.*

SALISBURY, Lazarus (born c. 1813), *hatter,* Burslem.

LS was born in Ireland about 1813. By 1851 he was established as a hat manufacturer, Market Place, Burslem and in 1862 he had premises both at 52 Market Place, Burslem and in Tontine Street, Hanley.

By his wife Alice whom he had married about 1848 he had two children. He served on the Burslem Board of Health from 1856 to 1862.

Census 1861; Dir. 1851, 1862; Oldham.

SAMUDA, Jonathan (1805-82), *railway company secretary,* Stoke upon Trent.

JS, son of David Samuda, was born in Tottenham, Middlesex, on 23 November 1805. A Jonathan Samuda, merchant, of 11 Angel Court, Throgmorton Street, London, is listed in 1840 and 1847. In 1833-4 Samuda and Ricardo, brokers, occupied 23 Finch Lane, London. It is reasonable to suppose that the Samuda connection with Ricardo helped JS to get the job of secretary to the North Staffordshire Railway at its inauguration in 1845. He held this post for 30 years. At his appointment, on 21 May 1845, his salary was £400 a year.

He was elected a Stoke upon Trent improvement commissioner and served as chief bailiff in 1869. His special interest was smoke abatement.

On 16 May 1849 he married Jane Bromley, daughter of Charles Bromley, a shoe manufacturer, of Stone, Staffs. He was living at Stonefield House, Newcastle Road, Stone, at the time of his marriage, and from 1851 until his death lived at Longfield Cottage, Hartshill, Stoke upon Trent. He died there on 13 October 1882, leaving in his will £30,000. He was buried in Hanley cemetery. There is a memorial tablet to him in Hartshill church.

Public Record Office, Rail 532/3; *Staffs. Advertiser* 19 May 1849; *Staffs. Sentinel* 15 October 1882; Stoke upon Trent Improvement Commissioners' minutes; Stone parish registers; gravestone in Hanley cemetery.

SAVAGE, Warwick (1843-91), *printer,* Burslem.

WS was born in Mansfield, Notts., in 1843. About 1865 he bought the stationer's shop at 28, Market Place, Burslem, where he also did general printing and lithography. From 1867 he printed the Burslem Board of Health annual reports. At first he and his wife Mary lived on the premises with their daughter and two sons, but later they moved to Wellington House, Burslem. WS was a member and pastmaster of the Sutherland Lodge of Freemasons. He died on 15 May 1891.

His sons, Warwick Savage (1871-1959) and George Savage carried on the business and expanded it into one of the largest in North Staffordshire. Warwick Savage II was president of the North Staffs. Master Printers' Association, president of the Midland Alliance of Master Printers and president of the Ceramic Printers Association. In 1891 new works were built in Wedgwood Place. Most of their printing was for the ceramic industry but they also had a bookselling trade. WS II formed a partnership with James Davies, trading as the British Transfer Company. The partnership was dissolved in 1919 but WS II continued until the 1950s. Since about 1974 the business has become Messrs. Waspe, stationers.

Census 1871; *Pottery Gazette* April 1959; R and S; *Staffs. Advertiser* 16 May 1891; *Staffs. Sentinel* 15 May 1891.

SCHOFIELD, Samuel Barton (1807-68), *minister of religion (Congregationalist),* Burslem.

SBS was born in 1807. He studied at Blackburn Independent College, and at Ashton, Lancs. He arrived in Burslem in July 1833, preached for four Sundays and was then invited to become pastor of the Congregational chapel in Nile Street, Burslem. He was ordained on 27 August 1833 and served as pastor for 34 years. In 1835 the name of the chapel was changed from Zoar to Salem. A new chapel and schools were built in 1837 in Queen Street, and thanks to SBS's fund-raising efforts the debt was almost negligible by 1866.

By his wife Mary, whom he had married by about 1834, he had two daughters, Margaret and Mary. In 1851 the family was living at Bleak Hill and in 1864 in Waterloo Road.

A tablet was erected to his memory in the church. Queen Street church was replaced in 1906 by the present church in Moorland Road.

Congregational Church, Burslem, 150th Anniversary Booklet 1821-1971; Dir. 1864; VCH viii.

SCRIVENER, Alexander (1852-1921), *architect,* Hanley.

AS was born on 19 April 1852, the son of Robert Scrivener (q.v) and his wife Elizabeth. He trained as an architect and was the third son to enter the firm of architects founded by his father in the early 1850s in Shelton. The firm acquired an extensive practice, designing public, private and industrial buildings. Among those buildings designed by AS was St. Paul's church, Newcastle under Lyme.

Among the interests of AS were music and archaeology. He was choirmaster of Endon church, and a member of the executive committee which organised the North Staffordshire Triennial Music Festivals. He twice served as president of the North Staffordshire Field Club (in 1895 and 1905) and was awarded the Garner Medal in 1905 in recognition of his archaeological work. He published numerous papers on archaeology and on church architecture in the *Transactions of the North Staffordshire Field Club* and in other journals. He was Conservative in politics.

He married Anne Twyford and had five children. He died on 17 December 1921.

Journal of the British Archaeological Association, New Series vol. ii, part 1, 1896; *North Staffs. Field Club Transactions* 1921-2; *Staffs. Advertiser* 24 December 1921.

SCRIVENER, Robert (1812-78), *architect,* Hanley.

RS, the son of William Scrivener, a carpenter and master builder of Ipswich, was born on 29 March 1812. He served an apprenticeship and became a master carpenter like his father. About 1850 he came to Hanley and acquired a brickworks by the canal in Shelton. The works later changed to the manufacture of pottery. RS then set up as an architect and surveyor in Shelton, buying land in Shelton and building two houses which became the offices of the firm. By 1856 he was sufficiently established to prepare evidence on ward boundaries for the inquiry before the incorporation of Hanley. His public buildings included the Queen's Hotel, Hanley (1869), which later became Hanley town hall, and the Mechanics' Institution. In 1868 the firm became Robert Scrivener and Son when his eldest son, Edward Elvine joined the firm, to be followed by Robert George and Alexander (q.v).

RS was a prominent member of Bethesda Methodist New Connexion chapel, serving as a trustee and superintendent of the Girls' School, and as a Sunday School teacher.

By his wife Elizabeth née Elvine, he had four sons and four daughters. He died on 19 April 1878 and was buried in Bethesda churchyard.

Bethesda Chapel records; N. Pevsner, *The Buildings of England; Staffordshire;* E. Warrilow, *A Sociological History of Stoke on Trent;* information provided by members of the Scrivener family and by Messrs. Scrivener and Sons, Wellesley St., Shelton.

SELLARS, William (1776/7-1833), *occupation not known,* Stoke upon Trent.

WS was born about 1776. Nothing is known of his parents or occupation. For more than 20 years he was a superintendent of the Stoke Wesleyan Methodist Chapel Sunday School and leader of the choir. He was a gifted musician and with his brother George composed, among other works, Jubal's Lyre, a set of psalm and hymn tunes in four parts arranged for organ and pianoforte. He died, apparently in humble circumstances, at Honeywall, Stoke upon Trent, on 21 April 1833, leaving a widow and eight children. An address at the graveside was given by the Revd. Sir W. Dunbar.

A. Curtis and E. Beech, *A History of Wesley Chapel; Methodism at Cross Street Chapel (Stoke) 1799-1949: Staffs. Mercury* 27 April 1833.

SHAW, Anthony (1827/8-1900), *earthenware manufacturer,* Burslem.

AS was born in Cheddleton, Staffs., about 1827. By 1851 he was established as an earthenware manufacturer at Newport Works, and living at Newport House. He had established the Mersey Pottery, Middleport, by about 1860, and the business was carried on, from 1882, as Anthony Shaw and Sons. A new manufactory, built about 1866, was equipped with machinery by a Scottish engineer, Dundas Porteous. The firm specialised in white granite-ware and cream-coloured ware for the United States, and printed, lustred and painted goods for South America. AS was awarded a medal at the Paris Exhibition in 1855. The firm was taken over by A. J. Wilkinson about 1898.

AS served as chief bailiff of Tunstall in 1857 and was on the Burslem Board of Health 1862-72. By his wife Jane, whom he had married by about 1844, he had three children. He gave the site at Milton for the building of a new Wesleyan Methodist chapel in 1862.

AS died at Bank House, Buglawton, on 19 January 1900.

Jewitt; A. Lamb, 'The Application of Steam Power in the North Staffordshire Pottery Industry, in *North Staffs. Journal of Field Studies* 1977 (vol. 17) quoting *Staffs. Advertiser* 10 February 1866; *National Index to Wills and Administrations;* Oldham; VCH viii.

SHAW, Charles (1832-1906), *minister of religion (Methodist New Connexion),* Tunstall.

CS, the sixth of eight children of Enoch Shaw, painter and gilder, of Piccadilly Street, Tunstall, by Ann née Mawdesley, was born between 5 and 11 August 1832. He attended a dame school run by Betty Wedgwood in Tunstall, then began work as a mould runner to an apprentice muffin maker, earning a shilling a week. When he was eight years old he moved to another factory, possibly Samuel Alcock's, as a handle maker. In 1842 his father lost his job as a result of his participation in a strike, and the family were forced into Chell workhouse. Shaw later wrote vividly and movingly of his experiences in the workhouse, and this and the other events in his early life were used by Arnold Bennett in his novel *Clayhanger.* CS was in the workhouse for about four or five weeks, then his father found a job and Charles was released. He went to work with a toymaker, George Hood (q.v). His elder brother, Edwin, gave evidence to the inspector, Samuel Scriven, who reported on the employment of children and young persons in the Staffs. Potteries in 1843; Edwin is called Evan Shaw in the report.

The Shaw family attended the Methodist New Connexion chapel in Tunstall. At the age of 18 CS joined a Mutual Improvement Society and by 1853 he was on the New Connexion local preachers' plan. He entered the ministry full time and was stationed in Oldham, Sheffield, Mansfield, Huddersfield and Aston during the 1850s. He resigned from the ministry in 1861 and entered the family business of his wife, Jane née Halliwell, at Radcliffe Mill, Grotton, near Oldham. On his wife's death, before 1870, he became co-owner of the mill. He carried on this business for a number of years, also writing leaders for the radical weekly newspaper, the *Oldham Express,* under its editor, Alfred Butterworth. In 1868-9 CS was prominent in support of the movement to disestablish the Irish Church.

He married, as his second wife, Maria Arthington, at the Methodist New Connexion Church, High Street, Huddersfield. He re-entered the ministry in 1897 and was stationed in the Isle of Wight and Bangor, Co. Down. His autobiography, *When I was a Child,* appeared as a series of anonymous articles in the *Staffs. Sentinel,* in 1892-3, and was first published in book form in 1903. He died in poverty in March 1906 at Springhead, near Oldham.

Children by his first marriage included Charles Mawdesley Shaw, a Methodist New Connexion minister who subsequently became a Christian Scientist, and Alfred Halliwell Shaw, manager of Radcliffe Mill. By his second marriage he had Joseph Bramwell Shaw, an industrial chemist, and Arthur Mawdesley Shaw, a research engineer, who designed the ventilation system for the Mersey tunnel.

O. Beckerlegge, *United Methodist Ministers and their Circuits; Daily Despatch* 9 March 1906; W. H. Chaloner, 'Two Anonymous Nineteenth Century Books', in *Proceedings of the Wesley Historical Society,* vol. xi, 1975; C. Shaw, *When I was a Child* (Caliban Books 1980); Tunstall Wesleyan Sunday School, admittance register; information from Mrs. Muriel Barritt, Nottingham.

SHAW, Simeon Ackroyd (1785-1859), *schoolmaster/author,* Hanley.

SAS, the son of Edmund Shaw, millowner, and his wife Betty née Ackroyd, was born on 17 April 1785 in Salford, Lancs. He came to the Potteries to work as a printer and compositor for the *Pottery Gazette and Newcastle under Lyme Advertiser* but by 1818 he was running an academy for young gentlemen in Northwood, Hanley and a commercial academy in Piccadilly, Hanley, by 1822. By 1834 he had a large academy in Market Place, Hanley. A linguist, with a wide knowledge in many fields, he published numerous works. These included *Nature Displayed* (6 vols. 1823), *History of the Staffordshire Potteries* (1829), *The Chemistry of Pottery* (1837), and later *Wonders of the Heavens and Earth, Grammar of the English Language, Grammar of Philosophy* and others. He began to issue instalments of a local history *The Borough of Stoke upon Trent in 1838.* Eight parts had been issued when financial difficulties arose between Shaw and his printers. W. Lewis and Son, and Shaw had to mortgage his book and rights. John Ward completed the work in twelve more parts, the last being published in 1842 and the whole work being published in book form in 1843. Ward later claimed that Shaw had contributed little apart from his name to the original eight parts and that Shaw had used his, Ward's, collections of material.

SAS was at least partly instrumental in the founding of the Pottery Mechanics' Institution in Frederick Street, Shelton, in 1826, although Ward does not include him in the list of founders.

SAS married twice, (1) on 13 June 1809, Elizabeth Simpson and (2) on 25 December 1821 Harriet Marsh Broad. He described himself on the title page of his book *Nature Displayed* as a doctor of laws. Increasing worries, both domestic and financial preyed on his mind, and these, together with overwork, led to his mental breakdown. He died on 8 April 1859 in the County Lunatic Asylum, Stafford. He was buried in Bethesda churchyard, Hanley.

E. and D. Beech, 'Simeon Shaw' in *Journal of Ceramic History* No. 7, 1974; *Bi-Monthly Review,* November 1951; Census 1841; M. W. Greenslade, *The Staffordshire Historians; Simms.*

SHELLEY, Percy (1860-1937), *pottery manufacturer,* Longton.

PS was born in Longton in April 1860, the son of Joseph Shelley and his wife Ann, daughter of George Mitcheson (q.v). The Shelley family had been potting in Longton since at least 1748. PS was educated at Queen's College, Taunton and Owen's College, Manchester and graduated from the University of London. His father had been a partner in the firm of Wileman and Co. since 1872 and PS joined the business in 1881. On the death of his father in 1896 he took control.

He employed Frederick Rhead as art director and Rowland Morris (q.v) also designed for the firm. The firm changed its name to Shelley and to publicise the new name a "Shelley girl" statuette was designed in 1926. At this time the firm were spending £10,000 a year on advertising. From 1926 the firm used the designs of Mabel Lucie Attwell on its children's ware. About 1930 Shelley's produced tea wares in Art Deco designs. PS incorporated the business in 1929 and retired in 1932.

He was involved in argument in 1905 when he suggested that German potters be invited to set up a factory in Longton to teach local manufacturers better techniques. He was president of the Liberal Party in North Staffs. and chairman of the election campaign in 1906 which won all five local seats for the party. PS was a supporter of federation and his motion approved by his fellow Longton councillors in November 1905 paved the way for its eventual success, although he failed to gain a seat on the new council.

He married Emma Jane Mayer in 1890 and there were three sons and a daughter of the marriage. PS was a pioneer of tennis in the district and laid down one of the first private hard courts at his home, Southlands, Trentham Road, Longton. He later lived at Tittensor before retiring to Bournemouth where he died on 28 August 1937. He is buried in Blurton churchyard.

Evening Sentinel 28 August 1937; C. Watkins, W. Harvey and R. Senft, *Shelley Potteries* (1980).

SHERRATT, William (1853-1919), *music dealer,* Stoke upon Trent.

WS was born at Biddulph in 1853. He took over the business of musical instrument maker and music teacher founded by Rolfe Medina (q.v) in the 1880s. He served as organist of Stoke upon Trent parish church for 40 years, was organist and choirmaster of Biddulph parish church until 1879 and conducted for the Stoke upon Trent Orchestral Society.

He died in June 1919.

Staffs. Sentinel, series of articles on North Staffs. Music Festivals 1896; *National Index to Wills and Administrations.*

SHERWIN, James Cartlidge (1835-99), *music dealer,* Hanley.

JCS, the son of George Sherwin and Louisa Emma née Cartlidge, was born in Burslem on 8 July 1835. He opened a music shop in Swan Square, Hanley, in 1855, then moved to the Market Place and finally in the 1880s to Hanley, on the corner of High Street (Town Road) and Empson Street. Though blind from birth, he was a talented organist, playing for Burslem St. John's in 1853, Bethesda New Connexion chapel 1866-91 and the Tabernacle from 1891-9. In 1867 he was listed as professor of music, 14 King Street, Hanley.

He died at Camden House, 21 High Street, Hanley, on 29 May 1899.

Dir. 1855-67; *Staffs. Sentinel* 29 May 1899.

SHIRLEY, Henry Benjamin (1858-1910), *potter's miller,* Hanley.

HBS, son of Jesse Shirley, was born at Etruria on 24 June 1858. He was educated at Northwood Acadamy, Hanley, and at Malvern. With his brother Jesse (q.v) he was in business as a potter's miller and manufacturer of agricultural manures by 1880. He was elected to Hanley council in 1893 and served as mayor in 1902-3. He was a Wesleyan Methodist, a Conservative in politics and president of Hartshill Cricket Club.

He married Gertrude Patti Beresford, of Belper, Derbyshire, in April 1894 and had two children. He died at the Ashlands, Hartshill, on 17 January 1910 and was buried in Hartshill cemetery.

County Biographies 1901; Dir. 1880; *Hanley Borough Year Book* 1902; Huntbach; C. Penn, *Staffordshire at the Opening of the 20th Century.*

SHIRLEY, Jesse (1848-1927), *flint grinder and bone merchant,* Hanley.

JS was born in Etruria on 17 November 1848. He was educated at Alfieri's Academy, Northwood, Hanley, and by 1880 was in partnership with his brother, H. B. Shirley (q.v) in the firm of Jesse and H. B. Shirley, bone and flint mills, Etruria.

He was elected to Hanley council in 1880, served as mayor in 1885 and became an alderman in 1892. As chairman of the parks committee he promoted the scheme for the purchase and laying out of Hanley park, 1892-7 sited on 63 acres of Stoke fields, waste ground on each side of Victoria Road. JS was also elected to the local bench of justices of the peace.

He married twice and had at least six children. He lived at Etruscan Villa, Etruria. He died on 8 August 1927.

Census 1861; Huntbach; C. Penn, *Staffordshire at the Opening of the 20th Century;* VCH viii.

SIBARY, George (1810/11-98), *chemist and druggist,* Longton.

GS was born in Rotherham about 1811. From about 1834 he was in business as a chemist and druggist in Market Street, Longton. He was registered as a pharmaceutical chemist on 1 August 1868 under the Pharmacy Act of that year, as having been in practice as a chemist prior to that date. Later he became a grocer.

He married twice, (1) Emma Lucretia Jackson, on 26 September 1842, by whom he had at least one child and (2) Elizabeth probably née Moore by whom he had probably two children. He died at Stamford House, Dresden, on 27 February 1898.

Census 1841; Dir. 1834, 1851, 1860, 1872; IGI Staffs.; information from Pharmaceutical Society of Great Britain; St. John's church, Longton, memorial inscriptions.

SIMMS, Rupert (1853-1937), *bookseller,* Newcastle under Lyme and Longton.

(RS properly belongs to Newcastle under Lyme but is included here because his research covers the Potteries).

RS, the son of John Sims (the second 'm' in the surname was added later), brickmaker, and Elizabeth née Mellor, was born at Consall Forge, near Ipstones, Staffs., on 31 July 1853. He attended local National schools in Longton, Silverdale and Wolstanton. In November 1862 when taking a meal to his brother at the Daisy Bank Brickyard, Longton, he was caught in the perforating machine and lost his left arm and right hand. Although the machine was unguarded the owners paid only 9d. in compensation. When the family moved to Silverdale in 1863, Rupert, with the aide of a schoolteacher, Mr. Smithyman, learned how to write despite his handicap. After some time as a tea-dealer in 1883 he set up as a second-hand book dealer in Friar Street, Newcastle under Lyme. He also bought furniture and pictures and in 1899 moved to new premises at 27, The Ironmarket, Newcastle. He was the editor or author of a number of books and articles. His chief work was *Bibliotheca Staffordiensis,* published in 1894, a list of books and articles published or printed in Staffordshire or written by Staffordshire authors or relating to Staffordshire. The book was not a financial success and the publishers, A. C. Lomax, of Lichfield, lost money. Simms also wrote 'The Parliamentary History of the Borough of Newcastle under Lyme', but this was never published.

RS married Mary Ellen Reynolds in 1878 and had a number of children. He retired in 1932 and died on 1 August 1937, in Newcastle under Lyme.

E. Beech, 'Bibliotheca Staffordiensis' in *Six Towns Magazine,* January 1971; M. W. Greenslade, *The Staffordshire Historians; Staffs. Advertiser* 14 May 1921 and 7 August 1937.

SKERRATT, Richard Thompson (born c. 1810), *engraver,* Fenton.

RTS, the son of Samuel Skerratt and Susannah née Thompson, was baptised at Wolstanton church on 2 December 1810. In 1851 he was described as a copperplate engraver and farmer and was living in Heron Cross. He had a shop and workshop in King Street in 1869.

He was an improvement commissioner 1851-73, chief bailiff 1858-63 and a member of the local Board of Guardians. On 21 January 1835 he married Margaret, daughter of William Sorton of the Stafford Arms, Newcastle and had at least two children. His daughter later married Joseph Forsyth, a civil engineer, who designed the lay-out of Hartshill cemetery in 1884.

Census 1851, 1881; Dir. 1862, 1869; Fenton Improvement Commissioners' Minutes; IGI Staffs.; *Staffs. Advertiser* 24 January 1835 (marriage notice).

SLANEY, Thomas Charles (1852-98), *schoolmaster,* Hanley.

TCS, the son of Charles Slaney, a coachman and ostler at the North Staffordshire Hotel, was born on 9 February 1852 and baptised at Stoke parish church in 1854. He attended St. Peter's school, Stoke upon Trent, and then trained as a teacher at St. Peter's College, Saltley. He taught at Boothen schools, St. Peter's school, Stoke upon Trent, and became head of St. John's National school, Hanley. He lived for some time at 2 Mollart Street, Hanley. He was captain of Stoke Football Club 1874-83, and secretary 1874-83. He founded and served as secretary of Staffordshire Football Association (1877) and after retiring from active football became a referee. He was also secretary of Staffordshire County Cricket Club 1889-93. For over 20 years he was a member of the 1st Volunteer Brigade, North Staffs. Regiment, and was its financial secretary in 1893. He relinquished the post of president of Staffs. F.A. in 1894 owing to pressure of business, having become a commercial traveller for Johnson Brothers of Hanley.

TCS was a Conservative and, with A. H. Heath, was the founder of the Unionist Club in Frederick Street, Hanley. He was a member of the Menturia Lodge (Hanley) of Freemasons. He married and had three sons and two daughters. He died at Wall Grange, near Endon, on 5 March 1898.

R. Speake, *One Hundred Years of County Football 1877-1977; Staffs. Advertiser* 12 March 1898; *Staffs. Sentinel* 1874-1900 (various issues).

SLATER, John (*floruit* **1877-1914),** *art director, pottery works,* Burslem.

JS was the fourth son of William Slater. He served an apprenticeship at Mintons and later became art designer at Pinder's, Burslem. When the firm was taken over by Doultons, in 1882, JS became art director of that firm. He retired in 1914.

JS came from a dynasty of pottery painters, gilders and designer founded by William Slater (1784-1864).

C. J. Noke, *John Slater, Art Director of the Royal Doulton Potteries, 1877-1914;* W. Scarratt, *Old Times in the Potteries;* ex inf. D. J. Morton (Royal Doulton).

SMITH, Edward John (1850-1912), *ship's captain,* Hanley.

EJS was born on 27 January 1850 in Well Street, Hanley, the son of Edward Smith, a potter and his wife Catherine Hancock, née Marsh. He was educated at Etruria British School. On leaving school at the age of 12 he worked at Etruria Forge, and eventually was in charge of the Nasmyth steam hammer. In 1871 he went to Liverpool to meet his half-brother, Captain Hancock, who commanded a sailing ship. EJS was apprenticed in Liverpool to A. Gibson and Co., and by the age of 24 had gained a master's certificate. He commanded a sailing ship, the *Lucy Fennel,* for four years, then in March 1880 joined the White Star shipping line. He served in various grades and in May 1887 was appointed to the command of the *SS Republic.* He subsequently commanded the *Baltic, Celtic, Coptic, Adriatic, Cufic, Britannic, Germanic* and for nine years the *Majestic.* During the South African war he made two trips to Cape Town and Durban with troops and was awarded the Transport Medal and the South African Clasp. In 1888, aged 38, he took an extra master mariner's certificate which qualified him as a captain in the Royal Naval Reserve. He was awarded a Royal Distinction in 1910.

By 1912 EJS was the Commodore of the White Star company line, and took command of the SS *Titanic,* built in the Harland and Wolff shipyard, Belfast, for her maiden voyage to the United States. She sailed from Southampton on 10 April 1912. At 11.40 p.m. on 14 April she struck an iceberg and at 2.20 a.m. on 15 April sank, with a loss of over 1,500 lives. Captain Smith went down with his ship.

A memorial tablet to EJS was unveiled in Hanley Town Hall on 16 April 1913. The tablet was removed in 1961 to Etruria Middle School, where it was placed next to a portrait of EJS subscribed for by the old boys of Etruria school and unveiled on 24 April 1913. Subsequently the tablet was returned to Hanley Town Hall. A fund was opened in 1913, most donations coming from Liverpool and America. There was some opposition in the Potteries towns to the idea of having a statue to Captain John Smith and eventually one was erected to him in Beacon Park, Lichfield. The statue, by Lady Kathleen Scott, widow of the Polar explorer, was unveiled on 29 July 1914 by Captain Smith's daughter, Helen Melville Smith after a speech by Millicent Duchess of Sutherland (q.v). The remainder of the fund was used to install a stained glass memorial window in Liverpool cathedral and for a cash grant to the Seamen's Orphanage, Southampton. A tablet was also erected to Captain Smith's memory in the New Seamen's Church Institute, New York.

EJS married Sarah Eleanor Pennington and had one daughter, Helen Melville Smith, later Mrs. M. R. Cooke.

Many books, newspaper and magazine articles have been written about the loss of the Titanic, a number of films and television programmes have been made and even music has been written about the disaster. Legends and myths have developed and there is still controversy and criticism about certain aspects of the event, such as the apparently excessive speed at which the ship was proceeding through iceberg-bound waters, the proportions of first and third class passengers saved, and the number of lifeboats carried.

L. Beesley, *The Loss of the S.S. Titanic* (revised edition 1973); W. Lord, *A Night to Remember; Staffs. Sentinel* 24 April 1913 and 1 August 1914; *Evening Sentinel* 14 April 1978.

SMITH, John, (died 1840), *coal and land owner,* Fenton.

JS the son of Jeremiah Smith and Elizabeth née Jervis was descended from a former bishop of Coventry and Lichfield and from John Smith of Heath End House, Keele, whose iron grave tablet is in St. Giles' churchyard, Newcastle under Lyme. JS inherited Great Fenton House and estate, owned Hallfields Colliery, Northwood and Goldenhill Colliery, Fenton, as well as coalpits in the vicinity of Northwood Park. About 1820 he built a reservoir at Birches Head to provide Hanley and Burslem with water. The water was pumped from a disused colliery, the waterworks being sited on the Caldon canal between Ivy House Mill and Dresden Mill. The works was bought out by the Staffordshire Potteries Waterworks Company after 1849.

JS built Foley Potteries about 1827, leasing them to Elkin, Knight and Bridgwood. The pottery made good quality Willow Pattern and other blue-printed ware, and had a steam engine and flint mill.

By his wife Elizabeth née Turner JS had three sons. He lived at Elmhurst near Lichfield. He died on 6 May 1840 and was buried in Stoke upon Trent churchyard. The family name is commemorated in Smith's Pool, Fenton.

T. Pape, *Newcastle under Lyme in Tudor and Early Stuart Times; Staffs. Advertiser* May 1840; VCH viii; Ward.

SMITH, Rodney (Gipsy), (1860-1947), *evangelist preacher,* Hanley.

RS, son of Cornelius Smith and Mary née Welch, both gipsies, was born on 31 March 1860 in Epping Forest. Like his father and uncles he was 'converted', the date which he assigned to this being November 1876. He joined the Salvation Army and was sent to Whitby, where he married Annie Pennock in 1879. He moved to Chatham, then to Hull and Derby, and came to Hanley in December 1881. His mission was so successful that he was asked to remain, and his second son, Hanley, was named after that town. In 1885 he was accused of breaking the Salvation Army rules by accepting a gift, and he resigned from Hanley Mission. In 1886 he began his campaigns throughout England and later overseas. He was appointed official Free Church evangelist in 1897. He received the M.B.E. for his work in France during the First World War. His first wife died in 1937 and he married Mary Alice Shaw in the following year. He spent the 1939-45 war in America and died aboard the *Queen Mary* on 4 August 1947. His grave is marked by a granite memorial in Epping Forest.

His appeal as a popular preacher was based on his singing, his appearance and his oratory.

His nephew, George Bramwell Evens (1884-1943), was 'Romany' of the BBC Children's Hour.

W. Addison, *Portrait of Epping Forest;* Biographical News Cuttings vol. 1 (HRL); D. Lazell, *From the Forest I came;* R. Smith, *Gipsy Smith, his life and work.*

SMITH, Sampson (1813-78), *pottery manufacturer,* Longton.

SS, the son of Sampson and Elizabeth Smith, was born in 1813. He was working as a pottery decorator by 1846 and is described in 1851 as a lusterer and ornamenter, of Upper Hill Street, Longton. In 1853 he moved to Garfield Pottery, High Street, Longton and in 1859 set up his own business at the Sutherland Works, Barker Street, Longton. He became one of the largest local manufacturers of Staffordshire figures, including china dogs, castles, toby jugs and portrait figures. Some models were made for the Latin American market.

Liberal in politics he represented St. John's ward on Longton borough council from 1865 to 1872. A philanthropist himself he encouraged his workpeople to contribute to deserving causes. By his wife Elizabeth, who died in 1872, he had at least two children. The family lived at Meir Villa, Weston Road.

SS died on 26 December 1878. He and his wife are buried in St. James's churchyard, Longton. The business was continued for some time by his executors, then by

Adderley and Tams, and later still by John Adderley and W. H. Davies until 1918, when figure-making was abandoned. Barber Brothers took over and revived the manufacture of figures about 1948, using some of the original moulds.

Jewitt; M. and H.; memorial inscription, St. James's churchyard; K. Woolliscroft, *Sampy* (catalogue produced for Gladstone Museum Exhibition Nov.-Dec. 1978).

SMITH, Theophilus (died 1801), *pottery manufacturer,* Tunstall.

Nothing is known about TS's early life and productions. About 1788 he bought the Furlong estate and built the hamlet of Smithfield near his house and pottery works. Domestic trouble caused him to neglect his business, and he was declared bankrupt in 1800. Either in June or July 1800 he attempted to murder his friend John Wainwright, a Liverpool merchant, whom he suspected of having an affair with his wife. The attempt failed, Smith fled to London but was arrested in Pall Mall and committed to Bridewell. While in prison in Stafford he shot his wife, who was visiting him in the prison hospital, then shot himself. His wife subsequently died of her wound.

The Smithfield estate was sold to John Breeze who renamed it Greenfield. The hall was demolished before 1908 and the site is now occupied by a housing estate.

E. N. Stretton, 'Theophilus Smith, Potter of Tunstall' in *Apollo,* vol. lxxi, March 1960; VCH viii.

SOLON, Louis Marc Emmanuel (1835-1913), *pottery artist,* Stoke upon Trent.

LMES was born in Montauban, Tarn et Garonne, France, in 1835. Ill health prevented his studying law as expected and he attended the Atelier of Lecoq de Boisbaudrant, Paris. Some of his etchings were published while he was at Lecoq's studio and this led to his joining the Sèvres Pottery, where he experimented with the pâte-sur-pâte process. A vase thus decorated was the Sèvres entry in the 1867 International Exhibition.

Solon moved to Minton's, Stoke upon Trent, just before the Prussians besieged Paris in 1870. There he was encouraged by Colin Minton Campbell to continue with his pâte-sur-pâte work. He and the assistants he trained produced many items which are now acknowledged masterpieces, including Queen Victoria's Jubilee Vase. Solon's decoration has been described as 'a curious blend of fantasy, Renaissance and Classical styles and discreet eroticism'.

LMES retired in 1904 but continued with his artistic work and his hobbies. He assembled a large collection of pottery, especially salt-glaze ware. He wrote a number of books on pottery and amassed a collection of works on ceramic history of over 3,500 volumes. His published works include *A Brief Account of Pâte-sur-Pâte* and *The Art of the Old English Potter.*

About 1873 Solon married Maria, daughter of Léon Arnoux, the art director of Minton's, and they had eight sons and one daughter. The family lived at No. 1, The Villas, Stoke upon Trent, where he died in June 1913. He and his wife Maria, who died in October 1910, were buried in Hartshill cemetery. His son Léon Victor Solon was art director of Minton's 1900-9.

Solon had sold his collection of pottery in 1912, and after his death his library was sold to the Central School of Science and Technology, later the North Staffs. Technical College and the North Staffs. Polytechnic.

The pâte-sur-pâte process for which Solon is chiefly remembered, involved laying slip on to a Parian clay body which had been coloured by metallic oxides. The slip is applied in successive coats. Then the piece is scraped, smoothed, carved and incised by iron chisels. Solon often spent 50 hours or more on the decoration of an individual piece.

P. Atterbury, *The Story of Minton;* Census 1881; *The Connoisseur* vol. xxxv, Jan.-April 1913; G. Godden, *Victorian Porcelain; Pottery and Glass Magazine* March 1951; *Pottery Gazette* 1 March 1906; *Staffs. Sentinel* 23 June 1913.

SPANTON, William Dunnett (1840-1922), *surgeon,* Hanley.

WDS was born on 27 September 1840 in Castle Street, Holborn, London, the son of John Spanton. He was educated at Loughborough Grammar School, then studied medicine. He was appointed an assistant house surgeon at Sheffield General Hospital in 1862 and in 1864 became house surgeon at the new North Staffordshire Infirmary. In 1866 he entered general practice in Hanley, living in Charles Street and later at Chatterley House, Old Hall Street. He continued as consulting surgeon for the North Staffs. Infirmary. He became a medical officer to the Werrington Boys' Industrial School, a medical referee under the Workmen's Compensation Acts, chairman of the House committee of the Staffs. Nursing Institute and of the Hanchurch Convalescent Home. In 1872 he was elected president of the North Staffs. Medical Society. In 1898 he was elected a Fellow of the Royal College of Surgeons. He acted as doctor to the Sutherland family when they were in residence at Trentham Hall.

He was a founder member of the North Staffordshire Field Club of which he was elected president in 1883. He lived latterly at Parkfield, Tittensor, and was appointed a county justice of the peace in 1892.

He married Ellen Victoria Bates in 1867 and they had three sons and three daughters. He wrote numerous articles and pamphlets on medical subjects. He retired to Hastings in 1911, dying there in May 1922.

C. Penn, *Staffordshire at the Opening of the 20th Century;* Simms; W. D. Spanton, *The Story of My Life; Staffs. Advertiser* 20 May 1922.

SPENCE, Robert (1816/17-69), *licensed victualler and gas works manager,* Burslem.

RS was born in Scotland about 1816. By 1851 he was the manager of the gas works, Holehouse, Burslem and in 1855 opened a shop in Burslem market place. He supplied fittings for Tunstall town hall in 1858. RS was also licensee of the Marquis of Granby public house, Burslem, which he gave as his occupation in 1861. He served on the Burslem Board of Health 1863-6. His wife Sarah continued as licensee of the Marquis of Granby after her husband's death on 13th August 1869.

Census 1861, 1871; Dir. 1851; Oldham; *Staffs. Advertiser* 22 September 1855; *Tunstall Board of Health Annual Reports.*

SPODE, Josiah, I, (1733-97), *pottery manufacturer,* Stoke upon Trent.

JS I the youngest child and only son of Josiah Spode of Lane Delph, was born in March 1733. His father died, a pauper, in 1739. JS was apprenticed in 1749 to Thomas Whieldon, for whom he worked until at least 1754. From 1762-70 he managed a pottery for William Barks and John Turner of Lane End. About 1760 he began in the pottery business on his own account, renting a works at Shelton, and later, in partnership with William Tomlinson, the Barks and Turner pottery at Lane End. The partnership with Tomlinson lasted until 1774. In 1776 JS bought the factory with the aid of a mortgage of £1,000 from the owner, Jeremiah Smith, who had bought it from

Barks. JS had another partnership with Thomas Mountford, which ended in 1780. The pottery produced cream-coloured earthenware, blue painted ware in the Chinese style and other wares. JS persuaded Thomas Lucas, an engraver, and James Richards, a printer, to leave the Caughley Works and enter his employment. On the basis of blue-underglaze transfer printing the business prospered and when Thomas Minton designed for him, from 1789-93, Spode's fortune was made. Late in life he began to experiment with bone ash in the manufacture of china, a method which his son Josiah Spode II perfected.

JS married Ellen Finley who had a haberdashery business, on 8 September 1754. He had seven children including Josiah Spode II, (q.v). He gave a number of houses to his daughter Sarah on her marriage and a pottery at Foley to his son Samuel on his marriage. He was an accomplished violist, his readiness to play giving rise to the old local phrase 'as ready and willing as Spode's fiddle'. He was a member of the committee formed in 1792 for the improvement of the Tittensor and Talke turnpike and a member of the committee which built the Newcastle canal, running alongside the Spode works.

He died at Stoke upon Trent on 8 September 1797.

G. Bernard Hughes, *The Story of Spode;* Jewitt; M and H; VCH viii; L. Whiter, *Spode, A History of the Family, Factory and Wares from 1733-1833.*

SPODE, Josiah II (1755-1827), *pottery manufacturer,* Stoke upon Trent.

JS II was the son of Josiah Spode I (q.v) and Ellen née Finley. He worked with his father in the factory in Stoke upon Trent, then from 1778 traded in London as a dealer in earthenware, glass and porcelain. To enter the business he became a member of the Worshipful Company of Spectacle Makers and was made a freeman of the City of London. He was still closely connected with the Stoke upon Trent factory and helped to form Harrison, Spode and Co., later Fenton Park Colliery, in order to secure fuel supplies. He returned to the Potteries on the death of his father in 1797 and lived at Fenton Hall. He joined with Thomas Wolfe and obtained the lease of the clay setts in 1799 on Carloggas Moor, Cornwall, despite opposition from the previous lessees, New Hall Pottery. He recognised the value of using rock felspar and produced Felspar Porcelain and stone china. He installed a steam engine in the works in 1802 and a larger, 36 h.p. engine in 1810. He eventually relinquished his share in the London business to his son, William, with William Copeland as co-partner. On William Spode's retirement in 1812 JS II resumed the partnership with William Copeland and in 1824 with Copeland's son, William Taylor Copeland (q.v.).

JS II built The Mount, Penkhull, in 1803, and lived there unitl his death. He erected houses in Penkhull Square in 1810 and in Ten Row, Nine Row and Penkhull New Road for his factory workers. He was appointed potter to the Prince of Wales in 1806, following a royal visit to his factory. He took a leading role in opposing government moves to impose a tax on pottery in 1811.

JS was chairman of the North Staffs. Pitt Club and commanded a troop of the Loyal Pottery Volunteers 1798-1805. He married Elizabeth Barker on 9 July 1775 and had two sons, including Josiah III, and three daughters.

He died in Stoke upon Trent on 16 July 1827.

F. Hayden, *Spode and his Successors;* G. Bernard Hughes, *The Story of Spode;* VCH viii; L. Whiter, *Spode, A History of the Family, Factory and Wares from 1733-1833.*

STAMER, Right Revd. Sir Lovelace Tomlinson (1829-1908),
Anglican bishop, Stoke upon Trent.

LTS was born at Ingram's Lodgings, York, on 18 October 1829, the son of Sir Lovelace Stamer, 2 baronet, and Caroline née Tomlinson. He was educated at Rugby School and Trinity College, Cambridge, B.A. 1853, M.A. 1856, D.D. 1888. He was ordained deacon in 1853 and served as curate at Clay Cross, Derbyshire 1853-4 and at Turvey, Bedfordshire 1854-5. He was ordained priest in 1855 and became curate-in-charge at Long Melford, Suffolk, 1855-7, then succeeded his uncle, J. W. Tomlinson, as rector of Stoke upon Trent in January 1858, retaining this position for the next 34 years. He was appointed rural dean of Stoke upon Trent in 1858, prebendary of Longdon in Lichfield cathedral in 1875 and archdeacon of Stoke upon Trent in 1877. He resigned his posts of rural dean and archdeacon on his consecration, on 24 February 1888, as suffragan bishop of Shrewsbury. In 1892 he became vicar of St. Chad's, Shrewsbury and rector of Edgmond 1896 -1905. He resigned the Edgmond living and the bishopric in 1905 and retired to Halingdene, Penkridge, Staffs.

He married Ellen Isabel, only daugher of Joseph Dent of Ribston Hall, Yorks, on 16 April 1857 and had five sons and three daughters. He became 3 baronet on the death of his father on 5 March 1860.

On his appointment as rector of Stoke upon Trent in 1858 he began the establishment of Sunday schools in Cliffe Vale, London Road, Mount Pleasant and the Mount estate. He allowed nonconformists to serve as pupil teachers in his schools. He was chairman of the Stoke upon Trent School Board from 1871 to 1888. He was largely responsible for the Stoke Rectory Act of 1889 by which the patronage and endowment of Stoke upon Trent rectory passed from his mother's family to the bishop of Lichfield, and which provided additional endowments for St. John's church, Hanley, St. John's Longton, Christ Church, Fenton, and other rural parish churches. In 1858 he introduced memorial tiles into Stoke upon Trent parish church and in 1888 he gave a new reredos to the church.

LTS was a vice president of the North Staffs. Infirmary committee and a trustee for nearly 50 years. He founded the Staffs. Institution for Nurses and supported the building of the nurses' home in Stoke in 1876. He helped to organise the fund in relief of the widows and orphans of colliers killed in the Talke-o'-the-Hill explosion in 1866. In 1870 he originated and for the next 38 years served as chairman of the North Staffs. Coal and Ironstone Workers' Permanent Relief Society. He supported the North Staffs. Discharged Prisoners Aid Society and helped to found an industrial home for discharged female prisoners and friendless women.

He died at his home near Penkridge on 29 October 1908.

DNB; F. D. How, *Bishop Sir Lovelace T. Stamer;* VCH viii.

STANLEY, Walton (1864-1947), *auctioneer and valuer,* Hanley.

WS was born in London in 1864 and educated at Ealing House School and King's College, London. He qualified as a solicitor and came to the Potteries in 1887 as managing clerk to Arthur Ellis, town clerk of Burslem. In 1891 on the death of Charles Butters (q.v) he joined the firm of Charles Butters and Sons. He achieved a national reputation as a valuer of old English pottery. He retired from business in January 1937.

He was elected to Hanley council in 1900 and acted as financial adviser to thé council in the federation proceedings. His scheme was preferred to that of Frederick Geen (q.v) by the Local Government Board, although the scheme finally adopted was a compromise between the two. He was elected an alderman of the federated borough but resigned in 1913.

He was recorder of the Ancient Corporation of Hanley from 1924-34, and was also president of the Hanley Society for the Prosecution of Felons, in succession to George Ellis (q.v). He was a freemason.

He married (1) Charlotte Jessie Burton, by whom he had one son and one daughter and (2), in 1943, Marjorie Keys. He lived at Lawton Hall, and before his death, in Curzon Street, Basford. Politically he was independent.

He died at Mount Vernon Hospital, Northwood, Middlesex, on 23 May 1947 and was cremated at Golders Green.

Evening Sentinel 24 May 1947; *National Index to Wills and Administrations; Staffs. Sentinel* 31 March 1910; information from Messrs. Charles Butters, Ltd.

STANWAY, James (c. 1835-1912), *pottery works manager,* Burslem.

JS became the manager of the Royal Doulton works in the late 19th century. He was a pioneer of the Co-operative Movement in Burslem, and was president of the Burslem Industrial Co-operative Society 1902-11. He died between June-September 1912, aged 77, the death being recorded in the Wolstanton registration district.

History of Co-operation in North Staffordshire; S. Josephs, *Sponges to Superstores.*

STEELE, James (c. 1764-1827), *engraver,* Tunstall.

JS was born about 1764. He was a cousin of Joseph Smith of Tunstall in whose house Methodist meetings were held from 1783. By 1785 the society's membership had increased to about 30 and JS became one of the leaders of the three classes formed. In the revival among the Harriseahead colliers of 1804, led by Hugh Bourne (q.v), JS played a leading part. It is believed that William Clowes (q.v) was among those converted at one of Steele's classes. JS almost certainly attended the first camp meeting held on Mow Cop on 31 May 1807.

As a camp meeting attender and for his participation in a love-feast JS was expelled from the local Wesleyan Methodist society on 16 April 1811. This expulsion led to the building of the first Primitive Methodist chapel in Tunstall. In this chapel, on 13 February 1812, the name 'Primitive Methodist' was adopted. JS became a local preacher and was first circuit steward of the Tunstall Primitive Methodist circuit. By 1819 this circuit covered an area as far south as Walsall.

JS died on 8 May 1827.

H. B. Kendall, *History of the Primitive Methodist Church; Primitive Methodist Magazine* 1827.

STEPHENSON, Joseph (1807-82), *colour manufacturer,* Hanley.

JS was born in Shelton in 1807. He may have worked in Rugeley where two of his children were born but by 1851 he was listed as a colour maker, living in Bethesda Street. He was elected to Hanley council in 1857, in 1869 served as mayor and in 1875 was appointed to the bench of local magistrates. In 1880 he had property in Ranelegh Street consisting of houses, a workshop and a kiln.

By his wife Ann he had at least four children of whom Alfred, the eldest, was lost at sea in 1877, aged 15. JS had a considerable collection of ancient and modern pottery.

He died at Richmond Terrace, Shelton, on 29 June 1882.

Census 1851; Huntbach; Rate Books, Hanley (HRL); *Staffs. Sentinel* 4 July 1882.

STEVENSON, Enoch (1814-65), *pottery worker,* Burslem.

ES was born about 1814. Orphaned at the age of nine he went to work in a rope walk, then at the age of 11 was apprenticed at Hall's Pottery, Burslem. Soon after becoming a journeyman at the age of 21 he was involved, as an active trade unionist, in the potters' strike of 1836-7, being one of the last to return to work. He supported the potters' emigration movement and held office on two benefit societies, the Ancient Order of Foresters and the United Free Gardeners. He worked for 22 years at Brownfield's, Cobridge, but in 1858, after being forced to enter the infirmary because of silicosis, he was replaced by another workman. He then worked for John Alcock, Cobridge and in 1860 for Cork, Edge and Malin. ES opposed the extension of the Factories Act in 1864 on the grounds that limiting the hours and age of child labour would adversely affect the workers in his union. He lost his job again following a dispute in 1864 about annual hiring and wages.

By his wife Ann he had four sons, one of whom, Herbert, enlisted in the army, and was bought out for £40. The family lived in Navigation Road, Burslem. ES found another job in Shelton, two miles from his home, but the walk to work during the winter and early spring of 1865 aggravated his ill-health. He died early in March 1865 and was buried in the churchyard at St. John's Burslem.

Census 1861; W. Evans, 'The Life and Death of a Working Potter', (1864) reproduced in the *Journal of Ceramic History* No. 3, 1970.

STEVENSON, Ralph (1776-1853), *pottery manufacturer,* Burslem.

RS, the son of Ralph and Ann Stevenson, was baptised, probably at Burslem, on 28 January 1776. He lived in Scotland with an uncle, John Adams, from about 1784 to 1800, then returned to Cobridge and set up in business as a pottery manufacturer. He went bankrupt in 1835.

By his wife, Mary née Mayer, of Hanley whom he married on 31 August 1807, he had two sons, Ralph Stevenson and John Adams Stevenson, both of whom became solicitors and clerks to Hanley and Stoke councils respectively. RS was involved in the establishment of the Potteries Mechanics' Institution in 1826. From about 1803 to 1818 he lived at Cobridge Cottage, situated off Elder Road, in the area of the later Grange Street. His house later became a convent, then the home of Samuel Alcock (q.v) and was eventually demolished in 1913.

Thomas Campbell, the poet, visited RS at Cobridge Cottage in 1805, commenting adversely on the condition of the local roads. RS died in Sandon in 1853.

P. W. L. Adams, *Notes on Some North Staffordshire Families;* IGI Staffs.; *Sentinel Summer Number 1910;* VCH viii.

STOCKER, Alexander Dingle (1839/40-94), *china clay merchant,* Stoke upon Trent.

ADS was born near St. Austell, Cornwall, about 1840. He came to Stoke upon Trent in 1860, and lodged with W. M. Grose (q.v) of The Villas, whose daughter he married and whose partner he became, trading as Grose and Stocker, china clay merchants.

ADS owned property in the centre of Stoke upon Trent. He pulled down Walker and Carter's factory in Church Street and erected a row of shops in its place. He was a member of Stoke upon Trent School Board from 1872, and was elected to the council in 1874.

He married Mary Hannah Grose and had numerous children. He died at The Hollies, May Bank on 11 January 1894.

Staffs. Sentinel 11 January 1894 (obit.).

STORY, Arthur John (1864-1938), *schoolmaster,* Stoke upon Trent.

AJS was born in Rochester, Kent, in 1864. He trained as a teacher of St. Peter's College, Peterborough, and later gained a diploma of the College of Teachers of the Deaf. He came to Stoke upon Trent in 1896 as headmaster of The Mount, Penkhull, the first residential school to be established by a local authority under the Blind and Deaf Act 1893. His wife was appointed matron of the school. He published a number of books in his specialist field, including *Speech for the Deaf,* (1900), *Language for the Deaf,* (1905), *Speech Reading and Speech for the Deaf,* (1915), which became standard works in Britain and abroad. He edited the professional journal *The Teacher of the Deaf* for 20 years.

His work for the adult deaf included helping to reorganise the North Staffordshire Mission to the Deaf; he helped to found the National Bureau for the Deaf (later the Royal National Institute for the Deaf) and acted as secretary of the Institute from 1925 after his retirement from The Mount. In collaboration with E. V. Greatbach (q.v) he helped to make ophthalmia neonatorum a compulsorily notifiable disease. He also supported Greatbach's efforts to set up the North Staffs. Workshops for the Blind, in Shelton.

He married and had two children. He died at Southsea on 11 September 1938.

Evening Sentinel 12 September 1938; *The Teacher of the Deaf* vol. xxxvi, No. 215, October, 1938.

STRINGER, Joseph (1810/11-73), *accountant,* Stoke upon Trent.

JS was born about 1811 in Northampton, possibly the son of Gabriel Stringer who died in 1851. About 1836 he was employed as accountant and secretary by Minton's, and acted as the historian of the firm, recording memories of old employees and giving information on the firm to historians including L. Jewitt. He was living in Liverpool Road, Stoke upon Trent in 1843, then lived in Hill Street, Glebe Street and by 1849 in Penkhull. In 1850 he was secretary of the Stokeville Building Society, in 1858 secretary of the Minton Memorial Buildings and the Borough Savings Bank. In 1864 he was living at Stokeville, and was described as potter's accountant.

By his wife, Maria, he had at least ten children, of whom his son, George Herbert Stringer, was an accountant for the North Staffordshire Railway and elective borough auditor for Stoke upon Trent from 1874.

Census, 1851, 1881; G. Godden, *Minton Pottery and Porcelain;* Stoke upon Trent Commissioners' Minutes; Stoke upon Trent Parish Registers; Turner.

STUART, Hackworth (1875-1909), *surgeon,* Hanley.

HS, son of the Revd. J. G. Stuart, was born on 23 December 1875 at Newton Abbot. He went to school in Nottingham, Bradford and London, trained at University College, London, then at St. Mary's Hospital, London, and in Paris, becoming M.R.C.S. (England) 1899, L.R.C.P. (1899), M.D. (London) 1902, D.P.H. (Cantab.) 1901 and F.R.C.S. (Edinburgh) 1906.

He held a number of posts. He was Assistant Demonstrator in Anatomy, Physiology and Histology at University College, London, Assistant Medical Officer in Fever and Smallpox Hospitals Metropolitan Asylum Board, House Surgeon London Temperance Hospital, Clinical Assistant Royal Eye Hospital and Pathologist and Bacteriologist North West Hospital.

He moved to Hanley by 1904 and became medical adviser to Hanley Education Committee, and medical officer of health to Staffs. County Industrial School, Werrington. He contributed articles to various medical journals and wrote *The Doctor in the Schools.* From 1904 until his death he lived at 8 Old Hall Street, Hanley. He died on 6 September 1909.

Information from Miss J. M. Aspden, Library Secretary, Royal College of Surgeons of England; C. Penn, *Staffordshire at the Opening of the 20th Century.*

STUART, Revd. Dr. Henry Venn (1864-1933), *minister of religion (Church of England),* Burslem/Stoke upon Trent.

HVS was born at Sudbury Hill House, Harrow, Middlesex, on 8 August 1864, the son of James and Mary Stuart. He went to Harrow School and Caius College, Cambridge, B.A. 1886, M.A. 1890, D.D. 1924. He was ordained deacon in 1887, priest 1888. He was appointed curate of St. Paul's, Burslem in 1887 and served in that office until 1891; he was vicar of St. James, Wolverhampton 1891-5, vicar of Cannock 1895-1903, rector of Stoke upon Trent 1904-24, Dean of Carlisle 1924-33.

HVS decided to work in an industrial parish while on a visit to his brother Charles Maddock Stuart, who was a master at Newcastle High School 1884-8. During his ministry in Burslem he campaigned on behalf of the movement for total abstinence and to prove his point spent a day at a pottery works in Longport drawing an oven, a week at Chatterley ironstone pits and a week on the coal face at Sneyd Colliery. He was actively involved in industrial and social welfare movements and helped to settle a dispute in the sanitary ware industry. He was president of the North Staffordshire Infirmary Committee 1915-17.

He married, on 10 October 1904, Marguerite Evelyn Bird. HVS died on 12 January 1933.

R. A. Cason, *Time and the Place; Staffs. Sentinel* 21 April 1924; *Evening Sentinel* 21 January 1933; Venn.

STUART, Michael (born c. 1824), *police officer,* Fenton/Longton.

MS was born in Roscommon, Ireland, about 1824. By 1851 he was a police sergeant in Longton and was promoted to inspector of police in Fenton. As such he also acted as lodging house inspector. In 1861 it was agreed that they should be paid the same salary as the inspectors of Longton and Burslem police. He resigned as inspector of nuisances, lodging houses and fire brigade in 1865, by which time he had also left the police force.

Census 1861; Dir. 1851; Fenton Improvement Commissioners' Minutes.

STUPART, John (1791-1860), *banker,* Hanley.

JS was born in Scotland about 1792. By 1834 he was employed as manager of the Manchester & Liverpool District Bank, Market Square, Hanley. By his wife Jane he had at least seven children, six of whom were baptised in Hope Chapel, Hanley, between 1842 and 1856.

He died on 2 October 1860.

Census 1841, 1851; Dir. 1834; Hope Chapel records.

SUMBERG, Colman (1874-1955), *tailor and furrier,* Hanley.

CS was born in Lithuania in 1874 and educated in Germany. He came to England in the same ship as Montague Burton, founder of the chain of men's wear shops. CS supplemented his income in his early years in England by assisting in the Wrexham synagogue. He opened a shop in Hanley in the early 20th century. He was the lay head of the Jewish community in Hanley for many years and a freemason.

I. Down, 'A History of Jewish Settlement in the Potteries' (Univ. of Keele, B.A. dissertation, 1984).

SUTHERLAND-LEVESON-GOWER, Cromartie, 4th Duke of Sutherland (1851-1913), *landowner,* Longton.

CS-L-G was born on 20 July 1851, the second son of George Granville William 3 duke of Sutherland by Ann Hay Mackenzie countess of Cromartie. His elder brother dying in 1858 Cromartie became marquess of Stafford, the courtesy title adopted by the eldest son of the duke of Sutherland. He was Liberal Member of Parliament for Sutherland 1874-86. In 1884 he married Millicent Fanny St. Clair-Erskine (see Sutherland-Leveson-Gower Millicent) by whom he had four children, Victoria Elizabeth (1885-8), George Granville (1888-1963), Alistair St. Clair (1890-1921) and Rosemary Millicent (1893-1930). He succeeded to his father's dukedom in 1892.

He served as mayor of Longton 1895-6, and gave the site for the building of the Sutherland Institute (opened 1899) in Lightwood (formerly Stone) Road. He supported federation and in 1907 offered Trentham Hall to the six towns on federation.

He died at Dunrobin Castle on 27 June 1913.

D. Stuart, *Dear Duchess.*

SUTHERLAND-LEVESON-GOWER, Millicent, duchess of Sutherland (1867-1955), Potteries and Newcastle.

Millicent Fanny St. Clair-Erskine, daughter of 4 earl of Rosslyn, was born in Dysart House, Fife, on 20 October 1867. Her mother was Blanche Fitzroy, formerly married to Charles Maynard, and descended from Charles II. Millicent married Cromartie Sutherland-Leveson-Gower (q.v), marquess of Stafford, and heir to 3 duke of Sutherland, on 20 October 1884. The marquess succeeded to his father's title and estates in 1892. The main family seat was at Dunrobin castle, Sutherland, and their other homes included Trentham Hall, Lilleshall Hall (Shropshire), a Stafford House (later Lancaster House), The Mall, London. Millicent was a noted society beauty and diplomatic hostess of the late Victorian and Edwardian eras. She early acquired a reputation as a social reformer with advanced views. She used her position and social and political contacts to advocate government restriction on the use of lead in pottery manufacture, and gained the nickname in the Potteries of 'Meddlesome Millie'. She was caricatured in several of Arnold Bennett's novels as the countess of Chell. In 1900 she founded the Potteries and Newcastle Cripples' Guild, from which developed the North Staffordshire Cripples' Aid Society which in turn expanded to become the North Staffordshire Orthopaedic Hospital. Trentham Hall was demolished in 1911 and Millicent rarely returned to the North Staffordshire area thereafter.

In the First World War, Millicent ran a Red Cross Hospital in France, and was decorated, among other awards, with the Croix de Guerre. The 4 duke, her husband, died in 1913, and Millicent married twice more, both marriages proving unhappy. She wrote a number of newspaper and magazine articles, novels, poems and plays. Her published works include *How I Spent My Twentieth Year* (1889), *One Hour and the Next* (1899), 'On the Dangerous Processes in the Potting Industry' in H. Owen, *The Staffordshire Potter, The Winds of the World* (1902). *Six Weeks at the War* (1914), and *That Fool of a Woman* (1925).

After the First World War Millicent spent most of her life in France. She was an incessant traveller, her most ambitious trip being across the Andes mountains in South America. By her first husband, the 4 duke, she had four children. On the death of her eldest son, George Granville, 5 duke of Sutherland (1888-1963), the dukedom passed to a distant cousin, and the earldom of Sutherland a separate title, passed under Scottish inheritance law to Millicent's granddaughter, the present countess of Sutherland.

Millicent died on 20 August 1955 at her summer home, La Maisou, Orriule, Sauveterre-de-Béarn, France. There is a memorial window to her in Dornoch cathedral. A portrait, by the local artist Ellis Roberts (q.v), is in Dunrobin castle and another portrait, by John Sargent, the American painter, is in New York.

D. Stuart, *Dear Duchess.*

SWEETING, John Hugh (1811-84), *superintendent of police,* Stoke upon Trent.

JHS was born in 1811 at Fivehead, Somerset. He was a farmer before joining the Metropolitan Police about 1831, later resigning and re-joining on 14 September 1838. He resigned again on 22 October 1839 to join the Birmingham police force. In 1843 he was appointed superintendent of the Staffordshire police. He transferred to the Potteries police force in 1845 as chief superintendent, retaining this position until his retirement on pension in 1873. He also held the posts of superintendent of the fire brigade and inspector of lighting for the improvement commissioners. In 1851 he was inspector of nuisances and later contracted to purchase the night soil.

On the incorporation of the borough of Stoke upon Trent in 1874 he was elected alderman and served as mayor 1878-9. In 1880 he was a member of the board of guardians. He was also a member of Stoke Conservative Club. In 1871 he was living at Rose Cottage, Field Place, Stoke upon Trent. As a member of Stoke Victoria Athletic and Cricket Club he offered to rent 11 acres of Sweetings Fields in 1877 for athletics, cricket and football. The area is now covered by Campbell Road, Book Street, Yeoman Street, Keary Street and Corporation Street.

He died at Weston-super-Mare on 30 September 1884.

Dir. 1871; *National Index to Wills and Administrations;* PRO, MEPO/4/333 List of Joiners 1830-42; Stafford County Police Force Book; *Stoke Improvement Commissioners' Minutes.*

SWINNERTON, Francis (1844/5-1920), *baker, confectioner and caterer,* Hanley.

FS was born about 1844 at Shebdon, High Offley. By 1871 he was in business as a baker and confectioner in Shelton, and by 1881 he was listed at Snow Hill Building, Hanley.

By his wife Emily Honor he had at least five childen. He lived at 16 Bryan Street, Shelton, in 1871 and at The Beeches, Barlaston Old Road, Trentham, where he died on 11 June 1920.

Census 1871, 1881; memorial inscription in Hanley cemetery.

TAMS, John (1837-1919), *pottery manufacturer,* Longton.

JT was born in Stafford Street, Longton in 1837, the son of John Tams and Ann née Procter. The family had been established in Shelton by about 1620. JT was apprenticed to a working potter. About 1865 he entered into partnership with Lowe, manufacturing in St. Gregory's Pottery, High Street, Longton. The partnership was dissolved about 1873 and in 1874 JT bought the Crown pottery, on the corner of Commerce Street and High Street. At first he specialised in the manufacture of imperial measured ware, mugs, jugs, etc., for hotels and public houses. The increasing use of glass and further government regulations forced him to develop new lines of production, including ornamental and general earthenware. JT retired from business in 1918. The firm continues today (1985).

He married Mary, daughter of Charles Kent, a draper, of Red Bank Cottage, Dresden, where JT and his wife were living in 1881. Later they lived at St. Edmund's Villa, Ricardo Street, and from 1898 at The Hayes, Stone. There were four children.

JT died on 17 May 1919.

G. Cope-Cartledge, *Pedigree of Tams* and article in *Six Towns Magazine*, November 1971; Jewitt; M and H; VCH viii.

TAYLOR, John (1769-1857), *town crier,* Hanley.

JT was born on 11 December 1769. He enlisted in the 8th King's Own Regiment, where he learned to play the French horn, drums and tambourine. Later his skills earned him the nickname of 'Tambourine John'. He was appointed town crier of Hanley, and performed his functions dressed in scarlet trousers, blue coat, white stockings and mounted on a pony. His duties were various and on one occasion he brought the bodies of Walklate, Toft and Collier, executed at Stafford in 1820 for murder, back to the Potteries for burial.

He died on 10 February 1857. His funeral took on the character of a public function, a crowd of over 12,000 accompanying the cortège to Shelton churchyard.

Staffs. Sentinel Summer Number 1907.

TAYLOR, Louis Alma (1857-1915), *auctioneer and valuer,* Hanley.

LAT was born in Leckhampton, near Cheltenham, in 1857. After working in London he came to the Potteries as assistant auctioneer to Charles Butters (q.v), in 1875. Later he set up in business on his own account in Lamb Street. He moved eventually to the Old Town Hall, using the former police office and court room in that building as his business premises. Subsequently his business was transferred to Tontine Street, Hanley. He is thought to have conducted over 5,000 auction sales during his 40 years in the Potteries.

He was elected to Hanley council in July 1881 and served until 1902. He received an illuminated address from the council for his success in selling building land around Hanley Park. LAT was an original member of the Hanley Horticultural Society, and a member of the Josiah Wedgwood Lodge of freemasons. At the time of his death he was chairman of the Hanley Christmas Hot Pot Fund.

By his wife Elizabeth he had at least two children. He died at 6 Sidney Street, Basford, on 11 July 1915, and was buried in Hanley cemetery.

Staffs. Sentinel 12 July 1915.

TENNANT, Frederick (1821-1914), *wine and spirits merchant,* Burslem.

FT was born in Mansfield, Nottinghamshire, in 1821. He came to Burslem about 1837 to work for George Baker and later succeeded to his business. He was at 14 St. John's Square 1867-80.

He was a member of the Board of Health from 1865 and served as chief bailiff. He also served on the Board of Guardians in 1867. He was a pioneer of the scheme to build a cemetery and supported the abolition of toll gates. He was the last member of the original Staffordshire Potteries Waterworks Company. He had been a special constable during the Chartist riots of 1842 and joined the volunteers in 1859. For 20 years he was a churchwarden of St. Paul's church, Dalehall. In politics he had Conservative opinions. He served as president of the Burslem Association for the Prosecution of Felons in 1873-4.

By his wife Mary née Bates he had two sons and four daughters. One son, Frederick Robert, born in Burslem in 1866, was senior science master in Newcastle under Lyme High School 1890-3, curate of Hartshill 1891-3 and Fellow of Trinity College Cambridge 1912-c.52. The other son became a professor at King's College, London. One of his students was Oliver Lodge.

FT and his family lived in Camoys House, Waterloo Road, Burslem and later FT bought Bradwell House, which had been built by his former employer, George Baker. FT died at Bradwell House on 23 December 1914. One daughter, Eleanor Victoria, married Arthur Ellis (q.v) town clerk of Burslem 1891-1910 and son of P. B. Ellis (q.v).

Staffs. Sentinel 24 December 1914; Oldham.

THOMAS, John Whitta (1826/7-1906), *schoolteacher,* Stoke upon Trent.

JWT was born in Liverpool about 1826. By 1860 he and his wife Susannah (by whom he had six children) were both teachers at Warmingham Free School, Cheshire. He was headmaster of St. Peter's School, Stoke upon Trent 1862-7 and of St. Thomas's School, Penkhull, Stoke upon Trent, 1867-72. Later occupations included business as a stationer, London Road, in 1870 and licensee of the Red Lion public house, Stoke upon Trent.

He played an important role as a sports administrator. He founded the Stoke Wakes Sports (Victoria Athletic Club) in 1868 and was secretary of the Stoke Victoria Cricket Club. Football was unknown in Stoke before 1862, and it is stated that the game was first played in the school yard at St. Peter's in that year. JWT and the other teachers founded Stoke Football Club in the following year, and the Victoria ground in 1869.

JWT was elected to the Stoke upon Trent council in 1876 and helped to establish the public library and the borough police force. He was clerk to the Stoke upon Trent school board from 1871-80, when he was dismissed. He served as the auditor to the mayor of the town and persuaded the Staffordshire Agricultural Society to hold its show in Stoke. He left the Red Lion in 1882 and also resigned from the council in that year. He was declared bankrupt in 1882.

He had been involved in a libel case in 1878 when he was accused by Charles Head, a Stoke upon Trent printer, of being drunken and dissolute and of stealing money given to him for teachers' salaries. JWT sued for £1,000 damages, the case went to Shrewsbury Assizes in July 1878 but was finally settled out of court, with Head withdrawing his remarks. Among JWT's many financial offices was that of treasurer to the Portland Lodge of freemasons.

JWT married twice. His second wife, née Kezia Anne Whippie, survived him. He moved eventually to London, where he died on 2 April 1906 at 6 Elspeth Road, Clapham Common.

P. Buxton, 'Busy Stoke Pioneer', in *Evening Sentinel Centenary Supplement,* 16 April 1973; Dir. 1876; IGI Staffs; *Staffs. Advertiser* 8 July 1882; *Staffs. Sentinel* 1868-82 (various issues); St. Thomas's School Log Book; F. E. J. Wright, *The Schools of the Parish of St. Peter ad Vincula.*

TIMMIS, Richard (born c. 1796), *printer, stationer and parian ear-drop manufacturer,* Burslem.

RT was born about 1796. He was in business in the Market Place, Burslem, by 1851, as printer, stationer, bookseller and parian ear-drop manufacturer, an enterprise which he had taken over from Mary Brougham (q.v).

He was a Methodist local preacher. By his wife Sarah he had two daughters, Mary and Sarah, the former being listed in 1851 as a school governess.

Census 1861; Dir. 1851, 1861, 1867.

TOFT, Charles (1831-1909), *pottery designer and manufacturer,* Stoke upon Trent.

CT, born in 1831, studied at Stoke upon Trent School of Design. By 1860 he was employed at Mintons as a modeller and worked on pâte-sur-pâte designs, but his name is chiefly associated with copies of 'Henri Deux' ware produced for Mintons. When these were exhibited at international exhibitions in the 1860s and 1870s it was reported that it was difficult to distinguish them from the originals. He left Mintons about 1877 and eventually went to Wedgwood as chief modeller. His 'War and Peace' vase was exhibited at the Paris Exhibition in 1878. He also designed silver and plated wares for Elkingtons of Birmingham. In 1889 he took over the Swan Works at Stoke, manufacturing rustic and slip decorated ware.

He married and had a son Albert who was born in 1862. CT died in 1909.

G. Godden, 'Victorian Ceramic Artists, V' in *Apollo* 1959; Jewitt.

TOMLINSON, John (1772-1838), *solicitor,* Stoke upon Trent.

JT, born on 25 April 1772, was established as a solicitor in Hanley by 1794. In 1801 he became a notary public (by appointment of the archbishop of Canterbury). He bought the advowson of Stoke parish church in 1817, obtained the lease of the tithes from the rector and succeeded, by means of his legal knowledge, in recovering the dormant rights of the church in the tithes of such commodities as hay, agistment and milk. He succeeded in getting the Stoke Rectory Act through Parliament in 1827 (predating the Tithe Commutation Act of 1836) which authorised the sale of tithes and certain glebelands and produced £50,000, which went towards the building of two new churches in Shelton and Longton. By 1829 he had taken his second son Frederick Wright Tomlinson into partnership. He acted as returning officer in the elections of 1833 and 1837 for the new parliamentary borough of Stoke upon Trent.

In June 1798 he married Margaret Wright and had at least four children, including John Wickes Tomlinson (q.v) and Caroline who married Sir Lovelace Stamer, father of Sir Lovelace Tomlinson Stamer (q.v). In 1810 JT bought Castle Cliff estate and built Cliffville, a two-storey mansion with classical porch (since the 1920s occupied as a girls' school). He made several charitable gifts to the poor while he was alive, and in his will he left an annuity of £5 for distribution to the poor at Christmas.

He died on 19 November 1838.

Dir. 1829, 1851; *Pottery Mercury* 27 April 1833 and 24 November 1838; *Staffs. Advertiser* 16 June 1798, 14 February 1801, 22 January 1820, 14 November 1835; VCH viii; Ward.

TOMLINSON, John Wickes (1800-57), *minister of religion (Church of England),* Stoke upon Trent.

JWT, son of John Tomlinson (q.v) and Margaret née Wright, was born at Cliff Vale, Stoke upon Trent on 4 August 1800. He was educated at Rugby School and Trinity College, Oxford, (M.A. 1823). He was presented to the living of Stoke upon Trent by his father on 31 October 1831 and remained the incumbent until his death. He made a printed collection of psalms and hymns in 1835 and published volumes of poetry in 1836 and 1843.

Dir. 1851; St. John's church, Hanley, baptismal registers; Simms; *Staffs. Advertiser* 9 July 1831; *Staffs. Gazette* 24 January 1814.

TOPHAM, Robert (c. 1818-90), *minister of religion (Church of England),* Hanley.

RT was born at Pateley Bridge, Yorkshire. He is thought to have spent some years in India with the army. He trained for the Ministry at St. Bees Theological College from 1848 and was ordained a priest in 1852. He served as curate of Penistone, Yorks. from 1851 to 1857, as curate of St. John, Sheffield from 1858 to 1860, became vicar of Biggin, Derbys. and chaplain to the Duke of Devonshire in 1860 and came to St. Matthews, Etruria, in 1864 as part of a three cornered arrangement by which the vicar of Etruria moved to Marazion, Cornwall and the vicar of Marazion to Biggin in place of Topham.

He was characterised as an eccentric and his activites caused much comment and amusement locally. It was said that his health had been impaired as a result of sunstroke during his days in India. He would marry couples for only a shilling and as a result the church was much used by people from a wide area. He was also unconcerned about observing the statutory time required for the publication of banns. He was the victim of at least one practical joke, when his clothes were stolen while he was swimming in the canal and he was forced to run naked back to the vicarage, and he was not above playing jokes himself.

RT retired from the living in January 1890. He married his wife Mary while serving at Penistone and there were three sons of the marriage, Richard, an architect, Robert, and George who became vicar of Long Melford, Suffolk.

RT died on 16 September 1890 at Richmond Place, Shelton.

The church of St. Matthews, Etruria built in 1847/8 and designed by Henry Ward (q.v) suffered greatly from mining subsidence and later bomb damage and after many restorations was demolished in 1978.

Census 1881; Crockford *Clerical Directory 1889; National Index to Wills and Administrations; Staffs. Sentinel* 20 Sept. 1890 (obit); E. J. D. Warrilow *History of Etruria;* information from Mr. L. Finn.

TREGORTHA, John (1759-1821), *printer, stationer etc.,* Burslem.

JT was born in Phillack, Cornwall and baptised on 15 December 1759, the son of John and Eleanor Tregortha. In 1796 he began a business in St. John's Square, Burslem as a printer, and in 1818 was listed as printer, stationer, bookseller and druggist, Market Street, Burslem. He published many books and articles, including works by Hugh Bourne (q.v).

Prior to his establishment in business he had been on trial as a travelling Methodist preacher, with appointments in Pembroke, Burslem, Macclesfield and Liverpool. After setting up as a printer he continued as a local preacher for the Methodist church in Burslem. He was a Sunday School visitor 1808 and a member of the committee 1812-18. It is recorded that Burslem youths would gather near his house on Sunday evenings and hold a burlesque service which included a mock hymn beginning

> Now old Tregortha's dead and gone
> We ne'er shall see him more.
> He used to wear a long frock coat
> All buttoned down before.

He became a symbol of antiquity and a Burslem saying was 'It's as old as Tregortha'.

He married twice. His first wife, Elizabeth died in 1791 and by his second wife, Elizabeth, he had nine children, all baptised between 1794 and 1810. Two sons were called Charles Gorst Tregortha and two were called William Lowe Tregortha. A Charles Gorst Tregortha appears in 1835 as a printer of Swan Square, Burslem. JT died in Burslem on 9 January 1821.

J. Beech, *Centenary of Burslem Wesleyan Circuit 1883;* F. F. Bretherton, article in *Proceedings of the Wesley Historical Society* vol. 21, 1937; Dir. 1818, 1835; R and S; *Staffs. Advertiser* 13 January 1821; *Staffs. Sentinel* 27 August 1925 (portrait by J. J. Maddock copied from life portrait by J.J.M.'s grandfather).

TUCKWELL, GLADYS (1861-1951), *trade unionist,* Hanley.

GT was born in 1861. She served as hon. secretary of the Women's Trade Union League from 1892 to 1905. In the period 1892-95 she investigated conditions of work in the pottery industry and in the white lead mill in Newcastle under Lyme. She helped to publicise the case for the use of leadless glaze in pottery manufacture and was active in the campaign to protect women workers in particular against lead poisoning.

She died on 5 August 1951.

Dictionary of Labour Biography, vol vi.

TUNNICLIFFE, Moses (1848-1901), *baker,* Hanley.

MT was born in the Leek moorlands in 1848. He was apprenticed to C. Sargeant, baker and confectioner, of Hope Street, Hanley. He eventually set up in business on his own account in High Street, Hanley, on the corner with Mayer Street, and later moved to Church Street. At his death he owned warehouses in Grafton Street, Hanley, and Liverpool.

He was elected to Hanley council in 1882 and served as mayor 1895-7. He was appointed a borough magistrate in 1897 and an alderman in 1899. He was also made a freeman of the borough.

He married and his son Frederick Moses Tunnicliffe, acted as executor of his will. He died at Florence House, Trentham, on 18 December 1901.

Dir. 1882; Huntbach; *National Index to Wills and Administrations; Staffs. Sentinel* 19 December 1901.

TURNER, George (1821/2-83), *printer etc. and earthenware manufacturer,* Stoke upon Trent.

GT was born in Burslem about 1822. He began work as a potter in Minton's, but by 1851 was established in Liverpool Road, Stoke upon Trent, as a printer, stationer, bookseller and music dealer, employing three men and two apprentices. In 1854 he printed one issue of the *Potteries Times* and in 1864 ran a circulating library. By 1872 he had given up his printing business and was in partnership with Hassell and Peake as earthenware manufacturers.

He served on the local highways board and was an improvement commissioner for Stoke upon Trent 1860-74. He was created an alderman in 1878 and served as mayor 1879-80. He was a vice-president of Stoke upon Trent Liberal Club, had somewhat anti-clerical views and was connected with the temperance movement.

He married twice and had four children. He died on 13 May 1883 at Prospect Villa, Regent Street, Penkhull.

Jewitt; *Staffs. Advertiser* 19 May 1883; M. J. Wilson, *The Temperance Movement in the Potteries 1848-60.*

TURNER, George Wardle (c. 1827-82), *pottery manufacturer,* Tunstall.

GWT was baptised on 2 January 1828, the son of Thomas Turner and Edna née Cartwright. Nothing is known of his early life. By 1861 he was in partnership with J. Tomkinson at the Victoria Works, High Street, Tunstall. The partnership ended in 1873 and the business continued as G. W. Turner and Sons till 1895. The firm also owned the Alexandra Works in Tunstall.

GWT was a member of Tunstall Board of Health from 1861 and chairman in 1870. By his wife Martha he had at least five children. He died at Chell Lodge, Little Chell, in 1882.

Census 1881; Dir. 1867; *Tunstall Board of Health Annual Reports.*

TURNER, John (1738-87), *pottery manufacturer,* Longton.

JT, the son of a Staffordshire lawyer, was born in 1738 at Brewood. Where he attended school is not known but he was sufficiently well-educated to be able to write his pottery chemical formulae in French to guard against industrial espionage. He was apprenticed to a Staffordshire potter, Daniel Bird, in 1753, and was established by 1756 in a partnership with R. Banks, making white stoneware, in a factory on the site of what is now Copeland-Spode, in Stoke upon Trent. He moved to Lane End in 1759. The earliest dated piece attributed to him is a 1762 teapot. About 1780 he discovered a vein of fine clay, peacock marl, at Green Dock, Edensor, from which he made a wide variety of ware of a cane colour. He also produced a blue glazed pottery similar to Japanese porcelain.

He was both a friend and commercial rival of Josiah Wedgwood. JT was a pioneer of the atmospheric Newcomen steam engine in the Potteries, installing one in his pottery in 1775. He was appointed potter to the Prince of Wales in 1784.

He married Ann née Emery on 15 October 1759 and by her had three sons and three daughters. His son William (q.v) and John later became his partners, continuing the business after his death on 24 December 1787. The firm was declared bankrupt in 1806. William continued on his own until 1829 when the factory was sold.

B. Hiller, *Master Potters of the Industrial Revolution—the Turners of Lane End;* A. Lamb, 'Mechanisation and the Application of Steam Power in the North Staffordshire Pottery Industry', in N.S.J.F.S. vol. 17, 1977; family tombstone in Brewood (Staffs.) parish church; information from Maureen Leese.

TURNER, William (1762-1835), *pottery manufacturer,* Longton.

WT was born in 1762, the son of John Turner (q.v). With his brother John he was in partnership with his father in the works at Lane End (Longton). After John Turner senior's death William and his brother continued the business. On 19 January 1800 they took out a patent for the manufacture of a new kind of stoneware called Turner's patent, which used Tabberner's mine rock. The firm was declared bankrupt in 1806 and William continued on his own until the factory was sold in 1829. The firm's productions were among the best wares of their day, equalling Wedgwood's in quality and sometimes being mistaken for them.

William was in Paris during the French Revolution, was arrested and escaped with his life only by the intervention of the British ambassador, the marquess of Stafford (later 1 duke of Sutherland). The effects of the revolutionary and Napoleonic wars contributed to the firm's financial collapse in 1806.

William, a rather more public figure than his brother John, was a major in the Longton volunteers in 1803. His bust, by George Ray, is in Stoke on Trent City Museum. WT died in Longton on 5 July 1835.

R. Haggar, *Staffordshire Chimney Ornaments;* B. Hillier, *Master Potters of the Industrial Revolution—the Turners of Lane End;* Jewitt; *Staffs. Advertiser* 11 July 1835 (obit.); information from Maureen Leese.

TWIGG, Joseph (1780-1861), *colour manufacturer,* Burslem.

JT, born in 1780, inherited a colour works at Velvet Croft, Burslem, started by his father, William, on land bought from William Adams.

JT attended Burslem church. He was elected chairman of the improvement commissioners in 1825. He married Ann, daughter of William Adams, on 15 September 1817. They had three sons, William Edward, Joseph (q.v.) and Francis. The family lived at Bank House, Burslem.

JT died in 1861, his son Joseph continuing the business.

Adams; VCH viii.

TWIGG, William Edward (1820-67), *solicitor,* Burslem.

WET was the son of Joseph Twigg (q.v) and Ann née Adams. He was born on 27 October 1820 at Bank House, Burslem. He was articled to John Ward, the local historian (q.v), and for a time was in partnership with Bishop, attorney of Hanley. He served as clerk to the Burslem, Lawton and Newcastle Turnpike Trusts, and to the American consul. He was elected to the local board of health in 1863, serving until 1866. After his father's death in 1861 he took over the colour works and the Legal Flint Mill in Velvet Croft.

He died unmarried on 2 August 1867 at the Overhouse, Burslem, to which his office was attached.

Adams; Dir. 1867; Oldham.

TWYFORD, Dora (1880-1924), *social reformer,* Hanley.

DT was born at Moor House, Biddulph, in May 1880. She was the daughter of Thomas William Twyford (q.v) and Susannah née Whittingham. She was educated at home and at boarding school. In January 1898 her family moved to Whitmore Hall and there she became joint Master of Foxhounds of the North Staffordshire Hunt. During the South African War 1899-1902 her parents helped to found the Hanley branch of the Soldiers and Sailors Families Association, and during the First World War Dora became secretary of this body. She was also active on the Pensions Committee. For her war services she received the O.B.E.

She helped to establish the Twyford Halls for Scouts and Guides in Newcastle under Lyme. In 1902 she became secretary of the Newcastle Cripples Guild, a branch of the movement founded by Millicent Duchess of Sutherland (q.v), with her office at 16 Ironmarket. She helped to found a new workshop in Wilmots Row and drew in the Countess of Torby from Keele Hall and the Harrisons from Maer Hall to further her welfare work. She founded the Hanley Infants Welfare Centre, housed in Twyford's old factory in Bath (now Garth) Street, and on her father's death she gave a block of cottages, adjacent to the original centre, to the Welfare Society. This became known as the Thomas William Twyford Memorial. She was president of the Red Cross Bazaar, last president of the Kitchener Club, a member of the North Staffs. Royal Infirmary and a director of the *Staffs. Sentinel.*

She did not renew the lease of Whitmore Hall on the death of her parents but in 1923 moved to The Sidway, Pipe Gate. She died there on 14 January 1924.

D. W. Adams, *Millicent Duchess of Sutherland and the Potteries and Newcastle Cripples Guild; Staffs. Sentinel* 14 January 1924; Twyford Archives, Cliffe Vale.

TWYFORD, Thomas William (1849-1921), *pottery manufacturer,* Hanley.

TWT was born in Shelton on 22 September 1849, the son of Thomas Twyford and Sarah née Jones. He came of a family of potters who had started making pottery in Shelton in 1680. In 1887 TWT opened his model factory in Cliffe Vale, considered by government inspectors as a pattern for the whole of Staffordshire. Prior to that date he had manufactured the ornamented Unitas one-piece pedestal closet in the factory in Bath (now Garth) Street, following the pioneer work of his father and in co-operation with Thomas Crapper, who engineered the cistern. In 1889 the first washbasins with overflows were designed. The ware won an international reputation. In 1901 the firm opened a factory in Ratingen, near Dusseldorf, but this closed in 1914.

Up to 1886 TWT was a Liberal in politics. Then he split with the party over the issue of Home Rule for Ireland and later became chairman of the North Staffs. Unionist Party. He contributed to the foundation of a Unionist newspaper, the *Staffs. Evening Post,* whose first issue appeared on 29 March 1892. Rivalry between the *Post* and the *Sentinel* lasted for four years, when financial losses induced the proprietors of the *Post* to agree to a merger with the *Sentinel.* TWT became chairman of the new company in 1896.

In March 1888 TWT was appointed to the magistrates' bench. He served as a deputy lieutenant of Staffordshire and in 1906 he became high sheriff of the county. The

Grand Duke Michael of Russia, who leased Keele Hall in the first years of the 20th century, conferred on him the Order of St. Ann. In the South African War he helped to found the Soldiers and Sailors Association, and in the First World War provided premises in Bath Street for the Hanley Infants Welfare Centre. He became a colonel of the local volunteer force and was a member of the North Staffordshire Tribunal. He was twice president of the Staffordshire Agricultural Society, a supporter of the allotment movement and a patron of Hanley Flower Show. He served as president of the North Staffs. Choral Society and was an authority on early Staffordshire pottery. He helped to provide premises for the Cripples' Guild in the Ironmarket, Newcastle under Lyme, and gave the cripples an annual treat at Whitmore Hall.

He married Susannah, daughter of Edward Whittingham in 1872 and had two children, Harold, who served in the South African War and in the First World War, and Dora (q.v). The family lived successively at Shelton, Endon, Moor House Biddulph and finally leased Whitmore Hall in 1898. Here TWT became a member of the North Staffs. Hunt and a successful breeder of labrador retrievers.

He died at the Chine Hotel, Boscombe, Bournemouth, on 21 March 1921, and was buried in Whitmore churchyard. There is a memorial to him in Shelton church.

W. Reyburn, *Flushed with Pride: the story of Thomas Crapper;* J. Hatton, *Twyfords, a chapter in the history of pottery; Staffs. Sentinel* 14 February 1922; *Staffs. Advertiser* 26 March 1921; Twyfords Archives; *The Sentinel Story.*

TYRWHITT, The Hon. Revd. Leonard Francis (1863-1921), *minister of religion, (Church of England),* Fenton.

LFT, son of Sir Henry Thomas Tyrwhitt, 3 Bt., and Emma Harriet Baroness Berners, was born on 29 October 1863. He was educated at Marlborough School, Magdalen College, Cambridge and Wells Theological College, B.A. 1886, M.A. 1890, ordained deacon 1887, priest 1888. He served as curate of Hanley 1887-92 and Hendon 1892-5, then was appointed vicar of Fenton in 1895 and held this post until 1907, when he went to Rolleston, Staffs., as rector. He was hon. chaplain to Queen Victoria 1869-99, and chaplain-in-ordinary 1899-1901, and chaplain-in-ordinary to Edward VII 1901-10 and to George V 1910-21. He served as chaplain on H.M.S. Renown 1905-6 during the royal tour of the Prince and Princess of Wales to India. He was a chaplain in the First World War and was twice wounded and mentioned in dispatches. In 1918 he was appointed Deputy Assistant Chaplain General. He was awarded the M.V.O. in 1906 and the O.B.E. in 1919.

In December 1903 LFT delivered two sermons which he called 'The Devil in the Potteries' and in which he criticised the moral behaviour of the local community. The sermons aroused much controversy and Arnold Bennett (q.v) commented that Tyrwhitt was well meaning but ill-informed and clumsy. Tyrwhitt replied in a sermon in January 1904. He said that he had been making inquiry as to who the gentleman (Arnold Bennett) was. He was assured in Fenton that the gentleman was a commercial traveller, although "out Burslem way" people said he was a writer of fiction. Tyrwhitt said that he was inclined to believe the latter, and described Bennett as a writer of the second-rate type.

LFT died unmarried at Windsor on 7 July 1921.

Burke, *Peerage;* J. Hepburn (edit.), *The Letters of Arnold Bennett* vol. ii; Venn.

VALE, Revd. Dr. Benjamin (1787-1863), *minister of religion (Church of England),* Longton

BV was born in London and educated at Christ's College, Cambridge. After ordination he went as chaplain to the convict colony in New South Wales, where he fell foul of the governor and was illegally court-martialled. On his return to England he presented a petition from the colonists protesting against the governor's arbitrary actions. He held several curacies in London, then in 1821 came to the Potteries as curate to Dean Woodhouse at St. Peter's parish church, Stoke upon Trent. About 1830 he started a school, held at first in the Wheatsheaf Hotel, Stoke, for the encouragement of virtue and the discouragement of vice, offering monetary rewards. He was appointed rector of the newly-formed parish of St. James the Less, Longton, in 1834. He had anti-Tractarian views and was also deeply opposed to the Chartists' ideas on the separation of church and state.

BV incurred the hostility of the local working classes. In January 1842 he was reported to have told some of his poorer parishioners that they could use dock leaves or broom seed as a palatable substitute for tea. His unpopularity may have prompted the attack on his rectory house, situated in the present Trentham Road, during the Chartist riots of August 1842. His wine-cellars were ransacked, his books and manuscripts burnt and his house was damaged by fire. Joseph Whiston, a potter and a Primitive Methodist lay preacher, is stated to have proclaimed that he was doing the Lord's work as he set fire to Vale's house.

The destruction of the manuscripts was not irreparable and Vale set to work immediately to rewrite his *Universal History*. He never forgave the local people for the events of 1842, and once described large congregations as 'ignorant as Hottentots, rude as bears and mischievous as monkeys'. He was a strong believer in self-help and mutual improvement, and supported the Longton Athenaeum and Mechanics' Institute as well as friendly societies. He was also a man of enterprising character, and made two balloon ascents, the second of which gravely weakened him physically.

His numerous published works included: *Authenticity of the Scriptures, A New System of Chronology, Geology in Miniature, Rhetoric in Miniature, The Early History of Egypt, Bible Commentary and Universal History, Philological Lectures, A Sermon on the Millenium* and others.

He died in March 1863.

Briggs; R. Fyson, 'The Crisis of 1842, Chartism, the Colliers' Strike and the Outbreak in the Potteries' in J. Epstein and D. Thompson, *The Chartist Experience.*

VARCOE, William (1833/4-1901), *china clay merchant,* Hanley.

WV was born about 1834 in St. Denis, Cornwall. He was in business as a china clay merchant in the Potteries by 1873, living at Northwood Cottage, Keelings Lane, Hanley and married to Mary née Walker. He had three sons and three daughters. In 1876 he was living at Highfield House, Hanley.

He died on 10 July 1901.

Census 1871; Dir. 1873; *National Index to Wills and Administrations;* P. Varcoe, *China Clay, the early years.*

VERNON, James (1809/10-80), *earthenware manufacturer,* Burslem.

JV, son of George Vernon, was baptised on 10 September 1809/10 at Burslem. In 1851 he was in business as James Vernon and Co. in Waterloo Road, Burslem, living in Bleak Hill. In 1867 he lived at 222 Grange Terrace. He served on the local Board of Health 1852-73, and was chairman and chief bailiff in 1853-4 and 1855-6. He was disqualified from standing for election in 1854-5 because of lack of proper property qualification. In politics he was a Liberal and Church of England by religious persuasion.

By his wife Julia he had at least five children. He died in Belmont Road, Burslem, on 30 March 1880 and was buried in St. Pauls, Dalehall.

Census 1851, 1861; Dir. 1851, 1867; Oldham; memorial inscription, St. Paul's, Dalehall.

VOYEZ, John (Jean) (c. 1740-c. 1800), *pottery modeller.*

JV is believed to have been born about 1740 of a family of engravers and metalworkers living near Amiens, France. He served an apprenticeship to a watchmaker and enameller. He came to London and worked for Philip Rundell, for whom he enamelled a watch and chatelain and vinaigrette bottle with peacock-tail style decoration. He qualified in 1766 as a master craftsman with a cameo of George III with a blue background. A sale catalogue of December 1767 lists two festoons of flowers by JV sold for £2.16s. In that year he was working in an artificial stone manufactory.

He was modelling for the Adam brothers, when Josiah Wedgwood discovered him. Wedgwood wrote to Thomas Bentley on 31 March 1768, 'I have hired a modeller for three years, the best I am told in London, he served his time with a silversmith, has worked several years at a china works, has been two or three years carving in wood and marble for Mr. Adam the famous architect, is a perfect master of the antique style in ornaments, vases, etc. . .' Wedgwood brought Voyez to Burslem, and provided him with a house and studio. JV worked for Wedgwood for only a few months, however, and in the spring of 1769 was charged at Stafford Assizes with drunkenness and disorderly conduct and sentenced to a whipping and three months' imprisonment. While in prison he carved an ivory plaque representing Prometheus. On his release JV returned to the Potteries where he was associated with Humphrey Palmer of Hanley, for whom he modelled a vase bearing the Prometheus motif. It is alleged that JV produced imitations of some of Wedgwood's wares. Wedgwood sought to control the situation by paying JV 36 shillings a week for the remainder of his three years' term, and when this was of no avail tried to force him to leave the district and return to the Continent.

Voyez was for a time employed by T. Hales, potter of Cobridge. In 1773 he issued a catalogue of cameos and intaglios in which he described himself as 'J. Voyez, Member of the Royal Society of Artists of Great Britain'. In 1788 he made the 'Fair Hebe' jug for Ralph Wood, potter. Eventually he left for London with his wife and child. He is documented as being in London in 1791 but thereafter no evidence of his life and career has been found.

Apollo, vols. 5, 49, 67; *Connoisseur*, vol. 68; W. Mankowitz and R. Haggar *English Pottery;* E. Meteyard *Life of Wedgwood;* R. J. Charleston 'Jean Voyez' in *Transactions of English Ceramic Circle*, vol. v.

WADE, George (1864-1938), *pottery manufacturer,* Burslem.

GW was born in 1864 and educated at Nottingham Universtiy. He became chairman of George Wade and Son, Ltd., making ceramic goods for the Lancashire cotton industry, electrical porcelain and art figures and groups. GW also had a business interest in Chromo Transfer Co., of Burslem. Competition between the Wade company and Henry Hallen of Wellington Street works, Burslem, ended when GW bought the Hallen business and united the two concerns in a new factory called the Manchester Pottery.

GW served as secretary of the Earthenware Manufacturers' Association for a number of years. He was elected to Burslem council in 1895, serving until 1903 and again in 1906-7. He was chairman of the School Board 1898-1903 and in this capacity pioneered the correlation of art instruction in elementary schools with that in the art schools. He was involved in the financial dispute between Burslem and Tunstall over the cost of extra-district children's schooling. He favoured federation and gave evidence to the House of Commons committee, arguing that federation would improve teacher training and the provision of secondary and technical education in the area.

GW was Liberal in politics and attended the local Wesleyan Methodist church. He served on the local and county benches of justices of the peace. For over 30 years he was president of the Burslem Mutual Assurance Collecting Society. In 1910 he served as president of the Burslem Association for the Prosecution of Felons. He married and had one son, (later Colonel) George Albert Wade. He died at Westwood, High Street, Wolstanton, on 1 January 1938.

The Jolly Potter (Wade magazine) September 1951; Oldham; *Pottery and Glass Record,* January 1938.

WAIN, Edward Brownfield (1861-1925), *mining engineer,* Tunstall.

EBW, son of Joseph Renshaw Wain (liquidator appointed to run Chatterley Whitfield Mining Company in 1878 after its voluntary liquidation) and Louisa his wife (q.v) was born on 3 March 1861. In 1882 he became under-manager of Chatterley Whitfield colliery and manager in 1886. He instituted a welfare scheme known as the Ground Club in 1889 to which both miners and the company contributed a weekly sum. The club was disbanded in 1910 on the introduction of a new national scheme. In 1912 he formulated a project for building a modern village on land owned by the colliery at Ball Green. The First World War brought the scheme to a halt. By 1920 EBW was managing director with his son, Roger Clement Wain as assistant manager.

EBW was a member of the North Staffordshire Colliery Owners' Association and was also president of the North Staffordshire Institute of Mining Engineers from 1894-6. He pioneered colliery rescue work using self-contained breathing apparatus. He served on the North Staffordshire Miners' Welfare Fund Committee and chaired the joint management committee for the proposed miners' convalescent home at Rudyard. He was deputy director chairman of the North Staffordshire Employers' Insurance, and a member of the Institute of Civil Engineers.

EBW's hobbies included gardening and photography. He was a member of the North Staffordshire Field Club and recorder of the Old Nortonian Society (founded c. 1923). He died on 24 April 1925.

A. Pointon, 'Comment about Chatterley Whitfield' (Chatterley Whitfield Mining Museum); *Staffs. Sentinel* 25 April 1925 (obit.).

WAIN, Louisa (1836-1907), *household duties and benefactress,* Tunstall.

Louisa Wain née Pointon, related to the Brownfield and Keeling families of Hanley, was born in 1836. She married Joseph Renshaw Wain, managing director of Chatterley Whitfield colliery, and had at least nine children, the first of whom was born in 1859. The family lived in Scotia Road, Tunstall, in 1881. During the 1890s she instigated Sunday afternoon prayer meetings in her home (Hoster House), and from these grew the mission church of St. Chad. The church was built on a site adjoining Chatterley Crossings, the Chatterley Whitfield colliery giving both money and land to the project, and Louisa Wain laid the foundation stone. The Wain family made various other bequests to the church, including a high altar.

LW died on 13 October 1907 at Kirklee, Congleton. One of her sons, Edward Brownfield Wain (q.v), became manager of Chatterley Whitfield colliery, and another. Clement J. Wain, established a chemist's shop in Newcastle under Lyme and later was created an alderman of Newcastle council. A daughter, Margaret, born in 1874, married W. C. Hancock, secretary of Stafford County Cricket Club.

Census 1881; *St. Chad's Mission Anniversary Booklet,* 1907; *Staffs. Sentinel* 19 October 1907; VCH viii.

WALKER, Sampson (1871-1946), *oil and lubricants merchant,* Hanley.

SW was born in Milton, near Stoke upon Trent, in February 1871, the son of William Walker. In 1873 the family came to Burslem, where William Walker and his brother John founded an oil refining business at Cobridge. The business was transferred to Brook Street, Hanley (now Century Street), and Sampson was educated at the Charles Street Wesleyan Day School, Hanley. He entered his father's business in 1884 and became a partner in 1892. The business became William Walker and Sons, Ltd., in 1928 and is now Century Oils Ltd.

SW was elected to Hanley council in 1908 and was one of the few opponents of federation in Hanley. He was however elected to Stoke on Trent council and became mayor in 1920-1 and later alderman. He took a leading part in the movement for the relief of distress in Hanley caused by the 1912 coal strike and was in charge of local food distribution. Politically he was a Liberal. He stood for election for the Burslem seat in 1918 but was beaten by Samuel Finney (q.v).

As a young man he played cricket for Burslem, from 1890-1901, and topped the batting averages in 1891. Later he became a director of Port Vale F.C. He married a Miss Hocknell, daughter of a Hanley grocer, and had four daughters. The family lived at 29 Charles Street.

SW died in the June quarter 1946, when he was still a member of the city council and chairman of the finance committee.

Century Oils (HRL); *Evening Sentinel* cuttings library; *Staffs. Sentinel* 14 May 1907, 31 March 1910, 5 November 1920.

WALLEY, Edward (1810-1872), *pottery manufacturer,* Burslem.

EW was born at Hanley and baptised on 6 May 1810, the son of Edward Walley and his wife Elizabeth. He operated the Villa Pottery at Cobridge from about 1840 until 1864 initially with Elijah Jones (q.v) and from about 1856 with W. Walley. By 1860 he also worked the Scotia Pottery at Burslem.

He produced relief moulded jugs for the home market and exported ironstone ware, particularly to Canada, where he supplied churches with ware decorated with individualised markings. He employed 360 hands in 1861. After withdrawing from manufacture he was in business as a commission agent and potter's valuer.

EW was a member of the Burslem Board of Health from 1850 to 1863 and served as chief bailiff in 1860-1. In 1849 he complained of the inadequacy of the street lighting in Cobridge.

He married Margaret Turner and a son Edward was born at Hanley in 1837. By 1861 the family were living at Grove House,.Cobridge and later in Clifton Terrace, Waterloo Road, Burslem where he died on 13 December 1872.

Information from Mr. J. W. Bentley, Lytham St. Annes; Census 1861; Dir. 1851, 1860; IGI Staffs; Jewitt; Oldham.

WALLEY, Edward (1834-1910), *builder,* Burslem.

EW was born at Queen Street, Burslem, and baptised on 6 April 1834. He was the son of William Walley and his wife Lucy, of Park Street, Endon. At the age of 15 he was apprenticed to Thomas Money, builder, of Burslem. In 1857 he set up in business on his own at 61 Navigation Road, Burslem. Among the public buildings with which his firm was involved was the Market Hall, Queen Street, Burslem.

He joined the Burslem Permanent Benefit Building Society in 1869, and became secretary, serving until 1873 when he resigned. He also acted as president from 1890 to his death. EW was a member of the Burslem Board of Health, School Board and Wolstanton and Burslem Board of Guardians. In 1900 he was appointed a justice of the peace. He was a member of Burslem Conservative Club.

He died in 1910 and was buried in St. Paul's churchyard, Burslem. He had served as churchwarden of St. Paul's.

Census 1861; Dir. 1860; Oldham; *Staffs. Sentinel* 27 June 1910.

WALLEY, John (1842-1904). *canal carrier and flint merchant,* Stoke upon Trent.

JW was born in Wharf Street, Stoke upon Trent, in 1842, the son of John Walley, a writing clerk and his wife Maria née Jones. The family had moved to Middleport, Burslem by 1851 at which date John Walley senior was a canal agent and wharfinger.

JEW was associated with Henry Colsell (q.v.) in the firm of Colsell and Co., canal carriers, by 1867. The business, in Copeland Street, Stoke, had become Colsell, Walley and Co. by 1872. At what date the partnership ended is unclear, but by 1880 JEW had developed a second business as an agent and flint merchant. He purchased flint from beaches in south east England and northern France, shipped it to the River Mersey and then carried it from Runcorn to the Potteries in his fleet of barges. His son Albert continued the business.

JEW married Mary Johnson at Burslem in 1862 and there were at least six children of the marriage. The family lived in Harding Terrace, Stoke by 1881 and later at Cleveland, James Street, Stoke, where JEW died on 19 November 1904.

Information from Mr. J. W. Bentley, Lytham St. Annes (great-grandson); Census 1851, 1881; Dir. 1867, 1872; *National Index to Wills and Administrations.*

WALLEY, William Thomas (1836/7-84), *provision dealer and cheese factor,* Hanley.

WTW was baptised on 10 August 1834 at Shelton Congregational chapel, the son of William and Mary Walley. It is suggested that he was one of the 600 men in the Light Brigade at the battle of Balaclava. He was in business at Eastwood Place, Hanley, before 1880. He served as mayor of Hanley in 1881 and died on 5 March 1884. By his wife Fanny he had at least one child, Ambrose Caley.

Dir. 1880; Huntbach; IGI Staffs; memorial inscription in Hanley cemetery.

WARBURTON, Ann (1713-98), *pottery manufacturer,* Burslem.

AW was born in 1713, the eldest child of Thomas Daniel. She married John Warburton, of Cobridge, survived him by 37 years and became a pottery manufacturer in her own right. She introduced a number of improvements in pottery manufacture including a process which made on-glaze enamelling of cream ware possible. She took her eldest son Thomas into partnership as Ann Warburton and Son. With her brother Ralph she developed an export trade in salt glaze ware to Holland. This is said to have encouraged Dutch enamellers to come to Cobridge. Ralph Daniel is credited with the introduction of plaster of paris moulds, after a visit to France about 1745. She was also exporting to Russia by 1774.

She died in 1798 and was buried in St. John's churchyard, Burslem.

M. Berthond, *H. and R. Daniel* 1822-1846; Jewitt; S. Shaw, *History of the Staffordshire Potteries;* J. Thomas *The Rise of the Staffordshire Potteries.*

WARD, Henry (1801/2-84), *architect and surveyor,* Hanley.

HW was born in Wakefield about 1801. He was in practice as an architect and town surveyor, as Henry Ward and Son, at Eastwood Place, Hanley, by 1851, but had already been commissioned to design Stoke town hall in 1834. The building was still unfinished in 1850. The centre of the building was originally an open space used as a market but this was converted into a council chamber in 1888. The town hall, the most imposing building in the Potteries, is in Classical style. The King's Hall, seating over 3,000 people, was built behind it in 1910-11.

HW married, with two children, was living in Cheapside, Hanley in 1861 and Observatory Terrace in 1867. He was involved in a long dispute with the Tunstall Board of Health from 1848-58 over a claim for work done for that authority. The firm of Ward and Son designed numerous churches and other buildings in the six towns and elsewhere in Staffordshire.

He died on 10 August 1884 at Forebridge, Stafford.

Census 1861; Dir. 1851, 1867; *National Index to Wills and Administrations;* N. Pevsner, *The Buildings of England: Staffordshire; Tunstall Board of Health Annual Reports.*

WARD, John (1781-1870), *solicitor,* Burslem.

JW was born in Shawston, Leicestershire, in June 1781. He was articled to a solicitor in 1802 and admitted in 1809. He set up his practice in Market Place, Burslem, in that year. He served as clerk to the Lawton and Burslem Turnpike Trust, the Longport and Tunstall Society for the Prosecution of Felons, was the local agent for the Birmingham Fire Union and was a member of the market commission in 1826. He was elected chief constable in 1840 and used his office to control the number of liquor licences granted. He was appointed a commissioner to assist the three judges in the trial of the Chartist rioters at Stafford in 1842.

As a solicitor he was engaged in a number of disputes. Amongst these was an action in 1819 for defamation of character against Enoch Wood, the potter, over Wood's remarks about Ward's part in a land sale. Ward sought £1,000 damages but was awarded only £100.

It is as a local historian that John Ward's name is chiefly remembered. He published *The Borough of Stoke upon Trent* in 1843. The extent to which this was written by Simeon Shaw (q.v.) is a matter of some controversy. Shaw had produced eight parts of *The Borough of Stoke upon Trent in 1838,* got into financial difficulties with his printers, W. Lewis and Son, and they passed the work over to Ward to be completed, which he did, in 12 more parts, by 1842. Ward received no payment for this, any profits going to Shaw as the originator. Ward later claimed that Shaw had contributed little to the earlier parts except his name, as he Ward, had spent considerable time on editing Shaw's work.

Ward's other literary works included a poem *The Potter's Art* — 575 lines of rhyming couplets, published in 1828.

He married Anne Rice, of Ashby-de-la-Zouch, in 1811, and had an only child, William born in 1812. JW attended St. Paul's church, Dalehall, from its opening in 1832, and served as a churchwarden, local treasurer of the Church Missionary Society and secretary of the Burslem National Schools. He joined the local Longport volunteers. His son William married Susannah Harrison, daughter of a silk manufacturer, and had a son John. When William died of pleurisy in 1847 John Ward's hopes centred on his grandson. John did not qualify as a solicitor, however, and ran away with the daughter of a Derbyshire innkeeper, whom he never married. JW changed his will so that his grandson should have only the interest on the estate until he married someone of whom the trustees of the estate approved. William's widow, Susannah, later married Henry Meir, a pottery manufacturer, of Greengates, Tunstall. Among the local place names are Meir's Field, Meir Street, and Ward Street.

JW died in Burslem on 3 June 1870.

E. Beech 'Who was John Ward?' in *Six Towns Magazine 1971* and unpublished monograph in HRL: M .W. Greenslade, *The Staffordshire Historians; Staffs. Advertiser* 26 October 1861, *Solicitor's Journal and Reporter* 11 June 1870.

WARD, John (1837-1906), *draper,* Longton.

JW was born in Fenton on 11 August 1837 and was educated at Ivy House Academy, Northwood, Hanley. He was first employed as a clerk in the Goldenhill collieries of J. H. Goddard (q.v.) but in 1860 opened a draper's business in Stafford Street. In 1869 he became assistant to Thomas Turner, secretary of the Longton Athenaeum, succeeding to the post of secretary on Turner's death in 1891. JW wrote the history of the Athenaeum. He was an enthusiast for the free library movement and eventually persuaded the Athenaeum committee to give its collection of books to Longton to form the basis of a public library. He was elected to the council in 1872, created alderman in 1894, served on the Stoke Board of Guardians, and was appointed to the magistrates' bench in 1902.

His principal writings were geological. His interest in geology and fossils had been stimulated by specimens from the mines in which he had at first worked, and he was encouraged in his studies by Dr. Robert Garner (q.v.). He was elected a Fellow of the Geological Society in 1874 and won the Society's Lyell award in 1899, coming to be regarded as one of the world's authorities on fossil fish. Many of the specimens he collected are now in the Natural History Museum, South Kensington, London. JW was a founder member of the North Staffordshire Field Club and served as its president in 1876.

He married Eliza Cooke, by whom he had a daughter, Elizabeth Ellen. He attended the Stafford Street Wesleyan church, of which he wrote a history, and was a Conservative in politics. On his retirement from business he lived in Stone Road, Longton, where he died on 30 November 1906.

Briggs; Census 1881; F. Dennis, *Longton's Greatest Man; Staffs. Sentinel* 3 December 1906 (obit.).

WARD, John, C.B., C.M.G., (1866-1934), *Member of Parliament,* Stoke upon Trent.

JW was born on 21 November 1866 at Oatlands Park, Weybridge, Surrey, the son of Robert Ward, a plasterer. His father died when JW was two years old and the family returned to Appleford, Kent, from where they had originally come. At the age of seven JW began work for a local farmer. When he was ten he attended a night school and learned to read with the aid of a copy of *Robinson Crusoe,* obtained by collecting coupons from packets of tea. He eventually became a navvy, working on the Andover and Marlborough railway, and then as a construction worker on the Manchester Ship Canal, where he earned 5½d. an hour. In 1885 he went to the Sudan helping to build railways for the army. For his distinguished conduct under fire he was awarded the Queen's silver medal. While in the Sudan he came into contact with Kitchener, then a lieutenant.

On his return to England JW became involved in politics and with John Burns formed a branch of the Social Democratic Federation at Battersea. He was arrested for leading a demonstration of unemployed men in Trafalgar Square. Then, in 1889, he founded the Navvies, Bricklayers and Labourers Union, serving as both president and secretary. It was now he made his acquaintance with North Staffordshire, obtaining wage rises for local builders' labourers.

He became chairman of the National Democratic League, which body recommended him to Stoke Trades and Labour Council in 1906 as a suitable Labour candidate for the Stoke constituency. He was elected with Liberal support, and again in 1910.

On the outbreak of the First World War JW's acquanintance with Kitchener led to his being commissioned, and he rose to the rank of lieutenant colonel, commanding the 25th Middlesex Regiment, which was largely recruited from North Staffordshire and included many members of Ward's trade union. JW also helped to raise several other battalions. He was posted to the Far East. En route the troopship in which he was sailing was sunk, and for his conduct in the emergency JW received the King's commendation. In July 1918 his battalion was sent to Sibẽria to fight the Bolsheviks, and in the course of the campaign JW crossed Russia from Vladivostok to the Ural mountains, and was awarded the Croix de Guerre by the French government.

He returned to England in November 1919, having been re-elected member of Parliament for Stoke upon Trent in his absence. His wartime experiences influenced his party-political opinions: 'The war killed party for me', he said. He had also become strongly anti-communist, and denounced the Soviet government as a 'hellish dictatorship'. He became estranged from the Labour party, sitting in the Commons as an independent, with local Liberal and Conservative support and accepting the Liberal whip. At the Trades Union Congress of 1925 he supported the cause of non-political trade unions. In the election of 1929 he was defeated by Lady Cynthia Mosley, wife of Sir Oswald Mosley. In 1931 she stood down to allow her husband to fight the election on behalf of the new party he had created, but was defeated.

JW's health now deteriorated, and he lived quietly at his home Omsk, Weyhill, Andover. He had married Lilian Elizabeth Gibbs in 1892, and there were four children of the marriage.

JW died on 19 December 1934.

Evening Sentinel 19 December 1934 (obit.); Sand L.

WARDHAUGH, Matthew (1813-88), *theatre proprietor,* Longton.

MW was born in Whitechapel, London, in 1813 and was early orphaned. He was first employed as a call boy at Drury Lane Theatre, then made a living by reciting and singing throughout England and Scotland. He came to Longton with a wooden van which served as a travelling theatre. This was replaced by a permanent wooden structure and, in 1867 by the Royal Victoria Theatre in Berry Bank, Stafford Street (now The Strand). He wrote at least 50 plays; a manuscript copy of his last play, 'My Little Wife or Nuts to Crack', is in the Horace Barks Library, City Public Library, Hanley.

In his early days he was a strong advocate of the temperance movement, was a Radical in politics, a Unitarian in religion and also a freemason. He served as a poor law guardian, and as mayor of Longton 1883-4. He died in 1888.

Briggs; VCH viii.

WARRINGTON, Henry (1838-1907), *colliery proprietor,* Fenton.

HW was baptised in Cheadle on 26 October 1838, the son of John Warrington and his wife Elizabeth née Hainsworth. He left school in 1851 to work for William Bowers at Berryhill Works, Fenton. He succeeded Bowers as proprietor on the latter's death in 1880. At the height of his business success he employed over 1,000 men. He also farmed 400 acres. By February 1900 the forges had closed and several hundred of his employees were idle.

He was injured in an accident in 1900 when his dog-cart collided with a tramcar. The damage to his health and the stress caused by the closure of his forges and by the illness of his son, Henry James Warrington, left him mentally distressed and he shot himself on 2 March 1907.

He had married his wife, Grace, about 1860, and there were two daughters and a son by the marriage. A Conservative in politics he represented Fenton on the Staffordshire county council. He attended the Wesleyan Methodist churches in Charles Street, Hanley and at Fenton. At the time of his death he was living at Fenton Manor House.

Census 1881; *National Index of Wills and Administrations; Staffs. Sentinel* 2 March 1907 (obit.).

WATKIN, Harold Gladstone (1882-1965), *dental surgeon,* Burslem.

HGW was born at Oak House, Waterloo Road, Burslem, (now a shop), in 1882, the son of an architect. His father died young and the family moved to Claremont House, Forthill. HGW went to school in Longport and also studied at the Wedgwood Memorial Institute. He qualified as an electrical engineer and helped to design the first fully automatic telephone exchange at the corner of Marsh Street and Trinity Street, Hanley.

He had many interests and in 1918 qualified as a dentist, at Liverpool University. After a period as a house surgeon he entered general dental practice in Durning Road, Liverpool, then in Kensington, Liverpool. Later he specialised in orthodentics and set up a practice in Rodney Street, Liverpool, one of the first such practices in the country. He acquired an international reputation as a designer of dental appliances and instruments, amongst which were the Watkin spot-welder and an oxygen anaesthetic apparatus. Between 1935 and 1947 he lectured at Liverpool Dental Hospital and at the Turner Dental School, Manchester, from 1937 to 1948.

He married Hilda Hayter, of Kensington, Liverpool and had two daughters, both born in Liverpool. He lived in Aigburth, Liverpool.

He died on 11 November 1965 and was buried in Burslem cemetery.

Evening Sentinel 18 January 1982; information from Mrs. E. M. Halpin, niece; *Transactions of the British Journal of Orthodentics,* 1933 and 1983.

WATKIN, John, (c. 1825-80), *builder,* Burslem.

JW son of Francis and Mary Watkins (sic) was baptised on 26 April 1825. In 1851 he was in business as a joiner and builder in Regent Street, Burslem, and was living in King Street. In 1867 his business was in Chapel Square and he owned a brickworks in Silvester Street.

He served on the Burslem Board of Health from 1857 to 1873 and on the Board of Guardians from 1867. By his wife Jane he had at least one child, James. In 1875 the family was living at Adbaston House, Burslem. JW served as president of the Burslem Association for the Prosecution of Felons in 1863.

He died at 'Sunny Bank', Endon on 12 July 1880 and was buried in Burslem cemetery. There is a memorial tombstone in St. John's churchyard, Burslem.

Dir. 1867; IGI Staffs; Oldham.

WATTON, Revd. Alfred (1830-86), *minister of religion (C. of E),* Burslem.

AW was born at St. John's Hill, Shrewsbury, on 7 January 1830, the son of John Watton, a printer. He was educated at Shrewsbury School. He matriculated at Cambridge 1863, graduated B.A. 1860 (having been a member of St. John's, Trinity and Magdalene colleges), and became an M.A. 1863. He was ordained in 1862, having served as curate in Tunstall 1861-2 and in Sneyd 1862, followed by curacies in Somerset and Nottinghamshire. He married Eliza Morris, daughter of Dr. John Morris, patron of the living of Burslem, and became rector of St. John's, Burslem, in 1869, in succession to the Revd. J. F. Armstrong (q.v.). He purchased the living from his father-in-law in 1871.

In 1872 AW was criticised, mainly outside the Potteries, for his funeral sermon on W. F. Horry (q.v.), which had suggested that Horry, who had shot his wife, was a Divine instrument for staying the progress of a sinner, though he denied that he thought of Horry as a martyr. He defended himself by pointing out that he was an opponent of capital punishment. AW supported the movement for the restoration of the Burslem wakes, suspended for a year in 1879 and characterised by Arnold Bennett in *The Old Wives Tale* as an 'orgiastic carnival'.

The expenses of the living, which included St. Paul's, Dalehall, and Christ Church, Cobridge, together with the costs of the restoration of St. John's in 1878-9 and improvements to a farm owned by the church at Brown Edge, caused AW financial problems. He suffered from dyspepsia and insomnia, though he did not take medical advice. Depressed by these ailments and by his financial difficulties he shot himself in the Rectory at Middleport, on 20 January 1886. He may have been influenced by the similar suicide of Revd. Adam Clarke (q.v.) a day or so earlier.

Oldham; *Staffs. Sentinel* 6 April, 13 April, 20 April 1881, 6 May 1872 and 20 January 1886 (obit.).

WEBBERLEY, William (1816-92), *china manufacturer,* Longton.

WW was baptised in Stoke upon Trent on 28 April 1816, the son of William and Ann Webberley. He began work at Minton's. In 1841/2 he was in partnership with G. Shubotham at St. James's Place China Works. The firm dropped the manufacture of lustre ware in 1844 to concentrate on china. On Shubotham's death in 1847 WW continued on his own account, buying the works in 1888 and rebuilding it. On his death the factory passed to Coggin and Hill, and then in the 20th century was held by a number of companies. The building was demolished by 1960.

WW was chief bailiff of Longton 1857-8, 1859-60 and 1861-2. He was appointed to the local magistrates' bench in 1867. He served as churchwarden at St. James's church, was a benefactor and governor of Longton Cottage Hospital, which he helped to found in 1868. He also assisted in the foundation of New Cottage Hospital, Normacot, in 1889. He was a freemason.

He lived first in Terrace Buildings, then in Trentham Road, Dresden. He died at Meir House, Longton on 22 October 1892 and was buried in St. James's churchyard.

Dir. 1857, 1864, 1873; IGI Staffs; Jewitt; St. James's church memorial inscription; *Staffs. Sentinel* 22 October 1892; VCH viii.

WEDGWOOD, Enoch (1813-79), *pottery manufacturer,* Tunstall.

EW was born in 1813, the son of Isaac Wedgwood, bookseller and tea-dealer of Tunstall and a distant relation of Josiah Wedgwood I. His mother was Charlotte née Yorke. About 1835 EW became a partner in the firm of Podmore, Walker and Co. who rented three pot-banks in Tunstall. Later he became the principal of the firm and took his younger brother Jabez into partnership, trading as E. Wedgwood and Co. In 1860 EW operated the Swan Bank works in High Street, Tunstall and the Unicorn works (now Summerbank Pottery). The firm moved from Swan Bank to Pinnox works, Woodland Street, 1860-2, and were employing between 600 and 700 men in the 1870s. The firm's success—one of their original designs, Asiatic Pheasants, became a standard pattern in Britain and the colonies—prompted a move to a larger factory in Brownhills in 1899. The firm became a public company in 1900 and effective control passed out of the hands of the Wedgwood family.

EW was a member of the Tunstall Board of Health from that body's inception in 1855, and was also a member of the Board of Guardians. He was appointed to the first Potteries Arbitration Board in July 1868.

EW married (1) Mary Ann Little in 1833 and (2) Jane Mattison in 1837 and had at least four children, of whom a daughter, Charlotte, married John Henry Clive, son of J. H. Clive (q.v.) and became noted for her good works in the area. EW was secretary of Wesley Place (Wesleyan Mathodist) Sunday School in 1837. The family later became Primitive Methodists.

EW and his family lived at 'The Limes', Porthill, where he died on 30 May 1879.

British Bulletin of Commerce Survey 1955; Census 1871; E. H. Eardley, *Tunstall;* IGI Staffs; Jewitt; *Staffs. Sentinel* 30 May 1879; VCH viii; J. C. Wedgwood, *History of the Wedgwood Family* and *Wedgwood Pedigrees.*

WEDGWOOD, Josiah (1730-95), *pottery manufacturer,* Hanley.

JW was born in July 1730, the youngest of the 13 children of Thomas and Mary Wedgwood of the Churchyard Works, Burslem. He was educated in Newcastle under Lyme, and at the age of 14 was apprenticed to his brother Thomas, who had inherited the family business. Early in his youth he caught smallpox which left him lame in the right leg. Later in life his leg was amputated a little below the knee.

Wedgwood first set up in business in partnership with Thomas Whieldon (q.v.) of Fenton Hall, and immediately began experiments to improve pottery manufacture. In 1759 he was on his own in the Ivy House Works, Burslem, rented from his uncles John and Thomas Wedgwood. There his first major achievement was the introduction of a greenglaze, ideal for the naturalistically-moulded wares of the popular Rococo style. By 1764 he was able to transfer his rapidly expanding business to the Brick House, known locally as the Bell Works from the method used to summon the workpeople. He introduced an engine-turned lathe here in 1763. About or just before this year he had perfected a cream-coloured earthenware, which brought him the patronage of Queen Charlotte, wife of George III. It became known as Queen's Ware and Wedgwood was able to style himself Potter to Her Majesty. It was at this time, too, that he met Thomas Bentley, a Liverpool merchant, who was to become his closest friend, confidant and later partner.

JW bought the Ridgehouse estate in 1766 and built a new factory there, opened on 13 June 1769. This factory was the nucleus of an industrial village which he called Etruria. The initial size of the works and the concept of a self-contained industrial community constituted a milestone in pottery history. Much of the early production at Etruria was of black basalt.

Early in 1773 Wedgwood was commissioned by the Empress Catherine II of Russia to make a dinner and dessert service of nearly 1,000 pieces. Each piece was hand-painted with views of the English countryside. At this time he was also experimenting with the production of a new stoneware body, which he eventually called Jasper. The body, being able to receive a mineral oxide stain throughout could be decorated with white bas-relief in the neo-classical taste of the time. A number of artists including John Flaxman, George Stubbs and John Bacon, supplied models for the bas-relief. In 1786 Wedgwood with his two best modellers, Henry Webber and William Hackwood, started a series of trials to make a replica of the Portland vase. In October 1789 he showed the result to Sir Joshua Reynolds who pronounced it a true and fathful copy.

To drive his clay, flint and colour mills Wedgwood installed Watt steam engines. He also led the movement for better communications and in the process brought turnpike roads and a canal to the Potteries.

He married his cousin Sarah, daughter of Richard Wedgwood of Smallwood, Cheshire, and had a numerous family. Two sons, John and Josiah, carried on the business after their father's death, which occurred on 3 January 1795. Josiah

Wedgwood and Sons continued in business at Etruria until 1938, when they built a new works at Barlaston.

JW had completed Etruria Hall, overlooking his factory, in 1770. By the mid-19th century all traces of the original ornamental gardens and parkland surrounding the hall had gone as Shelton ironworks expanded. The hall eventually became the offices of the Shelton Iron and Steel Works.

Jewitt; A. Kelly, *The Story of Wedgwood;* E. Meteyard, *Life of Josiah Wedgwood;* N. McKendrick, 'The Victorian View of Midland History: A Historiographical Study of the Potteries', in *Midland History*. vol. I (1971) VCH viii.

WEDGWOOD, Josiah, II (1769-1843), *potter and Member of Parliament,* Hanley/Stoke upon Trent.

JW was the second son of Josiah Wedgwood I by Sarah née Wedgwood. He was born in 1769, and eventually succeeded his father as head of the pottery firm, his elder brother John having left the industry for banking and horticulture. JW's period in control of the business was a difficult one, attended by a decline in trade caused by wars and the post-1815 economic depression. JW took his son Josiah III into partnership in 1823 and another son, Francis, into partnership in 1827. JW retired from the business in 1841.

He was a Liberal in politics and was returned for the newly created constituency of Stoke upon Trent in 1832, retiring in 1835. He was of a puritan character and it is recorded that he refused to take the Prince Regent over the works at Etruria because of the latter's loose morals. JW was a charitable man, however, supporting his poorer relations, men of learning, and poets, including Samuel Taylor Coleridge.

JW married Elizabeth Allen and had three sons and a daughter, Emma, who married Charles Darwin the scientist. He died in 1843.

M and H; V and S: C. V. Wedgwood, *Last of the Radicals;* J. C. Wedgwood, *Wedgwood Pedigrees.*

WEDGWOOD, Josiah Clement (Baron Wedgwood of Barlaston) (1872-1943), *Member of Parliament, historian,* Newcastle under Lyme.

JCW was born in Barlaston, near Stoke upon Trent, on 16 March 1872, the second son of Clement Wedgwood and Emily née Rendel. He was educated at Clifton College and at the Royal Naval College, Greenwich. He worked as a naval architect for Sir W. G. Armstrong and Co., of Elswick shipyards, Newcastle upon Tyne. He served in the South African war from 1900 to 1901, rising to the rank of captain of a battery of guns attached to a cavalry brigade. After the war he returned to South Africa to serve as resident magistrate for the districts of Ermelo and Carolina, for about two years, then returned to England because of his wife's health. He bought Barlaston Hall and looked around for a political career.

JCW was adopted as Liberal candidate for the Newcastle under Lyme constituency in February 1905 and was elected in the sweeping Liberal triumph of January 1906. He became parliamentary private secretary to Walter Runciman, the financial secretary in the new government but resigned because he could not support a motion of censure against Lord Milner, whose administration in South Africa was being criticised. JCW was by this time a supporter of the 'Single Tax' ideas of Henry George. He represented the borough in Parliament from 1906 to January 1942, sitting as a Liberal until April 1919 when he briefly joined the Independent Labour Party, changing to the Labour Party in August 1919. He was vice-chairman of the Parliamentary Labour Party 1921-4, a member of the Labour Party National Executive in 1924, and was created a privy councillor in 1924, in which year he was appointed Chancellor of the Duchy of Lancaster.

Meantime he had had a distinguished career in the First World War. He was in Flanders as a lieutenant commander in the Royal Naval Auxiliary Service, was severely wounded in the Gallipoli campaign in 1915, winning the D.S.O., went to East Africa for a few months in 1916, then was back in England as Assistant Director in the Trench Warfare Department in 1917. In October 1917 he was sent by the War Office to Russia to locate Kerensky's government, advised against further support of the counter-revolutionary forces in Russia, and was recalled.

In the 1920s JCW pursued his researches into history, including the local scene. He served as honorary secretary of the William Salt Archaeological Society, in 1922 publishing *Staffordshire Pottery and its History,* and in 1925 *Wedgwood Pedigrees.* His major contribution to Staffordshire local history lay in the three volumes of the *Parliamentary History of Staffordshire* (Collections for a History of Staffordshire, 1917-18, 1922 and 1923 and 1933). He was mainly responsible for the launching of the idea of a parliamentary history on the lines of the *Dictionary of National Biography.* Two volumes were published, in 1936 and 1938, but the work remained incomplete because of financial and other difficulties. It was resumed in 1951 after JCW's death. Apart from history JCW published many articles, books and pamphlets on political subjects, including the *Road to Freedom* (1913), *The Seventh Dominion* (1928), and *Testament to Democracy* (1942). His own autobiographical works were *Memoirs of a Fighting Life* (1940) and *Essays and Adventures of a Labour M.P.* (1924). A collection of prose and verse entitled *Forever Freedom* was published by Pelican Books in 1940.

He had been a strong supporter of federation before 1910, and in 1930-2 served as mayor of Newcastle under Lyme. He married twice. His first wife was Ethel Bowen, whom he married on 3 July 1894 and by whom he had two sons and five daughters. A few days after his unopposed return for Newcastle in the election of December 1918 his wife was granted a *decree nisi* for divorce on the grounds of desertion and adultery. He was denounced by a local vicar from the pulpit and JCW wrote to the *Sentinel* defending his actions. The affair resulted in his advocating the reform of the divorce laws. JCW's second wife was Florence Willett, whom he married on 25 June 1919.

JCW was raised to the peerage as Lord Wedgwood of Barlaston in the New Year's Honour's List 1942. He died on 26 July 1943 and was buried at Barlaston. He himself had suggested that whoever wrote his life should call it *The Last of the Radicals* and that it should be a 'clarion call against the constructors of a safe and unjust society'. His niece, C. V. Wedgwood, who wrote the biography, summed up his life thus: 'A passionate love of justice and a contempt for caution — these were the strongest forces of his character'. She also wrote ' . . . for the last nineteen years of his life he made the best of his position as a free agent, untrammelled by party ties, political caution or hope of office'.

M. W. Greenslade, *The Staffordshire Historians;* S and L: C. V. Wedgwood, *The Last of the Radicals.*

WELSBY, William (c.1790-?), *workhouse governor,* Chell.

William Welsby gave his age as 50 on the 1841 census form, when he was shown as governor of Wolstanton and Burslem Union Workhouse, Chell. He could have been the governor who figures in Charles Shaw's *When I was a Child* presiding over the flogging of a boy, as Shaw states he entered the workhouse in 1842. Welsby's wife, Sonia, also aged 50, was the matron. Nothing more has so far been discovered about the Welsbys.

Welsby may have held this post until 1850, when Charles Wellum (q.v.) was the governor. Other known Chell workhouse governors were John Bennett (q.v.), in 1862, Edwin Hudson in 1876, William Sargent in 1892 and John Bodden in 1904.

Census 1841; Dir. 1841; C. Shaw, *When I was a Child.*

WENGER, Albert Francis (1837-1924), *colour manufacturer,* Hanley.

AFW, son of David Rudolphe Wenger and Elise Cesarini Richard, was born in Lausanne, Switzerland, on 2 November 1837. The Wengers were an old and noble family of potters. AFW learnt the art of pottery at Nyon, eventually running an earthenware and porcelain factory there. He came to England to work as a modeller and designer and established himself in business in Cobridge in 1870. Later the works moved to Hanley and continued there until 1900 when a large factory was built in Etruria, equipped with up-to-date laboratories.

AFW pioneered the manufacture of colours and chemicals for the pottery, tile, brick, glass and vitreous enamelling trades. The firm produced gold colours for on-glaze decoration as well as under-glaze colours. The products were sent to all parts of the world as well as Britain.

AFW was a member of the social organisation known as the Ancient Corporation of Hanley, to whom he gave the Corporation Yard Glass. He married Harriet Mary Cecilia Agnes Heady on 4 August 1875 and had at least eight children. In 1881 the family lived at 10 Jasper Street, Hanley. AFW died at Victoria House, Newcastle under Lyme on 25 February 1924.

British Bulletin of Commerce November 1954, Part I; G. Cope-Cartlidge, *Family Tree of Wengers (HRL);* Cox's *Potteries Annual and Year Book,* 1924-25.

WEST, John Gilbey Uvedale (c. 1845-94), *medical practitioner,* Stoke upon Trent.

JGUW was born in Hogsthorpe, Lincolnshire, about 1845, the son of a Lincolnshire physician who was a Fellow of the Royal Society. He was educated at University College, London, graduating L.R.C.P. (London) and M.R.C.S. (England). He was appointed house physician to the North Staffordshire Infirmary 1872-5, resigning to take up private practice, but remaining on the honorary medical staff as an ophthalmic surgeon. He was medical officer to Stoke workhouse and medical attendant to the North Staffordshire Nursing Institution. He served as financial secretary of the North Staffordshire branch of the British Medical Association.

He was secretary of the North Staffordshire Philharmonic Society from its foundation in 1876. Swinnerton Heap (q.v.) dedicated the cantata *Fair Rosamund,* first performed in 1890, to him.

By his wife, Annie, JGUW had a son and three daughters. He died early in March 1894 in Madeira. The pulpit in Stoke parish church was erected to his memory.

Staffs. Advertiser 17 March 1894 (obit.).

WHEATLEY, Samuel (1847-1919), *brick and tile manufacturer,* Stoke upon Trent.

SW, son of Samuel Wheatley, was born in Hampshire on 7 August 1847. When he was four the family moved to Butterton, near Newcastle under Lyme, where his father was employed as agent to Lady Pilkington of Butterton Hall. SW at first followed his father's occupation as agent to the estate of Sir Lionel Pilkington. Then in 1870 he took over Springfield Tileries, trading as S. Wheatley and Co., by 1880 as Wheatley and Cooper and by 1884 as Wheatley and Caddick. He served as chairman of the North Staffs. Brick and Tile Manufacturers' Association, and as vice-chairman of the National Association of Brick and Tile Manufacturers. The Springfield tileries still exist.

He was elected to Stoke upon Trent council serving from 1874 to about 1884. He was president of the North Staffordshire Chamber of Commerce 1897-8, and chairman of the Railway Rates Committee. He became an expert on carriage and freight charges in 1895 producing a book of tables of maximum rates of conveyance for most railway companies.

He married Eleanor Sheldon, but there were no children of the marriage. The family lived at Clayton Villa.

SW died in Newcastle under Lyme on 19 September 1919.

Staffs. Sentinel 1 October 1919.

WHEWALL, James (c. 1851-1909), *cobbler,* Hanley.

JW came from Kingsley, near Cheadle, Staffs. As a boy he sang in the parish church choir. He moved to Talke-o'-the-Hill and worked as a collier until an accident in the pit caused him to find employment as a cobbler and insurance agent.

JW formed the Talke choir which later became the North Staffordshire and District Choral Society. The chairman of Talke choir and later treasurer of the Choral Society was Arthur Bailey, choirmaster of All Saints church, Odd Rode, where Havergal Brian (q.v.) was the organist. JW's choir won many competitions, and gave first performances of major choral works by Bantock, Delius and Elgar. They performed the *Dream of Gerontius* in London on 6 June 1903. JW's successes included a performance before the king and queen at Windsor Castle and the first performance of Delius's *Mass of Life* under Sir Thomas Beecham in 1909. The choir won the chief choral prize at the Welsh National Eisteddfodd in 1901, 1902, 1904 and 1906, an achievement not afterwards surpassed.

JW was twice married. His second wife was Deborah née Andrew. He died at 114 Wellesley Street, Shelton, on 28 November 1909.

R. Nettell, *North Staffordshire Music, a social experiment; Staffs. Sentinel* 29 November 1909; *Staffs. Sentinel Summer Number,* 1911.

WHIELDON, Thomas (1719-95), *pottery manufacturer,* Fenton.

TW was born in Penkhull in September 1719. He had opened a small pottery in Fenton Low by 1740. A capable business man as well as a skilled potter he prospered and by 1750 owned a number of parcels of land in Fenton, eight dwelling houses and land associated with Fenton Hall, as well as his pottery. A number of people who later became famous potters began as his apprentices or employees, including Josiah Spode (q.v.). TW was in partnership with Josiah Wedgwood (q.v.) from 1754 to 1759. TW's products included salt glazed wares, agate ware and a cream-coloured earthenware which was later perfected by Wedgwood. Much of his pottery was in imitation of Chinese imports and, it has been suggested, gave colour beauty and even humour to the drab homes of miners and labourers. He also anticipated Wedgwood in the development of the specialisation of different processes within the industry.

By his wife Sarah TW had six children, his sons carrying on the business after his death. The family lived in Whieldon's Grove, Fenton, which TW built himself in the mid-18th century, a two-storeyed mansion of five bays with a pedimented doorway. Later a wing was added. By 1829 the house was abandoned. The premises were taken over by the North Staffordshire Railway Company in the late 1840s, and much altered.

TW died in March 1795.

The American Wedgwoodian, vol. 1, No. 8, May 1965, 'About Thomas Whieldon'; Thomas Whieldon's Notebook (City Museum and Art Gallery, Stoke upon Trent; Transactions of the English Ceramic Circle, vol. 3, part 3; M and H; L. Weatherill, *The Pottery Trade and North Staffordshire 1660-1760.*

WHITEHURST, George (1845-1917), *grocer,* Tunstall

GW was born at Mow Cop in 1845, being baptised by the Revd. Richard Jukes, a travelling preacher. His father was a member of the Primitive Methodist connexion and his mother was a Wesleyan Methodist. He attended the Church of England school at Mow Cop, run by a severe vicar and also the Wesleyan Sunday School. He was a scholar in the school attached to the new Primitive Methodist chapel erected at Mow Cop in 1862 and was 'converted' when he was about 16. He joined the Primitive Methodist connexion and remained a member until his death. He first appeared on the Congleton circuit plan about 1864, preaching his first sermon at Cloud chapel. It was suggested that he should study for the ministry but his father had died in 1862 and the family was too poor to pay for his training. He had been at work since the age of 12 in the local iron forges, an employment he later described as 'slavery'. He eventually succeeded in setting himself up in a grocery business, using borrowed money, and prospered sufficiently to be able to pay off the principal and interest. His earliest reading was the Bible and he bought himself a family Bible for 29 shillings, paying by instalments. Other reading included *The Adviser,* a temperance magazine, and other temperance literature. Eventually he aquired his own small library.

His preaching commitments took him all over the Congleton circuit and involved him in walking long distances. In 1882 he was appointed a society steward and in 1889 he became the treasurer at the Mow Cop Memorial Chapel. The costs of the alterations to the maintenance of the chapel always caused him concern, as the congregation consisted mostly of poor people.

He married Elizabeth Cumberbatch about 1872 and there was one daughter Annie. The family lived on Mow Cop, the house still (1985) standing but its original shop front altered. He held scripture readings and prayers in the living room every morning. He took the pledge to abstain from alcohol early in life and when he established his business felt so uneasy about selling tobacco that he gave it up. He disapproved of theatre going and card playing, and was not of pronounced political opinions, althought he did once go to Manchester to hear Gladstone, the Liberal prime minister, speak. He died in 1917.

'My Recollections': manuscript notes by G. Whitehurst in possession of his granddaughter, Miss E. Boon, who also provided further information.

WHITTINGHAM, Thomas (1794/5-1869), *baker and flour dealer,* Burslem.

TW was born in Cheshire about 1794. In 1835 he was in business as a baker and flour dealer in St. John's Square, Burslem. He was chief constable of Burslem in 1846 and served on the local Board of Health from 1850 to 1867. He was opposed to the indiscriminate adoption of water closets, arguing that the system was only a theory and was known to have failed.

In 1851 he was living in Waterloo Road and described as a retired tradesman. He died on 1 January 1869.

Census 1851; Dir. 1835; *National Index to Wills and Administrations;* Oldham; *Staffs. Advertiser* 5 September 1857.

WIGLEY, George (1808-89), *brick and tile manufacturer,* Burslem.

GW was born in 1808. He came to Burslem in the 1830s and by 1851 had set up a business as a brick and tile manufacturer in Sylvester Square.

From 1850 he was almost continuously a member of the Burslem Board of Health, and after incorporation in 1878, a councillor. Liberal in his political opinions he agitated against the imposition of church rates. He acted as registration agent for the Liberal party in the 1860s. Married, with a son and four daughters, he lived in Wolstanton in 1867 and at Bank House, Rudyard, in 1873. He died on 5 July 1889.

Dir. 1851, 1860 1880; G. Melly, Letters, XIII, 3333 (HRL); *Staffs. Sentinel* 5 July 1889.

WILD, Thomas Clarke (1864-c.1939), *pottery manufacturer,* Longton.

TCW was born in September 1864, the son of Thomas Wild, a platemaker. He began work as a half-timer before the age of nine at Barlows of Market Street. He was employed as a jigger/turner in the morning from 6 a.m. to 1 p.m. then attended St. James's School in the afternoons. He earned extra pocket money by carrying water from the springs to houses in the Normacot area. After working with his father at the Beaconsfield Pottery TCW was apprenticed to Barlows as a thrower. He was employed briefly at Taylor, Wain and Bates, then at the age of 18 joined Barlows as an under manager. Thrown out of work by the sudden closure of Barlows about 1884 he found work again with Jones and Howson, and also opened a fruit and confectionery shop. This business prospered and eventually he had shops in Stafford Street, Commerce Street and High Street. About 1894 he founded the Royal Albert Works. His business interests expanded further and he came to control 11 potteries in Longton and was owner of the Alhambra Cinema, Normacot.

On federation in 1910 he was elected to the new borough council, was created alderman in 1920 and elected mayor in 1927. He was the first to have the title lord mayor when the city of Stoke on Trent was established. He served as a director of the Longton Mutual Permanent Building Society from 1903 and was president in 1913.

He married Emily Trickett about 1884. She died in 1913 and he married again in 1915, his second wife being Ada Eaves. From 1916 to 1932 they lived at Blythe House, Blythe Bridge, then moved to Rhyl where he died about 1939.

Cox's Potteries Annual 1924; Jewitt; *Staffs. Sentinel* 23 September 1927.

WILEMAN, James Francis (died 1900), *pottery manufacturer,* Fenton.

JFW was the son of Henry Wileman, a London (Paddington) china and earthenware dealer who came to the Potteries about 1853 and went into partnership with Joseph King Knight at the Foley Potteries. James and his brother Charles joined their father from 1864 to 1868, when Charles took the new china works built by Henry Wileman in 1860 and James took the original works. Charles retired in 1870 and JFW assumed control of both potteries. He was in partnership with J. B. Shelley in 1872, trading as Wileman and Company. The factory produced household wares, most of the products going to overseas markets.

Both brothers served as Fenton improvement commissioners in 1864, and James was chief bailiff 1870-2 and chairman of the Board of Health in 1825. Eventually he became an alderman on Stafford county council, and served as chairman of the Staffordshire Potteries Water Board.

Dir. 1872; Fenton Commissioners' Minutes; Jewitt.

WILLIAMSON, Hugh Henshall (c. 1785-1867), *colliery owner,* Tunstall.

HHW was born in Longport about 1785, the son of Robert Williamson and Ann Brindley née Henshall. By 1828 he was operating Scotia and Pinnox Collieries, which after his death fell into decay and flooded. The lack of concerted pumping operations effectively brought an end to mining in Tunstall and Burslem by 1890, as successive pits, Bycars, Jackfield and Bank Top flooded. Only Sneyd, through the efforts of William Heath (q.v.) survived.

He was associated with his elder brother, Robert in the operation of Goldendale Ironworks by 1848. HHW was appointed high sheriff of Staffordshire in 1834. He married Anne Clowes of Porthill at Wolstanton on 1 March 1814 and the couple lived at Greenaway Bank which was bequeathed to HHW by his uncle Hugh Henshall.

HHW died on 3 December 1867.

Adams; IGI Staffs; VCH viii; Ward; *National Index to Wills and Administrations.*

WILLIAMSON, Robert (1780-1869), *iron master and colliery owner,* Burslem.

RW was baptised on 10 September 1780 at Burslem, the son of Robert Williamson and his wife Ann, the widow of James Brindley. With his brother Hugh Henshall Williamson (q.v.) he operated a pottery in Longport built by their father in 1773 and which they sold to the Davenports about 1840. The brothers owned a number of collieries including Ravenscliffe and by 1848 had opened Goldendale Ironworks. RW retired from active management about 1852.

He was chief constable of Burslem in 1833 and chairman of the Conservative committee for the borough of Stoke upon Trent from 1832. RW became a volunteer officer in 1797 and was major commandant of the Longport Volunteers with 500 men from 1808 until their disbandment in 1814.

He married Anne, daughter of Thomas Kinnersley of Clough Hall, Kidsgrove, a Newcastle banker. There were at least seven children born of the marriage. The family lived at Ramsdell Hall near Congleton, where RW died on 31 August 1869.

Adams; IGI Staffs; *Staffs. Advertiser* 4 September 1869; VCH viii; Ward.

WILSON, Janette (born c. 1799), *school mistress,* Stoke upon Trent.

JW was born about 1799 in Hanley. She kept a private school described as a ladies' seminary at 22 High Street, Stoke upon Trent from c.1846-c.1867. By 1851 she was widowed and was living with her half sister.

Census 1851; Dir. 1846. 1867.

WINDLE, Herbert (1843-1902), *police officer,* Hanley.

HW was born in Chesterfield, being baptised on 25 January 1843, the son of Mark and Mary Windle. he began his police career as a constable in Chesterfield, being promoted to the rank of sergeant in May 1862. He was appointed inspector at Hanley in 1870 on the formation of the borough constabulary and chief constable in 1875.

A freemason and connected with the Charity Organisation Society, he lived with his wife Sarah at 8 Gladstone Street, Hanley, where he died on 26 January 1902.

Staffs. Sentinel 26 January 1902; Huntbach; IGI Derbyshire; *National Index to Wills and Administrations;* VCH viii.

WISE, John Ayshford (1810-70), *landowner and member of Parliament,* Stoke upon Trent.

JAW was born in 1810, the son of Ayshford Wise, Member of Parliament for Totnes, Devonshire, and Mary née Whitby. He received much of his education on the continent, with a view to his entering the diplomatic service. He was appointed a deputy lieutenant of Devonshire in 1832 and for Staffordshire in 1837, in which latter year he married Mary, only daughter of Hugh Booth of Cliff Bank Pottery, Stoke upon Trent. He came into possession of Clayton Hall through this marriage. He became one of the largest landowners in the area, with property in Clayton, Trent Vale and Penkhull. He served as an improvement commissioner for Stoke upon Trent from 1839 and was chief bailiff in 1849 and 1865. In 1839 he was adopted as prospective parliamentary candidate by the Liberal party but stood down in favour of John Lewis Ricardo (q.v.). He petitioned the county magistrates in 1839 asking that Stoke upon Trent should be removed from the areas in which the County and District Constables Act would operate, arguing that the existing police force was sufficient. He later opposed, unsuccessfully, the purchase of Stoke market.

He entered Parliament in 1852, sitting for Stafford borough. He joined with W. T. Copeland (q.v.) in getting Hanley removed from the list of towns to which the Health of Towns Act of 1848 would apply. He sat for Stafford borough until 1860 when he applied for the Chiltern Hundreds. He unsuccessfully contested the election for Newcastle under Lyme in 1865, later claiming that he had been tricked into doing so in order that some voters could have the chance of financial gain.

In 1850 he served as president of the North Staffordshire Agricultural Society.

His first wife, Mary, by whom he had a son and two daughters, died in 1844, and he married Anna Mary Way in 1848. He died at Clayton Hall on 9 September 1870.

Burke, *Landed Gentry;* S and L; B and S; VCH viii; Warrilow.

WOLFE, Thomas (1751-1818), *pottery manufacturer,* Stoke upon Trent.

TW was born in 1751, the son of Thomas Wolfe and Elizabeth née Bell. Thomas Wolfe senior (1720-1800), was a partner in Bell and Wolfe, potters, of Lane End. In 1781 TW occupied a factory in Stoke upon Trent on the north-east side of the Newcastle canal (opposite the property which became Spodes), and later acquired more land stretching along High (later Church) Street where he built his Big Works. From 1784 he manufactured queen's ware, cane ware and Egyptian black ware, much of the output going to the American and Irish markets. Towards the end of the 18th century he bought another property opposite the Big Works, where he produced china. He was associated with the Islington China Factory in Liverpool, in partnership first with John Davenport (q.v.) then with Miles Mason (q.v.). TW was also in business partnerships with Josiah Spode (q.v.).

TW is said to have been the first manufacturer to employ steam power for grinding calcined flint, an engine being erected in the works about 1793, but a recent study does not mention this. After TW's death the Big Works was taken over by William Adams (q.v.) who began the manufacture of porcelain there. The Adams family continued to operate the factory until about 1862. In the 1870s Wolfe Street (the present Kingsway) was built and ran through part of the Big Works site.

By his wife Rachel TW had at least five daughters. The second eldest daughter married Robert Hamilton, who went into partnership with his father-in-law. TW built them a house in the centre of Church Street, on a site now occupied by Stoke market.

TW died on 19 October 1818 and was buried in Stoke churchyard.

A. Lamb 'The Application of Steam Power in the North Staffordshire Pottery Industry' in *N.S.J.F.S.* vol. 17—1977; M and H; *T.N.S.F.C.* vol. 58; VCH viii; Ward.

WOOD, Aaron, (1717-85), *pottery designer and modeller,* Burslem.

AW was born in Burslem on 14 April 1717. He was the son of Ralph and Elizabeth Wood and the third of nine children. In 1731 he was apprenticed to Thomas Wedgwood of Burslem for seven years and for a further five years from 1738. He set up his own business in 1750, sometimes working in a locked room to preserve his secrets. He modelled for most of the leading potters of his time. Examples of his work are in the British Library and the Victoria and Albert Museum.

He married Mary Meir (born 1717) and had eight children including Enoch Wood (q.v.). He died on 12 May 1785. William Caddick painted his portrait in 1747.

F. Falkner, *The Wood Family of Burslem;* M and H.

WOOD, Absalom Reade, (1851-1922), *architect and surveyor,* Tunstall.

ARW was born on 20 December 1851, the son of Absalom Wood, a member of the Wood family, the Burslem potters, and his wife Elizabeth née Colclough. He attended the Burslem Wesleyan Day School. Later he won a scholarship to South Kensington Art School which he did not take up. Arnold Bennett used this fact in connection with the character of Cyril Povey in *The Old Wives' Tale* and to some extent modelled the Orgreave characters in the *Clayhanger* trilogy on the Wood family. ARW was articled to Robert Scrivener (q.v.) of Hanley, and began his own practice in 1874 in partnership first with J. Hutchings and later with Goldstraw. His office was in Piccadilly, Hanley and eventually in Butterfield Place, High Street, Tunstall.

He designed many public and private buildings in the Potteries including the Primitive Methodist school, Tunstall (1875), Baptist Tabernacle, Burslem (1876), Congregational Church, Tunstall (1878), Primitive Methodist chapel, Wolstanton (1878), Town Hall, Tunstall (1885), Congregational church, Burslem (1885), St. Andrew's church, Porthill, (1886), transepts and chancel of Christ Church, Tunstall (1885-6), Free Library, Science and Art Schools, Fire Station, Public Library and Museum, Tunstall (1887-97), Victoria Institute Jubilee Building, Kidsgrove (1889), Clock Tower, Tunstall (1893), facade of Jubilee Wesleyan Methodist chapel, Tunstall (1906), School of Art, Burslem (1905-7), sewage disposal works, cemetery chapel and lodge, public park, Drill Hall, High Street school, Chell school, Tunstall and many more buildings in Tunstall (from 1907). The only local example of ARW's *art nouveau* style was a redesigned shop front (now a fish and chip shop) in Paradise Street, Tunstall. As an architect he stressed the practical aspects of a building, for example installing ventilation shafts, and thought that the aesthetic effect was of secondary importance. In 1875 ARW was appointed surveyor to the Tunstall Board of Health, a part time post which he held until 1910. He married Mary Holdcroft and had at least two sons and three daughters. The family lived at Wesley Place, Tunstall in 1876, and in 1890 ARW built 'Hillcroft', Wolstanton, as his private residence. He was a member of the North Staffs. Field Club 1888-1920 and was later elected to Wolstanton Urban District Council. He attended Hill Top United Methodist chapel, Burslem, and later Longport United Methodist chapel, where there is a plaque to his memory.

His son William followed his father's profession.

ARW died in Wolstanton on 21 December 1922.

M. Cawley, 'Absalom Reade Wood', (Dept. of Art, History and Design, North Staffs. Polytechnic 1981); Dir. 1876-1922; N. Malkin, *A Grand Tour;* N. Pevsner, *The Buildings of England: Staffordshire; Staffs. Advertiser* 31 Oct. 1885, 2 August 1890, 31 Oct. 1891, 23 November 1898; *Staffs. Sentinel* 12 January 1904, 10 Oct. 1907, 23 December 1922 (obit.).

WOOD, Arthur Thomas (1857-1943), *schoolmaster,* Stoke upon Trent.

ATW was born in Keighley, Yorkshire. He became a pupil teacher in a Methodist school and taught Pitman's shorthand at the age of 14. He was a Queen's Scholar at

Westminster Training College in 1875. His first appointment was to a Wesleyan school in Yorkshire, then from 1880-1922 he served as headmaster of Penkhull school. He went to Leipzig in 1892 for a course in woodwork, and on his return taught, and wrote three books on this subject. He acted as secretary for the University Extension lectures in the area.

He married Ann Eliza Waring and had at least two children. He attended the Wesleyan Methodist chapel in Stoke upon Trent. His sister, Sarah Hannah Wood, was a mistress at Penkhull school 1880-1910.

ATW died on 13 December 1943.

A. Curtis and E. Beech, *A History of Wesley Chapel.*

WOOD, Enoch (1759-1840), *pottery manufacturer,* Burslem.

EW was born in Burslem on 31 January 1759, the youngest of eight children of Aaron Wood (q.v.) and Mary née Meir. In 1770 he was sent to Liverpool to learn drawing and anatomy from his relatives Richard and William Caddick. On his return to Burslem he spent a short time at the Bell Works of Josiah Wedgwood and then was apprenticed to Humphrey Palmer of Hanley Green. He became a skilful modeller, in 1781 producing a bust of John Wesley during one of the latter's visits to the area. In the church of St. John the Baptist, Burslem, are two terracotta plaques modelled by Enoch Wood and the Wesley bust, moved here from their original location in the Wood family vault. At 24 he became a master potter and started his own works, in partnership with his cousin, Ralph Wood. From 1798 to 1818 his partner was James Caldwell and from 1818 to 1846 the firm traded as Enoch Wood and Sons. The name Fountain Place Works came from the fountain which EW constructed for the town's use in 1798, but the works themselves date from 1789. The castellated brick parapets give the impression of a fortification. Enoch Wood's own house stood near the centre of the site, with gardens sloping down to the Trent and Mersey Canal. The works produced figures, busts, jasper ornaments, blue-printed and other table ware and special ware for America. Fountain Buildings in Newport Lane were built by Enoch Wood's workers in 1824 with his encouragement.

On 16 December 1780 he married Ann Browne (1758-1841) and the couple had 12 children. In 1788 EW was a churchwarden of Burslem church, in 1798 he helped to organise the Burslem Volunteers against the threat from Napoleonic France, and in 1804 he became treasurer of Hill Top Sunday School. In 1807 he took out a patent for a new method of applying steam power to raise water levels. In 1818 he helped to establish the National School in Burslem, and was chief constable of Burslem in 1832 and 1835. He formed a museum of local pottery and a collection of local documents.

He served as president of the Burslem Association for the Prosecution of Felons 1822-3, and his son, Enoch Wood junior, was also president in 1824.

EW died on 17 August 1840 and was buried in St. John's churchyard, Burslem.

F. Falkner, *The Wood Family of Burslem;* programme of 154th Annual Dinner of the Burslem Association for the Prosecution of Felons (list of past presidents).

WOOD, Revd. Henry Sotheby (1817/18-93), *schoolmaster,* Stoke upon Trent.

HSW was born in Needham Market, Suffolk, about 1818, the son of the parson of Claydon, Suffolk. He graduated B.A. at St. Catherine's College, Cambridge, in 1841, was ordained deacon in that year and priest in 1842. From 1841 to 1846 he served as curate of Fenton, Lincolnshire. In 1846 he came as master to Stoke upon Trent Diocesan, Grammar and Commercial School, Market Place, Stoke upon Trent, where he remained until 1864. He was living in 1861 in Oakhill, and was described as a clergyman without cure of souls. He had played cricket for Trentham Cricket Club in 1856. From 1846 to 1873 he was chaplain of a Barnet home for boys. In 1873 he was appointed rector of Grindon, Staffs., where he remained until 1892.

By his wife Fanny he had four sons. He died at St. James's Square, Notting Hill, London, on 21 January 1893.

Census 1861; Venn.

WOOD, Ralph (1715-72), *pottery manufacturer,* Burslem.

RW, born in 1715, made salt-glazed stoneware, 'Whieldon' ware and figures and toby jugs in Burslem about 1754. His business was carried on by his son Ralph (1748-95) and his grandson Ralph (1781-1801), who were the first English potters to impress their names on their figures, which were entirely original and uninfluenced by either Dresden or Chelsea. John Voyez (q.v.) may have worked for the Woods and Josiah Wedgwood (q.v.) bought some of their figures. RW died in 1772.

F. Falkner, *The Wood Family of Burslem;* M and H.

WOOD, William (1833-96), *bookseller,* Hanley.

WW was born in Shelton in 1833. He learned the trade of a pottery mould maker and later became a trade union official. By 1882 he kept a newsagent's and bookseller's shop at 54 Piccadilly, Hanley. He was a member of Hanley School Board 1870-3, 1877-96 and chairman 1888-96. By his wife, Hannah, he had at least five children, George, Arthur, Harriet, Thomas and Harold. Mrs. Wood is mentioned in the novel by George Moore, *A Mummer's Wife* (1885), the story of which is set at the beginning of the book in a draper's shop in Hanley.

He died in 1896.

Anderton; Census 1881; R. Hampson, Arnold Bennett, George Moore and the Potteries in *Arnold Bennett Society Newsletter,* 1980.

WOODALL, William (1832-1901), *pottery manufacturer and Member of Parliament,* Burslem.

WW was born in Shrewsbury on 15 March 1832, the son of William Woodall and Martha née Basson. He was educated at the Crescent Congregational School, Liverpool. He came to Burslem from Liverpool Gas Company in 1857 to be manager of the Burslem Gas Company. He became a senior partner in the firm of James MacIntyre (q.v.) and Co. (having married MacIntyre's daughter), and was also chairman of the Sneyd Colliery Co.

By 1863 WW was sole secretary of the Wedgwood Memorial Institute Committee. The Institute had been conceived in 1859 as a free library, school of art and museum. WW organised a petition to apply the Public Libraries Act to Burslem, by which the Institute could be funded from local rates, secured W. E. Gladstone, the Liberal statesman to lay the foundation stone and persuaded the government to grant additional aid. In 1864 the Burslem Free School trustees were persuaded to support the venture, and an art exhibition and bazaar at Alton Towers raised £2,000. A national appeal was made in 1866, and Woodall, accompanied by the local Member of Parliament, H. R. Grenfell, succeeded in getting the Department of Art and Science, to increase its grant and finance the art work of the building. The Institute was opened in 1869 by Lord de Grey and Ripon, with WW as chairman of the management committee. In 1879 he gave the funds from a testimonial in recognition of his achievement towards the cost of a new wing to the Institute.

WW was elected to the Burslem Board of Health in 1867 and in 1871 was appointed chief bailiff. When the town was incorporated in 1878 he became a councillor. In 1873 he was largely responsible for setting up the North Staffordshire Society for Promoting the Spiritual and Temporal Welfare of the Adult Deaf and Dumb, and in 1874 was elected chairman of the Burslem school board. In 1880 he stood successfully as Liberal candidate for the parliamentary constituency of Stoke upon Trent, and was returned again for Hanley in 1885, 1886 (as a Gladstonian Liberal), 1892 and 1895. In 1886 he was appointed Surveyor-General of the Ordnance, and in 1892 and 1894-5 was Financial Secretary to the War Office. He served as a member of the Royal Commission on Technical Education 1886 and of the Royal Commission for the Care of Blind and Deaf Mutes 1886-9. He helped to reduce hours of work and increase minimum wages in ordnance factories. He supported Gladstone in the latter's efforts to achieve Home Rule for Ireland and made three attempts, in 1884, 1889 and 1891, to obtain legislation providing votes for women. He was made a Chevalier of the Legion of Honour.

WW's local official positions included President of the North Staffs. Institute of Mining and Mechanical Engineers and chairman of the Staffordshire Congregational Union. He was also a member of the Charity Organisation Society 1887-96 and the Pleasant Sunday Afternoon Society, a governor of the Haywood Hospital Charity, Burslem, and a justice of the peace for Staffordshire.

In 1871 WW was one of the first civilians to enter Paris during the armistice following the siege of the city in the Franco-Prussian war, and on the following day after the suppression of the Paris commune. He wrote a book about his experiences entitled *Paris after Two Sieges*. He also contributed articles to magazines, including the *Contemporary Review, Good Words* and the *Weekly English Illustrated Magazine* and for some daily newspapers.

In 1862 WW married Evelyn daughter of James MacIntyre of Burslem. She died in 1870. He lived at Bleak House, Burslem until his retirement in 1900 when he moved to Llandudno. He was made a freeman of Hanley in that year. He died at the house of his nephew, Dr. Woodhouse, in Llandudno, on 8 April 1901, and was buried in Llandudno. His portrait, by W. M. Palin, hung in the Wedgwood Memorial Institute, Burslem, and his memory is perpetuated in the Woodall Memorial Congregational Church, opened in 1906, which replaced the Queen Street church of which WW was a member.

Anderton; Burslem News Cuttings (HRL): S. Clews, 'The School Boards of Stoke on Trent and Burslem 1870-1903' (Univ. of Sheffield M.A. thesis 1964); DNB; Simms; *Staffs. Advertiser* 13 April 1901 (obit.); *Staffs. Sentinel* 3 December 1898; L. B. Stokes, 'The Work of William Woodall and the growth of technical and design education in North Staffordshire', (Univ. of Keele M.A. thesis 1980): V and S; Wedgwood Memorial Institute Minute Book (HRL).

WORTHINGTON, Thomas (1816/17-79), *earthenware manufacturer,* Hanley.

TW was born about 1816, the son of John Worthington. From about 1844 he was the partner of James Green in the Brook Street pottery, and in 1862 they owned a theatre in Brunswick Street. He stood for election to Hanley borough council on 20 August 1857, was unsuccessful on that date but was elected on 1 September 1857. He married three times, and in 1861 wasliving in 13 Mollart Street. He owned houses in this street and in Bethesda Street. He was a benefactor of Bethesda chapel. His second wife Mary laid the foundation stone of the Worthington Mission Hall, which he founded in 1874. He died on 1 June 1879.

Bethesda Chapel Registers; Census 1861; Hanley Rate Books (HRL); Huntbach; Jewitt; *National Index to Wills and Administrations;* Townley.

WRIGHT, Arthur (c. 1812-87), *china gilder,* Stoke upon Trent.

AW was born in Derby about 1812. He came to the Potteries by 1841 and was employed as a ceramic chemist and colour maker at Minton's. In 1851 his occupation was given as potter and china painter and in 1861 as china gilder.

AW was a founder member of London Road Baptist Chapel, Stoke upon Trent, in 1841. He was the librarian of Stoke Athenaeum from 1846.

By his wife, Priscilla, he had at least nine children of whom Albert, born 1848, became a noted china painter for Minton's in the 1870s, specialising in birds and fish.

Census 1851, 1861; Fenn, *Stoke Borough Almanack; London Road Baptist Chapel Centenary Booklet 1841-1941* (Birmingham Ref. Library); W. Scarratt, *Old Times in the Potteries.*

WRIGHT, HAROLD (1858-1909), *stipendiary magistrate,* Potteries.

HW was born in Handsworth, Staffs., on 13 April 1858, the son of John Skirrow Wright, Liberal Member of Parliament for Nottingham. He was educated privately by a tutor, with whom he travelled widely on the Continent, then at Pembroke College, Cambridge, where he gained degrees in law and arts. He was called to the Bar and joined the Midland Circuit in 1880. He intended to stand for election to the Stoke upon Trent parliamentary constituency in 1885 but withdrew in favour of W. L. Bright, son of John Bright, the Radical. He contested Chorley but was unsuccessful, and also at Greenock in 1886. He returned to the law and in 1893 was appointed stipendiary magistrate for the Potteries, a position he held until his death. He earned a reputation for the imposition of severe punishments for crimes of violence but of greater leniency for cases of petty theft committed through stress of circumstances.

He wrote a number of treatises on the Bankruptcy and Debtors Acts as well as a book on the office of magistrate. He married Rosa Martha Heaton in 1899 and lived at Aston Hall. He drew caricatures for the magazine *Vanity Fair* under the signature of Snuff, and was also an accomplished painter. A friend summed up his life thus: 'he was intended for a politician, he ought to have been an artist but the devil turned him out for a lawyer'. He died in Colombo, Ceylon, on 23 December 1909.

Pottery Gazette 1 January 1899, vol. 34; *Staffs. Sentinel* 18 February 1899.

WRIGHT, Samuel (c. 1783-1849), *cobalt refiner and tile manufacturer,* Hanley.

SW was born about 1783, possibly the son of Thomas Wright who is listed as a cobalt refiner in 1796. SW was in business as a cobalt refiner by 1818 and in 1830 patented a method of making encaustic tiles, whereby the tile was made in a plaster mould and the pattern impressed. The indentations so produced were then filled with different coloured clay slips as required. Although he executed several orders he made little profit and gave Herbert Minton a licence to produce tiles with his patent. Minton used brass moulds but required several years of experiment to achieve success.

In 1844 SW renewed the patent for seven years and sold a share to Minton and to Chamberlain of Worcester. His son Samuel Barlow Wright joined Minton to produce the tiles.

By 1830 SW was living at Prospect Place (now St. Mark's Street), Shelton and was chief bailiff of Hanley in 1831. He married Sarah Barlow at Acton Trussell and Bednall church on 23 October 1813 and the couple had five children.

He died on 19 April 1849.

Census 1841; Dir. 1818; Information from Mr. G. K. Beulah of Hessle, North Humberside; IGI Staffs; Jewitt; *Staffs. Advertiser* 21 April 1849; J. C. Wedgwood: *Staffordshire Pottery and its History;* Will of Samuel Wright (Lichfield Joint Record Office).

YOXALL, Thomas Reeves (1854-1911), *builder,* Stoke upon Trent.

TRY was born in Stoke upon Trent on 2 October 1854, the son of Peter Yoxall and his wife Hannah. He was educated at St. Peter's National School. He succeeded his father as head of Yoxall and Heath, builders and contractors, a firm much employed by the North Staffordshire Railway. The firm also built All Saints' church, Boothen (1887-8), where TRY became churchwarden, and they were also involved in extensions to St. Thomas's church, Penkhull, and the Lyceum Theatre, Crewe.

TRY was elected to Stoke upon Trent council and served as mayor for two terms, 1901-2 and 1902-3. He was a supporter of federation and was one of the minority on the council who opposed Frederick Geen (q.v.) when the latter proposed to fight the Local Government Board's draft order on federation. Yoxall argued that it was a waste of money to oppose the order. TRY was a director of Stoke Football Club and was vice-chairman at the time of the club's liquidation in 1908 and resignation from the Football League. He married Eliza Ann Hackney and had at least one child. The family lived in Park Terrace in 1880, one of ten houses owned by TRY's father (died 1888), then in Sheppard Street. TRY built a number of houses in Leadbeater Avenue, Stoke upon Trent, in 1908. He died on 22 April 1911.

Census 1861; *Staffs. Sentinel* 23 April 1911 (obit.).

APPENDIX

The People of the Potteries and the Struggle for Federation

(names followed by * are the subject of biographical articles)

"Artificial, vexatious and harmful" wrote Arnold Bennett in *The Old Wives' Tale,* describing the municipal divisions existing in the 'Five Towns'. The novel was published in October 1908, shortly before the Potteries Federation Bill became law. The successful conclusion of the campaign to unite the six towns was the culmination of several previous attempts which, though unsuccessful, paved the way for eventual success by gathering support for federation. Local pride and independence were major obstacles which had to be surmounted and although more and more people came to accept the principles of federation, local interests prompted objections to details in the schemes. This essay attempts to describe the attitudes and opinions of the people of the Potteries in the years 1907 and 1908 and to show how these were affected by outside influences.

Summary of previous attempts at federation[1]

The recognition that the area comprising the six towns had a common interest in a staple trade had given rise to its description as 'The Pottery' or 'The Potteries' by at least the beginning of the 19th century. The first attempt to establish a common government, however, came only after the Reform Act of 1832 and the Municipal Corporations Act of 1835. The first measure gave the area its own members of Parliament and the second allowed parliamentary boroughs so created to choose to be incorporated as municipal boroughs. The opportunity so provided was nevertheless lost. Although John Davenport, M.P., thought that the interests of the six towns did not conflict because they were united by the pottery industry, he lost the argument; Burslem especially did not believe that the extra benefits which could be expected from union were worth the additional expense; the major concern of the time was law and order, and it was thought that the appointment of a stipendiary magistrate could provide for this.

In 1850 a report to the Board of Health[2] recommended the establishment of a local board of health to cover the area of the Potteries from Longton to Hanley. Joseph Clementson* and John Ridgway* of Hanley used the recommendation to press for the incorporation of the whole Potteries district or at least of Hanley but failed to win the support even of their fellow inhabitants of Hanley. It was another 40 years before the Local Government Act of 1888, by which county councils were created, prompted another attempt to achieve local union. The desire of the Potteries towns to escape from the authority of a Stafford-based county council caused them to produce plans for a Potteries county council, but the decision by Hanley to accept county borough status wrecked the idea. William Woodall, M.P.* thought that Hanley would not accept the proffered status and a number of Hanley councillors believed they should not: George Bradford*, John Roddy Cooke*, John Bromley*, Charles Adams* and Edward Ridgway* maintained, as late as 1889, that Hanley was committed to a Potteries county council plan. The arguments of those who, like James Bebbington* and Herbert Coates*, wanted Hanley to become a county borough, prevailed: Tunstall's decision to remain with Staffordshire afforded a convenient excuse for Hanley to accept county borough status.

The next attempt at federation, originating in Stoke upon Trent in 1900, involved the Local Government Board, and progressed further than had previous efforts. The original plan was for a county which would include Newcastle under Lyme, Wolstanton, Kidsgrove, Audley and Smallthorne as well as the Potteries towns Douglas Coghill, M.P. tried to interest the Local Government Board in the plan, but that body pointed out that its powers only provided for extensions to the boundaries of existing boroughs, and that Hanley would have to take over the other areas. In March 1902 a meeting of representatives from the towns involved agreed in principle to the idea of an enlarged Hanley. Hanley presented a petition to the board in November 1902 by which the other five towns and Smallthorne, Milton, Bucknall, Trentham, Caverswall and Wolstanton would become part of an enlarged county borough. The Local Government Board recommended the adoption of a financial plan similar to that drawn up by Sir Hugh Owen for the London boroughs. This plan proposed a valuation of the assets of each of the six towns from which debts and liabilities would be deducted. The net assets would be calculated as a proportion of its rateable value. Any town with a deficiency of assets would be required to compensate those towns which had an excess of assets by means of differential rating.

Fenton, believing that such a scheme would inflict undue hardship on the town, immediately withdrew from the proceedings. Frederick Geen* now submitted a report on the practical implications of the scheme. In September 1903 Burslem, whose councillors had ideas of achieving county borough status for themselves, polled their ratepayers, and federation was rejected by a decisive majority of six to one. Stoke upon Trent decided that further support for the Owen scheme was fruitless and withdrew. Hanley and Longton could only follow suit. Tunstall, under the influence of John Nash Peake* was again lukewarm towards the idea of federation. Once again the whole scheme collapsed.

A fresh initiative was made three years later. In November 1906 Stoke upon Trent and Longton put forward a plan for an amalgamation which would also take in Fenton. The Local Government Board rejected the scheme on the grounds that such an amalgamation would prove to be only temporary. The board's inspector, Major C. E. Norton recommended that a scheme should be drawn up which embraced all the Potteries towns. The reaction throughout the six towns was favourable and Hanley invited the other authorities to a conference. This initiative prompted remarks that Hanley wanted to 'boss the show', and instead, John Burns, president of the Local Government Board, agreed to inaugurate the conference.

1. The history is told in more detail in *Victoria County History of Stafford,* vol. 8, pages 252-8.
2. R. Rawlinson, *Report to the Board of Health on Stoke Parish.*

Outline of proceedings 1907-8

A series of meetings began on 12 July 1907, Tunstall being the only one of the six towns not to participate. Norton, reporting to the Local Government Board, said that the Owen proposals of 1902, based on differential rating, were generally unacceptable and that local opinion favoured a new scheme drawn up by Frederick Geen of Stoke upon Trent. This too proposed a differential rate but over 20 years, during which time the fixed assets of the six towns, like gas and electricity works would remain to those towns which had originally provided them. No sooner was Geen's plan made public, however, than numerous amendments were proposed and Hanley especially expressed its dissatisfaction. On the due date for representations to be submitted, 30 November 1907, Hanley put forward new proposals drawn up by John Goddard Shaw*, Stoke upon Trent and Longton submitted Geen's scheme and Burslem made no representation at all.

The Local Government Board's inquiry was held in Stoke upon Trent town hall on 8, 9 and 10 January 1908. Burslem immediately withdrew, alleging bias on the part of the chairman, Major Norton. Walton Stanley* now produced a plan proposing to settle the differences between the six towns by having both a flat and a differential rate for the first ten years. This scheme won the support of Tunstall, whose ratepayers had now voted in favour of federation, and of Longton, who were accused of being willing to support anything. The board's officials rejected the scheme and once again reverted to the 1902 proposals. These became the basis of the scheme which, with the support of Hanley, Longton and Tunstall, were embodied in a Provisional Order and the federation bill in Parliament. Counsel and witnesses for Stoke upon Trent, Fenton and Burslem fought the order and the bill throughout the whole of the parliamentary proceedings. The House of Commons' committee considering the bill produced amendments which they hoped would satisfy both its promoters and opponents and the bill passed the Commons' third reading on 29 July 1908. The bill proposed that differential rating should apply for a period of ten years; any town shown by a valuation to have a deficiency of assets, and thus unable to make a substantial contribution to the new county borough's services, was required to make an annual payment equal to one tenth of such deficiency. Local reaction to these proposals was strong. Fenton, which by the scheme would receive no direct advantage from its payments, was completely opposed, and was joined in its opposition by Tunstall and Burslem; even Hanley and Longton were less enthusiastic. It was clear that the final struggle would be fought out before a select committee of the House of Lords.

Lord Cromer, a diplomat of wide experience, headed the Lords' committee. He reported that his committee would find the preamble of the bill, in which the principle of federation was embodied, proved, and were prepared to wait for agreement on detail to be reached between the six towns. To facilitate such agreement the Lords were prepared to override the conclusions of the Local Government Board and the House of Commons and revert to Geen's scheme, which had received the largest measure of public support. 'If local public opinion cannot decide about local government', Cromer stated, 'then there is no value in public opinion at all'. He added a rider that if the six towns still failed to agree on the details of federation, then his committee would make the decision for them and recommend to the Lords that the bill be passed. Cromer went on to comment on the varying attitudes he had found; Longton and Hanley, he said, would federate on any terms; Fenton favoured Stoke upon Trent's scheme; Tunstall's attitude, commented Cromer, amid laughter, he could not define; as for Burslem, that town would have to propose another scheme or be included in the federation by compulsion.

Faced by this threat Burslem put forward a scheme, probably the work of Sydney Malkin,* which brought the productive undertakings of the six towns into account but suggested that there should be no valuation of assets and no gas profits, gas being sold at cost price. Hanley now offered an equalisation factor to Fenton in the hope of securing that town's agreement to the levying of a joint flat rate for the whole of the proposed new borough. A composite settlement was arrived at on 15 December 1908. Most of the six towns made concessions, and the final scheme was a compromise between Burslem's ideas and Frederick Geen's original proposals. A last minute difficulty over Longton was smoothed out and the formalities completed in time for the Royal Assent to be given to the bill on 21 December 1908.

Council Attitudes and Opinions

Of the six councils Longton was the most consistently in favour of federation and Fenton the most opposed. On the Stoke upon Trent and Hanley councils there was little outward opposition to the principle of federation though on both there was a majority not prepared to accept a financial scheme promoted by the other town, even if this should mean a delay in the establishment of federation or the abandonment of the idea. Burslem and Tunstall councils were more or less evenly split in support and opposition, although in deference to the opinions of their ratepayers as expressed in polls Burslem opposed and Tunstall supported the principle of federation.

Hanley, already a county borough, believed it had little to gain from federation. There was general agreement that some sacrifices had to be made in order to gain the confidence of the other towns, who feared Hanley's domination. Within the council, however, there were also sharp differences between those, including Herbert Coates* and Jesse Shirley* who favoured Geen's scheme, and a larger number, for whom Walton Stanley* came to speak, who were opposed. One of the latter, Sampson Walker*, said that Hanley was not prepared to accept federation at any price. Walker was one of the few anti-federationists on the council; he believed that amalgamation would bring extravagance rather than economy and envisaged a situation of 'rudderless councillors lost in an ocean of officialdom'. Walton Stanley refused to accept that capital items purchased out of revenue should be included in the valuation of assets. Hanley councillors suspected the other towns of attempting to isolate them over the issue of gas. Hanley had no gas works of its own and objected to the plan by which the town would have to pay one third of the total rates of the new borough and yet not be able to share in any gas profits for 20 years. Hanley council however was publicly committed to supporting any scheme approved by the Local Government Board. Fearing that the board would settle for Geen's plan Hanley produced proposals of its own, drawn up by John Shaw Goddard. This scheme proposed that the productive undertakings of the area, such as gas, would come immediately under the control of the new county borough. Walton Stanley spoke to these new proposals and won a majority on Hanley council. The scheme was put before the Local Government Board, but rejected. The board's own proposals were broadly similar, however, and Hanley maintained its support for the provisional Order and bill which embodied the board's plan. Ultimately the settlement favoured Hanley; the removal of the proposal to meet capital expenditure out of revenue saved the borough £50,000.

Local Government Board officers noted that Stoke upon Trent was Hanley's chief competitor for the position of the leading town in the Potteries. Stoke councillors in general supported the principle of federation, though when the Local Government Board decided to revert to the 1902 scheme most of them agreed to oppose the bill. Ernest Brooke, a keen federationist, demanded that a public opinion poll be taken on the issue of federation and the council's switch to opposition to the bill. Until his death in October 1908 Brooke constantly harassed Geen at council meetings; when Geen objected to his remarks and rose to move a point of order Brooke called him 'Mr. Alderman Jack in the Box'. Thomas Reeves Yoxall* was another supporter of federation even should it cost Stoke more. Yoxall also paid rates in Fenton but argued that Fenton's rates should be increased to the level of those of the other towns. One of the main issues for Stoke was Burslem's proposals for a flat education rate. Stoke opposed this partly because it would cause a sharp rise in the town's rates and partly because it ran counter to Geen's idea of a differential rate. Stoke also objected to Goddard's scheme which did not allow for payment for goodwill on the takeover of productive undertakings. Stoke did ultimately send representations to the Local Government Board's inquiry but inserted a reservation that if all six town were not included in the new borough or if the board departed from Stoke's financial representations, then the town would withdraw its support. When the details of the Local Government Board's Provisional Order were made public Geen complained about the lack of discussion. He was subjected to severe cross-examination at the hearings of the Commons' committee and accused of injuring the interests of his town by his refusal to accept the rejection of his own scheme. When the Lords' select committee reverted to Stoke's original proposals Burslem put forward a substantial amendment, and this caused Stoke to rescind its agreement. Eventually a compromise was arrived at. Stoke agreed with the amendment because its view that Hanley and Tunstall ought not to share in gas profits was accepted. Geen suggested that once loans were removed from expenditure the financial effects on the various towns would not greatly differ. He believed that he had been vindicated and that his principle of differential rating had triumphed.

Burslem's decision to take a poll of its ratepayers was evidence of the wide differences of opinion which existed among the town's councillors. Anti-federationists argued that the town had all the services it required for the next 20 years and might even aspire to county borough status in its own right. They were accused by Sydney Malkin of not properly informing the ratepayers of the proposals which had been made, particularly the idea that education should become a common charge throughout the new county borough, a provision which would relieve Burslem of part of the high cost of maintaining its technical art schools. The earlier poll in Burslem, in July 1903, had produced an overwhelming majority against federation (2,670 to 457). The poll held on 22 November 1907 also produced a majority against federation though this time the federationists did better; there was a 74% turn-out; the figures were, against federation 3,240, for federation 2,040. This was the poll so vividly described by Arnold Bennett. On the basis of this result Burslem's counsel decided to withdraw from the inquiry, a decision which caused uproar in the council; Thomas Willett accused the town clerk, Arthur Ellis, of being prejudiced; Ellis said that he was disappointed by counsel's action, though he did not disapprove of it, and complained that the split in the council placed him in a position of great delicacy. Burslem continued the fight through the Commons' and Lords' hearings. Counsel for Burslem suggested that Burslem and Tunstall could be left out of the proposed federation immediately, with the possibility of their joining later if they saw that the new county borough was working effectively. Thomas Edwards* admitted that although he had been a supporter of the idea of greater unity in 1888 the large expenditure made by the town since then had caused him to change his mind. When the Lords' committee threatened coercion this was denounced in Burslem as 'unEnglish' and unprecedented. Challenged to produce its own scheme or face compulsory amalgamation Burslem at length submitted a number of proposals. The final scheme met the town's objections to some degree; productive undertakings were to be brought into the scheme but gas was to be sold to Burslem's inhabitants at cost price.

When arrangements for the conference were being discussed Arthur Cotton* had suggested that all councillors and other interested parties such as the Chamber of Commerce should be invited to attend. On the casting vote of the chief bailiff, Henry Smallman, however, Tunstall had decided not to attend the conference at all. This decision was in keeping with their views on a union of the towns in 1889, when Tunstall's opposition had ended hopes of establishing a Potteries county council. The councillors had to reverse their decision, however, when their ratepayers went to the polls on 30 December 1907 and opted for federation by a majority of 895 to 641. Tunstall thereafter supported Walton Stanley's amended scheme. In evidence to the

House of Commons' committee the Reverend Granville Bailey* vicar of Goldenhill and chairman of Tunstall Federation committee spoke in favour of the bill. Elections now produced an anti-federation majority in the council, and Tunstall's position became increasingly confused, a situation which prompted Lord Cromer's remark. Arthur Cotton, hitherto a federationist, now joined the opposition, an aboutface which brought a strong attack from Leonard Grimwade*.

Public Opinion and Federation

The pro-federation movement was well organised throughout the area. The Potteries Association for the Promotion of Federation was formed early in the proceedings. It took as its motto 'Unity is Strength' and its membership covered a wide spectrum of politics and class: the duke of Sutherland* was president, Cecil Wedgwood chairman, Thomas Twyford* treasurer and Leonard Grimwade* secretary and leading propagandist. The Association's membership included three mayors, five aldermen, 15 magistrates, the presidents of the Chamber of Commerce, the Trades and Labour Council, and the Potters' Union; and Henry Venn Stuart*, rector of Stoke upon Trent. The main argument used by the Association was that federation would result in greater economies and efficiency. Grimwade pointed out that the cost of maintaining the engineers' department in Nottingham, a unified borough, was only half that of the combined Potteries towns although the population of the two areas was similar in size. He suggested that municipalisation of the tramways could bring Tunstall and Fenton within 20 minutes of each other at the cost of 1d. fare. Grimwade printed 30,000 copies of the speech made by the president of the Local Government Board, sending one to every ratepayer. He issued an inquiry about people's views, and published the results in his *Book of Opinions;* he printed 160 replies favouring federation, and said that only three replies had been opposed. The Association took an active role in the campaign before the federation poll in Burslem. When Arthur Cotton defected to the opposition Grimwade launched a week-long attack upon him.

The federationists' campaign in Burslem was opened by Sydney Malkin* who stated that if it had been left to him there would have been no poll and that ratepayers should trust their elected representatives. Edmund Leigh suggested that without federation Burslem would be unable to take advantage of recent legislation which would allow it to improve workers' housing. William Owen* in a letter to the *Staffordshire Sentinel* discussed pottery exports and argued that by voting for a weak Potteries people would be voting for trade disaster. The duke of Sutherland offered Trentham Park and Hall to the six towns on federation, and read out letters supporting the amalgamation from the earl of Crewe and Bishop Stamer*. In Stoke upon Trent the federationists were led by Charles Lynam* who organised a petition to the council in an attempt to force them to hold a ratepayers' poll. The petition was rejected. Henry Venn Stuart believed that federation would be worth while even if it cost more: 'We must not huckster about a penny or twopence on the rates', he wrote.

Both employers and employed in the pottery industry in general favoured federation. A letter to the local newspaper signed by 'A Manufacturer', believed to have been J. C. Bailey of Doulton and Company, urged manufacturers not to allow shopkeepers to block reform for fear of losing 1½d. a week. Abraham Fielding* and Percy Shelley* stressed the likely beneficial effects of federation on education. Noah Parkes*, secretary of the Trades and Labour Council, presented a petition to the Local Government Board containing over 30,000 signatures, representing, he claimed, 75% of his affiliated members.

It was generally agreed by Fenton's councillors that the town's rates would rise no matter what scheme was adopted. It was pointed out that Fenton had no park, no market and no public baths, a situation which led Balfour-Brown, counsel for the promoters, to describe the town as 'cheap and nasty'. Fenton was opposed to any valuation as a basis for a financial settlement, as well as to the imposition of a flat rate throughout the proposed county borough. Philip Elliot* chairman of the council, claimed that low rates encouraged industry to settle in the town. Indeed the North Staffordshire Railway Company, Fenton's largest ratepayer, threatened to move its works from Fenton if federation came about. Elliot argued that federation would be calamitous for Fenton, who would be contributing to the repayment of other towns' debts without any compensatory return. Fenton, because of its low education rate, also rejected the Burslem proposal of a flat education rate. A majority of the council was prepared to accept Geen's scheme as least harmful to the town's interests, but insisted that a differential rate should apply for 20 years. Under no circumstances was the council prepared to leave the decision to the Local Government Board.

There was, however, a small group of councillors who favoured federation. Their leader was John Shaw Goddard* who foresaw that the Local Government Board would reject Geen's scheme and introduced a plan during the federation conferences by which the new county borough would take all the productive undertakings of the town under its control, based on a valuation and paid for by a differential rate over 20 years. This proposal failed to gain acceptance chiefly over the question of payment for goodwill, required by Stoke upon Trent, Longton and Burslem. Goddard was accused of favouring Hanley, where his pottery was situated. His scheme was similar to the Owen proposals of 1902, except that it applied to floating assets and to commercial undertakings. When the Local Government Board rejected this in favour of the full 1902 proposals, Goddard went into opposition to federation.

Since 1902 most of Longton's local government elections had been fought on the issue of federation. When Longton sealed its representation to the board's inquiry on 30 November 1907 there was a majority on the council for federation of 37 to three. Longton's councillors had at first raised objections to Geen's plan of differential rating: Percy Shelley* argued that this would delay the economies expected as a result of federation; Joseph Leak* feared the continuation of six separate towns; George Kent*, town clerk and the leading protagonist of federation, asserted that differential rating would perpetuate all the evils of the existing system without any compensating benefits. Kent was later a principal witness for the Local Government Board's bill whose provisions were based on the 1902 proposals. During the bargaining which brought about the final settlement Longton was isolated over the issue of its long-term debts; anti-federationists noted with satisfaction that here at last was something which even Longton would not accept.

By contrast with this well-planned campaign the anti-federationists' propaganda was weak. In any case the force of their arguments was diminished by the revelation that several of their supporters, even in Burslem, accepted the principle of federation, merely opposing on points of detail. It was pointed out by the federationists that James Edwards, secretary of the Burslem Anti-Federation League, had accepted the 1902 proposals, and that his father Enoch Edwards, was in favour of federation. Joseph Dawson*, a member of the League admitted that he objected only to the speed with which he claimed federation was being rushed through. Dawson was supplying Arnold Bennett with ideas and information which the latter used in his *Old Wives' Tale*. One of his chief characters, Constance Baines, 'knew nothing except that the people of Bursley now shopped in Hanbridge . . . And there were actually people who wished to bow the neck to Hanbridge, who were ready to sacrifice the very name of Bursley to the greedy humour of that pushing Chicago'. Bennett wrote that the electric trams had carried off 'the cream and much of the milk of Bursley's retail trade' to the 'grasping and unscrupulous Hanbridge'.

Burslem patriots wrote at length to the *Sentinel*. One letter advertised a pamphlet printed by Joseph Dawson entitled *15 Reasons why Burslem Ratepayers should oppose and vote against Federation*. One correspondent, who signed himself 'Burslem Workman', called on his fellow townsmen to defend the rights and privileges of the mother town of the Potteries. Samuel Robinson, a wholesale newsagent of Moorland

Road, engaged with 'Fairplay' in such a lengthy argument on rateable values and rents that the editor of the *Sentinel* had to end the correspondence. The *Sentinel* was keenly federationist and condemned those whose parochial attitude impeded the progress of the inevitable, pouring scorn on their ideas and questioning their motives. It described the first meeting of the Anti-Federation League, which had been formed on 24 October 1907, as a 'miserable fiasco'. At this meeting Alderman William Cartlidge stressed the main point in Burslem's case — the large expenditures undertaken since 1888 which had provided the town with gas and electricity works, a park, an isolation hospital, baths and a sewage plant.

In Tunstall, despite the pro-federation vote of December 1907, there was much opposition to the idea. William Walker charged John Burns, president of the Local Government Board, with interference. The Roman Catholics in the town were, it was alleged, solidly against federation. William Grindley* described Longton and Tunstall as far apart as the two poles. Arthur Cotton, commenting on the duke of Sutherland's offer of Trentham Park, said that this was not of much use to Tunstall, eight or nine miles away.

Noah Parkes'* claim that trade unionists were in favour of federation was disputed. Alderman Thomas Edwards* of the Ovenmen's Society, claimed that pottery workers who had signed the petition had been forced to do so by their employers, and John Locker of Fenton complained that the Trades Council had suppressed expressions of anti-federationism. Fenton, he claimed, was being coerced or cajoled into federation, and its property was being confiscated in what he called 'bare-faced robbery'. John Locker may have been one of those Labour supporters who persuaded Will Crookes, Labour M.P. for Woolwich, to claim that the House of Commons committee which considered the federation bill had been packed. William Walker, a Tunstall councillor, declared that while he was not in favour of the hereditary principle in politics, he could 'Thank God for the House of Lords'.

The Role of the Local Government Board

When John Burns, president of the Local Government Board, was asked whether any town which refused to join the federation would be compelled to do so, he evaded the question, saying he hoped the issue would not arise. Later, after the Burslem poll, he met a deputation and again refused to be drawn into a statement. The assistant secretary of the board, Noel Kershaw, and the board's inspector, Major C. E. Norton, would have liked the six authorities to adopt the scheme proposed in 1902 by Sir Hugh Owen, but only Hanley was prepared to accept this plan. Frederick Geen's scheme was discussed and Kershaw used George Kent as an agent to try to force amendments to Geen's plan. Kent put forward a scheme of his own, but Kershaw thought this, although a 'little less mischievous than Geen's scheme', would not work and that even if it did, would not be equitable.

Norton reported to the board that although there was opposition in the Potteries to Geen's scheme, no alternative solution had been suggested. Kershaw therefore concluded that the board itself would have to produce a scheme. He suggested to Norton that the latter should discuss the situation with the Potteries Association for the Promotion of Federation, who might be able to influence the outcome of the impending Burslem poll. Kershaw wrote 'I fear the financial proposals will cause us and the local people much trouble and expense'. In the event the poll did produce a majority against federation, although Kershaw was able to report that compared with 1902 support for the principle had increased.

Kershaw rejected as impracticable George Kent's suggestion that the financial details should be inserted in the provisional order, and waited for Norton's report. The latter advised him that no one could devise a scheme acceptable to all the Potteries towns, and that the board would have to decide the matter for itself. Norton wrote:

> Mr. Geen's scheme has been aptly compared to a bunch of live Christmas turkeys tied together by their necks but unfettered as to wings and legs . . .

He argued that differences which existed at the time should be faced up to, and that the generation which adopted federation should make itself responsible for the financial charges such a principle involved. He thought that Stanley's was the best of the schemes which had been presented but recommended that the Local Government Board should choose Owen's 1902 plan, subject to special consideration for Fenton. Norton's recommendation nevertheless was rejected by the board. Norton gave evidence to the Lords' select committee, when he stated that Stoke's scheme would defer federation for a generation. Lord Cromer commented that 20 years was not a generation and with that the board's case was defeated and the Stoke proposals returned to favour.

Conclusions

The consensus of opinion which promoted federation was broadly based but was led by the pottery manufacturers. Federation took place at a time when foreign competition was threatening the local industry. Manufacturers wished to reduce costs and increase the technical skills of their workforce and believed that the divisions and differing standards of the six towns did not serve their best interests. Leonard Grimwade had amalgamated his four factories, sited in Burslem, Fenton, Hanley and Stoke upon Trent, and secured economies. He saw a similar solution for local government in the Potteries. Federation came to be seen as both the salvation of the pottery industry and of the Potteries towns.

Even for many of its opponents federation was believed to be inevitable, both because of local support and because of the attitude of the Local Government Board. The passage of the bill through Parliament should have been relatively smooth. In the event it was the divisions among the supporters of federation themselves which forced an expensive contest through Parliament. The result of Burslem's withdrawal from the board's inquiry made a parliamentary contest probable, but had there been no dispute between Stoke upon Trent and Hanley it is likely that Burslem would have negotiated an agreement with its neighbours rather than face the costs of opposing the passage of the bill through the Commons and the Lords.

The kernel of the problem was therefore the differences between Hanley and Stoke upon Trent. Each town considered itself the centre of the area, and this was true in different ways. Hanley was the commercial and Stoke upon Trent the communications centre of the six towns. In practical terms there was only one essential difference between them: Stoke upon Trent owned a gasworks and Hanley did not. The costs of and revenue from gas were an important element in the plan put forward by Frederick Geen of Stoke upon Trent. He was able to muster the support of the gas-owning boroughs and in some measure to isolate Hanley. Hanley realised that the town had to make some sacrifice for federation but was not willing to be over-generous. John Shaw Goddard's scheme was an attempt to bridge the gap between the two positions; it failed because Goddard refused to insert an element of goodwill into the purchase price. This was his sticking point, just as a differential rate was Geen's sticking point. Walton Stanley disliked but was prepared to accept differential rating, but he categorically refused to accept Geen's proposal to include capital items purchased out of revenue in the valuation of assets. What Stanley wanted was probably control of the gasworks. The result of all these divisions was a protracted and costly parliamentary campaign.

The *Sentinel* afterwards printed its nominations for 'federation awards': George Kent was nominated for his hard work and enthusiasm; John Burns for his initiative; the duke of Sutherland for his influence; Norton for his tact; Cromer for his wisdom; and finally Geen and Stanley jointly for the ability, tenacity and good temper with which they had conducted their contest. The story of this duel has become an enduring part of the history of the Potteries.

Arnold Bennett in an article called 'The People of the Potteries' printed in *Cassell's Magazine* January 1911, sought to put the struggle for federation in historical perspective. He wrote:

> In my youth . . . there existed less than two miles of tramline in the entire district, and only two trams, drawn by horses and travelling between Hanley and Burslem, twice an hour. Now electric cars run about everywhere, from Longton in the south to Tunstall in the north, and from Newcastle in the west to Smallthorne in the east. And it was precisely the rapid cars which at last broke down the stubborn individualism of the separate towns and brought about their federation and the triumph of Hanley, the central and largest town: Another case of geography influencing history! . . . Useless to fight against the temptation of those cars! For a penny or twopence, in a quarter of an hour, the man or woman with money to spend could be in Hanley and not all his love for his native town would keep that man or woman out of Hanley. Thus a smaller patriotism was gradually overcome by greater patriotism and the tendency of the potters to think of themselves as one single community instead of half a dozen communities was strengthened. And although each town protests against losing its identity, its identity will undoubtedly have to go. Even Hanley, the victor, has had to sacrifice something. It would have liked the federated Potteries to be baptised with its own name; but in the struggle for nomenclature, Stoke upon Trent has won, and rightly, for it is the centre of the railway system and the postal system. To the outside world of the traveller and the addressers of envelopes the Potteries has always been associated with Stoke upon Trent and the association will properly remain.

Postscript: the new county borough

Fifteen months elapsed between the Royal Assent to the federation bill and the first meeting of the council of the county borough of Stoke on Trent. The new council put off making a decision on the question of where their home was to be situated for six months, finally deciding on Stoke town hall as the permanent council chamber and Hanley town hall for meetings of the education and watch committees. The choice of the first mayor of the new county borough was also disputed; Cecil Wedgwood was a popular candidate and was proposed by John Wilcox Edge*. Frederick Geen was also proposed, although Sampson Walker objected to this nomination as 'partisanship'. In the event Wedgwood was elected and Geen became his deputy. Elections for the new council resulted in the disappearance of some notable figures: Percy Shelley, whose proposal in 1905 had begun the sequence of events that finally led up to federation, was not re-elected; nor was Arthur Cotton, the 'leopard who changed his spots'. Many convinced anti-federationists were returned, some unopposed; W. W. Dobson*, Thomas Edwards, William Cartlidge and Philip Elliot were all elected aldermen. Plenty of federationists, including Frederick Geen, were anxious to economise, but the costs of promoting and opposing the bill and compensation to displaced officials produced a considerable increase in the rates. In the field of education, improvements in art and technical teaching were generally acceptable but Geen opposed municipalisation of water, thereby incurring the wrath of Labour and Liberal councillors and prompting the resignation in protest of Sydney Malkin. Geen rode out the storm and later had the honour of entertaining the king and queen at his home for lunch. He became 'Mr. Stoke on Trent' just as he had been 'Mr. Stoke upon Trent', and died in the middle of a speech in the council chamber in 1915, doing what he was most used to, answering criticism.

Attempts to municipalise the tramways operated by the Potteries Electric Traction Company, which had exercised the thoughts of the federationists and were continued particularly by Labour members of the county borough council, failed in 1920. Although supported by the majority of the councillors, led by the mayor, William Robinson (M.P. for Burslem 1923-24), poll of ratepayers rejected the proposal by 7812 votes to 4043 on 17 January 1920, the figures reflecting the lack of interest shown by the electorate of about 80,000. George Wade and Sampson Walker were amongst those supporting the purchase, but opposed were Phillip Elliot and John Shaw Goddard, both ex-mayors of the borough. Sydney Malkin, who had resigned from the council over the blocking of attempts to acquire the water supply was opposed to the purchase, not in principle but because the price asked, almost £750,000, was far more than the near obsolete plant and equipment (according to a report by an engineer from Liverpool) were worth.

The question of the gas supply and of its associated works which had caused so much dissension during the federation proceedings was more easily resolved. The county borough, faced by the need to spend large sums on their several works, decided to make overtures to the British Gaslight Company to take over the works at Etruria and to concentrate production there. The company agreed and the transfer took place in June 1922. Equally easy was the transfer of the water supply to public ownership on 1 January 1925. The water company raised no objections and a Bill passed through Parliament unopposed, after discussions between the parties concerned. The Staffordshire Potteries Water Board formed had twenty three members nominated by local authorities in North Staffordshire and Stoke on Trent provided ten of these.

In 1922, the area of the county borough was almost doubled by boundary extensions which took in Chell, Smallthorne, Milton, Bucknall, Meir, Blurton and Trentham, much of the area which Hanley wished to include in its representation to the Local Government Board twenty years before. Samuel Robinson of Burslem wrote to the papers again to protest against the plan; he recalled some of the words John Burns had used at the Federation Conference in 1907, "big fish eat little fish and little fish eat mud". Robinson argued that it might happen in the aquatic world, but it should not happen to people if they did not wish it.

On 25 July 1925, King George V, in the course of a visit to Stoke on Trent announced that the borough had been raised to the status of a city. The letters patent to confirm and to create the title of Lord Mayor became effective in July 1928 and Thomas Clarke Wild, then mayor, became the first lord mayor of the City of Stoke on Trent. Local government reorganisation in 1974 caused a transfer of powers back to Stafford county council. The six towns remained united in one local authority, the Stoke on Trent District Council, though they retained the privilege of being styled a city with a lord mayor. The old county borough council handed over a business-like and going concern to the new district council, together with a surplus of over £2 millions.

Sources:

Primary (in HRL unless otherwise stated)

Newspaper cuttings relating to consideration of the House of Commons of the Local Government Provisional Order (No. 3), Bill (July 1908).

Newspaper cuttings relating to consideration by the House of Lords of the Local Government Provisional Order (No. 3) Bill (November-December 1908).

Great Britain House of Commons: Minutes of Proceedings before the Select Committee on Private Bills on the Local Government Provisional Order (No. 3) (Stoke on Trent Order) Bill 2 July to 27 July 1908.

Great Britain House of Lords: Minutes of Proceedings before the Select Committee of the House of Lords Provisional Order (No. 3) Bill, 24 November-19 December 1908.

Public Record Office: Local Government Board records filed at HLG piece no. 732-737.

Staffordshire Sentinel — various issues 1907-10.

Miscellaneous Cuttings relating to Federation 2, vols. (1907-8) (1908).

Secondary

T. Allbut, *A View of the Staffordshire Potteries* (1800).

A. Bennett, *The Old Wives Tale* (1908).

A. Huntbach, *Hanley* (1910).

K. D. Miller, *A Brief Chronology of Local Government in Stoke on Trent* (1950).

Potteries Association for the Promotion of Federation, *Book of Opinions* (1907).

Potteries and Newcastle Directory 1912.

Victoria Theatre, programme of musical documentary *Six into One* (1968).

Victoria County History of Stafford vol. 8 (1963).

E. Warrilow, *A Sociological History of the City of Stoke on Trent (1960).*